Beyond Obedience

TRAINING WITH AWARENESS

FOR YOU AND YOUR DOG

Beyond
Obedience

APRIL FROST

AND RONDI LIGHTMARK

HARMONY BOOKS

NEW YORK

Published by Harmony Books, a division of Crown Publishers,
Inc., 201 East 50th Street, New York, New York 10022. Member
of the Crown Publishing Group.

Random House, Inc. New York, Toronto, London, Sydney,
Auckland www.randomhouse.com

HARMONY and colophon are trademarks of
Crown Publishers, Inc.

Printed in the United States of America

Design by JENNIFER DADDIO

Library of Congress Cataloging-in-Publication Data

Frost, April.
Beyond Obedience: training with awareness for you and your dog
/ by April Frost and Rondi Lightmark. — 1st ed.
Includes index.
1. Dogs—Training.   2. Dogs—Behavior.   3. Dogs—
Psychology.   4. Human-animal communication.   5. Dogs—
Health.   6. Holistic veterinary medicine.   I. Lightmark,
Rondi.   II. Title.
SF431.F75   1998
636.7'088'7—DC21   98-23059

ISBN 0-609-60248-9

10 9 8 7 6 5 4 3 2 1

First Edition

TO JESSIE

WITH ALL MY LOVE, THIS BOOK IS

DEDICATED TO ITS SOURCE,

THE ANIMAL KINGDOM AND ITS

SPECIAL EMISSARIES, THE DOGS.

CONTENTS

ACKNOWLEDGMENTS

I am grateful to Rondi Lightmark and Susan Lee Cohen, who first saw the potential for this book and for their part in making this book a reality. Also to Martha Haas and her ability to capture the energy of the book and the animals who are mentioned in it with beautiful illustrations. To Stephen Vieira for his photography skills.

To my daughter, Lara, I am proud you are my daughter.

A very special thanks to the following: Jacqueline Newport for her friendship, love, and total support on every level, not to mention her computer skills and the endless hours of typing; George Bibens for all her love and support working shoulder to shoulder with me, keeping the place going while I was working on the book. My love and gratitude go to Greg Whitehead for his clarity and guidance when I needed counsel and for nourishing my body, mind and soul, providing me with time outs that allowed me to renew my energy and focus. To Lynn Noyes for her belief in my endeavors and her support and guidance for the Center.

I would also like to thank Scott Pollak for his support, humor and advice. Bill Pollak DVM for his support and guidance and reviewing the holistic information. Helen McKinnon for her help and wonderful gift of assisting in making connections. One of the greatest pleasures of the work that I do is getting to know loving, dedicated people like the three of you.

My gratitude goes also to Susan Madzunovic, Bev and Gary Savoie, Donna Buinicky, Susan Deane, and Lauren Symons for their friendship and support over the years and their volunteer work helping with the rescued dogs. Thanks go also to Amanda Daigle for her youthful energy and exuberance and desire for a deeper connection with animals.

And as always my gratitude goes to those that have brought all these wonderful people into my life, the dogs.

Blessings, Love and Light
April

Thank you, April, for introducing me to your magical world and for sharing your dreams and challenges. Your vision is life-changing. Your shining and loving animals are the inspiration and the blessing.

To Robin Westen, my mentor, and to my agent, Susan Lee Cohen, heartfelt thanks for your friendship and for believing in me. Many thanks to my editor, Shaye Areheart, for support, good humor, and guidance in the big city; to my mother, Joyce Swanson, and my mother-in-law, Stella Chapman, for trust, wisdom, and good listening; to Sam and Targhee, two unconditional and forever dogs; to my children, Kyra and Marcus, for parenting me when I really needed it; and deepest love and gratitude to Jim, the person who set me on the road and who sent me the phoenix.

—Rondi

PREFACE

Beyond Obedience fulfills my lifelong dream to contribute something to people and animals that will empower both to fulfill their highest potential.

This self-empowerment happens as a direct result of the development of love, mutual respect, and communication in the relationship between you and the dog you have in your life.

My desire to share what I have learned is inspired by the Native American belief that it is not possible to own living things, whether human or animal, nor can we own the life force of a tree, a river, or the land. Each radiates its unique presence, which cannot be possessed any more than we can own the wind or the rain. We can enjoy them to the fullest only by sharing our own life energy with them.

When we fly a kite in the wind or lose ourselves while floating in the current of a river, we can become more than we were before, because these things are freely given, and their contributions can be experienced for their own sake. When I watch a breathtaking sunset, I am nurtured with a sense of joy, wonder, and peace. I do not own those colors; their beauty belongs to all of us, and nourishes our hearts and souls. At such times I like to share the experience of the sunset with a person or animal whom I love. When I do, it becomes a treasured event, because I know that exact moment will never be repeated, nor will there ever be a sunset identical to this one.

In much the same way, each animal that has come into my life has been unique, and each experience with animals has been freely given and deeply meaningful for its own sake. I do not own any of the animals, nor do I own the lessons that they have taught me. Because this knowledge belongs to anyone who is open to it, I only share what has worked for me, changed my beliefs, and filled my life with awe and wonder beyond anything I could ever have dreamed. When the energy of two separate beings can harmonize in a free exchange of love, trust, and communication, especially when each is of a different species and has a unique spiritual presence and perspective, there are no words to express the greatness of the gift. In humility, I offer you what I have learned of the beauty, energy, and love of dogs.

APRIL RANDALL FROST

INTRODUCTION

Several months ago I was teaching a weekend workshop on Awareness Training, an inspiring way to establish a bond of mutual respect and communication with your dog. People were sitting in chairs while I lectured, and a number of the dogs were resting in their crates until we practiced the next exercise—all except for a borzoi named Shamir, who was having a hard time relaxing in the strange new environment. He whined and complained and kept turning around and around in his crate. Shamir was making so much noise that it was difficult for people to hear, and I finally realized that I needed to do something.

We had already spent a number of hours exploring the concept that the energy within our thoughts and feelings has a powerful influence on those around us and, furthermore, that we can learn to project these thoughts and feelings in supportive ways while communicating and developing a relationship with a dog. Because dogs are extremely perceptive, they easily understand when a projection is clear and focused. Shamir was providing a perfect opportunity to apply this knowledge in a practical situation.

I said to the group, "Now I want everyone to focus for a minute on Shamir, and visualize him becoming calm." Silence fell, as all eyes turned to the dog and people created their own mental picture, as I had asked.

In less than thirty seconds Shamir had stopped pacing, stopped whining, and now stood peering out of his crate in our direction.

I went on: "Now see him lying down. See him being calm, quiet, and lying down." Again the room was stilled by the presence of one clear thought projected at the dog.

Shamir fidgeted for a moment, peered out at us again, then slowly lowered himself to the floor of the crate and lay there quietly while a video camera recorded the entire sequence for posterity.

As soon as Shamir proved the power of our silent intent by doing as we had asked, everyone began to exclaim in amazement, the concentration was broken, and he popped up again.

It didn't matter; my point was made. Communicating and bonding with any living being is multidimensional, with different degrees of sensory perception. The more the energy of intent is put into creating a bond, the less need there is for words or other physical tools for communication and understanding. Other sensitivities predominate; intuition is the medium of exchange.

After the experience with Shamir, his human companion spoke up, saying that her dog had been in a number of classes with another trainer who, despite some pretty forceful methods, had never been able to get the dog to lie down when asked. The woman was totally amazed that it had now been accomplished without even touching him. Her comment gave me a good chance to point out to everyone that dogs are very intelligent beings and that it is much easier to work with their brains and hearts than to fight with their bodies.

Dogs have an exceptional ability to perceive the thoughts and feelings of their human companions, which is one reason they are valued as guides, guardians, and saviors. Incredibly, this awareness is an untapped resource of self-development for the millions of people who live with them every day. Dogs are extraordinarily aware; people have generally forgotten how to be, but dogs can teach us to remember.

People who brought their dogs for training that weekend were learning that, through developing their own perceptions and using those perceptions to help their dogs learn basic behaviors on cue, their connection with their dog could evolve beyond anything previously experienced. As they practiced teaching their dogs to respond to their requests, using their entire being— mind, heart, body, and spirit, they were being empowered to use inner capacities they had never dreamed were theirs. They were discovering the potential of a new method of communication between two different beings who have long loved one another, despite a certain barrier between them.

That barrier was created as a result of a centuries-old belief in Western culture that animals are without emotions and psyche, less intelligent than humans, and in need of physical discipline to keep them under control. This belief is part of the mind-set that says nature exists for our benefit and exploitation. It is as though we humans have put everything that is not human on the other side of a one-way mirror, where we can see but not be seen. This creates a feeling of detachment and also of loneliness. We belong to nature, but we have forgotten how to participate; we observe and judge rather than becoming involved.

Despite the intellectual and emotional separation that our culture has made from nature, people have animals in their lives because, on a deeper level, we sense that animals, and especially dogs, can heal that very wound of isolation. We can achieve a level of connection with a dog that we cannot find in any other relationship—not with parents, children, a partner, or friends. It is totally unique to the energy of dogs. People who are "dog lovers" understand and recognize this connection immediately and are drawn to it as if to a magnet.

The essence of this connection is acceptance; dogs are constantly, deeply, and fully present in each moment, without judgment. Regardless of who is around and watching, they are always themselves, and they are completely honest about expressing their feelings. Although we humans tend to hang back from doing this, fearing humiliation or rejection if we reveal who we really are, dogs by their very nature, give us permission to be ourselves. We can express every emotion we could ever feel in front of our dog and he won't tell anyone. If we cry in front of our dog, we will not be judged weak; if we feel anger, he will not judge us bad people; if feel happy and do something totally silly, he will not consider us foolish but no doubt will jump right in and join us. There is also, on the part of dogs, complete, unconditional acceptance of who we are, regardless of race, sex, job, religion, IQ, or the size of our pocketbooks. A dog's total acceptance gives us something that connects us with our truest nature and gives us a better understanding of our place in the universe.

Because dogs do not see or experience the world through our limited view of reality, a dog can be your master teacher. This has been true, and it is true for me. Over the nearly three decades that I have been involved with dogs as a trainer, counselor, and healer, I have experienced nearly every kind of interaction, delight, and sorrow that a relationship with another species has to offer. I would not hesitate to repeat one minute of this history, because the lessons have been so valuable. Dogs have heightened my perceptions, expanded my intuition, and taught me to commit to the joy in each new situation while simultaneously detaching myself from the outcome.

It is in this spirit that I venture to offer this book as a guide for co-creating with the spiritual forces that work through the animal kingdom, in nature, and in all of us. I hope that by awakening people to the wonderful gifts that animals so unselfishly bring into our lives, we will be able to return a fuller measure of that love and joy to them.

Awareness Training is an adventure in unlimited thinking. It will challenge you to become more conscious of how your thoughts, feelings, and deeds affect other living beings. You will also learn how to become more responsive to the powerful eloquence and intelligence of life around you, allowing each relationship the freedom to develop on its own path to wisdom. It can be a wondrous, creative, and playful journey into a new realm of understanding and experience.

I hope to inspire you to rediscover your true place in the circle of life, where, if you take a deep breath and look around, you will see great beauty and friendship eternally reaching out to include you.

Dogs, who have rightly earned the title Our Best Friend, have long been willing to be our ever-faithful and loving guides for this journey.

I did not grow up knowing this, although I developed a close connection to animals during a lonely childhood in a household composed of my mother, aunt, and grandmother. Each had a different idea about how I should be raised, and all worked out of the home, so I was given a lot of responsibility for the cooking and cleaning at a very young age. I don't regret that I learned to work hard, but while other children played together outside, I generally toiled alone indoors, trying to meet numerous, often conflicting, very high standards.

I was a well-behaved child, but I had a strong inner life and was always happiest when I could escape to the woods in an old pair of jeans instead of wearing the frilly dresses that my mother insisted would turn me into the right kind of woman.

My mother's father was a full-blood Native American whose tribe is part of the Iroquois nation. I never knew him, but since the Native American way feels like home to my spirit, I have often wondered if his blood in my veins gave me my preference for being outside in nature, and my passionate connection with the animal world.

The story of my career with animals is too long to tell here. But the short version begins when I was about eight, with the making of butternut doughnuts, a family tradition which required that I go to the shed where butternuts were hanging in sacks and spend hours laboriously cracking the shells to get the meat.

One day I discovered that a pair of squirrels had gotten to a sack before me, and suddenly doughnuts were secondary and making friends was paramount. Over the weeks I gradually befriended the two and named them Perry and Porro, after two squirrels I had seen in a Disney program. Perry and Porro grew to trust me and would visit me in my upstairs room via a handy tree branch outside my window. They rode on my shoulders everywhere, and we played hide-and-seek in the backyard. All the time that our bond was forming, there was a deep welling-up of love for them coming out of my lonely heart, and I was always, in some way, silently being with them, letting them know how much I loved them and that I would never do them any harm.

I don't remember when I became aware that we could communicate; it just happened so easily. I could talk to Perry and Porro in the same way I could talk to people. I would speak out loud to them, but their answers would come as a "knowingness" of their thoughts inside my head. And the things they told me about would come true.

One time I came in on a gray, unsettled September day and cautioned my mother to stay away from a tree in the backyard. I said that the squirrels had told me not to play around my favorite old oak for a few days, because it would not be safe.

No one believed me; I was severely admonished and threatened with having my mouth washed out with soap if I did not stop telling lies. I found this reaction extremely confusing. I already had two imaginary playmates who were horses, and my friends and family were aware that I talked with them constantly. I could not understand why communication with make-believe friends was acceptable while talking with my real friends, the squirrels, was not.

I went to bed feeling very hurt and alone and lay awake all night listening to the wind rise. At about five o'clock in the morning I heard a huge *crack!* and then a thundering crash as the tree split and dropped half of its body to the ground.

Not a word was said at the breakfast table. Life went on as usual with its rigid rules and formal interactions.

Occasionally I would forget and make a comment about my special friends. I would be abruptly corrected: "You can't talk to animals!" I was punished and ostracized by my family and friends for believing as I did.

Weeks went by. Perry and Porro had told me they had a family that they would soon be able to share with me. One day their children came with them when the two squirrels came to visit. The youngsters were frisky but shy, because they did not know me. Perry and Porro assured me that soon they would be my friends too. I kept this exciting new development completely to myself.

Everything came to a shattering end one day when I came home from school and found the two squirrels' lifeless bodies curled up side by side on the lawn. They had been shot with a BB gun and their tails were gone. A few days later I saw two neighborhood boys ride by on their bikes, squirrel tails waving from the handlebars.

By this time, Perry and Porro's children were beginning to play around the house and approach me, and I remember how I ran after them, screaming, and throwing rocks to frighten them and make them go away. I blamed myself for having made their parents trust people. The combination of the loss and the constant conflict between my inner and outer reality was too much for me. I shut that door between our worlds tight. Over. Finished. Time to grow up.

Thirty years later I found myself standing outside my house in the dark, sobbing wildly and begging for that door to open again.

I had a significant reputation as a professional show handler of dogs and horses, having won ribbons all up and down the East Coast and in the Midwest. I had established a career as a trainer, groomer, and breeder of dogs and horses. I had maintained a close relationship with animals, but the door between my consciousness and theirs had remained shut.

Everything changed abruptly with the end of my second marriage and the loss of my health and ability to work. I had Lyme disease, probably contracted from working in my herb garden where there were feeders that attracted many wild birds, some of which, I later learned, carry the Lyme tick. Every joint in my body ached so acutely that I could hardly move.

"Why don't you ask the animals for help?" said Helene, a psychic healer. I found her advice intriguing. She was quite insistent I see her about one of her dogs, in spite of the fact that I'd warned her I had no energy to counsel anyone. When she came and saw the state I was in, she looked at me with amazement. "Do you believe animals have souls?" she asked me. "Yes," I replied with conviction, wondering what she was getting at. "Here you are," she said, "Surrounded by loving beings who are waiting to help you, and you aren't even listening to them. I don't mean just these animals here, I mean the collective consciousness of all animals. You have an incredible connection with their world already. April, all you have to do is ask."

I had nowhere else to turn, having reached the place in the road where, in the end, we humans finally come to terms with lost pieces of ourselves. I was so far down that I let go of my defenses and my limited ideas about how the world worked, and I became innocent again, willing to trust, experience, and learn.

The floodgates opened. I realized that I had always interacted with animals on an intuitive level without being able to define what I did. I had always cared about animals' needs, beyond the usual physical demands. But part of me had remained very cautious because of what had happened when I was young. I had been hesitant to trust that the connection could be deeper, could actually become real communication, could even go as far as nonverbal communication. As my spiritual path became more clearly defined, however, things began to change dramatically.

I turned from the conventional drugs that were killing me to meditation, holistic medicine, and prayer. I regained my health, money arrived, and Hearthside was once more up and running. I began to look around me and see miracles: an encounter with an injured fawn led me to explore my Native American heritage. When I learned the words "Mitakuye Oyasin," which the Sioux say in their ceremonies and which means "all my relations," I no longer found myself lonely and divided in my life. I was whole, in my rightful place, at one with my work. I began to feel what it was like to live in companionship with the natural world. I could allow my life to unfold, supported by the universal love and consciousness that link the cosmos and all creatures in it as one.

One of the great descriptions of the relationship between humans and the natural world was written in the 1800s in a letter to the American government from Chief Seattle of the Suquamish people, a Native American tribe of the Northwest: "Man did not weave the web of life," he wrote, "he is merely a strand in it. Whatever he does to the web, he does to himself."

When we don't acknowledge our gifts from the natural world, we spend our lives as takers. If we live only to take, we live without the experience of gratitude. Without the ability to recognize our blessings, we can't recognize miracles anymore, despite the fact that we encounter them each and every day.

As my own spiritual awareness grew, I came to realize how important it is to see animals as powerful beings in their own right, as beings worthy of respect. They have their own choices and reasons for being on this earth. This attitude is very different from the conventional view, which is that they are lesser beings who need our help and protection. It became more obvious that we were talking about two different things when I let go of old ways of thinking. And since this book is specifically about dogs, I want to focus on what I have learned about their role in our lives.

Dogs, in many people's minds, are here purely to serve our needs. Actually, this role for most dogs is perfectly wonderful, because they are very happy giving us their unconditional loyalty and love. However, when this gift is taken for granted, which it has been for thousands of years, we are the ones who lose.

Our language reveals a psychology of domination: we "own" our "pets," and we "discipline" them to follow "commands" from their "masters." We have to find a new vocabulary that supports a more enlightened point of view.

The animals are my teachers, companions, and friends. I own the responsibility for the animals in the eyes of society, but I don't own the animals who live with me. This is why I no longer call myself an animal trainer; it's too one-sided a term. My goal is to open the lines of communication and understanding between species; humans and animals have to do this learning together. So I like to call myself an animal communication facilitator. I do not do "obedience training." Awareness Training is communication training based on love and respect, and it must go both ways.

Old-style dog training was mostly about physically forcing an animal to do something, rather than working with its mind and heart. It was a tough, insensitive method that made no allowances for differences in temperament, in personality, or even in size between animals. What you did with a Great

Dane, you also did with a Chihuahua. Even before I developed Awareness Training, I saw that this method was hard on dogs who did not fit the norm, especially very sensitive breeds. It also was a difficult technique for people to use who were not assertive or strict disciplinarians.

Old-style methods did not take either human or animal psychology into account; it was taken for granted that humans considered themselves superior to animals. The definition of owning a dog was limited to caring for its needs, making use of its instinctive talents, and enjoying its company. All of the expectations tended in one direction. Although animal behaviorism is a growing field, with the result that it is more acceptable to speak of animals having emotions and a psychology, it is still very common for many people to use the old, limiting definitions of the relationship.

However, I challenge you to be more adventurous. If what I have to offer doesn't work for you, then turn to your dog for the answers. Ultimately he will be your best teacher. If you let go of everything you think you know or have heard about dogs and dog training, your dog will show you the best way to create a fulfilling relationship. If your dog has a problem, your dog also has the solution to the problem.

This brings me to a very important point: there is actually no one right way to work with a dog. Any approach that says all dogs can be trained using the exact same methods is simply wrong. Why? Dogs are individuals. Each has a distinct personality, as different as one human being from another. Every encounter between an individual human being and an individual dog will have its own energy, wisdom, and goal. If you have more than one dog in your life, you will quickly learn this. Dog raising is like raising children: there are certain basic approaches that often get results, but there is never an ironclad guarantee that what works with one will be successful with the next.

I've often noticed that when people want to learn how to raise a dog, or even a child, they tend to choose a method that either mirrors or totally rejects how they were raised. This is not necessarily the best way to make a choice of techniques. I suggest that any approach is fine as long as it is not inflexible or inhumane and as long as it encourages people to use common sense and to trust their intuition. I say this because it is very important to me to convey to every single person I teach that my beliefs and methods come from my own unique reality and experience. I am not intending to give people answers; I am offering tools, skills, and new ways of approaching the development of a fulfilling relationship with your dog. I do not have all of the answers. I am still in the process of learning and growing with every animal I meet, and I will be doing this for the rest of my life. Each person will have a relationship with a dog that is unique. This special relationship will be its own experience, and you will need to allow it to grow at its own pace.

You will also need to make your own choices as to which aspects of Awareness Training are the most helpful to you. You may be challenged to find your own way. It is important that you feel free to do so.

If I encounter a new idea, I always take a moment to see if it feels right for me. At the same time, I have learned to stay open and not reject recommendations or opinions simply because they don't fit into my current way of understanding the world.

It took me a long time to learn to value my own worth and trust my intuition. It is crucial that you find that same ability to trust your feelings about what is right for you, whether this applies to a situation, another person, a choice of direction, or even the best way to be in a relationship with a different species. I want this book to be a way to help you develop self-confidence, and I hope it will offer you a wide variety of options and inspirations for personal growth. If certain ideas and approaches do not feel right to you, don't use them; however, I do encourage you to explore and find a way that meets your needs.

Much of this book is designed to be experiential for a very important reason. It is not enough to learn something with your head; you must also practice new ways of being in your body and heart. You need to experience things from your dog's perspective. This will give you a much better understanding of why a dog responds the way he does.

We humans tend to think our way through our lives rather than feel, or experience, things. Dogs, however, experience everything very purely, and you will understand them better if you spend some time in their world. You also will find your world more vibrant and interesting if you explore your senses—sounds, smells, tastes, the way your body feels—and also your imagination—your inner theater, where you are the artist, producer, and director of unlimited richness.

Whenever you reach a recommendation or view in this book where your brain says, "I'm not sure I can do this," substitute "I give myself permission to experience something new," or "I am open to having a wonderful new experience." Allow yourself to enter fully into the ideas and exercises. Then you will best be able to evaluate whether they work for you and your canine companion.

I guarantee that every outcome will be unique, so let your process of learning evolve at its own pace. Some training books list lessons in terms of week-by-week goals. Instead of adhering to such a schedule, I suggest that you allow things to unfold in a way that is appropriate for you and your dog.

Realize that the things you accomplish with your dog may not be dramatic and may not happen overnight, although you will have those kinds of breakthroughs also. When I am working with a difficult animal, I frequently stop, look back, and see many, many small triumphs. Watch for these, so that you do not get discouraged and so that your dog does not become discouraged or restive. Each small achievement should be honored and celebrated.

In the end, you are the most important tool that you have to develop. You are a far greater influence on your dog's life than any piece of training equipment. The more you invest, the more you will receive in return.

1

THE DOG IN OUR WORLD

The key to a successful relationship with any living being, whether animal or human, is interest. The more curious you are to learn as much as possible about your dog, the greater the potential for a deep bond to develop between you, because after interest come respect, commitment, and love.

To help create this bond, it is important to begin by examining the relationship between dogs and humans. In this chapter I will take a look at the issue of how people and their dogs find one another. Then we will look at a typical crisis in a dog-human relationship. I'll offer some general information about how dogs' experiences of the world differ from ours, and I will make some introductory comments about training. You will find this chapter especially helpful if you already have a dog. If you are thinking about getting a puppy, this chapter will provide some important guidance, and you will find additional information in Chapter 15.

There are many different ways that dogs end up with people. Some people grow up with dogs; others acquire them only when they are older. Although I was passionate about animals from early childhood, I was not allowed to have a dog until my freshman year in high

school. My mother limited my choice to a toy or miniature poodle, partly because they don't shed and partly because she liked the image of sophistication that the breed projected. Although I was disappointed not to have other options, I got a frisky little poodle I named Kisty ("Kisty" was short for Conquistador), and we became good friends.

A friend who lived nearby also had a poodle, and once we realized that it took all of our baby-sitting money just to pay for grooming, we saved our money, bought a pair of clippers, and learned to groom the dogs ourselves. We started attending training classes and showing our dogs in obedience competitions. Soon we were caring for other people's dogs while they were away. Before long we were also being asked to groom dogs, so my career with animals actually began while I was still a teenager. By the time I was in my twenties I had already made the commitment to helping animals in need. My house became a haven for them, I had horses in the backyard, and I was busy training, showing, and breeding Irish setters, a breed I had long admired.

My animal family is still very large by conventional standards. At this writing, Hearthside Animal Center, in Cornish, New Hampshire, contains a dog pack of assorted breeds that numbers nearly thirty, plus nine cats, two cockatiels, six ferrets, a rabbit, and a guinea pig. There are four Arabian and seven miniature horses as well as chickens, turkeys, and doves out in the barn. Most of these animals have been rescued, and I am fortunate to have George, who has worked for me for four years, primarily doing repairs, maintaining the grounds, running errands, and assisting with animal care. In addition to her, I have volunteers who believe in my work and who come and help with their care and training.

Rescuing a dog is one thing. Choosing one is another. And then there are those dogs who make the choice themselves. Red, a client's dog whose timing was impeccable, was one such dog.

I first met Red when an elderly man named Charlie brought her to training classes. Charlie was a gentle giant who always wore a fedora, a flannel shirt, and red suspenders. His hands were enormous and had been used hard and well over the course of his life; he had a warm, compassionate disposition and a charming sense of humor.

Charlie was born into a family of culture and wealth, but he was adventurous and loved being outdoors, so he went out west when he was a young man to work on different ranches. Now he was too old for that life and had come back into genteel society where the furniture was polished and clocks with brass pendulums ticked out the long minutes of each day.

Charlie was finding life pretty dull when Red just walked into his yard one day and made herself at home. It was as if she knew that Charlie was looking for a spunky dog like her to liven things up. It was news to him, but he soon saw that she had a serious relationship in mind, and she fit his temperament well. They became inseparable.

Red had a strange build and the straightest legs I had ever seen on an Irish setter, which gave her a strange walk, as if she were on stilts. Extra clumps of hair grew like an old rug on her shoulders and hips. She looked like she was wearing chaps; maybe that was why Charlie found her so appealing. Red also had a crazy way of sitting, sort of askew on her haunches. She would hold that position, and when she was intent on something, she would put one leg out straight in front of her, as if she was pointing.

Red had a bit of the devil in her, which Charlie adored. He would correct her, but he'd shake his head and smile instead of getting angry when she ignored him. One time he took me aside after class and said, "So, April, do you think Red's ever gonna be a nice old lady?" It

"Red"

got to be a joke between us over the years, as our mutual appreciation of Red's unique personality drew us into a close friendship. I always replied, "Charlie, Red will be an old lady, but she's never going to be a *nice* old lady!" He seemed to find this reassuring.

I was right about Red; she had real integrity, and you just had to respect her for it. Incorrigible to the last, she left her awkward body at the ripe old age of fifteen. Charlie went downhill fast and died not long after. It was as though he had lost some of his zest for life, or perhaps he lost his reason for getting out of bed in the morning.

Not long before he died, Charlie gave me a picture of Red. In the photo she is sitting in a rocker on his front porch, looking right at the camera, with his old fedora perched on the top of her bony head, and her long, silky ears hanging down. She looks as though she is saying, "What a life, huh?"

Red chose Charlie, or maybe you could say they recognized that they needed each other. But there is no question that she filled his final years with friendship and style.

There are many wonderful stories about dogs who have turned up at special times in people's lives, either as friends when friendship was needed or as powerful opportunities for growth and learning. Frequent and inspiring as these stories are, they are not the norm. It is more typical for people to choose their pets than the other way around, and it is important to remember that this can be a life-or-death question for the dog.

According to a 1994 American Humane Society survey, as many as 60 percent of the 8 to 12 million dogs entering shelters that year were put down, usually because the dog had become uncontrollable due to human ignorance or neglect. This amounts to an average of over *six million* dogs a year! I know of one European dog breeder who refuses to sell his animals to Americans because he says we are a throwaway culture. My many years of experience

"The Sheltie Drill Team"

with rescue work have led me to draw the same sad conclusion: we live in a disposable society. When there are problems in the relationship, it has become more expedient for many people to say, "The dog no longer works for me; I'll just get a new one."

The number of dogs who are mentally unstable or physically unfit to be companions is small, however, compared to the number whose lives are held cheap. Our culture allows the indiscriminate breeding of millions of dogs. Those who don't make the grade, or who don't have homes because there are simply not enough people to adopt them, are killed. Even greater numbers die because of human ignorance: of the millions of dogs put down in the United States yearly, more are killed because of behavior problems than for any other reason. In one 1985 study, 10 percent had been euthanized for biting, 23 percent for aggression, 17 percent for house-soiling, 15 percent for barking, 15 percent for chewing, 7 percent for fearfulness, and 5 percent for digging. (These percentages include dogs who exhibited more than one undesirable behavior.) Tragically, most of these deaths could have been avoided through a combination of inspiration, education, and some kind of system that deals with the issue of accountability.

It saddens me when I hear of the loss of so much potential. I am even more concerned when I think about the inevitable repercussions of these attitudes. If we can be so indiscriminate about the killing of millions of dogs, let alone the millions of cats and other small animals whose lives are also cut short, is it not obvious that there will be repercussions elsewhere, particularly in our relationship to the environment and in our inner lives?

I do not often encounter this casual attitude with my clients at Hearth-side, because people who contact me for help are usually committed to working hard on the relationship with their dog. One memory, however, has always haunted me because the person was so out of touch with herself and with a soul-sustaining view of life. A woman I'll call Marnie came for a counseling session with her three young daughters and Spicer, a boisterous, ten-month-old golden retriever. The puppy had been her husband's idea, which was the first problem; she had no interest in having a dog or forming a bond with him. No one had done any training with Spicer at all, and it was obvious that the whole situation was just about the last straw as far as Marnie was concerned. She was a tense, unhappy woman, who seemed to be over-whelmed and caught up in a busy social life. Parenting and puppy training did not seem to be high on her list of ways to spend a day. This was made more obvious by the excessively polite behavior of her children, which I found eerie. They all sat like little robots in a row, hands folded in their laps, never making a move or speaking, except to say "Yes, ma'am" or "No, ma'am," when I asked them questions about the dog.

After listing her many complaints about Spicer, Marnie got up and began to pace, gesturing angrily at the puppy, who was whining and tugging at the leash held by Katie, the oldest child. "I was so annoyed with him the other day that I was thinking of having him euthanized!" she finished dramatically.

Katie, who was about ten, looked at her mother with alarm, "What does that mean?" she asked.

"Put to sleep," her mother said flatly. The child still did not understand.

"Killed," Marnie said, now sounding defensive.

I talked at length about Spicer's needs, but my suggestions seemed to fall on deaf ears. She did not really want any solutions; she just wanted the dog to disappear from her life.

When she left for a moment to get her checkbook, Katie broke my heart. She came up and stood in front of me, looking over her shoulder and asking her question quickly, before her mother returned. "If we do something bad," she said, "will Mommy have us put to sleep too?" She and her sisters all looked at me big-eyed for my answer.

I put my hand on her and shook my head emphatically, saying, "No, dear, of course not!" My stomach was in a knot; I felt that these children were living in an emotional vacuum and I was powerless to help them.

Katie was not satisfied. "Then *why* *would* they do it to Spicer?" she demanded.

I didn't know what to say. What kind of message does it send to children to dispose of a life because of a lack of convenience or understanding? Katie had already figured out that the implications were pretty clear: if you don't toe the line, you are sent away. I was sure that, unless there was a radical change, those children were probably headed for boarding school. Marnie had already euthanized them emotionally, and I couldn't do anything for any of them. Had Marnie shut down emotionally because of her own lack of inner fulfillment?

A lack of spiritual nourishment pervades our fast-paced culture. Because so much time is given to outer work, people have developed the habit of looking without really seeing and of hearing without really listening. Many are afraid or have lost the ability to trust or express their feelings. Perhaps this shutting-down comes about because of an attempt to ward off the negative influences of media, noise, unhealthy food, bad air, landscapes devoid of nature, fear of the future, and fear of being controlled and judged by unhappy, unfulfilled people. As I embarked on my own spiritual journey, I thought a great deal about this problem and about the negative impact it has on the lives of animals like Spicer. I realized that eliminating fear and judgment— and fear of being judged—would truly create heaven on earth. We are incredibly blessed to have animals, with their ability to fully accept us without judgment and as wonderful examples to help us.

This is why, while evidence of spiritual malaise is everywhere, there is hope. Many people are actively seeking, reaching out to nature in record numbers for soul-sustenance: to gardens, to travel in remote, untouched landscapes, and especially to those animals who are accessible because of domestication. Dogs are more popular than ever before, and they are being asked to play a big part in creating a deeper feeling of connection with the inner life.

This brings me back to the issue of how dogs and humans come together. If you are seeking a more conscious relationship to the animal world, and to dogs in particular, it is usually best to begin by choosing your dog consciously. Unfortunately, our culture offers little guidance in looking at the fundamental issues. It often seems to me that people spend more time thinking about which style of shoe to purchase than they do about choosing an animal to live with for the next twelve or so years.

If you already have a dog, take a moment to ask yourself why you brought that particular animal into your life.

Was it an impulse? Did you find yourself unable to resist a puppy who scratched at the glass in a pet shop window? Or did your seven-year-old bring one home and beg to keep it? Did it come from the humane society? Was it a present from someone who thought you needed company? Or did you research the breed, call around to find the best source, and then knowledgeably select the one you wanted?

Any of these approaches can work out (although some have more unknown factors than others) when the individuality of the dog is recognized and balanced with the expectations of what that dog will do and be for its human companion. However, there may be all of kinds of unidentified preconceived expectations, which the dog cannot fulfill because of issues like temperament, personality, type of breed, and stage of development, and these can be the underlying cause of dissatisfaction with the dog.

I am often called by people who have not done enough research ahead of time and who typically say things like this: "I'm a single woman and live out in the country, so I got myself a Rottweiler for protection." The problem, she says, is that Spartan loves everyone, and he never even barks. He is not living up to his job description.

Another caller might say, "We got a Lab puppy as a playmate for the kids. And now he's using them as chew toys!"

Unfortunately the kids are barely old enough to walk, but the puppy got that part down very quickly. He now weighs 70 pounds and has learned that he can outmaneuver and outmuscle them. He runs by, hip-drops them on the way, and knocks them flat. In winter, he grabs them by the scarf and drags them across the yard. The children's parents wanted a Lassie, and now they are complaining that they got a monster, not realizing that their dog is only being a typical puppy and playing with the children the way he would have played with his littermates. Since the family did not know enough about dogs to understand this, the puppy's future was in danger.

It is wonderful when relationships that begin on the wrong foundation can end up on the right one. However, in order to give your relationship the best chance to succeed, it is far better if you honestly examine, ahead of time, your reasons for getting a dog. Educate yourself so that you will know what to expect. (Chapter 2 will help you clarify your expectations when you create your dog's profile.)

I have at times been able to help out with an unfortunate match. I especially remember a frail elderly woman named Mrs. Sorin, who walked in with Ernest, a gigantic and very friendly Old English sheepdog. Her children had given the dog to her because her cardiologist said she needed to get out and walk more. She was a gentle, anxious-looking woman in her mid-seventies, with a certain poise and a lot of forbearance. She needed it. Her arm was in a sling because Ernest had enthusiastically bowled her over the day before, when he and Mrs. Sorin were on their way out for their morning haul up and down the road. It could just as well have been in a sling because of the strain of trying to keep the dog groomed; such breeds have thick, bushy coats that need a lot of attention.

Mrs. Sorin was followed by the Stevens family: three energetic brothers and their bouncy sister, all under the age of twelve, and their parents. Their new dog, Sadie, had come from the pound; she was a very shy, inhibited cocker spaniel with the same bewildered look in her eyes that Mrs. Sorin had in hers: there simply was too much family energy for her temperament, too much loving, hugging, patting, and wanting to play. Sadie looked as if she wanted to drape her long ears over her eyes and disappear, as the children tugged and argued over whose turn it was to smother her with affection.

As the same mismatched constellations of people and dogs returned to class after class, a conviction grew in me, and one night I asked Mrs. Sorin and the Stevenses to stay after. "I'm wondering," I said to them, "what you would think about swapping dogs for a while. Maybe you will find that you like the exchange and want to make it permanent." They looked at me blankly, and then from dog to dog. Sadie was halfway under Mrs. Stevens's chair, peering out from behind her leg. Ernest was leaning happily against Mrs. Sorin, wriggling with excitement, and drooling on her nicely polished shoes.

Mrs. Sorin looked at Sadie and raised her eyebrows. The oldest boy walked over to Ernest and squatted down on his haunches for a look. Ernest immediately flopped onto his back and begged for a belly rub. In another minute he was surrounded by kids and reveling in the attention. And Mrs. Sorin was bent over, peeking under the chair and extending a thin hand to Sadie, who was taking a tentative sniff.

It worked out beautifully. But I'm definitely not saying that big dogs go with big families and small, shy ones with elderly people. Although you always need to balance the animal's size and the level of maintenance required against the needs of your lifestyle, the dog's temperament and personality are even more important. Young, timid children can be just as overwhelmed by an Ernest as Mrs. Sorin was. And tiny dogs can be dropped by young children and have their legs broken easily by an unfortunate fall.

Perhaps you have done all of the research, are clear about your expectations, have all of the right intentions, and have a beautiful dog in your home, but things still aren't working out. Although great numbers of dogs are euthanized for behavior problems every year, this does not mean that all of the people who had those dogs were uncaring people. Yes, there is irresponsibility in many cases, but the greatest problem comes from a lack of understanding of how dogs think and behave.

It is very simple: *dogs only do what works*. Once a dog discovers a behavior that works for him, he will continue that behavior, because it is rewarding. Furthermore, a behavior has to work only once for a dog to learn its benefits and continue to seek them.

People get into problems with their dogs because they do not understand how or why certain types of behavior occur. The following story is a good illustration of this point. In this case, a dog learned an unacceptable behavior from her human companions, and because they could not understand where it came from, they were thinking about getting rid of her. Fortunately, this tale has a happy ending.

Sallie belonged to Mike and Janice. A young springer spaniel of good breeding, with a wavy liver-and-white coat, she had a mind of her own even in puppyhood. Mike and Janice were an older couple, and it was clear that Sallie filled a void in their lives after their children left home. When she was about ten weeks old, they brought her to kindergarten puppy training swaddled in a fuzzy pink blanket with only her nose and one bright eye peeking out. They would not allow her down on the ground, but passed her back and forth between them and coddled and marked her every wag and whimper. Part of this concern came from the fact that she had not been a healthy puppy; she had been treated for a urinary infection when they first got her; then she caught kennel cough, which was followed by another urinary infection. Although she worked through her health problems, she had experienced an overdose of attention and permissiveness in the process.

Little did Mike and Janice know that behind Sallie's physical weakness was a clever and assertive dog with a tendency to be dominant, who was feeling smothered by all of the attention. Because she had so little time or space to herself, she began to growl and snap at them when they cuddled her.

Sallie completed puppy class with moderate success, but I could see that Mike and Janice were not maintaining clear, consistent guidelines. They returned and took a junior level puppy class with her and they were still somewhat in control. Then they came to the advanced class. By this time, Sallie had hit her adolescent testing and rebellion period and was testing the limits at every opportunity.

Mike and Janice tried to work with her, but Sallie was out of control, sassy, and completely uninterested in their tentative attempts to get her attention. When we began off-leash work, she simply took off, running and barking around the whole training area, looking for other rebels so she could instigate a free-for-all. When Mike tried to catch her, with Janice in his wake and pleading for cooperation, Sallie escalated the game with relish, barking at both of them, glaring right at them as if to say, "Don't tell *me* who's boss here!" It became obvious that if the class was to proceed I would have to take charge.

I went over, took Sallie by the collar, looked deep into her eyes, and said, "Stop it. That kind of behavior is not acceptable." Sallie dropped her head, lowered her tail, and was led back to Mike.

By this time, both Mike and Janice had begun to see that they'd created a problem, but they still weren't taking it seriously enough. They shared a common fear that discipline—whether with animals or with children— would rob them of love. However, things were bad enough so that it was clear more definite actions were needed. Mike and Janice were beginning to say, "Okay, this isn't cute or funny anymore," and I hoped that things would turn around for them.

It was not going to be that easy. Some weeks later I received a fax from Janice saying, "*We need help!* Sallie is absolutely pushing us over the edge, and soon I'm going to find an edge to push her off instead! Call us as soon as you can!"

I did, and learned that Sallie had a new trick. She had figured out that barking got her all kinds of attention. Furthermore, she had begun urinating all over the house. I told Janice to first get her checked by a vet to be sure the urinary problem had not recurred. If the test was negative, then the problem was purely behavioral.

The test came back negative. I had Janice and Mike in for a private counseling session and began to do some sleuthing. There is frequently one particular incident or situation that triggers a behavior; I had to find out what it was.

It became apparent that Sallie was feeling displaced. One of Mike and Janice's sons had just moved back home. Unaccustomed to the diminished attention, she was doing anything and everything that worked to keep the focus on her, because that was the definition of her world that her human companions had previously given her. She did not know how to interpret their change in behavior, but she did know that it made her feel unsafe. She wanted things to go back the way they were.

Mike and Janice ran a consulting business, and they brought Sallie to the office to keep her from feeling lonely. No sooner would they sit down to work, however, than the yapping would start. At first they thought she needed to go out but when they let her out, she barked at the door. They would bring her back in, but as soon as they sat back down to work or to discuss something with a client, Sallie would begin yapping and demanding attention again. Janice finished relating this latest trial, her voice shrill with frustration.

"Sallie is not a little puppy anymore," I said. "And her behavior actually isn't much different from before; it just isn't cute anymore."

I pressed Janice to think back over the preceding weeks. "Something must have triggered this," I said. "Some incident made her realize that barking would get her the attention that you used to give her before your son came home. Dogs only do what works, and it only has to work once for a dog to grab on to it and use it, especially a dog like Sallie, who is smart.

Janice shook her head and looked blankly at me, then at the floor while she thought hard. Then she suddenly looked up and said, "Omigod!" The light had dawned.

"Yes?" I asked.

"About two weeks ago," she began, "Mike was reading the paper in the living room, and all of a sudden there was a gnawing sound. Sallie was chewing on the corner of the bookcase! She had never done that before. Mike got up from his chair and said, 'Cut it out, get away from there,' or something like that. But Sallie started gnawing again as soon as he went away, and so he turned around, stamped his foot on the floor, and yelled, 'Stop chewing!'

"Sallie just turned around and went, 'Raaa Raaa Reaaarr Rerrraaaar!' and we both started laughing; she was just talking back to us. It wasn't a bark; it was pure sassing, and it cracked us up. She went right back to chewing again, Mike yelled at her again, with the same results, and this whole thing got repeated three or four times."

"That's it! That's the trigger." I said.

Janice went on: "Then the other day Mike was in the office, and he told Sallie to stop doing something. She started barking, and she hasn't stopped since! It's gotten to the point where we can't get anything done! We've tried giving her a bone or toy to distract her, we've tried telling her to go lie down, but she will not shut up! I thought Mike was going to kill her the other day because we had some important clients in the office and she wouldn't stop for over an hour. At home she barks at me while I'm fixing supper, and she barks at Mike reading the paper and just barks and barks and barks!"

Janice finally wound down, took a deep breath, and looked at me with a mixture of triumph and exhaustion.

It was such a simple interaction: a bossy-minded dog has a cute way of complaining and she gets a laugh. Who could have guessed Sallie would get so much mileage out of it? However, one thing can very quickly escalate to another, and often people don't realize the consequences until it is too late.

"She's doing it to demand attention" I said, "and she's certainly getting it."

Janice nodded ruefully. "We've tried ignoring her, but then she gets worse and really pushes it.

"Be aware that when you give her a bone or a toy to distract her, it has to be before the fact, not after," I said. "Otherwise she will think you are rewarding her. If all else fails, have her do a repetitive series of Sits and Downs. This will give her attention, but not the kind she is looking for. Don't have her do just one or two, but enough of them so that she doesn't want to play the game anymore. And then make her do a few beyond that.

I gave Mike and Janice one further instruction that was the most important of all. "Above all," I said, "keep mentally telling her why she needs to be quiet and well behaved. Tell her how much she pleases you when she does as you ask. Holding those thoughts will help you be consistent in your expectations. Finally, make very sure to notice when she is being quiet on her own.

Praise and reward her. This will teach her that the best way to get attention is by being quiet and well mannered."

Maintaining a positive focus was crucial, because Sallie could easily pick up on what Mike and Janice were feeling. Their frustration with her behavior only added to her insecurity. They had to stop emphasizing those things that she was doing wrong, and instead hold a clear image of what they expected of her. This was essential in order for her to understand how to give them the right response.

I also gave Mike and Janice some flower essences for Sallie to help her through the repatterning process. I will explain more about this approach in my chapter on holistic health.

My solution for Mike and Janice did not involve punishing Sallie. It was aimed at changing her interest in the behavior by making it mildly unpleasant for her. She wanted attention, and even though she was getting negative attention, it was still attention. Furthermore, their yelling at her to be quiet amounted to a lot of barking back from Sallie's point of view. What fun! A bark-in! However, when the attention that Sallie got amounted to some boring work—which I would not advocate except in extreme cases—she said, "Whoops! That didn't work out right. Let me try something else." She found out that being quiet earned praise and attention and made her feel good.

In addition to changing the energy in the situation from negative to positive, Mike and Janice also learned to anticipate those times when Sallie was on the verge of repeating undesirable behavior and to provide other rewarding outlets well in advance of her usual attention-getting methods.

Some outdated training approaches might have suggested a no-bark muzzle, an electric-shock collar, or even severe physical discipline for Sallie. These devices and methods, which create a quick fix through physical punishment, may prevent the undesirable behavior for the moment, but they do not solve the underlying problem, which is not physical but psychological and emotional. This creates a high level of frustration in the dog and if the root cause of the problem is not addressed, the behavior will often be rechanneled to an equally undesirable outlet.

Sometimes I tell my classes, "Be careful, you could be the best pet your dog ever had." It can be quite common for dogs to end up in control of the household, especially when people get in the habit of being "on call" and responding to every request for petting, playing, feeding, and going in or out. It is not so much a case of a reversal of roles; it has more to do with those factors that create harmony and mutual respect in a relationship. Mike and Janice did not understand the signals they were giving to Sallie or how she was receiving them. They inadvertently taught her how to dominate them, and they ended up at the mercy of her desire to maintain the level of attention that had given her a sense of security. It was up to them, because it was their world into which the dog has been introduced, to ensure that there was balance. This is essential in all dog-human relationships.

The more you learn about dogs and how to communicate with them, the better chance you will have to create the loving relationship you envision. Here is some general information to get you started; in the next chapter, it will become specific for you and your dog alone.

THE WONDER OF DOGS

When we examine the similarities between humans and dogs, we see that one obvious distinguishing characteristic is that, like us, dogs are social animals. As in human tribal cultures, there is sharing of work and honoring of individual skills among group members. When a dog pack goes out hunting in the wild, no two dogs play the same role. Studies of wolves chasing caribou have shown that all of the pack members may start out at a dead run but after a short stretch, they spread out. The faster ones go to the front, and the slower ones begin to drop back. The ones in the front push the prey to exhaust it, while those who maintain a more moderate lope eventually come in and work to bring it down. Dogs in the rear stop the prey if it doubles back. The strengths of each animal are used. Each individual has a job and a place within the structure.

When you include a dog in your life, it is important to realize that the way he relates to you and to other members of the household is similar to his understanding of pack structure. He will have a certain perception of his place and the job he should fulfill. How this comes about will depend on the dog's own personality and the guidance and instruction—or lack of it—that he has received from the people he lives with.

Dogs maintain their group in pure Darwinian style in the wild. The higher-ranking eat first, the lower-ranking last. The weakest are sacrificed if there is not enough food. However, within the group, close bonds are often formed. Animals have a structure that they respond to, but within that structure there are attachments based on the need for protection and for propagation of the species. It can be challenging to separate an individual dog's consciousness from his instinctive group consciousness, and bring him into the human world. Something unique must be awakened, ideally when the dog is eight to twelve weeks old.

A dog communicates with other dogs by means of a vast array of signals. Although dogs do have many different ways of vocalizing, most communication is nonvocal, through body language. For example, bristling of hair on the back, flattening of ears, stiffening of the tail, narrowing of the eyes, and baring of the teeth generally indicate fear or aggression. Open eyes, pricked-up ears, a grin, and a wagging tail usually mean the dog is feeling safe and happy. Cringing generally means fear, and licking lips and rolling on the back indicates submission. Although these are common ways that dogs show their intentions, there are always exceptions. You will need to learn by observation the small details that make your dog unique.

ABOUT DOGS AND AGGRESSION

Most dogs are kind, gentle, and loving. There are, however, many causes for aggression in dogs, some of which are natural and some of which are the result of human genetic engineering, abuse, or treatment with drugs. People who work with aggressive dogs have a legitimate cause for fear, because such dogs are dangerous and unpredictable.

Aggressive behavior appears in a number of different forms, frequently involving the protection or defense of something or someone. Aggression, for example, can be maternally motivated, food-related, territorial, or exhibited in connection with something like a toy or a favorite resting place.

In addition to factors like selective breeding or abuse, aggression can also be learned from the example of other dogs or as a result of trial and error in dealing with humans. It is also taught as a benefit to serve human needs, or it can occur because the dog's human has unwittingly encouraged it. One common example can often be seen in the waiting room at the vet's office, where dogs who snarl and lunge at other dogs are petted and hugged sympathetically by their human companions. Although the desire is to calm the dog's fears of "going to the doctor," unfortunately, dogs who receive this kind of attention believe that they are being encouraged to continue aggressive behavior, and therefore it tends to escalate.

All dogs have an inborn plan of defense called the fear-flight-fight mechanism. Imagine a target with three concentric rings and the dog in the center. If a threat approaches the outer "fear" ring, the dog will go on red alert. If the threat is withdrawn, the dog will relax. If a threat penetrates the second "flight" ring, the dog will usually look for ways to escape and if he's successful, aggressive behavior will be averted. If the threat enters the bull's-eye, however, the dog will fight to defend himself.

Some dogs are called fear biters, and they are dangerous. Fear biters are in one of these three stages a good deal of the time. With some, these rings can almost be measured with a tape measure; in extreme cases, the three rings are almost on top of one another and are triggered simultaneously, so the dog can attack without warning. A dominant aggressive dog exhibits predictable behavior; a fear biter will frequently give a different reaction, or degree of reaction, each time, even to the same stimuli. These dogs attack whether the threat is real or not because they fear for their lives, not because they are big, bold, and dominant. The cause of fear biting in dogs is often genetic, and the problem occurs more in some breeds than in others, as well as in some lines of certain breeds. It can also be triggered by a single traumatic incident during a critical period of development, or it can develop if the dog has a fearful nature. Fear biters often attach to and trust only one person.

Although fear biters are dangerous animals, my heart goes out to them. To live in constant fear of people and new situations must be comparable to being afraid of snakes and living in a snake pit. If your dog exhibits any of these behaviors, it is imperative that you seek professional help immediately for an evaluation. The longer these problems go unaddressed, the worse they become.

BREED TRAITS AND CHARACTERISTICS

Humans have done an incredible amount of genetic engineering with domesticated animals over the years. Most of it is outdated; we no longer are a hunting or agrarian society, so most of us don't need dogs who are bred to hunt, herd, protect, pull sleds, and perform other tasks that were meaningful in past times.

The effects of enhanced traits dominate the dog's personality and responses, and behavioral problems may occur if the dog does not have a way to fulfill what he has been bred to do. Terriers, for example, were selectively bred to be feisty and to dig in the ground in order to catch vermin like rats or badgers. Living with a terrier usually means dealing with a feisty personality who loves to dig. If the dog has no outlet for that instinctive digging, then sometimes the couch is the target, particularly if it has a loose spring which sounds like a mouse squeaking.

TEMPERAMENT AND PERSONALITY

Temperament in a dog is generally defined as the way a dog deals with things over which he has no control: things like being in a city for the first time, learning how to swim, riding in an elevator, or meeting new people. He may be calm, curious, or extremely fearful in such situations.

Personality, or disposition, is generally defined as the way a dog deals with things over which he does have control, such as the approach of a person while he is eating, whether it is all right for someone to pick up his favorite toy while he is playing with it, and how he feels about having his tail accidentally stepped on. His responses will be open and friendly or defensive and aggressive, depending on his disposition.

A dog can have a good temperament and a rotten disposition or vice versa, and a dog who can handle things well when he is in control may totally freak out when something new or different is introduced. Soundness is a general term used to describe an ideal blending of the two. A mentally sound dog is one that is calm, steady, outgoing, and competent in both temperament and disposition.

THE DOG'S SENSES

The dog's sensitivity appears to be nothing short of magical. A partial list of the tasks they can be trained to perform include guiding for the blind and hearing-impaired, sensing and warning of the onset of epileptic seizures, detecting drugs in human body cavities as well as in all kinds of man-made structures, and detecting rats, termites, bombs, illegal kills during hunting season, missing persons, and bodies drowned or buried in snow or rubble. Recent research shows that dogs can even be trained to sniff out the presence of melanoma cancer.

When a client complains that his dog does not pay attention, it is often because humans do not realize that the dog is tuned in to levels of perception and reality that we have no easy way of entering. Dogs read their environment with senses other than sight, and this is very different from our experience, because we have become a predominantly visually oriented species.

Your dog trusts his sense of sight the least. If you want to prove this to yourself, notice how your dog acts when he sees you or a family member from a distance. It will be obvious that he is unsure who is approaching him. Many dogs typically begin to bark furiously at this point. When you start talking to him, he will be curious and unsure and will perhaps cock his head or shiver with nervousness. For that moment his eyes and his ears are in conflict. When you get close enough so that he can smell you, then he may lower his ears and act embarrassed, or he may jump madly around you with relief once he recognizes you. He always relies, above all, on his sense of smell.

Most dogs cannot see over distances the way we can, but their peripheral vision is better than ours, and they can better pick up on motion at a distance. Alertness to movement is especially heightened in the sight-hound breeds, which pursue their prey by sight rather than tracking by scent. Retrievers are trained to follow a directive hand signal and go in the direction that you point. Most dogs, however, will look at the end of your finger rather than beyond it. If you move your finger over to an object, their attention will follow the path you make to that object. If you raise and lower your hand, the dog follows your gesture with his head. You can train your dog to do directed retrieving in competitions or for fun, in which case you extend your whole hand and arm to signal the direction you want the dog to take.

Dogs also learn to pick up on very subtle motions. For example, some dogs who do tricks are signaled by almost imperceptible cues, like the trainer raising his eyebrows. For all of these reasons, I teach people to use a lot of emphatic hand signals when asking the dog to do something, because this makes the cue more accessible to the dog's mind.

Scientists generally agree that dogs cannot distinguish colors, but I am not so sure about this. I believe that matadors use red capes to incite a bull to charge because the intense color creates intense emotional reactions. My own work with colors and colored light has led me to believe that dogs actually can perceive and are sensitive to different wavelengths of light. Since different colors are of different vibrational frequencies, it is possible that the dog senses the frequency rather than the actual color.

Dogs do have better night vision than humans. (This is due to a prevalence of tapetum lucidum cells in their eyes, which admit and magnify light at night.)

Dogs' hearing is far more acute than that of humans. Humans can hear sounds between 16,000 and 18,000 oscillations per second. The average dog's range extends to 30,000 and 40,000 oscillations per second. Some dogs can hear up to 100,000 oscillations per second. Dogs can locate rodents by their high-frequency squeaks, which are well above human hearing range.

The dog's perception of his environment is predominantly influenced by his sense of smell. The dog's olfactory sense membrane commonly covers an area 10,000 times larger than that of the human, and breeds with long or large muzzles generally have a better sense of smell than short-muzzled breeds. Dogs constantly receive "scent-pictures" of their environment. As with humans, receiving scent information simultaneously with pain or pleasure can leave a lasting impression, and a reoccurrence of that scent can trigger emotional and psychological reactions.

Upon entering a room, a dog can tell who has been in there, how many people were in the room, whether they were male or female, whether there were children, whether they had a snack of tuna fish or peanut butter, whether there have been any male or female dogs in the room, and much more. This sensory stimulation is incessant. It is the dogs' reality, their world. They can't shut it off.

Dogs use their senses to assess their environment. The information a dog receives through his sense of smell usually influences his decision-making to a greater extent than does either his sight or hearing. This hierarchy of senses is highly functional. Acting upon olfactory clues, the dog can respond correctly to a danger that it did not detect through sight or hearing.

Finally, body sensitivity differs from one dog to another. Also, the pain reactions of each individual dog vary according to circumstances. When a dog is startled, for example, by having his tail stepped on, he may yelp and carry on as if seriously injured. However, if his mind is totally absorbed in something else, like winning a fight or running away from danger, he will temporarily ignore the pain, no matter how extreme, and become aware of his injuries only after the event is over.

Although we humans, especially in modern culture, do not use our senses to the extent that dogs do, we are nevertheless capable of accessing a greater range of sense information than we generally use. Professions like wine-tasting, or perfume-sampling, for example, require a refinement of taste and smell. People who have lost their sense of sight become able to hear much more acutely than the average person, and they can refine their sense of touch to decipher the small raised patterns in Braille. Isolating a single sense will heighten your ability to use it.

The following simple exercise will increase your awareness of your own senses and also help you understand why a dog can sometimes be overwhelmed by the number of sense impressions he receives in a given moment.

Read this list into a tape deck and then play it back for the greatest benefit:

- Get into a comfortable position; you may choose to sit, stand, or lie down.

- Take several deep breaths, relax your body, and close your eyes. This will help you focus more clearly on your other senses. We have become a very visual society. The more we use our eyes, the less we perceive in other ways.

- Shift your awareness to your sense of hearing. Notice what you hear in the room, now that you have focused on that sense. Are there high sounds? Are there low ones? Which sounds feel comforting and which annoy you or don't register any emotion at all? Can you feel a sound vibrate in parts of your body other than in your head? Can you identify all of the sounds? Do any sounds evoke certain feelings, especially sounds you cannot instantly identify? With the shift in focus, be aware of how much more you can hear than before.

- Now project your listening beyond the walls of the room. You don't have to identify all of the sounds; just be aware that you can do this. Airplanes, birdsong, and car noises may suddenly seem louder when you shift your focus. Again, notice how this feels in your body. Don't limit your experience to your ears and brain. Are you aware of any emotional reactions to the sounds you are hearing? Are any of them disconcerting, annoying, nostalgic, confusing, or soothing?

- Keeping your eyes closed and remaining relaxed, shift your awareness to your sense of smell. If there is another person in the room, can you smell the subtle difference in odors from one human body to another? Can you distinguish those scents from food smells or smells given off by furnishings or by air coming through an open window? How many scents can you isolate? If there are any food smells, can you identify each one? Can you smell dust, cologne, fabric softener, the fragrance from any plants? If there is an open window, which smells are coming from nature and which from cars and other machines?

- Focus on your sense of touch for a moment. Experience how your body feels where it is in contact with the chair or the floor. Experience how different parts of your body feel. Feel your glasses on your face and your watch on your wrist. Are there places where you feel tension or discomfort in your body?

- Stretch as you end this experiment, and feel how your muscles respond. See if you can remember how a dog stretches after resting or sleeping. How does he reawaken his body?

- Shake your arms and hands or even your whole body and notice how that feels. Pay attention to the times when your dog uses that shake, not because he is wet but to wake himself and become ready for action. Dogs also will often give themselves a good shake to release tension—after receiving a reprimand, for example.

I hope this sensory exercise has shown you something about the possibility of expanding your own awareness and has increased your appreciation of the wonderful uniqueness of another species.

BASIC TRAINING TRUTHS

Dogs who share their lives with humans need guidance, direction, structure, and limits, because those things occur naturally in a pack. Because two different species are sharing one environment and social structure, it is necessary to clarify the different roles in the relationship. I prefer to think about this issue in the following way:

Life is a game, and all games have rules. We could say that we have taken the dog from his natural playing field and put him on ours. If, however, we do not teach the dog the rules for our environment, then there will be problems, because the dog has no way of understanding how to function. If the dog is going to be on my playing field, I need to regard him as a teammate, not an adversary. It falls to me to be the captain, because I know the rules for my game, and the dog doesn't. I need to teach him the plays in order to help him act in a socially acceptable way in my world. I also need to teach him that I require an immediate response to those plays, so that when there is an emergency or crisis, I can keep him safe. I do not agree with training books that tell you you have to think and act like the alpha dog, the leader of the pack. Dogs are not stupid; they know we are not dogs. We don't even have tails!

You need to give your dog guidelines and limits, but there are many ways to earn his respect without setting up an adversarial relationship. If you think of yourself as needing to dominate, you are always going to be worried about being overthrown, and your reactions will be defensive rather than loving and understanding. Furthermore, it can be ruinous for certain high-strung dogs to experience an alpha shakedown—a move that asserts the human's domination over the dog. If you perform a dominating move with a dog, you are not only asserting yourself, you are also calling the dog to the mat for a fight. This should absolutely never be attempted by someone whose dog is already growling and snapping. If you don't know what you are doing, you may end up with a multitude of stitches in your face.

It is much easier to work with a dog's mind than to fight with his body, and it is far more rewarding to work for harmony, respect, love, and mutual communication.

How Dogs Learn

A domesticated animal like the dog is a mixture of instinctive behavioral drives and learned behaviors. A learned, or cognitive behavior is something that we teach the dog to do. However, you need to be aware that no matter how much training a dog has received, instinctive behavior is always there, right under the surface.

Most instinctive behavior is directly associated with survival. Major areas include hunting and scavenging; carrying away, stashing, and defending food; self-defense; the seeking of safety, especially while at rest, for self and progeny (this includes the search and preparation of a suitable den area); and breeding and reproduction.

There are three main classes of learned behavior: (1) that which the puppy learns through association with its own kind, such as vocalizing, posturing, and the meanings of these postures; (2) that which the dog learns independently, through trial and error, such as not to repeat acts that are unsuccessful; and (3) patterning, or that which is taught by humans, such as certain behaviors.

Dog training is generally based on the principle of conditioning, the teaching of a specific behavior in response to a certain stimulus. Behavior can be deliberately taught, as in training, or it can evolve out of human-dog interactions and communication as each attempts to satisfy his own needs. (My story of Sallie, the spoiled springer spaniel is an excellent example of the latter.) There is always an underlying motivator, some kind of expectation created, either of something pleasant or desirable to be gained or of something to be avoided.

We condition the dog to perform in certain ways by using physical, oral, mental, and emotional cues. Here are some basic training guidelines, which I will repeat over and over in this book:

- Dogs are born knowing how to bark, bite, dig, chew, chase, jump up on one another, eliminate when they need to, and snarl when they feel threatened. It is a challenge to get a dog to suppress or modify his instincts in order to make human existence more pleasant. If the dog reverts, you need to remember that that these acts are not malicious; the dog is simply doing the best he can with the information he has been given about living with and behaving in a socially acceptable way toward a totally different species.

- Dogs can learn whatever you can find a way to teach them, so long as it is within their physical capability to perform.

- Dogs, like humans, take the path of least resistance; they only do what works well and easily to satisfy their needs and desires. If it is a self-rewarding move, they will repeat and escalate the behavior, whether that behavior is in harmony or conflict with your wishes.

- Every dog has its own point of motivation, a trigger that will evoke a response and awaken its desire to respond to its human.

Most behavioral problems people experience with their dogs are the result of a lack of early patterning, socialization, and training. If you haven't given your dog the right information about living with humans very early in its life, there will be a void, and the dog's instinctive behaviors will become stronger as he matures. In order to prevent this from happening, early training is critical. Even at three months, if a dog can learn the wrong thing, he can also learn the right thing. By the time puppies reach six months of age and have reached the teenage testing and rebellion phase of their growth, they often have lost a lot of their cuteness and appeal and things have begun to get out of hand. Then, at ten or eleven months, many dogs with behavior problems are sent to the pound.

I like to start working with puppies the moment they are born, because I find that puppies who have received constant attention and association with people tend to develop the fewest behavior problems. Eight weeks is generally considered to be the accepted age for adopting out or selling puppies, and in my own state of New Hampshire, it is against the law to sell or give them away before that time, because of the behavior problems that arise when they leave their mothers and littermates too soon. I will speak more about puppies in Chapter 15.

The number of rescued dogs who are living with me, as well as those I have retrained and found homes for, is testimony to the fact that it is possible to teach an old dog new tricks. Even so, it takes longer to change a habit that has become ingrained or to erase a learned behavior pattern and substitute a new one.

Once an acknowledged and accepted behavior is learned, it can be very hard on the dog if his job description changes. I had a client who was in the midst of a very ugly divorce; she acquired a mastiff because she was afraid of her ex-husband. She was very nervous every time a car went by her house, so it made her feel safer if her dog barked wildly when someone came to the house. A year later, after the divorce was final, she came to me because she had opened an inn and the dog was scaring away all of her guests.

We had to take the dog through a series of repatterning exercises to make it clear to him that his companion now felt safe. We used flower essences to help with the emotional aspects of the problem, and friends practiced coming to her door. I taught her to project the emotion that she was happy to have visitors, so that her dog could receive a clear message that she was not afraid, while at the same time she rewarded him with praise and affection for not barking.

It is very common for people to tell stories of dogs being vindictive. For example, if a dog with a destructive chewing problem takes the house apart in the person's absence, the person may say, "That dog destroys things to get even with me because I left him alone!"

In fact, for most dogs, destructive chewing is the result of boredom or separation anxiety. They have nothing to do when they are left in the house all day. Chewing is a normal dog pastime. A dog tends to target your favorite things in your absence because those items are heavily permeated with your scent, and he finds this reassuring in your absence.

Some people may find it hard to accept that dogs don't feel the negative emotions that we do, especially when you walk in the door, see a puddle on the floor and the dog cringing and anxiously wagging his tail, because he has been conditioned by prior experiences to expect negative reactions from you. But why should a dog express behaviors that we interpret as guilt, if it does not deliberately, intentionally misbehave?

We learn guilt from society, from our parents, and by comparing ourselves to other humans. Canine culture doesn't have these teachings; dogs always do the best they can, and if their performance isn't perfect, they don't agonize over it, because they have nothing to prove. They have a far more expansive scope of reality, and they don't get hung up on ego issues.

I have rarely seen an instance where I felt a dog was being deliberately spiteful or malicious. I believe that dogs are beyond these emotions, which require harboring resentments, calculating for the future, and worrying about self-image. The fact is that dogs live for the most part in the present moment; they live in the here and now with their entire being.

Experiencing the way an animal lives in the present is one of the most wonderful, powerful, and precious gifts that our dogs give to us. It's very hard for humans to stay in the moment; we tend to obsess about what happened yesterday or a year ago, or what is going to happen tomorrow. But dogs are very much "now" creatures.

This makes it critical that the guidance you give your dog is clear and consistent, because he processes each new piece of information in each moment. Dogs do not mull things over afterward while lounging on the front stoop. When they are lounging, they are totally present and relaxed in body and mind. A great lesson for all of us!

Being in the now is your only point of power. It's one of the most wonderful things that my animals remind me of over and over. I am who I am right now. You're not the same person you were yesterday; I'm not the same person I was an hour ago. Everything is always changing; it's changing in the now.

The inevitability of change is, of course, a factor in living with your dog. When clients ask me how long it will take to train a dog, I reply with a chuckle, "Forever! Learning and communication never stop!" Because life never stands still, learning, communication, and the cultivation of awareness and mutual respect between you and your dog will always be an ongoing process, a give-and-take that responds to the inevitable changes in the environment, your relationship, and your needs.

A dog can learn the basics fairly quickly, but he forgets if his human companion does not maintain the same level of interaction. If the rules change, the dog falls back on his instincts, and feelings of stress, confusion, and anxiety can arise and create disharmony in the relationship. Therefore, once the groundwork is covered, there should always be an ongoing process of monitoring and fine-tuning to ensure that the structure of expectations that has been created is maintained. A consistent interest in the dog's learning can also be especially rewarding for people who want to see how deep their level of communication can become.

When you bring a dog home, hopefully it is with the intent to make a commitment to that dog for life. This also applies to the issue of breeding dogs. I believe that far too many people allow their dogs to have puppies and then assume that the responsibility stops after the puppies are given away or sold. The amount of indiscriminate breeding in America today is a major factor contributor to the decline of healthy, intelligent, long-lived animals. When I bred Irish setters and Shetland sheepdogs, all of my puppy buyers had to sign an agreement stating that if they decided to give the dog up, they had to return it to me.

Whether you breed dogs or simply bring one home, if you begin with consciousness and responsibility, you will have the best chance of finding solutions to any problems.

2

YOUR DOG

In this chapter I'll try to help you get a clear idea of who is, or will be, sharing your life. It is important that you be very specific in your analysis, be clear about your expectations, and compare this information with the dog you have or think you need. Once you do this, you will be able to understand what can be changed and what must be respected as an aspect that is part of the dog's individual and genetic makeup.

If you already have a dog, take a moment first to appreciate fully where you are in your relationship with your dog right now. Think about the lessons and experiences you have already shared. Go for a walk or just sit outside and observe your dog in a fenced-in area where he is safe. Notice how completely aware he is of his environment, how tuned in to the energy of life all around him, whether it is the motion of a bug, the sound of a bird or squirrel in some dry leaves, or the exhilaration that comes from a sharp wind.

Look at your dog as though you are seeing him for the first time or as if he belonged to someone else. This will fine-tune your observation of the details. For example, how does he carry his body when he is relaxed? Note how his body signals differ when he is agitated, suspicious, or fearful. How does he normally carry his tail? How does he respond to different pitches of your voice? If you speak quickly in a high voice, does he get overly excited or does it just make him happy? All praise should be sincere and enthusiastic, but frequently and particularly during stationary exercises, your voice will need to be low and calm. You will be telling your dog through the music in your voice to lower his energy. How does your dog respond if you try this now?

Look for things in your dog that would indicate any underlying physical problems. When he walks, is there a stiffness in a certain part of his body? Does he shake his head a lot? Does he scratch a lot?

Is his skin dry? Does he have the kind of trouble getting up that might indicate a hip problem such as dysplasia? Does he seem to tire quickly, even though he's not old, which might indicate an underlying heart or health problem? All of this information will contribute to a depth of understanding of who your dog really is.

After you have done this part of the exercise, get to know the dog behind the eyes. When you are in a relaxed state, gaze softly, without staring, into your dog's eyes. Those things that you observe, both physically and intuitively, give you insight into his personality. You may get a sense that the dog tends to be a worried, assertive, or happy-go-lucky, joyful being. Try to develop a deep sense of how the things that he does with his body and the moods that he expresses through his eyes are expressions of a unique being.

Look into your dog's eyes, but at the same time, look at the whole dog and blink languidly, slowly, and purposefully, like a cat. Stay relaxed and absolutely do not stare. Smile as you gaze at your dog. Become even more relaxed. See if you perceive any intuitive messages or emotions coming from your dog.

Here are some other things to check: Is your dog more responsive to verbal praise alone? Does he become distracted or too excited if you touch and pat him, or does he enjoy that touch and find it comforting, calming, and reassuring? Is he more motivated by a food reward or by an object like a toy or a ball? Does he have a favorite toy?

Now do a different analysis of your dog and look at everything else that constitutes who your dog is. Consider breed characteristics, temperament, stage of development, and disposition. You'll find a form later in this chapter for you to fill in after you have read the basic information.

STEP ONE: RESEARCH YOUR DOG'S BREED

Read an appropriate book or magazine, or do a search on the Internet, to find out what your dog was originally bred to do. Don't get stuck on descriptions of the perfect appearance, because looks are important only for show dogs. I can say this after many years on the show circuit as a professional handler. For companion dogs, it is far more important to put the emphasis on good temperament, disposition, and mental soundness.

Hawk, an Australian shepherd who lives with me, cannot be shown because one of his ears has a tendency to stand up rather than to fold over for a show-style look. This, of course, in no way affects him as far as his temperament, soundness, and conformation are concerned. In fact, the wonderful thing about Hawk is that he has so much to offer: a working dog's weather-resistant coat that never mats or tangles, so it needs minimal grooming, correct conformation and a very athletic body, a sharp intelligence, and a lovely personality. These details should be the priorities for a family dog.

After you learn what your dog was originally bred to do, you will have some insight into which training exercises will be easy for the dog and which might be more difficult. Greyhounds, for example, are a galloping breed originally used for hunting and running prey to ground. They are heavily muscled in the hindquarters with a natural arch in their back so it can coil like a spring. They often have difficulty sitting because of their build.

You may wish to compete in various dog sport activities, but be aware that your dog may not be able to fulfill your expectations. Some dogs are natural athletes and make great agility dogs. If your dog has structural problems, however, agility exercises may cause him pain or discomfort. Even if he is structurally sound, he may not enjoy the mental challenge of running an obstacle course. It can be very frustrating for the dog if you decide he is going to become something that he does not have the natural desire or ability to do. Perhaps this same dog likes to use his nose to seek out things and could make a superb tracking dog.

All dogs, like their human counterparts, have something that they are good at and especially love doing. When you dream about the times you will share with your dog, focus on activities that will enhance his natural abilities in order to experience the fulfillment of the potential that your dog brings to the relationship. My goal with every animal I have is to see how far we can go together in our level of communication and mutual enjoyment of activities. The more I commit to learning about and nurturing the animal's gifts, the more I receive in return.

STEP TWO: RESEARCH YOUR DOG'S TEMPERAMENT

In most books about specific dog breeds, there will be only one tiny paragraph labeled "Temperament and Personality." This is the most important paragraph to read if you are looking for a good companion! It will give you the best indication of what you are likely to be dealing with.

If you already have a dog, read that section to see whether your dog fits the description of the breed. Is she supposed to be friendly and outgoing? Is she supposed to be very dedicated to her human companion and aloof with strangers? Aloof doesn't mean shy or a fear biter. It simply means the dog would rather be with you than give attention to a stranger.

If you have a mixed-breed, look up each of the breeds in your dog. What you see on the outside will not necessarily dictate what is on the inside, because of dominant and recessive genes. If you have a collie-shepherd mix, for example, he could look mostly like a German shepherd, but mentally his behavior patterns and personality could be more like those of a collie. As a matter of fact, out of all of the puppies in a litter, no two will have exactly the same genetic packaging. There is generally no such thing as half-and-half. It's like rolling dice: you can come up with a different genetic combination every single time. Temperament and disposition can also vary widely in a litter, because dogs are individuals.

This fact was very evident in a group of fourteen Shetland sheepdogs that I showed professionally. After winning many ribbons, I saw that the dogs were getting bored with competition, so I trained them to perform as an exhibition team called the K-9 Drill Team. We gave benefit performances for different animal causes in the Northeast and Canada. Six of the Shelties would pull a cart while two sat in the driver's seat; one dog would go over high jumps carrying a raw egg in his mouth without cracking it, and another would jump over a side-by-side row of ten of his teammates. There were numerous other demonstrations of their intelligence and athletic ability. I bred these dogs myself and was fascinated to see how different they were from one another. This meant that, although I needed them to work in unison, I had to take each dog on its own terms.

Shiloh, a big male, was serious even as a puppy. I used to joke that when Shiloh was having fun, he was seriously having fun. Duke by contrast, was always humorous. He would rather get a laugh than win a ribbon in the show ring. And Tarl was unusually conscientious. I never had to raise my voice with him if he made a mistake. If I even looked slightly disappointed, he was devastated. He was extremely precise and careful about everything and basically a happy dog, but, like some people, he had to have everything just perfect.

Do I think there are "good" and "bad" breeds? No. I have seen a broad spectrum of both desirable and undesirable qualities in every breed. All dogs are individuals with a wide range of temperament, disposition, and personality combinations. It is very important that these characteristics are compatible with their human companions. We have to get rid of the term "bad dog." I dislike generalizations, particularly because dogs that are called bad are usually blamed for things that are not their fault.

TAWNY THE TERRIBLE

If, after all of your research, you find that your dog doesn't fit the descriptions, you may have drawn a wild card. When it comes to temperament and personality, the story of Tawny is a good example of a unique dog.

Many of the dogs who live with me are too challenging for the average person to deal with. Tawny is such a dog. He came into my life in the following way: a woman named Lorna called me about her family's new dog, who had come from the humane society. She was at her wit's end with him.

As I listened to her describe all of the problems she was having with him, a strange thing began to happen. I suddenly realized that I had a clear image of the dog in my head. His face, even the expression in his eyes, was as clear as if he were sitting in front of me. He was small, probably a dachshund mix, with a short ginger-colored coat, dangling ears that were pricked up, so that his forehead wrinkled in a comical way, and dark eyes that were full of energy and a steady, impish gaze. I focused on this vision for a moment and then blinked. It disappeared as my attention was drawn back to Lorna, who was explaining that her family had never owned a dog before. Obviously, this was a lot of dog. He didn't just bark; he also shrieked. If he was let out of his crate, he would tear the house apart and nip at anyone who tried to take things away from him that he had grabbed or chewed up. If they put him in the crate, he would urinate and smear it with feces. This last was unusual, because dogs instinctively keep their den area, or the place where they sleep, clean.

I kept listening to Lorna talk, and the strange premonition lingered. This was the first time I'd had that experience, and I was very curious about it. She had not described what the dog looked like. Why could I see him so clearly?

"Well, I'll have a look at him," I said. "I don't know if I can do anything." I should have known.

Her car pulled up, and out came a whirling dervish on a rope. He was, to the smallest detail, exactly what I had seen. I have never had that experience with a dog before or since. He was little and cute, but full of the devil. His name at that time was Beau, which to me sounded too much like "no," a word the dog had heard incessantly since he'd joined Lorna's family. I took his lead from her, and she beat a hasty retreat. He looked at me for a second as if to say, "Okay, I'm finally here—where's the party?"

He had every bad habit a dog could have. It took a month to work through crate training so he would keep his crate clean and stop the incessant screaming when he was confined. But he had charisma which was good, because otherwise no one would have cut him any slack at all.

I renamed him Tawny, and he quickly taught me that there is no such word as "can't." He absolutely does not grasp the concept of obstacles. He's a little dog with big courage, and anything he puts his mind to, he does. He can undo crate latches, turn doorknobs with his teeth and open doors, and find his way into anyone's car if the window is open just a crack. No gate can keep him in, and there is no fence that he can't leap over, including the smooth six-foot vertical-board fence around my backyard. People will come to Hearthside and

"Tawny"

be stopped dead in their tracks when a furry fifteen-inch missile comes flying over the tall fence to check them out.

Tawny's personality was not about to be changed, but he has learned to coexist and compromise without ever giving up who he is, and this is the biggest lesson he's taught me. Of course, I had to compromise also, by giving up the idea that he was ever going to stay where I put him when he had another agenda.

Tawny is not the dog for everyone, but his story is a good example of the importance of accepting the entire dog and not just the parts you like. If there are aspects of a dog that you wish were different, you will have to be realistic and see what actually can be changed, as opposed to what you will simply have to accept as an authentic expression of who the dog is.

STEP THREE: WHAT IS YOUR DOG'S STAGE OF BEHAVIORAL DEVELOPMENT?

Even if you have a dog like Tawny and have finally attained a harmonious coexistence, remember that with animals, as with people, nothing stays the same. You are not the same person you were last week; you've learned more; your feelings and reactions have changed. It is the same with dogs, plus they, like humans, go through various behavioral development stages that are quite predictable. Knowing this will help you understand any possible speed bumps that might occur in training. Dogs go through fear imprint periods, protective aggression stages, and periods of adolescent testing and rebellion, but these periods do not last as long in dogs as they do in people. This is why, for example, your dog can grow overnight from a cute little puppy to a testing teenager at about four and a half weeks of age.

As you read the following section, see if you can determine your dog's current stage of development:

Birth to three weeks: Newborn puppies need warmth, food, sleep, and are totally dependent on their mother. They are neurologically very primitive, responding by reflexes. Even simple body functions such as urination and defecation are reflex responses to their mother's licking. At this time there is no capacity for real learning.

Four weeks: Puppies are still dependent on the bitch, but this is a critical period of extremely rapid sensory development during which they become acutely aware of their surroundings and begin to interact with their environment. Puppies are very vulnerable to psychological trauma at this stage; therefore this is the wrong time for weaning.

Five to seven weeks: Puppies are still dependent on their mother and their littermates. Dogs that are removed from the litter at this time tend to be unable to socialize well with other dogs later on. Resulting problems can include aggressive behavior with other dogs, neurotic behavior, and refusal to breed. They also tend to become overdependent on their human companions, which leads to overprotectiveness, excessive barking, biting, and general unresponsiveness to discipline. If left with the mother, however, they learn to respond to authority and to accept discipline, which she delivers swiftly, firmly, and lovingly. They learn that hard biting usually brings swift retaliation, which teaches them to develop an "inhibited" bite. At this age puppies practice body posturing, vocalizing, and biting with their littermates.

Seven weeks: The brain is now completely developed. The puppy's learning capacity is that of an adult; however, his attention span is still short, like that of a young child. Concentration is very limited and he is easily distracted. Everything the puppy comes in contact with now leaves a lasting impression, as he enters his time of greatest learning. Because he is assimilating information so rapidly, it is important for safe, nonstressful socialization with people and other animals to begin. He needs to become aware that there is a whole world beyond the familiar confines of his den area.

Now the puppy enters into a series of frequently overlapping stages:

Eight to ten or eleven weeks—fear imprint period: Anything traumatic that happens during this age will leave a lasting impression and will provoke defensive reactions throughout the dog's life. Things such as elective surgery or shipping should be postponed.

Eight to twelve weeks—optimum socialization period: This is the time when the puppy should be exposed in a nonthreatening way to everything and everybody he will encounter in adult life—children, men and women, other animals including livestock and especially cats, experiences like riding in cars (to pleasant places, not just to the vet). This is also a good time to begin kindergarten puppy training. Puppies can learn basic communication cues, but their attention span is still short, so training should be adjusted accordingly.

Twelve to fourteen or sixteen weeks—period when serious training should begin: Puppies are now beginning to assert themselves; any nipping or displays of dominance toward people need to be addressed immediately. The onset of puberty also occurs now, frequently accompanied by experimental sexual mounting. Males begin having erections.

Sixteen to thirty-two or forty weeks—period when adolescent testing stage begins: When told to "come," a puppy of this age will often scoot off in the opposite direction. A puppy who up to now has followed his human companion everywhere will suddenly refuse to follow and start venturing off on his own. (This is about the time that my phone starts ringing!) This is also the beginning of protective and territorial tendencies, such as barking at strangers. Leg-lifting in males usually begins at this time.

Twenty-four to fifty-six weeks (six to thirteen months)—second fear imprint period: Dogs may begin acting suspicious or afraid, even of something or someone familiar. Many dogs, as a result of this insecurity, display the protective-aggressive behavior characteristic of the fear biter. A general persistence of behavior problems becomes apparent, and corrections for these become more difficult as time passes. It has been my experience that this second fear imprint period occurs at different times in different breeds. I see it occur around six to seven months in basenjis, for example, and around ten to eleven months in shelties.

One to four years—maturity: This period can bring purposeful protective-aggressive behavior and renewed testing of leadership. Problem behavior can become habitual, especially if it becomes self-rewarding. By this age, dogs that have received proper socialization, training, and direction throughout their earlier development stages are reliable, responsive companions. Dogs that did not receive proper guidance during these periods are locked into patterns of "problem" or "neurotic" behavior that may be very difficult to change.

STEP FOUR: IS YOUR DOG EXCITABLE OR INHIBITED?

Your dog is going to have a tendency to be either excitable or inhibited, though things can change, depending on the situation. Excitable dogs vent things outward. They jump on doors and people, pull on leads, bark at things, and express everything outwardly when they are excited or stressed.

Inhibited dogs can become very introverted and can literally become unable to function.

STEP FIVE: DOES YOUR DOG HAVE ACTIVE
OR PASSIVE DEFENSE REFLEXES?

All dogs, in certain situations, can—and most will—use their teeth to assert or defend themselves. When you evaluate your dog, recognize that I am not talking about a dog that is being unduly stressed. Decide how ready, willing, and able your dog is to use his teeth either to assert or to defend himself on a daily basis. Does it take a little or does it take a lot? I have dealt with some dogs who would have liked to take a chunk out of me if I made direct eye contact. Other dogs, no matter how much physical abuse they have endured, will rarely use their teeth to defend themselves. Dogs with active defense reflexes and those with passive can occur in the same litter. Animals are individuals: you need to know your dog! You need to know his limits and how he thinks and responds.

STEP SIX: WHAT IS YOUR DOG'S LEVEL OF
SIGHT, SOUND, AND TOUCH SENSITIVITY?

Understanding your dog's response level to external stimuli will allow you to be more effective if corrections are needed. It will also enable you to predict any unusual sensitivity that might create a difficulty during training. Evaluate these on a scale of one to ten, with one as the lowest, ten as the highest.

Sight: If your dog sees something he hasn't encountered before, and he doesn't know what it is, what is his reaction response? Does he become hysterical and bark wildly? Does he startle at first, and then get curious and cautiously check it out? Or does he calmly look at it, possibly check it out, acknowledge it, and then put his attention on other things?

Sound: What is your dog's reaction to sudden loud noises? If you drop a metal pie plate or a pan on the kitchen floor, does she take off, kii-yii-ing out of the room and refuse to come back in? Does she startle and run at first, and then quickly come back to see what made the noise? Or does she turn around and check out the cause of the noise?

You also need to learn how your dog responds to different tones of voice. Does she pay better attention, for example, to deep voices or to high ones?

Touch: (A warning: if you are aware of the fact that your dog has particularly sensitive feet or becomes hostile when his feet are handled, omit this exercise.) Assess your dog's sensitivity to physical stimuli by gently taking his paw and applying moderate to firm pressure to the webbing or skin between his toes with the tips of your fingers (not your fingernails). Start to use firm pressure, and begin to count. Some dogs will react by the time you get to two. (As soon as you get a response *stop* applying pressure at once.) Other dogs will yawn and watch you count to ten and beyond while your fingers go into a cramp. Touch sensitivity is not a matter of size. I have worked with Great Danes who were so touch-sensitive that I could walk them with the leash draped over my finger and guide them with the slightest crook of that finger. I have also contended with small Jack Russell terriers who required several fairly firm corrections to begin to get their attention.

STEP SEVEN: WHAT IS YOUR DOG'S POINT OF MOTIVATION?

This information will help you to know whether it will take a little or a lot to get your dog's attention when the two of you begin training. Your dog's point of motivation is the volume and tone of voice, eye contact, body posture, and corrections needed to gain the immediate desired response.

Your dog was born with that level of sensory motivation. It is dictated by his level of sensitivity, independence, social attraction to you, and desire to please. Most dogs are a mixture of these, but occasionally there are those dogs who reach extremes on either end. If you end up with an extremely touch-sensitive dog who is very willing and eager to please no matter what you do, then you can consider yourself among the blessed. You have what is known as a soft dog. If you have a dog, however, who does not seem all that interested in whether you have a connection with him or not, and who has the touch sensitivity of a football, you have your work cut out for you!

This is not a question of whether one dog is better than the other. It's a question of *what is*. It's about learning to work with and accept what you have.

A dog's point of motivation doesn't stay the same, although you will learn to predict most of his reactions. When your dog is calm and relaxed, you will find that you can easily get results with a soft to moderate tone of voice and, if needed, some guidance with the leash or some other direction. If, however, something gets him excited and his adrenaline starts pumping, his point of motivation will be radically different. If you do not adjust your communication skills, you will find yourself completely ignored. In fact, if you are under or below your dog's point of motivation, your lack of ability to communicate will often cause him to intensify his focus. He will tune you out because he will find you slightly distracting, like an annoying mosquito.

FILL OUT YOUR DOG'S PROFILE

Each member in the family who interacts with the dog and is participating in the training process should now fill out a profile, preferably without discussing the answers with other family members. After these are completed, there should be a round-table discussion and comparison of answers.

Sometimes the results can sound as if there are several different dogs in one family, even though there is really only one. These differences in perception—along with conflicting needs and expectations, or different enforcement or lack of enforcement of rules—can create a lot of problems and stress for the dog. This, in turn, can cause him to exhibit inconsistent or disruptive behavior, which is upsetting to the family.

Family consultations, where everyone learns to cooperate and compromise can help to resolve some of these differences, especially after they are out in the open. This kind of learning, on behalf of a beloved family member who happens to be your dog, can be a wonderful experience for everyone.

DOG'S NAME:

AGE:

SEX:

BREED(S):

PURPOSE OF BREED:

DESIRED TEMPERAMENT AND PERSONALITY FOR THE BREED:

MY DOG IS _____ TYPICAL _____ NOT TYPICAL.

DOG'S AGE AND STAGE OF BEHAVIORAL DEVELOPMENT: _____

_____

DOG IS _____ EXCITABLE _____ INHIBITED.

DOG HAS _____ ACTIVE _____ PASSIVE DEFENSE REFLEXES.

SENSITIVITY ON A SCALE OF ONE TO TEN: _____ SIGHT
_____ SOUND _____ TOUCH

ON A SCALE OF ONE TO TEN, HOW RESPONSIVE IS YOUR DOG IF YOU NEED TO GET HIS ATTENTION WHEN HE IS EXCITED OR DISTRACTED? _____

HOW RESPONSIVE IS HE WHEN HE IS RELAXED? _____

MORE LESSONS ABOUT GETTING TO KNOW YOUR DOG

The exercise in this section is a wonderful way for you to increase your powers of observation and learn more about dogs in general.

Dogs have many ways of using their bodies to show each other what they are thinking. Some of these movements are general, and some are specific to the individual dog. If a dog shows his teeth, for example, it can mean he is angry, annoyed, or fearful and ready to bite, or that he is doing a submissive grin. Amy, my old greyhound, greets visitors with a submissive grin and chatters her teeth to tell you that she just loves you to pieces. Sometimes visitors back way off when they see this, which simply crushes her. They do not know the difference between a grin and a snarl because they are not understanding the rest of her body language, which indicates that she is relaxed and wriggling with eagerness to be patted.

It is difficult to read the signals in dogs who have no tails or who are so shaggy that their eyes are covered with hair. The Old English sheepdog, who has no tail, and whose ears and eyes are covered with dense hair, is a good example. I always make sure that this hair is lifted off the eyes and held back with a rubber band or a barrette when I work with them, to be able to communicate better with them.

The general lack of knowledge about the meaning of dog body language in an individual dog sometimes creates labeling and dangerous situations. For example, a common belief is that Irish setters are friendly and that German shepherds can be dangerous.

I had a big male Irish setter named Rebel who did not fit that stereotype. He was very protective of me, my daughter, and our home. I also had a very large, completely black male German shepherd named King. He was very scary-looking; when he opened his mouth, all you saw was a set of big pointy white teeth in a very black face. And he just loved everybody.

If a car pulled up and King was out in the yard, he always barked excitedly, prancing and wagging his whole self up to the fence to say hello. People would not even get out of their car when they saw him! King would get quite deflated, never understanding why his greetings were not immediately returned.

When Rebel was out in the yard, his whole body stiff and vibrating with a low, deep, ominous growl, people would come right up to him without fear. He would relax once I indicated that it was all right for the person to be there, but it amazed me all the same that the notion "Irish safe, German shepherd dangerous" was such a strong influence on the way people behaved.

When I have a new dog in my home and I don't know anything about him, I begin our relationship by sitting quietly and observing. In addition to doing the kinds of observations described at the beginning of this chapter, I try to learn how to predict the dog's behavior. I watch to see how he uses his body to communicate and how he responds to different stimuli and to a variety of interactions that I initiate.

It would be ideal if you would spend some time doing this observation every day until you feel very secure in your knowledge of your dog and her typical responses. Share the project with family members; if you have more than one person in the household, it can be fun to see who can make the most accurate predictions. In the final analysis, your ability to read your pet and respond appropriately and intuitively is ultimately the greatest test of your knowledge and awareness.

The following story illustrates how my awareness of a dog's behavior, as well as my acknowledgment of the importance of mutual respect in a relationship, enabled me to decide exactly how to act at a crucial time.

I had seen a notice in the papers that said "Special dog with problems needs an understanding home." The dog was described as an Australian shepherd. Somewhat curious (because I have a soft spot for Aussies), I clipped the query out and saved it; I was going to call, but got busy and didn't.

Several weeks later a woman rang, identified herself as Janine, and spoke quickly, sounding rather desperate: "I hear you do Australian shepherd rescue? I have a dog I need to place. Can you possibly take her?"

I asked for the dog's history. Janine explained: "She belonged to a couple who lived way out in the wilderness on top of a mountain, and they raised these dogs; they had about fifteen of them. Because they owned the whole mountain, they allowed the dogs to run loose. They didn't want them stolen, so they taught them to be afraid of strangers. They were quite proud of the fact that they were the only ones who could get near them."

"Then they had to move and they couldn't take all of the dogs, so they sold this one to me, and I got her sister too. I named this one Pretty Girl, and the two were very shy when I got them, but I thought they'd both settle in eventually."

They hadn't. Both dogs were constantly breaking free from their collars and tie-out chains and running off. Finally the dogs were taken to an area humane society. Within a half hour both had scaled the fencing and were gone. It was January. The dogs lived on their own in the wild for the rest of that month and all of February. Janine and her collie got near them several times but could not catch them.

"They eventually ran into a porcupine and Pretty Girl's sister got so badly quilled in the mouth that she couldn't eat or drink, so she died. I was able to catch Pretty Girl then, because she was weak and starving. But now,"

Janine continued, "my husband is adamant that we can't deal with her any-more, and the humane society said if they took her they would just put her down because she is not placeable. I would hate to have that happen. It's not her fault that she was raised to be afraid!"

My respect for Janine had grown considerably in the course of the phone call. Obviously she had made an enormous effort to try to save this dog. I sud-denly remembered the ad I had saved and asked her if she had placed it. "Yes," she replied, "but none of the people who called sounded as if they could handle a dog like her."

Janine came over. As soon as her car stopped, the door flew open and a medium-size black, white, and brown dog leaped out of the car and began to twist and pull frantically on the end of the lead. She had obviously been very carsick, and now she had a massive attack of diarrhea.

I went up to the pair and said, "Can I help you?" Janine was a harried-looking woman in her forties, who said, "I'm the person who called with the Australian shepherd."

"Where is she?" I asked.

Janine looked at me blankly, gestured at the dog, and said, "Right here!"

"Well, she may be an Australian something, but she's definitely not an Australian shepherd," I said. "I have a couple of Aussies, and she does not look at all like them."

Janine was deflated. "You're probably not interested, then," she said, still standing there, looking at me hopefully.

I looked at the poor dog, shaking all over, drool dripping down to the ground, eyes like saucers in her head, and said, "If you want to leave her with me and sign the release papers, I'll begin working with her, but I can't guar-antee that I can place her."

She agreed. We went to the training building, Janine signed the release form and was gone, and I was left hanging on to a very miserable-looking dog. She looked to be about a year and a half old. I could see that she was proba-bly predominantly Australian cattle dog—a different breed entirely—and built strong for long, hard days of working out on the range. She had short hair, erect ears, a strong squarish muzzle, and the typical tricolor markings, with the black and brown ticking spots on her white patches. Her eyes were full of fear, and her coat was dull and dirty. She cowered and strained against the leash whenever I glanced in her direction.

Neither of us saw Janine leave. We were too busy sizing each other up.

I brought Pretty Girl to the house, put her in a kennel crate to give her time to get used to her new surroundings while I went to care for some of the other animals, and all of a sudden I heard a terrible racket. I went back into the room and saw that she had torn the crate apart and was loose in the room. It was a fiberglass crate, and she had literally chewed her way out. I got hold of her, gave her some flower essences to help her calm down, and put her in a sturdier crate. She was frantic. I went through three crates in the first few days.

Then I tried another tack. Thinking that maybe a crate was too confining, I put her in my bedroom and closed the door.

Bad idea. She tore the molding off the windows and chewed more off the wall, trying to find a way out.

Obviously she could not be left alone. She was teaching me fast that she was both smart and determined. All of her body language and the energy radiating from her, however, told me that she was terrified of me. I decided to "umbilical cord" her and kept her on a leash attached to my belt, so that she had to stay near me at all times. At night I kept her in a crate next to my bed. She did not try to escape when I was right next to her.

I did not do a lot of interacting with her; I had to pretend that she was not there. Meanwhile, wherever I went, she had to follow. She had to smell me, watch me, hear my voice right near her, observe me preparing food and caressing the other dogs. As long as I didn't acknowledge her or even look at her, she was okay. But if I reached out to touch her, she would bolt to the end of the lead and scramble furiously to get away.

Days went by. George and I were sitting out by the pond having lunch one afternoon. I had Pretty Girl attached to me as usual. She had been on flower essences for a while, and I had been able to do some massage work with her. She was beginning to allow me to reach out very slowly and touch her. She would accept the contact, but she pulled away from any real caress.

Now the sun came out from behind a cloud and shone on the dog's deep black back. "George, look at her coat!" I exclaimed. It had been dry and dull at first, but she'd been on natural foods and vitamins for more than a month and now within the black, there were gleaming iridescent metallic purples, roses, and greens. We changed her name that day to Rainbow.

I found I could now allow her the run of the house off lead. To my great relief, she was fine with the other dogs and did not attempt to escape or do any damage. It was obvious that she was becoming comfortable with me, but she would still flee if any other person entered the house.

Out-of-doors was another matter. I kept her on a long line, because I knew if she could clear the fences at the humane society, my six-footers weren't going to mean much to her.

I soon found out I was right. A client showed up at a busy time, and because some of my dogs were asking to go out, I opened the door for them. I was in a hurry and just pushed it shut without checking to make sure it was latched.

"Rainbow"

While in conversation in the reception area, I suddenly realized that the house was full of dogs again. They had pushed their way back in, leaving the door, which swung inward, wide open. I looked out to see that Rainbow had obviously jumped the fence and was headed down the driveway. "Oh, no! I exclaimed. "There she goes."

I dashed outside and stood watching her. She turned to look at me, and the expression in her eyes said, "I'm free; I'm going," and she took some more steps away. In the months we had spent together, I realized I had fallen deeply in love with her spirit, and now the thought of losing her, as well as the knowledge that she very likely would die on her own, made me desperate. I began walking after her, but it was clear that she would only run if I pressed her. I thought, "This is stupid, April! The harder you try to catch her, the faster she will run, and she's heading down toward the main road."

Now came the moment of truth: had any bonding taken place at all?

I squatted down and held out my hand to coax her. She stopped and looked at me, then looked back down the drive. I could see the tremendous conflict inside her. I crouched there in the road for a long time, my heart pleading with her to stay. But at last I had to accept that she probably had no intention of doing so. Everything in her body said that she was leaving. The life she'd had with me didn't seem to be enough to overcome her need to be free. I had to let her go.

"Okay," I finally called to her. "You could have had a wonderful life here, and I love you, but if being confined is not your cup of tea and you choose to leave, there's nothing more I can do. You know I can't catch you, and if you're not happy and don't want to stay here, that's your choice. Have a good life; stay out of the road; don't get into any more porcupines. Good-bye. Blessings."

I turned around and started walking back up the driveway, grieving that in spite of all my efforts, she had not been able to trust me. I really loved her, and she was going. What was going to happen to her?

I was nearly back at the house when I could suddenly sense that she was coming along very tentatively behind me, but keeping a safe distance. My heart leaped when I realized this, but I didn't dare look back. I just kept walking, desperately holding on to the hope that any bond we had established would be strong enough to influence her final decision.

When I reached the house, she was still behind me. My mind shifted suddenly from letting her go to trying to figure out how to catch her again. I knew I couldn't get her to come in the front door, because with all of the other dogs, there would be too much confusion. So I walked all the way around to the backyard. I went through the gate and stood inside the fence. I left the gate open, thinking that if I could get her to follow me onto the lawn, maybe I could run through this door and out the other door and get behind her and shut the gate.

Then I realized that was ridiculous. Obviously she had escaped over the fence to begin with, because all of the gates had been shut. I was just trying to be clever and trap her. Did that make sense, given the level of communication I hoped we had established?

Rainbow stood outside, framed in the open gateway, her ears pricked up, and all of her body tense. Our eyes met, and she looked intently into mine.

I affirmed again that I acknowledged her need for freedom and that the choice was hers, simply saying, "Well, what's it gonna be?"

Completely ignoring the opening, Rainbow turned slightly and took a huge leap over the fence and back into the yard. Her act said it all: "I'm choosing to stay, but do not forget that I can leave anytime. I don't even have to come through this gate if I don't want to.

I just started laughing; her statement of independence was so plain. And I had been wasting my thoughts on all of those devious ways of cornering and snaring her. Our relationship wasn't going to be about outwitting each other. She proved her point right then and there that our relationship would be based totally on trust and respect: "In your dreams, lady! Don't forget who you're dealing with!"

From that day on, I couldn't keep Rainbow on a long line outside anymore, out of respect for her statement. She became more and more attached to me, although she was still wary of physical affection. However, she began to hang around me more and more by choice.

One day I returned from somewhere, and all of the dogs crowded around, happy to see me, and I was patting them. All of a sudden, I heard a strange noise behind me—a very deep "Wooaaoaohhh." I turned around, and at first I thought it was my imagination.

This happened again a few days later; I walked in the door, and the dogs crowded around and were asking for affection. And I heard it again: "Whooooaaaaahohhh. Whooooaaaahhhoohh." I wondered who could be doing that. I couldn't figure it out.

I turned to include Rainbow in my greeting, and she stood there wagging her tail, but when I put my hand out to caress her, she drew back, saying, "Nope, that's too much." She kept her distance, but it was clear that she had, in the meantime, deeply bonded to me. If George opened the door to let the other dogs out, Rainbow would jump the fence and find me anywhere on the property. If I was in the training area giving a private consultation, she would come scratching at the door. She'd follow me anywhere, but it was still hard for her to trust.

One day I was coming up from the training area, having worked all day. The dogs had just been let out, and Rainbow cleared the fence and came down and joined me. It was getting cool, and it was a lovely afternoon. As we came up the driveway together, all of a sudden she bounded ahead and began circling, prancing and dancing around me. And that funny sound came out of her, like a little happy song: "Whooaahh, woooahhha, wooooahhooh!"

It was so low, not a growl or a moan. Her own special voice.

That was when I realized the strange sound was her happy talk, what now I affectionately call her bear talk because it sounds like a bear's woof. She was happy that I was coming home. And she knew what "home" meant by now too.

Next to Jessica, an Australian shepherd I had taken in years before, Rainbow and I probably have the deepest psychic connection. If I have to leave for a day or so, Jessica always knows when I'm coming back and is looking out the window as I drive in. I worried when I had to leave Rainbow at first, because she is so strongly bonded to me. I was afraid that she would try to come find me. But she stays home.

And often when I return, she is waiting for me right at the end of the driveway, as if to say, "At last!"

The beauty of the exchange between Rainbow and me comes from love and mutual respect—a phrase I use over and over. We have a level of recognition that is beyond the ordinary. I see who she is—I can "read" everything about her: I understand what she needs from me to feel acknowledged. In turn, she gives back to me her loyalty and deep appreciation of who I am.

I've asked you to do a deep study of your dog. Now I'm going to ask you to take a look at yourself.

3

YOUR SELF

Since the fundamental goal of Awareness Training is to bring the energy of two different species into a mutual exchange of respect, love, and communication, it is important to acknowledge that we need to examine ourselves also. In this chapter we will begin that process by exploring some of the typical ways that dog and human relationships become problematical.

One of the most unfortunate and unfair aspects of a relationship between a human and a dog occurs when the dog is used to promote an image. For example, there are those who acquire genetically aggressive dogs to serve as a macho alter ego. The current popularity of the Rottweiler, pit bull, and Akita is evidence of a high degree of fear and sense of powerlessness in our culture. This kind of dog is frequently trained by force, and goaded and encouraged to frighten people; he usually lasts only until his human companion is threatened with a lawsuit. Then I get a call. This is my least favorite kind of case; it may surprise you, but dog trainers actually do sometimes lose their lives while counseling people with vicious dogs.

In past years, before I learned my present approach to working with animals, I was unexpectedly and seriously bitten by dogs a number of times. One time in particular stands out as the moment when I really thought it was all over for me.

A man came to me with his extremely aggressive Rottweiler and a terrified girlfriend. The dog did not even have a properly fitted training collar on, and the sheer brawn of the man on the end of the leash was the only thing that kept him from making mincemeat out of anyone who looked at him sideways.

What did this deeply angry guy, whom I'll call Gary, name his vicarious killing machine?

Satan.

Gary's girlfriend, Sue, was terrorized by his big dog. The day before, he had left Satan in the house with her and their eleven-month-old baby, and the dog had suddenly appeared snarling at the bedroom door, where Sue was making the bed. She was barely able to slam the door in time, but then she heard, to her horror, that her baby was awake and crying in her crib in the other room. The Rottweiler kept Sue trapped for nearly three hours in the bedroom. There was no phone nearby, and it was a second-floor apartment, so she could not go out of the window. She was sick with fear that her baby would be attacked, but she couldn't open the door without having Satan lunge at her each time.

Gary eventually showed up and laughed heartily at Sue's predicament, before grabbing the dog's collar and letting her out of her prison. Ol' Satan sure was tough, he boasted.

Then ol' Satan lunged over the side of Gary's open pickup truck, which was parked in a supermarket lot, and grabbed a woman by the shoulder as she was putting groceries in her car. The injury required sixteen stitches, and Gary was being sued.

Now we sat facing each other in the training arena, Gary with his chin and belly stuck out, sprawled casually in the chair, one hand on Satan's leash. Sue sat nervously nibbling at her nails, her feet tucked under her chair, away from the dog. Satan crouched at the utter limit of his lead, eyes glittering, watching my every move.

I am always on red alert in these situations, and remained so while I heard the dog's history. Gary gave it grudgingly; Sue chimed in when she dared. Then I dropped my pen and relaxed my guard to lean over and pick it up.

Instantly Satan tore the lead out of Gary's hand and went for me, but stopped three feet away as I sprang to my feet and faced him down, my reflexes on automatic, knowing what was likely to happen next if I did not have the strength to hold him there. I knew I had to maintain an eye contact that communicated awareness but neither fear nor challenge. I called upon every force of nerve and calm that I could muster. If I wavered, it would be all over.

Sue began to scream, "Oh, my God! Oh, no! Oh, my God!"

Satan's eyes were slits, his ears flattened against his head, a thick ridge of hair bristled down his back to his stiff, quivering tail. And all I could see was the way his many, many teeth glistened in the light from the window.

"Susan," I said very precisely, barely moving my lips, without changing my position or my intense focus on the snarling dog, "Shut . . . up." I did not have time to be pleasant.

Sue closed her mouth and began to whimper. I felt Gary's consternation and utter inability to do anything. My brain was whirling with shock and fear. I couldn't even collect myself to pray; all I could do was think, "This is it, April," and "The dog must have been taught something. What can I say to him that will reach him?"

I spoke again, very firmly and emphatically, never moving my eyes from his. "Satan," I said, "sit."

Satan deepened his growling and began making quick feints at me, body rigid, lips drawn tight back against his teeth.

I stood immovable as a statue and sent my gaze boring into the center of his skull. Pulling even more willpower out from some reservoir of experience in my gut, I put it all into my voice, "Satan. Sit,"

Satan sat. And nervously licked his lips.

Without shifting my gaze, I spoke to Gary, very slowly and deliberately: "Get hold of his leash and take him *out of here. Now.*"

Once Gary had put Satan in the car and returned, I tried to give him a comprehensive series of things he would need to do to help Satan overcome his aggression. Gary listened in a sullen manner but scheduled another appointment before he left. I heard soon afterward, however, that Satan had again been left in the back of Gary's truck and had lunged out and bitten someone even worse than before, with the inevitable result that the dog was euthanized.

Gary and Satan were a bad mix because they brought out the worst in each other. Satan's genetically aggressive and protective nature took over for Gary's inability to meet the world with strength and sensitivity. With another human companion, that same dog could have been prized for his intelligence and loyalty or for his independent and assertive nature, and with proper training he could have lived a long and happy life.

The following cases illustrate some other human-personality aberrations that are hard on a dog:

CASE ONE: CONTROLLING THROUGH
PAIN AND FEAR

People like Gary deal with fear by dominating those around them with a vicious dog. There are also those who take out their fears on the dog directly. Sometimes they don't know any better, and sometimes their behavior is a reflection of the way they were raised, or of a situation wherein they feel powerless.

Mark, a rather gray-looking and stiff man in his late thirties, came to me for private counseling because Doc, his hound-shepherd mix had suddenly begun behaving aggressively toward him. As we talked, I learned that he had used very forceful and heavy-handed methods with the dog since puppyhood. It also came out that Mark felt like a victim; he hated his job and was very lonely, having no meaningful friendships in his life.

It seemed that the only thing Mark thought he had control over was his dog, and now that he was losing that structure, he was in a panic. The first incident of retaliation had taken place a month before; he had lost his temper and been very physically abusive because Doc had resisted lying down when Mark told him to. Doc, no longer a puppy and now nearly a year and a half old, had growled, shown his teeth, and snapped at Mark as soon as Mark began punishing him. This had set Mark back on his heels, and Doc had learned, for the first time, that he too had power. Things had escalated since then. Each physical reprimand and each angry shout provoked an immediate, aggressive-defensive response in Doc. Now that he was older and larger, he wasn't taking any more abuse.

When I asked Mark to work Doc a bit, I observed that there was no joy in the dog's responses. I suggested to Mark that there was a different and less stressful way of working and that it was not necessary to be so aggressive. Mark doubted that Doc would respond to "soft, cutesy training methods." I took the lead and began to walk with Doc, gently guiding him with very light corrections if he did not immediately comply with my cues. I kept projecting a strong feeling of encouragement and already saw in my mind that he was responding correctly. Within minutes Doc was smiling up at me and giving me his full attention. I had not demanded or forced anything from him, and he was completely happy and willing to follow my lead. He was a dog with a good heart, and I felt sure that there was a lot of potential for him and Mark to become close.

Mark watched the joyful way Doc and I interacted, and something in him suddenly opened up. He agreed to attend regular group training classes, and eventually I saw a wonderful change take place, not only between him and his dog but also in his relation to the other members of the class. As they all chatted with Mark, applauded his efforts, and admired Doc's spirit, the tension in his face began to soften, his way of moving relaxed, and by the end of the course, he had gained new friends, not the least of whom was Doc, the one who had brought him there in the first place and who had loved him all along.

Mark was one of many people who believe that the only way to relate to a dog is through physically forcing the animal to do everything. There is a big difference between giving a correction that makes a behavior mildly unpleasant to continue, and giving a correction that causes pain or trauma.

Relationships based on coercion, domination, and fear, whether they are with people, or between people and animals, are always limited because there is no respect. Relationships rooted in trust, mutual respect, and love grow and deepen without limit, because they are based not on the output of one being but on an endless give-and-take *between* beings.

CASE TWO: CONTROLLING BY YELLING

It's not uncommon to see people attempt to get their dog to behave by bellowing at the top of their lungs. I think the psychology is similar to that of the person who yells at someone who does not speak English, thinking that a louder voice will break the language barrier!

Often this habit begins rather innocently, as it did with a woman I'll call Beth.

Beth stands before Taffy and says, "Taffy, sit," in a normal tone of voice.

Taffy looks at her, wagging her tail and panting happily.

Beth tries again, raising her voice a little: "Taffy, I'm speaking to you. I want you to sit."

Taffy grins and wiggles, then searches for something to sniff so she will look busy.

Now Beth really wants her attention, so she raises her voice again: "Taffy! C'mon, now! Sit!"

Taffy glances Beth's way and wags her tail again, looking friendly but totally unimpressed.

Now Beth is frustrated and out of patience: "*Taffy, when I tell you to sit down, I mean* SIT DOWN!" She physically forces the dog into position and then dispenses some token praise: "Good dog." Lesson over.

Time goes by, and Beth needs Taffy to sit again. She begins the sequence all over again, and Taffy listens patiently until she hears a decibel level that tells her, "Well, she's getting close." That's her signal, and that is when Beth gets what she is asking for.

This approach unintentionally teaches the dog that until you are yelling and screaming, you are not willing to activate to elicit a correct response. You are also, without realizing it, teaching her a pattern of resistance. When you develop a habit of repeating directions over and over, without getting an immediate response from your dog, it becomes a head game from the dog's perspective: who is going to outwait, outthink, and outmaneuver whom?

Constant repetition is unproductive and feels negative, because nothing creative is going on. If, however, you elicit an immediate response from your dog, you can quickly switch to praising her and create a pleasant, memorable experience. You can yell and gesture very dramatically, but if you are not 100 percent committed to the dog's response, you will usually get less than you ask for.

CASE THREE:
CONTROLLING WITH FOOD AND CODDLING

This person basically manipulates the dog to fulfill a deep emotional need for a substitute child or partner. There is an attempt to control through coaxing, fondling, and yummy treats. Often the dog is made so emotionally dependent that she thinks she cannot survive or function without her human companion, which often leads to destructive behavior on the dog's part in the person's absence. While usually interpreted as a malicious act, this behavior is actually a result of acute separation anxiety.

In one of his books, the famous Scottish vet and storyteller James Herriot did a wonderful job of poking gentle fun at a wealthy woman and her fat, overpampered Tricky-Woo. There are many benign versions of this kind of relationship, to be sure, but I have seen some tragic ones as well.

I will never forget a middle-aged woman named Dora who came to see me after making an appointment. She sounded quite upset on the phone and said she was afraid of her dog. From her description, I expected a monster to walk through the door, but in came Candy, a quiet, sweet-natured miniature poodle, who was twelve or thirteen years old and getting creaky in his bones. I could tell from the way he moved that he had calcification of his spine, and I guessed that the condition was probably quite painful for him.

My heart went out to him; he was a wonderful dog, and Dora had had him since he was a puppy. She had a small craft shop and took him to work with her every day, where he was reportedly adored by her help and all of her customers.

Dora, I could see, was an extremely needy person, who kept Candy in a stranglehold on her lap during our session and would not give him a moment's peace, fawning over him, kissing, hugging, and patting him incessantly. He had bitten her severely several times, most recently in the face, causing a wound that required three stitches.

"Has the dog bitten anyone else? I asked.

"No," she replied airily, "and I have a cat who bites and scratches me too!" She looked at me for sympathy and then hugged Candy tighter and nuzzled him aggressively.

"Does the cat bite anyone else?" I asked, beginning to see a pattern.

"No," she said, and then added with an injured expression, as if the world was against her, "I also have a horse who is really mean. Whenever I get on her, she tries to run away with me. And sometimes she won't even let me in her stall; she just tries to kick me! I'm getting rid of her, but I can't *live* without my dearest little Candy." She grabbed his muzzle and squeezed, looking passionately into the little dog's eyes.

I counseled Dora for three hours, suggesting some repatterning exercises, neutering—the dog was scent-marking all over the house—and some help for his spine. Dora half listened, but seemed interested mainly in gaining my sympathy about Candy's lack of tolerance, all the while continuing to maul the poor animal in her clutches. At last, Candy reached the end of one of his ropes and growled to make her back off. "See?" Dora exclaimed, looking at me triumphantly. "He does this to me all the time!"

"First of all," I said, in as even a tone of voice as I could manage, "you have him in your lap. That's a very dominant place for him to be. Secondly, if he is growling, why do you insist on sticking your face in his and kissing him? You have to give him some space!"

Dora barely let me finish before protesting, "He's affectionate! He likes being patted and kissed!"

"But maybe not every minute of the day!" I said. I felt that I had to talk to her as if she were a child: "What's your favorite kind of pie?"

"Chocolate," she replied, with a question in her voice.

"And," I went on, "if I brought in twelve pieces and told you to eat them all, would you?"

"No," she said, looking at me, mystified.

"Well," I said, "Candy doesn't have the option of saying no to all of the sugar you are pouring all over him all of the time. It's too much."

"He's affectionate, he likes it," Dora repeated stubbornly.

We scheduled another session; I outlined exercises for her to use to work toward resolving some of the issues, and I hoped that by the next time things would have improved.

This was not to be. The following week a friend of Dora's called to cancel and say that Dora had decided it was easier to take Candy to the vet and have all of his teeth pulled. I was barely through gasping over this senseless cruelty when he went on to say that something had gone wrong under the anesthesia and now the little dog was blind.

Dora now had a dog totally at her mercy, without sight or teeth, in pain from a chronic back problem, who would be eating mush for the rest of his days. I was so infuriated, I just sat there and cried. It shocked and amazed me to see the extent to which she was willing to go to avoid the problem, rather than take responsibility for the way her behavior was stressing her elderly companion, who had spent his life enduring her unstable personality.

This happened years ago and now, rather than feeling anger, I am sad, realizing that Dora, desperate for love and completely unable to handle any form of rejection, was too afraid to look at herself. I've learned that it is not my place to judge people in these situations, but to try to help where I can. I also have learned to trust that animals have their own wisdom; I believe that sometimes they endure certain things in order to give people the opportunity to change or learn. Perhaps in Candy's case, it was to make a lonely woman's life more bearable.

CASE FOUR: BEING AFRAID TO DISCIPLINE

My story of Janice, Mike, and their dog, Sallie, in Chapter 1 is another, less extreme example of a relationship where a dog is acquired to fill a void in a person's life. In their case, problems occurred because of a lack of clear guidelines and structure, and because they were afraid that if they reprimanded the dog, they would lose her love. This is a common problem in many a dog-human relationship, and the reasoning is exactly opposite of the truth. It goes back to the concept of respect: the more your dog respects you, the more he trusts you; the more he trusts you, the more loyalty he gives to you, because that's the way it is in the pack.

All dogs have tremendous allegiance to one another, and in particular to the alpha dog and the alpha bitch, who set the rules and keep the pack together and functioning. Discipline doesn't mean whips, chains, and thumbscrews; it is more about attitude, consistency, rules, and guidelines. And dogs, like children, need to have them so that they know exactly what your expectations are and how to meet them.

CASE FIVE: TRAINING BY HEARSAY

I sometimes meet people who use a little of all the advice they've ever heard when trying to train a dog but who never actually spend time studying their dog's individual needs. The main problem here is the lack of consistency. This is, again, contrary to the dog's experience in the pack. In a pack situation, the dogs behave quite consistently—especially the higher-ranking dogs—so that the lower-ranking members can count on them and can know exactly what is expected of them and how to fulfill those expectations. Pack dynamics do change, but they change with a certain predictability. Consistency is crucial for the dog; it is inherent in his understanding of the world.

I often find myself telling clients who are inconsistent that it is better to be consistently wrong than always to be changing the program on their dogs. Inconsistency stresses a dog, because he never knows where he stands. One day he is reprimanded for a behavior, and the next day that same behavior is ignored, laughed at, or even encouraged. This can happen particularly when different family members have different rules for the dog; this creates a *very negative* situation.

The other problem with always switching training approaches on the advice of nonprofessionals is that the solution for a friend's dog could be a total disaster for your dog. A certain recommendation could be very useful, or it could totally destroy your dog's confidence in you.

Many people may be quick to offer advice when you and your dog are having a problem, but it is best to get professional help right away. If you even think you have a problem, that's the time to address it, because the longer you wait, the more time, effort, and money will be needed to turn things back around.

If you ask your veterinarian for advice about training or behavioral issues, be sure that this is the vet's area of expertise before you follow through with suggestions.

ABOUT BURIED ISSUES

In an earlier chapter I spoke of a woman who got a Rottweiler for protection and another family that chose a Lab puppy as a companion for their young children. Both of these expectations were common enough; if there had been more knowledge about dogs, neither family would have run into problems. When deep, unrecognized emotional issues exist, however, there can be some very big challenges to creating a healthy relationship.

I once had an elderly couple I'll call Mr. and Mrs. Markham in class, and they had a very nice big white Samoyed named Snow. He tried very hard to please, but he received only a token amount of praise, hardly ever any patting, and never a hug.

This lack of affection began to bother me, so one night after class I asked the Markhams if there was a problem or anything that I could do to resolve issues they had with Snow. The story came out; they had not chosen the dog. Snow had belonged to their daughter, who was now unable to keep him. Because Snow was beloved by the daughter, the Markhams had agreed to take care of him.

They had been looking forward to enjoying their retirement by doing some traveling, but now they felt tied down, raising another "child." This, however, was not the main problem. The real issue was the hair—drifts of Snow hair all over their clothes, house, and car. They were rather meticulous people, and Snow, being a double-coated Arctic breed, shed constantly. It drove them crazy.

Actually, they did not realize how much it bothered them until I invited them to share their feelings about the dog. This had been a buried issue, except for the fact that they did not want to touch Snow for fear of creating further hair-in-the-air.

I asked the Markhams why they did not brush Snow, and Mrs. Markham explained that she brushed him every day. I asked about the brush, and realized that it was totally inadequate for that type of coat.

The Markhams came for a special grooming lesson. I showed them how to use a water spray bottle to dampen Snow's coat, so that the hair would not fly all over when they brushed him. I gave them the right brush, one that would get down into the coat and remove the loose dead hair. In a few weeks they had the hair problem under control, and Snow was getting the affection he deserved.

The Markhams had not been conscious of the fact that their inability to enjoy Snow was focused on such a small issue. The forms in this chapter and in Chapter 2 can help you avoid these kinds of problems.

Buried emotional issues can be a major reason for a relationship between a dog and a human companion to fail to work out. There are also numerous cases where only one family member wants a dog, as well as cases where each family member has a different expectation of the dog's role. For the sake of the dog, it is imperative to keep track of any differences and try to resolve them.

CASE SIX: DOGS IN THE MIDDLE

Ray loved dogs, but his wife, Gloria, like the Markhams, was super-meticulous, and disliked the idea of any animal in her immaculate home. They compromised, and Buster the beagle was allowed in the kitchen and mudroom only and nowhere else. A gate stood between him and the rest of the house where there were untouchable things like rugs and couches.

But Buster, it seems, was a real sneak, because Gloria, who had a very busy life outside the home as a volunteer, was always finding dog hair on the couch or recliner when she returned home. This was outrageous! Ray claimed that he had never seen Buster get over the gate, although he was home a good deal of the time. And the strange thing was, Buster usually had bouts of severe diarrhea after these hair manifestations. The vet had checked him out and found neither parasite nor infection, so the dog was referred to me to see if there was a behavioral issue.

Ray and Gloria, who were in their mid-fifties, sat with Buster between them, and the beagle looked innocent as could be. Gloria, who was immaculately groomed, ranted and raved about the dog hair, and Ray, who had to be reminded to pull up his socks, did so and then kept his gaze on his shoes.

"And every time I return home, that dog is always sitting in the kitchen," Gloria finished, "I just know he hears me coming when the car pulls in, and if he's in the house, he just runs back to the kitchen before I open the door. And then the mess!" she continued, wrinkling her nose in disgust, "I take him and show him the couch and then really yell at him and shake him and punish him, but he just won't get the point!"

"In order for reprimands to be effective, you have to catch him in the act," I said.

My first guess was that stress-anxiety and punishment-after-the-fact were causing the intestinal distress, but I was mystified as to how all this was happening, since the dog had never shown any interest in jumping or climbing the gate at all when they were around, or at night when they were sleeping.

The truth came out in the following session, when Ray came alone. Gloria had another committee meeting, and she had sent him to work on the problem without her.

He seemed to be a shy man, very vague, somewhat sheepish. He fumbled with Buster's leash and checked out his shoes some more after I asked him how things were going. Then, "It's me," he blurted out, "it's all my fault," and got bright red all the way down into his collar.

"It's you?" I asked.

"Buster and I watch football together," he continued painfully, turning his hands palm upward in a gesture of supplication. "On the couch," he added.

I wanted to laugh and cry for him all at the same time. "And then what?" I asked.

"Well, I feel bad for Buster when she yells at him," he said. "I wish I had the nerve to tell my wife, but I don't."

"What happens after Buster gets all the blame?" I asked, beginning to guess already.

"I feel bad," he repeated. "I pet him and apologize to him. I give him some ice cream or some hamburger."

"How much ice cream and how much hamburger?"

"Oh, sometimes a carton, sometimes half a pound," he replied, with a tone in his voice that said that if Buster could have eaten more to assuage the man's guilt, he would have tried to get him to do so.

After promising never to reveal the truth to Gloria, I explained the ramifications of this kind of reparation on Buster's digestive tract, and talked about the emotional stress that after-the-fact punishment and anger caused in the dog. We brainstormed ways to create companionable, guilt-free football watching, and finally found the solution: a television was added to the family room in the cellar, and with a certain amount of tact, the idea was posed to Gloria that Buster be allowed down there, as long as there were sheets on the furniture. Believing that this would solve the "stress diarrhea," she agreed, and harmony returned to the home, because everyone's needs were met.

Joanne's story is another example of a conflict in needs among two people and a dog. Joanne's new husband, Tom, brought his Great Dane Christy, with him into their marriage, and Joanne was not sure to whom he was most wedded. The dog always got the first kiss when Tom came home, and there were nightly battles over whether Christy was going to share the bed with them. When the dog won, she would lie right between them, which was fine with Tom, who could not understand why Joanne was so jealous.

Christy knew who loved her and who didn't; she obeyed Tom instantly and ignored Joanne's directives completely. Joanne brought her to me for private counseling, but I could see that she really would have been much happier if Christy had been an old girlfriend that Tom had given up when he married. Since she didn't want a relationship with Christy at all, it was very difficult to get them to interact. However, I had to give her credit for realizing that she and the dog had to solve the problem, since Tom was not about to help. She said, only half joking, that she knew if he had to choose between them, she would probably lose.

Although Joanne and Christy never became as strongly bonded as Christy and Tom, they did reach a good point of understanding through working together in a training class. Joanne was able to get Christy to listen to her, and Christy had to accept that Joanne had authority and equal space in Tom's life.

A final example of how dogs function in a family dynamic concerns a different expression of a buried issue. Dogs can be a barometer of the health of relationships in general and can be part of the way the family communicates to outsiders. For example, when the human members of the family don't want to express emotions, it is not unusual for their pets to do it for them.

Sadie, who belonged to a retired couple I'll call the Gordons, was a Lhasa Apso who did this very efficiently. The couple's older daughter, Sandra, had married David, and they disliked him intensely and frequently bad-mouthed him when he was not around, creating lots of negative energy. When David visited the house, however, they put on their company manners, except for Sadie, who was without guile and persisted in growling, slinking around him, and attempting her own form of backbiting! They finally had to confine her to the garage during his visits.

The Gordons worried that Sadie was a biter, and Sadie wondered why her human companions kept changing the signals. Fortunately David and

Sandra moved away; otherwise the dog might have paid a price for trying to uphold the truth.

YOUR MATCH

Take a moment now to compare your dog's temperament and personality with yours. Did you choose a dog that has similar personality and temperament traits, or opposite ones? Are you someone who enjoys prolonged periods of calm and quiet, but find yourself with a high-strung, energetic dog who won't leave you alone at the end of a long day? Do you like to run ten miles every morning, but you got yourself a bulldog who doesn't have the stamina or the respiratory capacity to keep up with you? Whether you already have a dog or are planning to add one to your life, the following personal questionnaire will help you find a good match:

Describe in detail your temperament, your likes and dislikes, and your favorite ways to spend your leisure time:

Describe your dog's temperament, likes and dislikes, and preferred ways of playing and relaxing:

How did you acquire this particular dog?

List the traits you believe are the most positive in your dog.

List the traits that you believe are the most negative in your dog.

What do you like most about your dog?

What do you like least about your dog?

If you could change only one thing about your dog at this time, what would it be?

What lessons has your dog taught you?

Give a brief description of where your personality and your dog's personality match and where you clash.

List other demands in your life that compromise the way you want to be with your dog:

This analysis will have helped you to clarify your thoughts and feelings toward your dog. When you begin to set your training goals in Chapter 8, you will be using this information.

What if you discover that you have made a real mistake in your choice, or that your dog is incompatible with other members of the household or with your lifestyle?

Hopefully, you will be able to be flexible and compromise; you will have to decide what you are willing to settle for. Be realistic; you are not going to turn a hyperactive border collie into a snooze-loving basset hound. If you made a bad choice of breed, you must acknowledge this. I see many cases where there is nothing wrong with the dog and nothing wrong with the human companions, except that they are going to drive each other crazy.

If this is your situation, then you have a tough decision to make. Dogs know if you don't like them. Is there a workable compromise? Are you willing to make adjustments on an ongoing basis? If not, then perhaps you should assume the responsibility for finding the dog a good home, which will be in your mutual best interests.

"Lack of time" is one of the first responses to the last question on the form, as is "the demands of other relationships." Since we are no longer an agrarian culture, the dog's role has diminished, like that of children whose labor used to be an absolute necessity in the functioning of the household. Kids watch television nowadays, and dogs lie on the rug with them like stuffed animals, or spend long hours alone each day confined in the house or in a crate, waiting for their human companions to come home and take them for a quick walk.

Quality time is an issue for dogs, just as it is for children. However, quantity time is also an issue, because a dog needs plenty of physical exercise and mental stimulation to stay healthy.

There are other ways that you and the course of your life can profoundly affect your dog; these are the tragedies over which you usually have little control:

DOGS AND DIVORCE

Dogs suffer from the breakup of a family, just as children do. They get caught in custody battles and bounce back and forth between households.

I worked recently with a woman and her male and female cocker spaniels who had been spending six months in Massachusetts with her and six months in Utah with her ex-husband. Each person had different expectations and rules for the animals, and the dogs, just like children in such situations, were suffering from the lack of consistency.

Both dogs had taken on a great deal of the anger surrounding the breakup and were very stressed. This stress had evolved into a health issue for the female dog; she was sweet and anxious to please, but even though she ate well, she was losing weight, and she kept developing chronic ear infections. The vet had not been able to find any physical causes. Meanwhile, the male had gotten irritable and snappish and had bitten someone. Unfortunately, the ex-husband never reprimanded him, and his behavior was rapidly worsening. The woman realized that there was a need to do something, but sadly, little could be accomplished because the rules were going to change in a matter of weeks, when the dogs would be flown back to Utah.

DOGS, ILLNESS, AND DEATH

It is not at all unusual for a dog to take on his human companion's illness. My friend Scott, who manufactures an excellent brand of dog food, frequently counsels people who call to purchase from him. He reported that "A man called to order, and I asked him why he wanted the food. I always talk to my customers to be sure that they get the support they need in helping their dog to switch diets. The man explained that his poodle awakened around two or three every morning and cried as if in pain. He thought perhaps she needed a different diet."

"Does she eat well?" Scott had asked. The answer was yes, and also yes to his questions about her looks, elimination, and enjoyment of exercise.

Then Scott surprised himself by asking, "Is somebody sick in your house?" It was a spontaneous question, but prompted by many conversations with his brother, a holistic veterinarian who firmly believes that dogs—especially dogs who are very closely bonded to their human companion—can be profoundly affected by that person's physical problems.

The man was silent for ten full seconds before confirming that his wife was very ill, bedridden in fact, and that the dog was her baby.

"Where does the dog sleep?" was Scott's next question.

The dog had slept at the foot of the bed for nine years, and now she insisted on sleeping by her mistress's head. And she cried in the middle of the night.

"I believe that dogs are here to lighten the burdens of people," Scott told me. "If someone is sick or dying, the dog is there to give love and support, to help ease the stress, and even sometimes the actual disease. I told the man to ask his wife to hold her dog for a bit each night before she went to sleep, and to tell the dog that everything was okay, to reassure her. I'm not sure why I said this, but months later the man called me back and said that my suggestion had helped immediately. The dog had gone back to sleeping at the foot of the bed and had not cried any more. And both the dog and the man's wife were much improved."

When I heard this from Scott, I was reminded of the famous story of Greyfriars Bobby, the steadfast Skye terrier who, after his master died, kept a vigil on the grave for *fourteen years* before dying himself, and who now has a monument to his faithfulness erected in Edinburgh where he lived. It seemed in Scott's story as though the woman's dog also felt that he had to keep watch, perhaps even to howl away at the fears that come to an ill person in the middle of the night.

The bond between a dog and its human is, in many cases, stronger than death or fear, but when it comes to loyalty and devotion, a dog is unparalleled in its infinite flexibility and forgiveness, despite all human failings, buried issues, fears, and inconsistencies.

Then there are dogs like Rainbow, who challenge one to find resources of grace and resolve that one could not have imagined one possessed. The following story of a massive rescue operation was the biggest test of my expertise and self-awareness in my entire career. I hope my experiences in this story may inspire you to know what is possible when you fall in love with dogs.

4

WHAT DOGS CAN TEACH

In May of 1994 I received an urgent call from a woman named Patty who was involved in animal rescue work. Would I help out by taking a couple of dogs who needed a home right away? If I couldn't, they were going to be shot.

She gave me a brief description: a Vermont woman had been keeping a large pack of dogs in a homemade wood-and-wire pen half the size of a basketball court next to her trailer. The town had demanded that the dogs be licensed and rabies-vaccinated, but a local veterinarian had been unable to get near them to give the shots. The woman had thrown up her hands and told the town officers to come and shoot them all. Patty was representing a local humane organization that had been asked by the town to help resolve the situation.

I told her I would help by taking four dogs until homes could be found for them, and I loaded my station wagon with four dog crates. I was just reaching for my rabies pole—a long metal pole with a retractable noose on the end used for catching animals—when Patty called again, more upset than before. The intervention involved more dogs than they had anticipated; they needed more crates—could I bring all I could spare? I called for George—once called Georgiana—my right-hand helper.

George was born in the mid-1940s and raised by a father who was a carpenter and a mother who worked a night shift as a nurse. While her mother caught up on her sleep, George's dad had baby-sat his infant daughter on the job by sitting her on the roof and driving a nail through her diapers to keep her in place! Little Georgiana had loved it all—loved wood and hard work, and grew up "in the trade." Since she wasn't taken seriously as Georgiana in a man's occupation, she'd cut her dark hair short and changed her name and her wardrobe, just like the stories of adventure-loving women who sneaked aboard sailing ships to be cabin boys in days gone by. In this way, and by ducking her head and muttering, she was able to earn her living by getting hired on building crews.

Of old Vermont stock, possessing a kind and gentle disposition, George had been with me doing the heavy work of the center since December. Now she helped me haul nine more crates out and agreed to follow in my van. At that moment my friend Susan drove up, and after I filled her in, she volunteered to join us. We headed west, crossing the Connecticut River on the covered bridge at Windsor, Vermont, and then turned south. My curiosity mounted as we drew near our destination. I found the rutted dirt road as described and turned in, eventually pulling up next to a group of cars parked by a trailer that had seen better days.

The first thing that struck me after I got out of my station wagon, was the eerie silence. This was unlike any rescue scene I had previously experienced. Where were the dogs? Usually there is a din of barking when strangers approach large groups of dogs. Yet here there was not a bark, yelp, or whimper to be heard. Behind the trailer, about a dozen people stood unmoving with their backs to me, gazing into a wire enclosure. We walked over and joined them.

The sight that greeted me was extraordinary: a large pack of dirt-caked dogs of mixed breeds and color were streaking silently up and down inside the pen, eyes staring, hackles up, their tails clamped tight between their back legs. Now that I was closer, I could hear an undercurrent of low, fierce growling. The amount of terror radiating off of them made me suddenly shiver. "My God," I exclaimed, "these dogs are completely wild!"

George moved close to me and, speaking in an undertone, filled me in: "I used to know this person," she said. "She wanted to breed keeshonden, and I guess some beagles, Labs, and terriers got added to the mix. But she just left them out here without any human contact. It's been this way for years."

I shifted my gaze from the frenzied animals and surveyed their home. The filth and squalor were incredible. The "earth" in the pen was packed excrement, and it was deep. There was a dilapidated plywood shed in the center, with other sheets of plywood leaning against it for additional shelter. Under the shed, I could see that the dogs had dug deep holes for dens for their puppies, as they would have in the wild. What I saw in this pen however, had little to do with the intrinsic balance that exists in nature.

Under normal circumstances there is a hierarchy in a dog pack, with one dominant member of each sex, and the status of the remaining members ranked in descending order. The place a dog holds within the structure is determined by its individual personality and qualities of brains and/or brawn. Generally there is minimal, if any, inbreeding and the frequency of mating is regulated by the seasons and the food supply. Wolves, for example, generally have only one litter a year, and only the dominant male and female breed, though even they do not breed if the food supply is low. Human intervention has changed this picture with domestication and genetic alteration of the dog's instinctive drive for economic advantage. Dogs with more frequent fertility cycles have been selected over the centuries, and lots of line breeding and cross breeding have given us the wide variety of species that we enjoy today. It also has given us dogs who come into heat about twice a year, no matter what the season or the amount of food available.

Without a doubt, a lot of uncontrolled mating had gone on in this pen, and there had been bloody life-or-death fights for supremacy. Although I could not tell whether there were puppies in the dens, the absence of very old and very young dogs in the pack that was visible could mean only one thing: the limitations of food and space had created a grotesque Darwinian experiment where only the toughest and strongest had survived. For the rest, the old adage, "dog eat dog" had been brutally played out. Even one brief look was enough to detect the ravages of terrible battles on the dogs' bodies. They were in a desperate situation, with death the only hope of liberation.

It was daunting to figure out how to approach this maelstrom of panic. These dogs had only known one kind of life, savage as it was. And we humans were about to take their world apart.

Since the dogs could move freely about in the pen, we needed a strategy for catching them. Knowing that this would be very traumatic for dogs who had never known human contact, I wanted more than anything to minimize their terror. I took a deep breath and turned to the other volunteers, suggesting that a few of us bring food and sit quietly in the pen to try and be a calming presence. If any dogs approached us voluntarily, it would make the job much easier.

Three of us sat silently, while the dogs sped madly around us or came, wild-eyed and trembling, to within six feet of the food we held out to them. After thirty minutes went by in this fashion, it became obvious that bridging the gulf between our worlds needed more than we had time to give, especially because the large crowd of strange people around the pen created a frightening distraction. We would have to take our rabies poles, chase the dogs down, and snare them.

It took us nearly seven nightmarish hours. The dogs were incredibly quick to evade us; our nerves frayed with the constant stress of stalking and missing a catch. Once noosed, each dog would go into paroxysms of terror, urinating, screaming, and frantically clawing the air as we forced it into a crate. Our compassion for their plight and our aversion to causing them so much distress was strangely contrasted with our constant fear of being bitten, as panic-stricken dogs, in a final act of desperation, often charge when cornered. A jittery local constable stood protectively by with his gun, adding to the tension.

At last the pen was empty, but somehow I knew that there were still more dogs to be found. We turned to the dens beneath the shed and knelt before the holes. I aimed the beam of a flashlight down into the darkness—and caught the intensity of eyes blazing back. I counted four more dogs. We had no choice but to force them out with water from the garden hose and to snare each dog as it burst forth, soaking wet, filthy, teeth flashing, eyes rolling in terror, from its hole.

I checked one more time. There was still one dog deep in a hole, its dark, matted coat barely illuminated by the searching ray of light. We thought perhaps it was dead because it was not moving. Everyone wanted to give up, but I couldn't bear the thought of leaving it there without knowing for sure.

We tried everything we could think of to flush it out, but without success. People were tired and getting impatient. Tempers were flaring. Then George suggested that we could probably get at it through the floor of the shed. The two of us, along with a humane society worker named Ellie, went in, lifting piles of old hay saturated with urine and excrement from the rotting floor. We had no tools, so we ripped the boards up with our bare hands. I peered down through the gap. Yes, I could just reach the dog's inert body. I put my hand down and touched its side. I felt a faint warmth and a slight quiver in reaction.

It took three of us with our feet braced to pull him out, he had wedged himself in so far. When his pitiful, emaciated form came out into the light of day, Ellie burst into tears: "Oh, God! I wish I had brought my euthanasia kit to put him out of his misery!"

My first thought was that she was right. The dog was obviously the low man on the pack totem pole, and who knows how long he had been down there, trying to save himself from the hungry jaws of the stronger pack members. No doubt he would not have survived another day. He was in deep shock, his limp, dehydrated body a mass of wounds and sores, his eyes half open and glazed over, his breathing so shallow it was barely perceptible. Through the muck, I saw a keeshond-like coat of fur.

This was my first encounter with Mephistopheles—later called Stoff—the dog who came from the gates of the underworld.

The dog was laid in a crate, and as I knelt by him, I called to George to bring my bottle of Animal Emergency Care Flower Essence from the car. I had been introduced to "energetic" medicines like homeopathy and flower essences several years earlier and had doubted their efficacy until a number of dramatic incidents with animals demonstrated their worth. I now swear by my own formula, which I use on animals who have suffered trauma, injury, or shock.

I reached into the crate, opened the dog's mouth, and dripped some of the clear solution under his tongue. I felt for his pulse, which was weak and thready, then gently placed my hands on him, holding different parts of his scrawny body.

I began giving him Reiki, a form of hands-on healing I had been practicing for several years. Voices behind me warned that I was taking a huge risk by touching one of these dangerous and unpredictable dogs, but I didn't think he had enough life left in him to be a threat. I could sense through my touch how close he was to death.

There's been talk about the laying-on of hands for centuries, but our modern culture finds it difficult to accept that something so simple can be effective, that it is possible to channel energy into another being and help renew its will to live. Yet how many of us remember the healing touch of a parent when we were ill in childhood? Sometimes it was all that was needed in times of sickness or sorrow. Maybe the most important thing anyone could do for the barely breathing dog in the moment was to hold it with compassion. I ignored the warnings of my colleagues and leaned over, listening with my whole being.

Five or ten minutes passed while I knelt before the open crate in a circle of silent watchers, and then suddenly I felt the dog's energy shift. He stirred and raised his head. Someone gasped. A moment later he gave a sudden heave and sat up, looking dazed, as though he had just awakened from a heavy sleep. I withdrew and carefully closed the wire-mesh door, in case he suddenly became fearfully aggressive as he came to fuller consciousness in his new surroundings. I heard people around me exclaim, expelling their held breath in great sighs, and then the click of a camera shutter. "I had to record this for posterity," said a man who had arrived on the scene. "I never would have believed you could bring that dog back."

Ten of us had arrived to remove the dogs at nine in the morning, and it was now almost five in the afternoon. A basic intervention had turned into an extremely bizarre, challenging, and exhausting drama. At least we had managed to catch all of the dogs. Now it was time to divide the pack up among the various volunteers and animal shelters. Some of the people looked in the crates, however, saw the flashing teeth, and the hideous wounds, and began backing out of their commitments, deciding that such completely wild and battered animals could not be rehabilitated. They recommended euthanizing the whole pack.

I could not justify giving up so soon; I hoped that the dogs would be capable of different behavior after they got over their initial fears. I found myself with Susan and George, heading home with more than half of the pack in our two vans—all thirteen crates full.

The stench was so nauseating, I had to keep my head halfway out of the van window on the way home. In addition to the odor of feces that the dogs brought with them, many immediately became carsick. Their terror caused them to repeatedly blow their anal sacks, the small glands on either side of the rectum which secrete tiny amounts of fluid when dogs defecate. The oily, highly odiferous secretion contains scent pheromones that serve to mark a dog's territory. When released in fright, copious amounts are secreted at one time; the smell is truly awful, and it permeates everything.

All the way home, my brain was spinning with questions: how was I going to heal the terrible injuries and infections sustained by so many, let alone bring them across the great gulf that divided them from our world? I knew that, except for George, I was going to be pretty much on my own. Local veterinarians and humane societies were still reeling from the effects of another rescue operation involving over a hundred animals, and their resources were stretched to the maximum.

I kept thinking that these dogs had had a horrific introduction to people. For all they knew, they had been raided by Martians and were now trapped in a spaceship. Furthermore, the stress and trauma visited on them in their debilitated physical state could not have been less helpful for future physical and emotional healing. If George and I had taken fewer dogs, we could have dealt with them differently and given each animal lots of time and energy. However, adding thirteen to those already living with me instantly more than doubled our workload. How was I going to hold everything together?

We arrived home totally spent, but without the possibility of rest. As soon as I got out of the car, I found myself going on automatic pilot. George and I cleared out a large room next to my living room and hauled in the crates, putting the new dogs in quarantine from the other animals to avoid the potential spread of any parasites or viruses.

We were like a front-line MASH unit. Our first order of business was to get collars and leashes on the rescued dogs, so that we would have some control when we began cleaning them and tending their wounds. Because of the danger of being bitten, we had to use the rabies pole to get each terrified dog out of its crate. Once a dog was out, it sometimes took us more than an hour to get it calmed down enough so that we could approach it and get the collar and leash on. Over the next months, I was to go through over fifty leashes as dog after dog chewed desperately through a lead in only two bites. In addition to the screaming, snarling, and biting at the end of the pole, the terrified dogs constantly emptied their bladders, bowels, and anal sacks. The cleanup after each collaring was unremitting.

George and I just kept moving, the desire to create a rudimentary sense of order overriding all else. When we finally were able to step back and survey the results, it was the middle of the next day and my friend Donna was knocking on the door, bearing grinders—submarine sandwiches—from a local deli. We wolfed them down, ravenous. It was then I realized that we had not slept or eaten since the previous morning.

Other offers of help came from friends and former clients who loved animals: Bev and Gary, Lauren, Brad and Jane, and Heather. In addition to George and Susan, they became my principal team over the next months.

Once I had some control over each dog, I began to assess its physical state. One by one, each was given flower essences to minimize stress, as well as a mild tranquilizer obtained from a local vet, to help it endure being handled while it was bathed and its wounds were tended. Each dog took several washings before I could even get the soap to lather. Meanwhile I was discovering the true extent of their injuries—the abscesses, deep lacerations, and open sores, beneath the crust of excrement that covered their bodies. Most of them also had terrible ear infections from mites, and their toenails were so long that it was impossible for them to stand correctly. Given the horrendous nature of their wounds, and the psychological and emotional trauma they were experiencing, I wondered how many of them were actually going to make it.

Several days passed. George and I were going to sleep at one in the morning and rising again at five, and still we felt we were barely keeping up. We found working in the atmosphere of constant terror emotionally draining. I recalled going to the doctor as a child and hearing him say, "Now, this will only hurt for a minute and then it will be over." I wanted so much to be able to say this to these terrified dogs, to tell them that there would indeed be an end to what must have seemed like our constant assaults with muzzles, water and scrub brushes, blow dryers, clippers, and medications. I had spent all of my life trying to release animals from fear and pain. Now it seemed that I would never get beyond being the cause of it.

The stress came to a head one night late in the first week. Even though they were starving, the dogs would not eat in front of people and cowered mutely in the back of their crates in a state of anxiety during the day. The food and silence disappeared at night when they were alone and the lights were off. Then they would bark and howl incessantly. It seemed that they were calling out to one another for reassurance that the pack was still bonded and intact, even while releasing all of their pent-up cries of exile and confusion into the night. I could get no rest.

One evening, as I was staggering with exhaustion, Lauren's son David walked in with his guitar and a notebook. David is a composer. "Go to bed," he said, seating himself in the middle of the dogs' room. "I do my best work at night."

David softly played his guitar and wrote, the dogs were quiet in his presence, and a blanket of peace settled over the house at last. I lay in bed, but could not let go into sleep. It was my first chance to think hard about what I had gotten into. Was it really in the dogs' best interests to continually subject them to the stress of handling and our attempts to introduce them to a world that was totally alien to everything they had known? How many were really capable of making the transition? Yet the only alternative was mass euthanization. It seemed incredibly unfair not to give them a chance, especially after everything they had already been through.

In all my years of working with animals, I had never encountered anything remotely like this. It is one thing to work on establishing trust with an animal that is open to knowing you or who at least has been around humans from an early age. That makes it easier to say you have proof of the unity of all beings within the circle of nature. But here we were outside of natural laws, and instead of the possibility of unity, there was a wall, a relentless force of fear and bewilderment that had to be dismantled in order for mutual respect and communication to begin.

My knowledge about dogs, my belief in the mysterious and powerful workings of the spirit, my work with meditation, my holistic remedies, and my trust in my intuitions and in the guidance I believed came from the spiritual world—all of this was being put to the test. I could not release the tension from my body until I thought this through. What actually did I have to work with? A *pack* of dogs, an already tightly bonded group of animals who had little sense of themselves as individuals. They had a collective consciousness, a group intelligence. Anything that affected one animal would affect the whole, which was dramatized every time we took a dog out of its crate to treat it. As soon as it began reacting in fear, every other dog in the room would simultaneously begin to tremble, whine, or growl. This made it extraordinarily difficult to build any trust, because although we were working with many individual personalities, the group identity and mind-set of total rejection overrode all else.

Normally when a puppy is developing, a small window of opportunity between the age of eight and twelve weeks is the optimum time for bonding and socialization with humans. That window had never opened for these dogs. I knew that it would be almost impossible to break through the pack mentality and ask an individual dog to change its focus to my direction. I was a foreign invader; they had no need or use for me.

Furthermore, these dogs were "initiative smart." Like all wild dogs, they were canny, used to figuring out how to ensure their survival. Domestication has minimized this trait in many breeds, producing dogs that present less of a challenge to work with. These "trainable smart" dogs are able to learn the task you train them for, but they're less likely to take the initiative to change or modify the program in order to succeed if an obstacle is put in their path. Given their circumstances, the dogs I was working with had been forced to hone their survival skills to a high art; they were the hoods, the toughest and cleverest of the bunch. I knew that if they ever got over their fear, they would try to outthink me at every turn.

I recognized all of this. I don't give up easily, but something more than force of will was needed here. I felt a wave of frustration wash over me, and I tossed and turned.

Then something shifted. Something more solid moved into my gut, something that felt like an old memory, an inborn knowing of the reason for my life. "There is only one way to meet fear," said a voice inside my head. "You know that love is greater and stronger than all of this. Take one day at time, and trust that you will know what to do."

I slept deeply, the sleep of rocks that sit for centuries, holding the world together.

I woke, and it was dawn. I found myself making plans. At least the dogs were small enough to give me some advantage in terms of physical control. I canceled all of my private lessons, and I didn't board any dogs for over six months—a decision that nearly broke me. Yet I've never stopped to ask myself whether I can afford to do anything if an animal is in need. Somehow, something always works. These feral dogs, through no fault of their own, had been slated for execution. I was their only hope; until the universe told me otherwise, I was determined to see if each dog could be healed of its physical and psychological wounds and become someone's loving companion.

Later that morning, after feeding the dogs and tending their wounds, I gave myself the luxury of a cup of coffee and a moment alone. The phone rang. It was a woman I barely knew named Marjorie, and she sounded upset. I had met her the day before, when she had stopped by and offered to volunteer. I had asked her to assist with crate cleaning, and she had witnessed the amount of effort it took to accomplish minimal tasks with the dogs.

Although it would have been easier to deal only with the dogs' health issues before I began to take their training on, this was impossible because of the issue of elimination. We don't tend to think about it, but the dog is the only domesticated animal whose bodily elimination needs are subject to the convenience of its human companions. If I was going to find homes for these dogs, they needed to learn to control their bowels and bladder in a crate and indoors, and they had to get used to eliminating on-leash. This took enormous efforts on our part during the first weeks. Whenever we took a dog from its crate to go outside, it required two collars and two leashes with two people holding the leashes like a V, in case one person was attacked or a leash chewed apart during the dog's struggle to escape. Terrified of leaving those of its pack members still in crates, each unwilling dog was taken outside, where it was confronted with the sight and the strange foreign texture of grass. One female who had been put out by herself, with her leash attached so that we could catch her again, had actually clawed through the bottom half of the metal door while trying to get back inside.

Although Marjorie had only helped with cleanup the day before, she had watched George and me struggle with this exercise. She had left abruptly, without saying good-bye.

Now I could hear the agitation in her voice: "I think you are out of your mind to waste so much time and energy on such useless animals," she fumed. "There are plenty of better dogs out there that need your help finding good homes. Why ruin their chances by setting someone up with a dog that will only have to be euthanized in the long run?"

I couldn't blame her, having asked myself the same questions the night before. But I had made a commitment, and there was no going back. Although I did not realize it at the time, I was talking about a profound spiritual test that had little to do with anything I could do for the dogs physically.

"Everything I know about dogs is on the line here," I said as diplomatically as I could. "I don't know if we are going to make it, but I'm not ready to give in yet. I have been learning about animals for as long as I can remember." I continued. "And I know what they are going to need to help them feel safe. I know how to love them. These dogs deserve a chance, so I'm going to try to rebuild their world."

"Forget it," she retorted. "Dogs aren't capable of starting life over, let alone a wild pack of dogs that has never been around humans. That saying, 'You can't teach an old dog new tricks,' means just that. It's a terrible waste!"

I was getting impatient. Life is too short to waste on negativity; I've always believed in moving forward and staying focused, instead of worrying about all the things that could go wrong. I tried to explain why I could not agree with her. "Dogs experience the world differently than humans do, but there are important similarities. Scientists are even beginning to agree that their psychology is similar to our own. They just use different tools. Because we think with our heads more than with our senses, we find it hard to comprehend their incredible awareness. . . ."

I was going to continue with my appreciative speech, but she had already hung up on me.

The fact that dogs *are* so aware was the solution to what I aimed to accomplish—that was why I felt so hopeful. Rather than having Marjorie's limited view of their capabilities, I often end up questioning my own. If people had the dog's ability to hear so acutely that they could recognize the sound of a familiar car over a half mile away, or a sense of smell so keen that they could locate a body at the bottom of a pond, perhaps subjects like psychic awareness and telepathic communication would be more easily accepted.

In addition to their amazing sense of smell and hearing, dogs read body language and eye contact as a way of determining intent. Their interpretation of subtle messages—a certain stance, the lift of an eyebrow, or the chemical change of body odor from someone in relaxed state to one of fear—can be extremely astute. These wild dogs, in their wounded and psychologically displaced state, were raw and open, and their awareness posed an incredible personal challenge.

There was also the issue of my own awareness. I knew that I was good at reading dogs' signals and ways of communicating with one another. I would have to apply this knowledge in trying to awaken each dog to its sense of itself as an individual. This is what bonding is about: aligning the consciousness of two individuals. I would have to shift each dog's allegiance from its pack to me, and then ultimately help it learn to love and trust the person who wanted to give it a new home.

Although most dog lovers already know that their dogs are individuals, it still sounds strange to talk about them in this way because science has only recently made the leap to acknowledging that animals have emotions. In fact, there would be no way even to determine the hierarchy in a pack in the wild were it not for the expressions of individuality of its members. By the same token, these rescued dogs had very distinct personalities and temperaments, and I had to be sensitive to those differences in every interaction. My knowledge of how to use myself—my voice, my body, my own emotions, my experience and training skills—was a critical element. It wasn't just a matter of being smart at figuring the dogs out. I had to become acutely aware of the emotional needs of each, because that was the foundation on which the bond of trust would be established. Nothing could be accomplished without trust; it was the critical first step.

Above all, there was the question of my willingness to commit to the dogs on all levels of my being. It was not enough for me simply to use my expertise to tend to their physical needs while allowing my inner state to be taken up with worry, insecurities, and fears. Whenever I dealt with these dogs, I had to be positive, focused, and consistent all the way to my core, because if I was not, the dogs would without a doubt sense it. And then they would never allow me in.

I'd posted records on the dogs' crates from the very beginning, with brief assessments of their worst wounds and sketches of their treatments. My approach was different from that of conventional medicine. Although I gave a mild sedative in the beginning to help the dogs deal with being handled, I did not use antibiotics, steroids, or anti-inflammatory agents for any of their wounds, fevers, or infections. I had been using various holistic healing remedies for several years after healing myself from Lyme disease. I believed that if anything was going to do the job, it would be the approaches that I had already tested with great success.

Because the dogs were in such a wretched state, I marshaled these and every other healing tool at my disposal. Although I am not a veterinarian, I have a considerable knowledge of healing from my years of animal care, and I am able to administer basic care to all of my dogs; the only veterinary care any of the dogs had over the next months was for spaying, neutering, and rabies-vaccinating.

The holistic approach was not an experiment in my mind. It was an exercise of my deepest convictions. I worked holistically in every sense of the word, because these dogs were almost out of reach, not only on a physical level but also mentally and emotionally. Each dog's ability to heal completely would depend on whether I could bring all three levels into wholeness within the context of a new reality.

I began with structure. Dogs live in the present moment. They interpret their reality according to the information given them, and their reactions are based on their understanding of what will keep them alive and safe. They do not plan for the future, and although their bodies can store memories of past experiences, particularly bad ones, that memory bank can often be overridden through good experiences. Therefore, a predictable routine would help them process their new reality. I made sure that we fed and dealt with them in the same order at the same time every day. This became the foundation of their existence and greatly reduced their stress, because they quickly figured out what was expected of them and began to be able to accomplish it on their own. For example, after having been taken out of the crate, led on a leash across the room to the door and out to the exercise yard in exactly the same way each time, as well as experiencing the process in reverse, it was eventually possible to eliminate the leashes and just open the crate door. Each dog figured out that this was the signal to go out, and each knew how to find its own crate when it came back in. Life began to make sense. This routine built the foundation of their new existence.

I put the dogs on a nourishing diet to build up their bodies and create a sense of well-being, which would enable them to feel more capable of responding to the changes in their environment. They had been starved. Instead of synthetic vitamins, I gave them fresh raw meat and vegetables— carrots, beets, kale—foods with natural enzymes. I added garlic, lots of vitamin C, a supplement high in lecithin, B-complex vitamins, and digestive enzymes.

Every dog had some kind of wound or infection: lacerations, punctures, and tears. I treated these with herbal medicines made from plants that I grow in my gardens or gather in the wild: tinctures of oat straw, chamomile, and Saint-John's-wort for depression and to support the central nervous system; herbal poultices; infused oils and salves containing rosemary, plantain, flaxseed, burdock, or calendula to treat the wounds. We treated their ear mites daily with olive oil infused with garlic, rosemary, and rue. And I used homeopathic remedies: aconite for stress, staphysagria for rapid healing of incision-type wounds, Ledum for punctures. Homeopathic remedies, like flower essences, are a potentized solution: the liquid with the material in it is diluted so many times that only the essential quality of the substance remains.

Some of the dogs were running a fever from their infections. I had long been interested in the use of colored light to stimulate sensory reactions and the immune system, and I used it here because it is simple and noninvasive. I hung droplights with colored bulbs on the crates, flooding the interiors with colored light. The color of the bulb and the length of time varied from dog to dog; I gave the feverish ones regular doses of blue light. I gave every dog a color bath in green light—a color that balances and stabilizes the energy of the system—for at least ten minutes a day. Stoff, who had been pulled from beneath the shed, was exposed to red light for ten minutes a day to build up his vitality; then he received ten minutes of green light for balance.

I added a variety of sensory stimulants for the dogs' emotional states— and for ours as well. Since dogs are incredibly sensitive to the moods and intentions of humans, I played soothing music constantly in the room— Mozart, Handel's *Water Music*, Native American flute music, and other kinds helpful for meditation and relaxation—to help all of us, dogs and humans, stay calm. I also used aromatherapy, diffusing the scents of plants or minerals. The sense of smell is one of the most profound pathways to the brain and the neurological system; burning incense or heating scent-infused oils can stimulate certain things like memory, can calm or enliven moods, and like the taste of food, can serve as a kind of nourishment for the nerves. I heated lavender oil because it has calming qualities and vetiver because it has an earthy smell and is helpful for emotional stability.

To help alleviate stress, I put my flower essence remedy in the dogs' drinking water every day. Flower essence was one of the first holistic healing tools I ever tried, and the results were so convincing that I began using the essences regularly to treat various emotional states.

It was especially frightening and sometimes painful for the dogs when we touched them, which we had to do in order to treat them. For this reason, after we completed the daily treatment of their wounds, we would spend another ten or twenty minutes doing massage work, as well as a combination of different modalities that promote healing on the mental, emotional, and spiritual levels: Reiki, acupressure, and physical touch therapies like TTouch, and Therapeutic Touch. (Yes, they are different.)

TTouch was discovered by Linda Tellington-Jones, a renowned animal trainer and therapist. It was inspired by a kind of body work called Feldenkreis and is based on the fact that every cell in the body has its own intelligence. Each cell stores a certain energy pattern, which can be altered by emotional reactions. By breaking up the pattern with various forms of touch therapy and Reiki, it is possible to help a person or an animal change old habits or find relief from pain. It is also a way to create and establish a new response.

When I worked on repatterning these dogs, I especially wanted to change the habitual contraction of the muscles in their hindquarters, where anxiety had caused them to walk in a constant crouch with their tails clamped tight between their back legs. If I could get those muscles to release, they could begin to release their fear.

Most dogs find comfort in physical contact, but this was not so for these dogs. The work took hours of patience, but as time went by, we began to see results as the dogs gradually realized that gentle, nonthreatening touch could make them feel better, something that they could not do for themselves. It seemed as though a part of them wanted to enjoy the experience, but their fear of humans would not allow them to relax. Nevertheless, it took less time each day to achieve a little letting-go by the end of a session.

It was early July. George came in from collecting the mail, chuckling with great satisfaction. She had just been stopped on the road by a stranger, who had peered at her warily out of his car window and then, gesturing with his head toward the house, asked, "Is that the place with the witch doctor?"

I could laugh too: Call me anything you want, I thought, and then come look at these dogs. In fact, we were making exceptional progress with their healing and had seen constant improvements from the very beginning.

Stoff was a prime example. His wounds were completely healed, his body had filled out, and his thick coat was beginning to shine. Lucy was another. After she had spent a week in a catatonic state, I heard Lauren, a friend who came to volunteer and help with caring for these dogs, call out to me early one morning: "The female is lying down!" We all knew immediately which female she meant. Lucy had stayed in one position with her head facing the back of the crate for a week and then she had turned and faced out, following our every move with wary sidewise glances. But every day she was more and more alive, curious, and interested in her new surroundings.

Navaho had also recovered, and now, when we took the dogs outside, he and Lucy were inseparable. This was not the only bond that was evident in the pack. As the dogs became more accustomed to their new environment, it became apparent when we put them outside together that there were deep friendships as well as long-standing issues of animosity and aggression among them. One thing, however, still united them above all else, and that was their profound sense of displacement and their utter rejection of humans.

Every day I had evidence of the pack's deep depression when I went into their room. Although the look of utter panic and terror had left the dogs' eyes, they hung their heads with a dullness, and their gaze was vacant. They no longer snapped at us when we reached out to them, but each still cowered in the back of its crate when someone reached out to give it a pat. They tolerated human contact, but that was all.

As I was able to shift my focus from the dogs' physical needs to their emotional states, I contemplated how far we still had to go. The approaches that are normally used to establish trust and communication in a relationship with a dog—eye contact, verbal praise, caresses, and food for rewards—would not work as motivators here. I began to go into their room in the evening and meditate and ask for guidance. I believe that everything that happens in the physical, happens first on a nonphysical level, and that was where I would have to go to do the real work. I needed a breakthrough.

I had already been trying to communicate mentally all the time. Each time I approached a dog, I would take a moment to get myself relaxed and calm. I would create a picture in my mind of what I was going to do, and I would imagine that I was showing the dog a mental image of what was about to take place, in order to help prepare us for the experience. I also had been especially focused in my work with Reiki, channeling healing energy into each dog, not only when I touched it but also when I sat among the dogs as a group.

One evening as I was sitting in prayer and meditation, an inspiration came to me. Reiki practitioners work mentally with certain sacred Japanese symbols to help them access and direct healing power. Now I created a new symbol of my own and filled it with all of my love and hope for these dogs, until my whole being was energized with a sense of power and conviction. I projected the symbol like a shining gift to each dog in the room.

The change in the atmosphere was almost immediate.

I could feel that the love I had sent out through the symbol was being returned. It was coming from the dogs. The sensation was so intense that I could feel wave after wave of gratitude wash over me. We had finally found a common ground, and it was not of the physical world but of a brilliant, unifying spiritual reality. Love had conquered the fear. As I began to realize the full impact of my discovery, I wept with joy.

I continued to use my symbol every evening and saw that it was a powerful tool. I had discovered a level of communication that they were willing to accept; we had reached a new dimension of awareness. Some time was still to pass, however, before I saw the results manifest in the visible world. Now if only one of the leaders would spontaneously approach us in friendship and trust, I knew that such a positive example would ripple through the rest of the pack.

I made a new plan. I decided that the dogs needed more room to run and more mental stimulation than they had been getting in the small pea-stoned yard just off their room. I have three securely fenced acres of lawn and woods for my other dogs, as well as a large spring-fed pond for swimming. I knew that we might have trouble catching the Vermont dogs if we let them free in such a large area that they did not know well, so I began putting a few of them out at a time, each one dragging a 50-foot-long line. This would enable us to catch them more easily, since none knew how to come when called.

One day I also decided to introduce them to some of the other dogs, hoping that the example of being well-adjusted, bonded with people, and happy would be influential. I turned to special members of my household for help, choosing three Australian shepherds: Jessie, who is the highest-ranking among the dogs who live with me; fun-loving and playful Flicker; Black Hawk, who was now a boisterous six-month-old teenager; and my thirteen-year-old Shelties, Brechen and Vixie.

A few of the Vermont dogs were near the house. That group included Lucy, who was obviously a high-ranking female in her pack. When my own dogs were let out, Jessie was the first to touch noses with Lucy. A blue merle with a thick silvered coat with black splotches, Jessie is the self-appointed mother of all in my household. Every evening she visits each of her pack mates as they lie about on my living room floor, and she carefully cleans their ears with thorough, attentive licking. This nighttime ceremony, which is like a good-night kiss, is so important to the other dogs that if she forgets any one pack member, that dog will follow her around the house like a neglected child until Jessie performs the rite. She is extraordinarily loving, and I had great hopes that she would be a big influence on the cringing pack we had brought out in the sun on a beautiful summer day.

At first there was a lot of ritual display between the two females, with curious sniffing, stiff body posturing, and tails quivering as if an electric current were running through them. Shaggy Jessie dwarfed compact, red-coated Lucy, but that didn't mean much, since the smaller dog had already been to hell and back and knew how to defend herself. I stood by, not sure what was going to happen but keeping my expectations positive.

The ritual was thorough. Then came acceptance. Once Jessie signaled her approval, my other dogs crowded in to be introduced.

Hawk gave a joyful, openhearted leap in the air in front of a long-haired black female we had named Ebony. "Go, Hawk!" I whispered to myself. "Take that pup for a run!" But Ebony shrank back, and although the two packs mingled together for several minutes, at a certain point they resumed their strange division of worlds. I sat on the grass with George and Susan near my pond, and my longtime dog companions gathered around us like a loose furry skirt, to dream lazily in the summer heat. The other pack slunk about under the trees.

I continued to put the two packs out together on a daily basis for weeks. The Vermont dogs' spirits improved with their new freedom; however, they continued to keep their distance. The same thing would always happen: I would emerge from the house, and my dogs would rush up to me joyfully, tails high and and eyes bright. The other pack would watch intently, then move off in the opposite direction. It was like watching two schools of fish in a pond. The two packs remained divided, same species but very different cultures.

One day there was a humorous development. I headed out to round up the dogs that were on lines, knowing it was going to be a chore because they were unwilling to be caught. It had been taking two and sometimes three of us at least an hour to accomplish the task since we had begun letting the dogs loose in this way several weeks before. I felt, however, that it was worth the effort.

As we began to corner dog after dog and gather up the lines, Black Hawk suddenly seemed to grasp the purpose of our efforts. He ran across the lawn and grabbed a line that was connected to Jamie, a small female with beagle-type ears and a short red-and-black coat. I immediately praised Hawk and told him to come to me. As he started toward me, Jamie put on the brakes, which stopped Hawk short. He turned around, faced her, and gave a huge tug on the line, which so surprised her that she began moving again, following

"Hawk Catches a Vermont Dog"

Hawk's lead. I doubled over with laughter. It was the first time I had ever seen a dog give another dog a correction with a leash.

Hawk enjoyed the praise, and because he is a working breed, he seemed to be delighted with the fact that he had just created a new job for himself. Life immediately got easier. The dogs would still run when a human approached, but they were totally at ease with the approach of another dog. From that day on, when it was time to call them in, Hawk would gather up line after line. He would have trouble getting some of the bigger dogs to do his bidding, but he would grab the line and hold on, or sometimes even wrap it around a tree until we could get to him to take charge.

So my dogs helpfully began to get involved. The summer wore on.

In late August one of my greatest hopes was fulfilled. George and I were sitting on the back stoop. The Vermont dogs were out in the yard, by now able to go without long lines because they had learned the habit of coming whenever I said "Inside," since I had been focused on getting them to understand verbal cues from the very beginning. They would head in to their crates if I stayed well out of the way.

On this soft summer morning, some of them were milling about near the house, and Lucy was casually sniffing the ground, doing regular doglike things with all of the wonderful smells of the great outdoors. Navaho was attending her as usual, his thick black, silver, and white coat nearly doubling his size now that he had recovered. It still was a mystery to us why he had been in so many fights when he seemed to have such a gentle disposition.

As always, George and I were keeping our bodies sidewise, not looking directly at any of the dogs in order not to seem aggressive, holding our hands out casually behind us with treats in them, and appearing not to notice if any dog came close enough to take an exploring sniff. These hesitant investigations were happening more often now, especially if we were sitting down, because our reduced body size was then less threatening.

Lucy seemed to be circling, now shy, now inquisitive, now rather off-hand. "She's coming to check me out," whispered George, and she began to talk to Lucy in a low, friendly way: "Hey, little love," George crooned. We remained casual. Lucy mounted the stoop. George and I ignored her and moved into a conversation, making plans for fall, philosophizing about the end of summer. The dog moved behind us and took a careful sniff of George's back, then inched closer. Close enough. She reached up and gave George a tiny, tentative lick on the cheek.

George does not cry easily, but she did then, bursting out with, "Oh, you little princess!"

It was the first time any of the dogs had indicated any good feelings for us. Lucy was crowned with the noble title of Princess, and she became our bridge-builder and anchor dog. From then on, if she stayed calm in a new situation, the rest of the pack would also, and the shift in their collective consciousness could be used to help the training and repatterning process work for us instead of against us. I knew that things would now begin to move more rapidly.

A week later, when the dogs were out running and playing, Princess came across the lawn to me, dragging her hindquarters. I was stunned; was I about to lose my best ally? I took her to the vet and had her X-rayed, knowing that her condition had to be a spinal problem. The slides showed that it was a ruptured disk, possibly due to mating, more probably from fighting. The amount of calcification indicated that it was one of a number of reoccurrences of an old injury.

As we headed home again, I kept wondering how a dog, even with her high rank, could have survived in a paralyzed state, given the harsh laws of the pack. If she'd shown any sign of weakness, she ought to have been destroyed by the starving dogs.

The knowledge burst in on me. "Navaho!" I exclaimed aloud. Now I understood why her devoted companion had been so horribly battered. He was her valiant warrior champion, and he had fought for her, offering his life each time her crippled condition had diminished her power. I could only imagine the bloody battles that had raged over her huddled form.

But Navaho and Princess had made it; they would never again have to fight with other dogs to stay alive. Princess had bonded with us and had begun asking for attention. Yet the shadow of depression lingered. When would the knowledge that life was more than a regular meal truly sink in?

Nearly six months after these dogs came into my life, I saw the long-looked-for sign that the shadow had lifted and tolerance had turned to trust.

A number of us were standing outside on a brilliant fall afternoon. The crisp air had the house dogs romping and chasing one another, and I wanted to run and play with them, but I knew this would frighten the Vermont dogs, so instead I sat down and watched as their pack, with Navaho and Princess in the lead, went swarming silently down toward the pond. "Oh, come on guys," I pleaded silently. "Can't you be happy?"

And then, all of a sudden, it happened.

It might have been the snip of autumn breeze that ruffled the surface of the pond, sending sparks of light dancing across its surface. It might have been the distant, humorous gobble of my tom turkey herding his mate around the barnyard. Good smells, familiar all's-right-with-the-world sounds, and already somewhere there was a supper that could be counted on to appear. . . . I suddenly saw Navaho's tail come out from where it had been locked tight and safe between his back legs since he had arrived. It became a waving plume. It was more than a tail that had remembered what tails were for; it was a glorious flag of surrender to joy.

Navaho gave several exuberant bounds and began to run, not away from anything at all, but for the pure, wild feeling of release.

I wanted to do a leaping victory lap with him around the yard; I wanted to give a celebratory whoop, but I didn't want to risk scaring that beautiful symbol away. I looked over at George and her eyes followed my pointing finger. We reached for each other and hugged and cried. Except for Princess's shy overture, it was the first time we had seen one of those dogs find joy in this new life.

I knew then that they could make it. All of the hard work, all of my willingness to trust and believe in the power of love and commitment, was finally manifested in that bounding animal.

And over the following months, dog by dog, that banner was carried through the pack.

Out of the original pack, only those dogs who came home with me survived. I had chosen those who had the worst injuries and the most challenging personalities, while other dogs, who seemed more tractable, were sent to various facilities where they were kept in kennel runs. Unlike my place, where the dogs have to be handled to put them in and out, in these kennel facilities they can be fed, watered, and let in and out by by opening a sliding door, so they never have to be touched. This meant that although their physical needs were met, they did not receive any one-on-one attention. The assumption was that the dogs would eventually come around, but in fact, they never could because they did not know how. The psychological and emotional support was lacking. They were not met where they were, and then guided onward. This lack was especially dramatized by the fate of one dog who stayed at one of these facilities for months without any change in behavior. I was eventually asked to take him on, but I had to refuse because I was at my limit, so he was sent to another good and qualified trainer for obedience work. The dog was able to learn the basics, and a home was found for him, but within a half hour of being there, he escaped and was never seen again.

The saddest story involved the fate of five who were sent to a facility in northern Vermont. They were chained to doghouses and immediately broke away and escaped into the woods, dragging their chains like death sentences behind them. One male was eventually found; he had been hit by a car and had to be put down. There is little doubt that the others also met with tragedy.

Ebony, Princess, Jamie, and a dog named Tyler remained with me, while a number of the others were adopted by the volunteers who had worked with me over the long months. Their eagerness to continue to work with the dogs in their own homes was particularly the result of my discoveries about the purposeful focusing of the mind and emotions in training. As I taught each person how to apply some of my new techniques with the various dogs, strong bonds began to form between individuals, and lifelong commitments were made. These people also had other dogs, which was an important factor, because they would provide companionship and support and serve as an example while the new dog continued to adjust.

Stoff, whose life had nearly ended at the bottom of a black hole in the ground, remained a loner in respect to his own kind, but he became the treasured friend of a young man who likes to hike and adventure. The two of them are still exploring the world, and they are inseparable.

Once the dogs were settled in their new homes, their human companions brought them to my group training classes to continue the lessons of basic obedience. On the first night of class, I stood in the center of the room, filled with emotion as I watched each proud but anxious person enter with a nervous but willing dog. Despite the nervousness, the bonds of trust held, and after a few sessions, no one could tell the difference between the once "wild" dogs and their classmates.

Four of the Vermont dogs could not make the switch to our world.

They were three of the older dominant males and one female: tough, scrappy, and eternally lost without their roles. Although they received the same ministrations and behavioral repatterning as the other dogs, they could not deal with their new situation and remained aggressive, unpredictable, and distrustful of people. I agonized for a long time, but finally decided that I had to respect their choice to reject us. Since there are no other options for such animals, sending them back to spirit seemed the kindest and most humane thing to do.

Champ and Streak left first and, later, a male we had named Crusader and a female named Fox, who had been at another facility. I felt the tragedy deeply, because their physical wounds were completely healed. I had considered giving them an outside pen to live in with minimal human contact, like they had before. Ultimately, however, it came down to an issue of freedom and respect; keeping them like zoo animals made no sense.

George and I took Champ and Streak out by the pond. The humane officer followed, and she put them down.

It was incredible. Within a few minutes after the dogs' spirits left, all of the other dogs at Hearthside began to howl. A white cloud of doves came from the barn and flew three times around us in great circles. This incident was repeated a week later when Crusader and Fox left.

Later that evening, I buried Champ and Streak near a stand of white pines, ancient tree elders who guard the entrance to my land. As I stood in the gathering dusk, I heard George call me. She was standing in the driveway, pointing to the sky. I stepped out from the darkness under the trees and looked in the direction of her pointing finger. Near the deep blue horizon line, I saw the shape of two rosy-pink dog clouds running, headed east. I knew then that I had made the right decision. Champ and Streak were free at last.

One year to the day after the Vermont rescue, we had a reunion. Sixteen people came, out of a number who had adopted forty-five dogs that I had rehabilitated, including the Vermont dogs. Other people who could not attend sent cards and good wishes. Thirty well-mannered and happy dogs played or lolled in the circle of chairs while their human companions told their stories. It was fun watching the dogs' happy reactions at seeing one another again, but the biggest highlight of the gathering was to hear all of the people speak proudly about their dogs' progress. The love and sense of accomplishment in the room could be felt by all.

Newspaper reporters wrote furiously as we talked, and then I brought out a cake I'd constructed of dog food in the shape of a giant dog bone, with cream cheese frosting and thin slices of liver spelling out "love" on the top. Princess dived in and got cream cheese all over her nose, and so did the rest. As I took in the whole event, I wanted to set off fireworks over New England.

When the reporter's story came out, she called me a "miracle worker." This assessment was inaccurate. I guess I've been around animals too long to take credit for what happens between us; the exchange is mutual. If I had looked at the wild pack as a group of dogs who had gone wrong and who would serve no purpose, bring no enjoyment to humans, and contribute nothing, how much I, and the people who worked with me, would have missed. The whole draining, time-consuming, often frustrating, and ultimately rewarding experience was a deeply satisfying validation of a new approach to training animals through working with nonphysical communication.

"George and Lucy"

The ability to bridge the gap between the self and the animal world is within each one of us. I am fortunate to have been chosen to assist in that process. Although at the time of the rescue I had spent my entire adult life with dogs and many other animals, I had never before been challenged to focus predominantly on communicating with my mind and emotions. Without this essential capacity, none of my other methods—my extensive knowledge as a trainer, or my work with holistic medicine—would have created the will to trust and communicate. Despite the dogs' continual rejection, I had to maintain a mental discipline and a peaceful, loving energy in every encounter. I had to really stretch myself—to draw on every method I had ever tried, every intuition that came to me—in order to break through the barriers created by fear.

The most powerful gift that dogs bring to humans is their ability to be unconditionally loving. The only way that these dogs could become loving pets and companions was to receive the same unwavering trust and unconditional love from humans. Because the roles were reversed, this experience, more than any other in my life, made me appreciate the real meaning of love without condition, judgment, or expectation. I had to give love for love's sake only, to experience it in its purest form.

Through healing these dogs, I was taught to value the tremendous spiritual potential in a mutual exchange between species. Now I want to share what this can mean for you.

5

YOUR MIND AND THE ENERGY CONNECTION

The next four chapters contain the basic elements of Awareness Training, an approach that has been profoundly influenced by my dramatic
encounter with the Vermont dogs. Although I learned a great deal
from that experience, it did not immediately occur to me to incorpo-
rate certain elements of that knowledge into my ongoing training
classes until I became frustrated with hearing people tell me that I had
such a magic way with animals. This would often occur when there
were disruptive dogs in the class that people were barely able to control. I would walk over, look at the dog, and give it a verbal request and
a hand signal to sit. It would immediately do so happily, making eye
contact and wagging its tail. I'd turn around to resume the lesson, and
within minutes the dog would be out of control again.

Since I knew I couldn't take every dog in the world home if its
owner gave up on training, I saw that I needed to teach people something more than the basics. I stopped and analyzed what I was doing
that was different; there was something instinctive within me, something that didn't exist with most of my students.

I finally realized that the crucial missing ingredient was attitude,
and how that attitude was experienced by the person and communicated to the dog. I had a lot of faith in my abilities, had a clear expectation of what I wanted, had automatically visualized the result in my
mind before I even approached the dog, and I was already projecting
positive energy about his response to my intentions. By contrast, I
could tell that most people expected the worst from themselves and
their dogs. They were riddled with self-doubt, negativity, and fear.
They were creating psychological and emotional blocks that their
dogs found confusing and, in some cases, even frightening.

I committed myself to figuring out how to share my realization.
I discovered that I needed to show people a specific way to access

their inner power through consciously using the energy of the mind and the heart.

In my story of the rescued Vermont dogs, I related the essential truth that was the turning point in my relationship to those animals who were so out of reach. I used my psychological and spiritual resources as a training tool. This inner work, more than any other reason, created the breakthroughs that began with Princess and traveled through the pack. As I showed the dogs how to join our world, I established a link with each one by creating an energetic awareness between us. I validated the spirit of each individual, and each became more receptive and responsive to my expectations.

Even though I had already been introducing the importance of attitude in my training classes, I was more convinced than ever after the Vermont rescue experience. The more I tried out some of my ideas, the more dramatic were the changes in my clients' relationships with their dogs. People began to tell me that the approach was also a positive influence on their lives. I concluded that it was a wonderful, nonthreatening exploration of the power of our inner life. In addition, I find that people who might not otherwise have explored purposefully directing the mind and emotions are willing to do so, especially because their efforts are confirmed by the changes in the behavior of their animals.

Awareness Training: Part One—The Energy of Life

When you formulate a thought, you instantly project it out into the universe. We think countless numbers of thoughts every day, but most of them arrive and disappear without creating much impact in our lives. If, however, a thought has a strong emotional charge, whether positive or negative, the energy of that thought can become a highly influential and creative force.

When I speak of the energy in the thought, I am referring to universal life force, an invisible energetic flow that is present in all living things. It is within and around us and is constantly in a dynamic state. It is a unifying force, connecting all things that are alive. Because of this connection, every living being is influenced by the changes in life energy of every other living being. It is why we are able to say that we are all one. Nothing in the universe operates in isolation.

Awareness Training is mindful work with life energy. Your attitudes and beliefs are energies that you project into everything you create in your life and into those things you attract to you. When you project fear or doubt, you attract similar energy. When you project an attitude of calm and energy that is positive, you attract more of that energy. Worry, fear, and doubts create tension, stress, and the feeling of being "down." The energy of those emotions can affect the people around you, and it can affect your dog. This is also true when you are feeling happy and confident. Because dogs are so sensitive, they can easily perceive and respond to these contrasting states, and they will usually reflect them right back to you. Energy flows both ways.

Contemporary philosopher Deepak Chopra, who is at the forefront of discussions about the mind-body connection, defines life energy as an intelligence comprising everything that holds the universe together, from the structure of atoms to the genetic code, to the functioning of the human immune system and the ability of each cell to fulfill its own particular job.

Because energy is intelligence, says Chopra, it is also mind. In his book *Ageless Body, Timeless Mind*, he describes how an emotional state like fear will create a biochemical reaction with the production of adrenaline. The mind sends the body a message to produce a certain reaction in order to sustain itself.

The work of Chopra and others is creating a revolution in modern medicine—for example, in the control of pain in cancer patients and in the lowering of blood pressure through the use of biofeedback. It is now generally accepted that a focused mind can consciously control many bodily functions and that the practice of certain mental disciplines, such as meditation, can increase this control.

Knowledge of life energy has been around for centuries. In India it is called *prana,* and in China and Japan it is called *chi.* In the West, philosophers of the eighteenth and nineteenth century called it the etheric or vital force. Explorations of life energy have created practices like meditation, acupuncture, Tai Chi, Qi Gong, the use of potentized solutions as in homeopathy, and certain forms of body work like Reiki and polarity therapy. All of these are based on the experience that energy can be controlled and directed in such a way as to affect the functioning of a living being. One can, for example, use one's own life energy to affect the energy of others, as though certain forms of body work like massage or healing touch, or one can control one's own energy exclusively, as in Tai Chi.

You can experience your own energy field without too much difficulty. Try the following experiment:

Rub your hands briskly together in a clockwise circle for a few moments and then separate them at a distance of about one inch. Gently move them closer together and farther apart. It may help to close your eyes so that you can focus your attention only on the sensations on your palms. Like most people, you will probably feel a sort of fuzzy or spongy density in the space between your hands. You are feeling the vibrations of your field.

Another way you can feel your energy field is to have someone walk up and stand close behind you. Generally, people can feel a sensation along the back of the body when the other person gets within a foot or so.

Energy in the human body, and also in dogs is localized in energy centers, or chakras. We have seven major centers, located at the vertical midline
of the body, and each is associated with a color. Briefly, they are (1) the root
chakra, red, located at the bottom of the trunk between the legs; (2) the belly
chakra, orange, located at the bottom of the belly in the region of the spleen;
(3) the solar plexus, yellow, located behind the navel; (4) the heart chakra,
green, located in the center of the chest; (5) the throat chakra, blue, located
in the neck; (6) the brow or third eye chakra, indigo, located between the
eyebrows; and (7) the crown chakra, violet, located at the top of the head.

When you do healing work on people or animals, these energy centers
are important reference points for bringing balance back into the body. They
also can be focal points for drawing in or sending out energy, and this is how
I use them in Awareness Training. I will explain more about this in Chapter
13, and have given references for further reading in the appendix if you want
to do more research.

Humans have the ability to create with universal life energy; we can manifest our ideas in the physical world. Whenever we decide to act outwardly,
there is an incredible amount of inner activity, which is a combination of
thoughts and feelings. Purposefully organizing and directing those invisible
thoughts and feelings is what allows ideas to manifest on the visible plane.

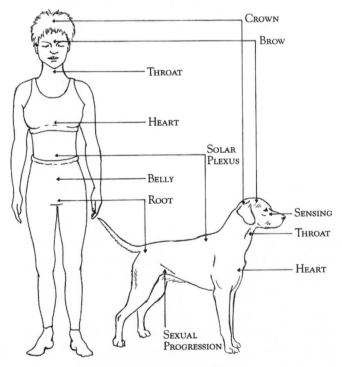

"Human and Dog 'Energy Centers' "

We act on our thoughts and feelings by using the power of our will, which is what it means to be purposeful, or to have intention. We also make choices among those things that we want to manifest. Some we accomplish with our hands, like the creation of a garden; some we create with our minds, like the solution to a math problem; and some we create with our emotions, like nurturing a child to develop confidence by giving her lots of love. Some things are never actualized in the physical, but fade away because there is not sufficient energy to bring them forth. On the other hand, simply maintaining a high level of purpose and a clear image in your mind of the object of your desire can bring that object into manifestation.

This is why I always say to my students, "Behind the word is the thought; behind the thought is the intent; and within the intent lies the power."

Your intention is your creative power. The relationship between your thoughts and your feelings is the essential dynamic in each creative act. By being objective, you are attempting to free your thoughts from the emotional energy of your feelings. If, on the other hand, you are subjective, you are allowing your feelings to be the guiding principle. Emotional energy is the most influential energy of all, which is why, if it is not controlled with purpose, it ends up controlling you.

Creating thoughts that have the emotion of fear or anger attached to them manifests a life energy that can be a powerful negative influence on the health of a situation or another being. Thoughts that are charged with the desire for good can have a powerful positive influence. This is why there are so many stories of people who, when facing great obstacles in their lives, have expressed that the most important factor in their ability to succeed, was that another person believed in them, especially at a time when they were finding it hard to believe in themselves. When positive energy is sent to you, it helps you to reconnect with it in yourself, because it resonates at the same frequency.

This knowledge is of great significance when applied to communicating with animals. When you do awareness training, you consciously work with life energy; you give your dog physical cues with tools like your voice, posture, and the leash, but most important, you cue him mentally and emotionally by showing him your intent for the situation. You create the concept, empower it with positive emotional energy, and if necessary, guide the dog physically. I will be giving you specific guidelines for how to do this, but first I would like you to have some fun playing with energy and with some of these ideas.

A very simple way to experience the influence of your psychological-emotional state over the energy in your system is through the practice of kinesiology. The principles of kinesiology were discovered in 1964 by George J. Goodheart, a midwestern chiropractor who observed relationships between the amount of strength in a muscle and other physical-emotional conditions in the body. If there is a weakness in a certain organ, it can be discovered by testing those muscles that have a relationship to that organ. It was also discovered that the presence of negative thoughts and emotions can affect the body's energy in obvious ways—fear, for example, will make your knees weak—and in more subtle ways—if you don't tell the truth, your deception can often be detected by a subtle shift in the energy of a muscle.

Kinesiology, like dowsing or a lie detector test, demonstrates that the influence of whatever you mentally and emotionally project or absorb is manifested in the muscular strength of the body. If you project anger, your body alters itself chemically to deal with the emotion. If you project love, the same thing happens. If you hold a cigarette in your hand or a quarter teaspoon of sugar under your tongue, your body prepares itself for the influence by creating a reaction, and this can be recorded through testing a muscle. For this reason, kinesiology is used in various holistic health practices to collect information about bodily imbalances. It can be used to determine the source of an allergy, the need for a certain vitamin, the cause of a chronic illness, and even the presence of tooth decay.

I do kinesiology with people to demonstrate that their thoughts and emotions, particularly as expressed through their words, have creative power. Once people have a direct experience of this, it becomes more clear why directing energy through the sending of emotion-charged thoughts can have a dramatic effect on the behavior of their dogs, on their own lives, and on the energy of other living beings. Some of these techniques were shared with me by Dr. Heather Ann Harder, an educator, philosopher, and politician interested in human consciousness. I adapted them for use with animals.

The kinesiology exercises are important because, although it may not be hard to grasp the concept of energy fields, it is hard to understand that we have some control over an invisible force. The exercises can show you why the conscious control of energy is so important, but ultimately your dog is the one who has the power to convince you when you do Awareness Training. When you consciously control the energy that you send to your dog, you will experience a dramatic difference in the way that he responds to you, and that is more convincing than anything else!

To try these experiments, gather a few of your like-minded friends together, people who will not undermine your testing with negative attitudes. If someone is feeling skeptical, that's okay; it's not uncommon for people to question these ideas. Just be sure that everyone has an openhearted desire to explore.

You can use any muscle in the body for the exercise. I like to use the deltoid, which supports the arm when it is held straight out to the side, because it is so easy and obvious to see how well it works as a barometer.

Note: Because energy fields affect other energy fields, be sure that you and your partner do not stand too close to other people when you are trying these exercises.

THE FIRST TEST

Part one: The purpose of the first part of this exercise is to discover what a person's normal energy is when the muscle of the arm is put under moderate stress; the arm should be held up with ease:

1. Have the person who is going to be tested raise one arm (either arm can be used) and hold it straight out to the side, slightly below shoulder height. The person should keep the hand relaxed, fingers loose and extended.

2. Face the person, keeping your body slightly off-center so that you are not directly face-to-face. Do not look at the person during this test.

3. Place two fingers lightly on top of the person's outstretched arm, just behind the wrist. Put your other hand gently on the person's other shoulder.

4. Ask the person to resist and then steadily apply light to moderate (2 to 5 pounds) downward pressure on the arm. Press just hard enough to feel the person's ability to resist, hold for a moment, and then stop.

5. Take a moment to compare notes with your subject. How much energy did the person need to keep the arm horizontal? How much pressure were you using in order to feel the quality of the resistance?

Part two: The purpose of the second half of this exercise is to demonstrate that normal strength in an organism can be disrupted when an energy center is blocked.

1. Repeat the exercise, but this time, take the hand that was on your partner's opposite shoulder and hold it about three inches from the person's brow chakra—that is, just in front of the area between the eyebrows. Have your other hand in the same position as before, two fingers resting lightly on top of the arm, just behind the person's wrist.

2. Say "Resist," and using exactly the same amount of pressure, test again.

3. Stop and compare results. Most people find that the amount of energy required to keep their arm up is considerably greater. Some people's arms drop immediately to their side! Some people may have the feeling you are pushing harder, although you were using the same amount of pressure as before. Remember, this is not a test of physical strength but a means of developing aware-ness of subtle shifts in energy. This is a sensitivity exercise to discover how easy it is to keep an arm up in response to down-ward pressure.

4. Compare notes. It will be different things for different people; the energy shifts can range from subtle to dramatic.

THE SECOND TEST

Part one: The purpose of this part of the exercise is to demonstrate that energy is truth. By this I mean that you will be able to see that your energy is weakened by any statement that is false.

1. Repeat the first part of the opening exercise, but this time, ask your partner to say his or her first name: "My name is ————." Make sure that the name used is the familiar one; in other words, if your partner is known best by a certain nickname, that is the name to use.

2. Ask your partner to resist and test the strength of the arm as before. There should be no problem maintaining position.

Part two:

1. Now have your partner say a different name, choosing one to which he or she has no emotional attachment and that is also of the opposite sex, for the most dramatic response (Chris, for example, is either a male or female name, so it is best to choose a different one). For example, instead of saying, "My name is April," I might say, "My name is Fred."

2. Test again. Your subject will usually find it more difficult to resist the downward pressure of your hand.

THE THIRD TEST

Part one: The purpose of this test is to show how positive or negative thoughts can affect your energy.

1. Repeat the test from Test One, Part One.
2. Now ask your partner to say enthusiastically three times, "Yes! Yes! Yes!"
3. Test for resistance.

Part two: Saying "No" can sometimes be positive (for example, "Say No to Drugs"). Clearly state before you begin that for the purpose of this exercise, "No" represents something negative.

1. Repeat the test, but have the person say three times: "No. No. No." Most people experience diminished energy when you test. If you would like to, you can now switch roles with your partner.

Now that you are familiar with kinesiology testing and are becoming aware of how your thoughts and words affect your energy field, play with some further exercises, which may be even more enlightening.

THE FOURTH TEST

When energy is focused and directed: The purpose of this test is to allow you to see for yourself that even inanimate objects can be affected by negative energy. If this is so, you can begin to be aware of how your dog can be affected if you are angry and upset with him.

1. Take two or three identical objects, such as spoons or ballpoint pens.
2. Have the person who will be tested hold one object at a time, bringing it in close to his or her body. Test the person each time with each object. There should not be any noticeable difference among the objects as far as affecting the person's energy. Generally, the person's energy is not affected.
3. Place the objects at least 3 feet apart and at 6 to 10 feet from you and your partner.
4. Ask your partner to relax for a moment. Without discussing what you are about to do, close your eyes and get in touch with an

intense negative emotion. As you experience the intense feeling of anger, fear, or another negative emotion strongly in your body, visualize *one* of the objects. Visualize that one object located where you placed it, and link that emotional energy to the object. Continue to do this intently for a full minute.

5. Ask your partner to pick up one of the objects and then test her energy level. If she picked up a neutral object, there should be no change in her energy. Place the object aside, well away from the other objects not yet tested; continue to do this with each. When your partner holds the object that has the charge of negative energy, she will usually experience that her arm is weakened.

After you finish the experiment, be very sure to clear the negative energy from the object. To neutralize the energy, first take a moment to clear your mind of thoughts. Then have the intent to call back any negative energy that you sent out. Pause for a moment, and then say to yourself or aloud that your intention is to remove all negative energy from the object and transmute it to positive. Get in touch with a positive emotion, and beam that emotion at the object in the same way that you did before.

Now, without letting your partner see, mix up the order of the objects and perform a final test with all of them again. You should discover that your partner will no longer have her energy diminished when she holds the object.

THE FIFTH TEST

When energy is spread by proximity: The purpose of this exercise is to demonstrate that your energy can have an effect on people standing next to you. You will need three people, in addition to yourself.

1. Have your helpers stand at least three feet from one another, and do a simple energy test on each of them.

2. Select one person to be the focal point of the exercise.

3. Explain that the person will say something that he or she does not really believe, but you will be able to see that your brain believes everything that you tell it. This is why large corporations and professional athletic teams have motivational speakers give workshops on positive thinking and how it can affect performance.

4. The person should repeat three times, "I am not worthy, I am not important."

5. Test the person's energy again. It is usually considerably weak-ened.

6. Have another person stand shoulder to shoulder with the person just tested, and test his energy. It is usually diminished.

7. Repeat with the next person. This person's energy, too, is usu-ally diminished.

When I do this exercise in my classes, I make a long line of people, and there are usually lots of exclamations of surprise as it is discovered that a per-son standing at the end of a line of twenty people also has weakened energy.

If you have ever felt good and then walked into a place where there were depressed and angry people, only to discover that you, too, felt a loss of vitality, this exercise shows you why. You absorbed negativity without even knowing it.

8. Test the first person again to see if spreading negativity around has helped. Usually that person's energy remains weakened.

9. Ask the third person you tested to say aloud, "I choose to allow only good things to affect me." Test, and you will usually find that his energy is back to normal.

10. Ask other volunteers to think the same sentence without speak-ing it aloud or to imagine that they are surrounded by a beauti-ful protective bubble that shields them from negativity. Give them a few moments to do this, and then test. You will usually see that energy is restored.

When I want to shield myself from negative energy coming my way from other people, I envision a protective bubble and create another bub-ble beyond that, which is programmed with my intention to transmute any negative energy deflected off my shield to positive when it returns to its source!

Unfortunately, this does not mean that bad things will never happen to you. I wish it were that simple. It does mean, however, that you do not have to let your life challenges affect you on an energy level. Listen to your intu-ition, and you will usually be able to tell when you need to "bubble up."

The point of this part of the test has been to demonstrate that we can choose how we want to be affected by energy from other people. This is why, if a person decides not to allow any kinesiology test to affect him at all, you will always get the same reading!

11. Return to the first person and test his energy again. It is still diminished, because that person chose to diminish his energy with his statement of unworthiness.

12. Have the person say three times, "I am worthy, I am important." Test, and his energy will be fully restored.

If you believe that you have been open to learning from the exercises and you still could not get a clear reading, your energy flow could be temporarily out of balance. Many things—being tired, stressed, coming down with a cold, and so forth—can drain your system and put it out of balance on a given day. You could, for example, need more water in your body. You can sometimes reactivate your system by drinking a large glass of water, or you can do the following exercise: touch your tongue to the roof of your mouth, just behind your teeth, and at the same time tap the indentation that is approximately one inch below your breastbone about ten times. This stimulates your thymus and often helps to rebalance your energy.

Now that you have some experience with the way thoughts and feelings can affect your energy system, realize that you can direct and control your energy. Purposefully directing your energy is about creating your own reality and manifesting things you desire. An important principle to remember about controlling energy is that where the attention (or focus) goes, the energy flows to create more of what is happening. This is the law of attraction, which can be observed when you start thinking about someone, and a short time later the phone rings and the person you were thinking about is on the other end of the line.

When I work with a dog, I purposefully create a consistent and powerful positive energy in order to attract a positive response from him.

It is important to say that this does not give me the power to dominate or control the dog. Rather, I am projecting my intent out into the universe, creating the space and possibility for change to occur. I am willing to accept that it may not happen, because every individual dog has a choice of whether to respond. Some, like the four Vermont dogs, will not. Nevertheless, I was not controlling any of them; I was maintaining an energy to allow for a change to take place. This is a very important point to remember when you work with energy. It is not about controlling others. It is about maintaining an energy to attract additional energy of a similar vibration, in order to create something new.

Pay attention to what you are expecting, because your expectations are what you are attracting. Writer Shakti Gawain says, "We always attract into our lives whatever we think about most, believe in most strongly, expect on the deepest levels, and/or imagine most vividly." You need to be very careful of the energy in the words you choose and the feelings and thoughts that you live with, because they attract more of the same.

Thoughts set energy into motion. This is not judged by the universe; it just is. All words that we speak are a manifestation of our thoughts, which, in turn, set energy flowing in a certain direction. The vocabulary you use with your dog represents your beliefs, and if you look objectively at those beliefs, you will see the kind of energy that you are attracting.

You also need to think about how certain energy influences you. I caution my students to be very careful about the kind of energy they absorb through things like books, music, and the media, because the brain wants to believe everything it is told. Think of a time when you were watching a movie and were deeply emotionally involved in the experience. Part of you was aware it was only a movie and not real, yet if your brain did not want to participate, why did you weep or laugh or experience fear? Your energy became involved with the energy of the event, and your thoughts, emotions, and beliefs were affected.

Although you can consciously choose how you will let things affect you, it is important to realize that dogs cannot. The same openness that dogs bring to being unconditionally loving and forgiving also means that they absorb whatever we send in their direction. This is also true of young children. This is why it is critical that you make every possible effort to be aware of how your energy affects those who are naturally vulnerable. I work with many adults who still carry emotional scars and tremendous lack of self-esteem because of something a parent or teacher said to them in childhood.

When constructive training is not given to a dog at an early age, people can often fall into a lot of negative self-talk, making belittling references to the worth of the dog. If family members say, "No! Bad dog! Look you've done it again! Don't jump! Don't chew! Don't steal food off the table!" and so forth, eventually everything that is said about the dog becomes an affirmation. The person's brain says, "Okay, the power of my words has convinced me that I really have a stupid, rotten dog, so I had better get rid of it and get a new one." Our humane societies are full of dogs who are victims of human self-talk in combination with an overall lack of training and communication skills.

Practicing these ideas with your dog will help you realize how easily you can unwittingly create some of your own problems in training and why it is more productive to stay focused on positive training vocabulary and on your goals rather than on the impedances. I sometimes say in a stern voice to my clients, "Whatever you do in the next ten seconds, I don't want *any* of you—you hear me! I really mean it!—I don't want any single one of you to think about a monkey!" People immediately begin chuckling, as they realize that, in spite of being told firmly not to do something, they did it anyway. I point out that this is another example of the way that negativity attracts more negativity. This is why it is important to affirm to yourself that your dog is happily playing and chewing on his own toys when you leave the house, rather than to nurture the thought that he will probably destroy the house on your return. It is an unproductive use of energy to say, "Now, behave yourself and don't chew up the rug while I'm gone!" Dogs "see" our thoughts as pictures; when you say, "Don't do such-and-such," you are sending your dog the message to do the opposite of what you really want. This is because, like the monkey example, when you say, "don't," your mind is imagining the subject of the negative statement and putting energy into creating it.

If someone is already feeling very negative about something and is spreading that negativity around, the typical response is to become defensive and send the energy right back, even though that is the last thing that person needs. This is another example of the law of attraction, which needs an energy boost to get it flowing in a different direction.

This point was beautifully illustrated by Nancy, a young woman who came to a private counseling session. She was having a very difficult time getting her dog, Sadie, to come to her, and it made her frustrated and angry, with the result that her dog began barking at her and generally ignoring her every effort. She finally burst out, "Sadie makes me so angry, I could just scream! Her behavior can absolutely ruin my whole day! She is making me a nervous wreck!"

I waited until she had calmed down a little, and said, "Then you have one of the most powerful dogs I have ever worked with."

A look of surprise crossed Nancy's face and she asked, "What do you mean?"

"When Sadie does something that upsets you, is she forcing you to respond that way, or are you choosing to do so?" I asked.

Nancy looked at me blankly for a moment, and then she began to laugh. "You're right," she admitted. "I do have other options, don't I? I just wasn't aware that I did!"

We repeated the exercise, and Sadie again refused to cooperate. This time Nancy remained calm and focused and held in her mind a vision of Sadie responding correctly. She sent her lots of love for doing so. As soon as Nancy's energy shifted, Sadie came right to her.

This is a perfect example of the difference between throwing more negativity into an already blocked situation and choosing consciously to help transform the energy.

Directing and transforming energy with your intention is a skill that anyone can learn. There are a few simple tools that will help build your confidence. The first one, which is the easiest, is to relax your body and mind. You have to get out of the way so that energy can flow! Clear your mind, let go of your emotions, just be.

The second thing to do is to create a clear thought form of your intention. If you want to train your dog to sit, you will want to clarify all of the things you and your dog are going to do to bring this behavior about. You will do this through visualizing—doing a mental run-through ahead of time. In order to prepare yourself in every way to keep your energy and intention flowing, "see" your dog in front of you, listening to you and responding correctly to your desire that she sit. Avoid blocking your intention by creating doubts or lack of understanding of the steps involved. Finally, increase the level of positive emotional energy around your visualized intent, which will provide impetus and support for both you and your dog.

In several of my stories, I've described times when I have "held an image of a dog sitting calmly" or "seen the dog being happy." This is similar to how top professional athletes use visualization in their practice and play. They sit quietly, with eyes closed, and they imagine themselves making the perfect shot or doing the perfect combination of sequences off the diving board. They do this exercise over and over and over and over again, without actually physically doing the activity. Because every single cell in your body has its own intelligence, by doing visualization, you are programming your brain to teach your body what you want it to do.

Visualization helps *you* clarify what you are going to ask of your dog. If you can imagine what you need yourself to look and sound like in order to communicate effectively, and if you can imagine how you want your dog to respond, you will create the kind of energy that will support your training. When you consciously visualize your expectations to your dog, he can read your energy and your body language even better than when you give only a verbal direction or pull on his body for a response.

This ability to sense intentions never ceases to amaze me. Dogs are attuned to energy all the time, and I often observe some very sophisticated readings when the dogs are outside playing in the three fenced acres behind my house.

For example, they have one game that I call fox-and-hounds. It can be an average day in the yard. All of a sudden several dogs will fan out and take a stand in different places, just as if they were playing hide-and-seek. Some of them can't see one another, and the unwitting "fox," who is one of the other dogs, comes diddley-bopping up from the back side of the pond, passes through the gateway, starts out across the lawn, and all of a sudden goes, "Uh-oh. I'm it!"

That dog know he's the chosen one because he suddenly feels that the five or six other dogs, who have fanned out, are watching him intently. Some

of them are beginning to go down into a crouch. Others are stiff with attention. The air is electric with expectancy.

Although some of the waiting dogs are spaced out of sight of the others,
at the exact same second, every dog activates and launches himself toward
the "fox." And the game of chase is on.

How do they do this instantaneously when they can't even see each other?
They sense a shift in one another's energy and the energy around them. Unfortunately, many dogs are used to getting mostly static from their humans
because people have a problem being clear in their expectations—for example,
"I wish he would come when I call him, but I know he won't." One thought
cancels out the other, sending the energy of confusion to the dog. If you don't
know what you want him to do, it is very hard for the dog to figure it out!"

It is hard for people to be clear and positive in their expectations because
we have lost contact with our understanding of energy. Many of us abandon
imagination in childhood and have most of our images handed to us through
the media and other cultural institutions, instead of creating them ourselves.
Many people never develop the knowledge that there is a clear connection
between what they can imagine and what they can actually create and
accomplish in their lives. Visualization practice can help you in all aspects of
your life, especially in improving your relationship with your dog.

Images have power, just like thoughts. As a matter of fact, thoughts are
twice as potent if they have an image attached to them. If you have a thought
and then combine it with a strong emotion and a fully realized inner picture,
you create a dynamic energy and set it in motion in the world.

Visualization exercise: You can record the following exercise on a cassette
tape so that you may listen to the sequences as you practice them, or you may
simply want to read through these pages several times until you are comfortable with the sequence.

It is important to be relaxed when you are doing a visualization exercise
in order to receive the maximum benefits. Choose a quiet time of day when
there are few distractions and turn the telephone ringer off. It is best, if at all
possible, to perform the actual exercise with your dog—such as taking him
for a walk or feeding him—immediately afterward, while it is still fresh in
your mind, so that you can compare the accuracy of your visualizing.

- Sit comfortably and take deep breaths, breathing in through
  your nose and out through your mouth. After a few breaths,
  focus your attention on sending your breath not only into your
  chest but also all the way down into your abdomen.

- Imagine that your mind is becoming as calm and clear as a
  reflective mountain lake or an uncluttered, brilliant blue cloud-

less sky. Feel yourself becoming still and serene. Now that you are calm and relaxed, allow your mind to create another image.

- Begin to imagine what your dog looks like. Pay attention to small details, like the look in his eyes, how he is holding his ears and tail, the texture and colors of his coat, the way he stands and moves his body.

- Begin to bring yourself into the picture. Begin to visualize yourself there with your dog, as if you are watching yourself on a home movie that someone has recorded for you.

- Now select a typical daily routine that you do with your dog. Select something simple, such as preparing to go for a walk or perhaps getting ready to give him his dinner.

- Take your time and visualize every detail and each step of the process as clearly as possible, from beginning to end. If you have chosen going for a walk, see if you can add the sounds, such as the noise the leash makes when you pick it up or the sound that the closet door makes when you open and close it to get your coat. Remember to visualize what the dog is doing as well as what you are doing. If you selected something like feeding your dog, add the sound of the dishes or the can opener. See if you can remember what the food smells like, the color of the food bag and the dog's dish. Remember to also include what your dog is doing in anticipation of or in response to what you are doing. Remain still for a few minutes of silence.

- When you have completed all of the steps and put in as many details as possible, slowly begin to allow your mind to shift back into your room. When you are ready, open your eyes and become fully aware of the shift from the reality of your imagination into your everyday reality. Take a moment to allow this to happen and perhaps take a good stretch to refocus and rebalance the energy in your body.

When you are ready to focus on your dog, don't be surprised if he is already anticipating the activity that you visualized earlier—a walk or a meal, for example—since many dogs will be able to connect with the mental and emotional energy that you have been using.

It is inspiring to experience a response from your dog after a visualization, but if this does not happen, don't worry about it. You are both learning a new way to communicate with each other. If the dog doesn't respond, it does not mean that the visualization didn't work or that he didn't get it or that you didn't do it well. The primary purpose of the exercise at this point is to become comfortable with visualizing and with the idea of using it as a tool to help you clarify and focus your intentions in training.

Some people find it difficult to formulate pictures in their mind. This, too, is nothing to worry about. It may be easier for you to just "know" what the exercise will be like or to "hear" yourself speaking to the dog and to sense his response. Any and all of this sensory input is appropriate and useful.

If you still have trouble and feel an energy block, it is usually because of fear or some kind of inner resistance to the whole idea. Whenever you experience fears or doubts, rather than trying to ignore them or push them into the background, it is important to acknowledge them. Fears are generally a defense mechanism to help us avoid something we are not sure we can do successfully, or something we have been told is not good for us. Fears can also come from memories associated with painful events in the past. Acknowledge that you have them, and that they are trying to protect you but at the same time let them know that you no longer need them on those terms, that you have received the lesson from the experience and no longer need to dwell in the emotions around it. Let fear become curiosity and doubt become openness. This will help you move beyond any limits in your thinking and be open to a totally new experience. Feel free to embrace the new possibilities and opportunities that the present moment holds for you. Remember you are the one who chooses what your relationship to the new opportunity will be.

I am sometimes asked if visualization alone will solve established behavior problems. Generally not; repatterning exercises will be necessary as well. However, sending the right image and keeping positive energy flowing will move you forward farther and faster than a negative program.

One of my clients once showed me a beautiful example of turning fear into strength, and the family dog was her companion in this journey:

Sarah was a woman of about thirty-eight, but she looked ten years older. She was shy, gray from her hair to her unstylish dress to the color in her face. She sat hunched over and twisting the leash of the dog she'd brought to me for training.

Oscar was a big-chested Labrador retriever who was strong and dominant. Sarah couldn't do a thing with him. He jumped on her, challenged her by growling and barking at her, body-slammed her, and dragged her all over when she walked him on leash, even though she was the one who placed his food dish under his nose every night. Sarah's three hulking sons could handle him very well, because they could physically overpower him, and they would jeer at their mother when the dog ignored her. They had learned this behavior from their father, who was alcoholic and verbally abusive to Sarah. So the pattern in all of them was ingrained: Mom was the doormat they all wiped their feet on. If you could have examined a printout of her inner life, the words "I am not worthy; I am not important" would have been repeated several times at the top of each page.

I had to work with Sarah quite a bit before I could even get her to make direct eye contact with Oscar, because subconsciously she was so used to averting her gaze. Oscar was basically a good-natured individual, but he had picked up on the way things were in the family, and he had learned his bullying well.

But Sarah learned how to see clearly in her mind the kind of behavior she wanted from that big, intimidating dog. She practiced visualizing herself interacting with Oscar. She imagined a different Sarah, someone who stood up straight and was direct, firm, and clear. She also learned what it felt like to send Oscar positive energy, to praise him when he did what she asked, to move into her fear with the power of love.

And Oscar began to respond happily to what she asked of him. The first time the connection was made, I don't know which of the two looked more surprised. Something that was dead inside of Sarah came alive; something that was stuck began to move.

The last time I saw Sarah, she was looking right into my eyes and smiling. This was a year from the time that we had worked together. She had left her domineering husband and was going to school to become a teacher. "I want to give to children what you have given to me," she said.

In this chapter, I introduced the concept of the bountiful energy of life that is around and within all things. The quality of energy that you put into every thought that you formulate is the crucial element in Awareness Training. Positive energy will create more positive energy because of the law of attraction. It is important to realize, however that "thinking" a positive thought is impossible. A positive thought is one that is filled with a positive emotion. You have to *feel* a positive thought, and then the energy in your thoughts is directed from the right place: your heart. This is the subject of the following chapter.

6

THE HEART CONNECTION

Caroline Myss, the author of *Anatomy of the Spirit* says, "The mind has no power without the heart. If your emotions are not engaged with what you do and what you want, you cannot create anything. Your emotional energy is the electromagnetic field through which the laws of cause and effect and magnetic attraction operate."

Training a dog with conscious heart-filled intention is the key to creating a deep bond. Once you have accomplished this work with another species, think what you can do with your own. The Zen masters practice flower arranging or calligraphy or archery not for the benefits of the skill alone but because doing one thing well has a ripple effect on the rest of one's life. In the same way, Awareness Training is a spiritual practice. As you practice achieving a harmonious, mutually respectful relationship with your dog, you are practicing a harmonious, mutually respectful relationship with all living beings on the earth.

To fully attain the benefits of Awareness Training, it is important that you see your dog as an equal, and not as a lesser being. This book is a guide for co-creating; Awareness Training is something that you and your dog will accomplish together. You will learn to blend your two energies harmoniously through increased understanding and awareness, which will allow you to experience the world from the perspective of another being with very different needs, talents, and individuality. Awareness Training is an experience of *practicing* mutual respect with your dog.

Religions like those of Native Americans and other indigenous cultures, which honor the concept of wholeness rather than separateness, have always included animals in their forms of worship. This stems from the belief that animals have certain powers to share with humans and that each animal species holds or contains a specific kind of energy or intelligence on the planet. For this reason, tribes and individuals choose an animal totem as a guardian spirit. Choosing to become aligned with a certain animal's energy is considered beneficial and empowering.

Our culture also believes this to a certain extent: sports teams and cars are named for animals that symbolize certain qualities. Madison Avenue would never try to sell a car called a Snail, but driving a Lynx immediately calls up the image of "lynx power"—something fast, sleek, and alluring.

There is a big difference, though, between the psychological and emotional relationship our culture has with animals and that of cultures in which animal totems have long had a sacred role.

In our culture, the degree of respect, emotional involvement, and sacredness accorded to animals is frequently nonexistent and certainly less than in totemic cultures. Our love for animals is all too often based on how we can use them for our own purposes, instead of looking for the special and unique things that we can learn from them. There has been a tendency to foster a hierarchical separation and subjugation of animals, instead of being nourished by their compassion, wisdom, and kinship.

Opening yourself to creating a different relationship to the animal world is fundamentally heart work. Practicing with your dog is a safe and wonderful place to begin.

Your mind alone does not create the kind of energy you need to do Awareness Training. Your mind creates the structure, but your heart creates the content. You have to wake up your heart by energizing your thoughts with authentic emotions. Sending loving energy takes focused attention, repetition, and practice until it evolves into a consistent expression of its power in your life.

The following story is an illustration of a typical relationship that had all of the right structure but none of the content necessary to create a real bond between a man and his dog:

Martin Burke was about thirty years old, and he had never wanted for anything. His car was flashy, his clothes were expensive, and Flint, his borzoi, came from a top breeder on the West Coast. But Martin was very frustrated. He sat in front of me, gesturing angrily at the dog, who lolled by Martin's chair wearing a friendly, but supremely bored expression. Flint was wearing an expensive collar of the finest leather and was immaculately groomed.

"I don't understand what's the matter with this dog!" Martin was saying with disgust. "I buy him the best of everything! He has an eighty-dollar bed, I always buy top-of-the-line food; his crate was imported from Germany . . ."

I found it interesting that Martin could not refer to Flint without mentioning all of the money he had spent on the dog's behalf. And now it seemed that Flint was ungrateful.

"He ate his bed," said Martin, "He tore up my two-thousand-dollar leather sofa, even though I spent three hundred dollars on toys for him. He won't come when I call, he lifts his leg on the furniture, and whenever I let him out, he runs away. He has everything, and still he won't do what I ask. I'm fed up with him." Flint wrinkled his brows at me and then yawned widely before putting his head down on his paws.

"It's very nice that you are able to provide all of those toys for your dog," I said, "but you know, he would be just as happy with an old stick. He doesn't have the same appreciation of material things that you have."

Martin looked at me blankly.

"The only thing that I haven't heard you mention that you give this dog is your time," I went on. "How much time do you spend every day with Flint? What do you do with him? What kinds of games do you play?"

"I spend almost a half hour with him whenever I can," Martin replied, looking threatened. "Anyway, he has everything he needs!"

"No, he doesn't," I said, shaking my head, "He's alone ninety percent of the time, and when you're there, you're too busy to interact with him. That's why you keep trying to buy him off!"

Martin opened his mouth, but I stopped him with my next question, "Is it really important to you to keep this dog?"

"Well, yeah," he said defensively.

"Why?" I asked. "You just told me that you spend less than a half hour a day with him. You buy him all of these fancy things when what he really needs is you, and that's the one thing you are not willing to give him. Let's be realistic! Perhaps what he really needs is a different home."

Martin looked down and got very quiet. All of a sudden I realized he was crying. I had obviously hit a nerve. He got up and abruptly left the training area. Flint disinterestedly watched him go and then put his head down again, while the clock ticked and we waited.

After a bit Martin returned, having regained his composure. He sat down and looked at me hard. His voice was ragged, but he spoke with conviction. "You know, until this moment I never realized that I have been treating this dog exactly as I was treated as a kid. I could always have anything and everything that I wanted, but my parents were too busy for me and they were never there." He looked down at Flint as if he was afraid to touch him. Now that everything was out in the open, perhaps Martin feared that all was lost between them.

"What would you really like to happen with Flint?" I asked gently.

"I want you to help me train him," he said keeping his eyes on Flint as if seeing him for the first time, "and I guess it's important for me to learn that he probably is one of my best friends. I can't believe what he has to put up with from me. Until now I never understood how lonely he must be."

We began to work. Martin had never spent any time with Flint; his dog had just been another ornament around the house, and now that Flint was in his teenage rebellion period, things were rapidly deteriorating.

Training would be a challenge for both of them, since they had so few communication skills. Flint had learned that he could get away with a lot. Martin's heart had been shut down. He was a very lonely person who struggled with feelings of worthlessness in spite of his wealth, so he found it difficult to trust his own inner resources and his ability to turn Flint around. People can give love only to the extent that they feel it for themselves.

If Martin wanted to connect to Flint, he could no longer put off coming to terms with his emotions. People can be stuck in loveless relationships for years, but they don't shred sofas or urinate on the rug to express their desperation and loneliness if things don't get resolved.

We took things slowly, working step by step. Martin continued to practice creating a clear image in his mind of the behavior he wanted from his dog, while energizing that expectation with positive emotions. As soon as Flint responded in even the smallest way to Martin's directions, Martin practiced opening his heart even more and pouring on love and encouragement. He had to confirm to both himself and his dog that there was unlimited potential in the relationship, and he had to keep his feelings genuine. At first he felt very vulnerable. It was challenging for him to be so emotionally flexible.

Flint, like all dogs, was without judgment. As soon as Martin began to give him honest energy and emotions, Flint's spirit radiated love in response. He restored Martin's sense of self. No matter how awkwardly Martin approached him in the training lessons, Flint was ready to help, as long as Martin's energy flowed toward him in a positive and loving manner.

After several weeks of private lessons, Martin took a group training class, and in each session, I could see how the bond between him and Flint continued to grow. The best moment was when we practiced calling the dogs to us. I watched Martin run to the other end of the training field, squat down, and hold his arms out wide for Flint, who was being restrained at a distance. "Flint, come!" Martin called, with real joy and recognition in his voice, recognition that he was the most important person in that dog's life. When I released him, Flint gave an eager whine, leaped forward, tore across the grass like there was no tomorrow, and went barreling into Martin's embrace.

Flint was a blessing in disguise for Martin. I felt sure that Martin learned a lot about things that money can't buy, and there was a good chance that he would not repeat his learned pattern of emotional isolation in the future if he started a family of his own. Flint had said, "Look at me, dammit! I'm here! I need your love! I'll make you notice me!"

Martin's conflict with his heart and his sense of self is a common one. In general, our culture does not tend to know how to control, or use, or even recognize emotional energy—and especially heart energy—very well. As Caroline Myss says, emotional energy is the most powerful force of all, far more powerful than mental energy alone.

The healing energy of dogs *is* love energy. Animals can heal wounds that their humans have not been able to identify, let alone resolve in their lives. Furthermore, interacting with animals is an absolutely safe way to begin exploring and trusting feelings. Whether it is through the basic connection between a dog and his human, or through more formal means such as a companion program for the elderly, for abused children, for convicts, or for any other emotionally wounded part of the population, animals have always been ambassadors of the heart.

One of the most beautiful examples of this occurred a number of years ago when I used to visit local convalescent homes with my two greyhounds, Strut and Army. Strut came to me from off the track when he was five, having been retired after a very successful racing career. He was always, from the first time I met him, a kind and gentle soul. I used to tell people that if he were a human being, he would be tall, thin, and silver-haired, generally attired in a smoking jacket and puffing on a pipe filled with very high-quality tobacco. Amy, who is still with me, is more playful, and also has an abundance of grace and love to share.

One afternoon, after visiting one particular home and spending some time with a number of the elderly residents in their common room, I was asked if I would bring Strut and Amy upstairs to visit some of the people who were bedridden. I was happy to do this, and the dogs were warmly welcomed as they went from room to room. Then, when our visit was nearly over, Strut veered and pulled me toward a half-open door to a room we had not yet entered. I turned and asked a nurse if it was all right for us to go in and visit. She pulled down the corners of her mouth, saying, "You won't get much out of it, and neither will she. She just lies there and rants and raves and screams and hollers half the time. She drives all of us crazy. I wouldn't waste the time, myself."

"May we go in anyway?" I asked, my curiosity piqued. Besides, Strut was halfway in already.

The nurse shrugged and walked away. We went in. There was a wisp of a woman with snow-white hair, lying on her back in bed. Her eyes were squeezed tight shut, her jaw was clenched, and she was so thin that she barely made a lump under the covers. The guard rails were up on the bed, so that she lay in a sort of metal pen. Her delicate arms were imprisoned by restraints, and her hands were enveloped by big hospital mittens.

Strut headed for the bed, just as another nurse came in, a kind-looking woman, who leaned against the wall and watched the dog approach.

"What is her name?" I asked, gazing with a mixture of sadness and pity at the bound figure.

"Eva," replied the nurse. "She's been here a couple of months. The mittens and restraints are because of self-mutilation and because she tries to pull out her I.V.'s. All she's done since she came is yell and scream," she added, looking sympathetic and also frustrated. "You've arrived during one of her breaks."

"Hello, Eva," I said gently to the silent figure on the bed. "I've brought someone to see you."

The woman's eyelids fluttered a few times, but remained shut.

"Actually, I've brought a dog," I explained, just as Strut pushed his head purposefully between the bars of the guardrail and nuzzled Eva's arm. Amy was right behind him, and also gave her greetings. Both dogs seemed very interested and very pleased to see her.

Eva did not respond, and then Strut insistently pushed her arm again with his nose, asking for a caress.

Eva's eyes opened, and they were incredibly blue. But that was all. There was a vacant stare, and then they closed again. We stayed a few more minutes, and then left.

We returned the following week. This time, we heard the screaming: incomprehensible sounds of rage, like a wounded animal, coming from the room. Strut was not taken aback in the least, went right in, got his head through the guardrail again, found the one place on Eva's arm that was not covered, bound, or poked with an I.V., and gave her a welcoming lick. He looked at the woman expectantly. Eva stopped screaming. Her eyes opened. Then shut. And that was all.

The following week, Strut was eager to push his head through the bars again, and Amy pushed near and wagged her tail. They had never received any response whatsoever, and yet at each visit they were more and more loving. This time, at the first nudge, Eva opened her eyes, looked at Strut, then at me, and was there, for the first time. She made an effort to turn toward the dogs. I hurried to find the nurse, "Do you think we could unstrap her, just during our visit?" I asked. I yearned for her to have a little freedom; it pained me to see such fragility so immobilized, as if her body could break with the pressure of the straps that held her down. As I sat in the chair and watched the interaction between Eva and Strut, I couldn't help but wonder how I would react if I found myself in her position. I have always been physically active and very independent. I wondered what kind of person had ended up like this.

Eva's arms were freed, although the mittens were left on. Her face relaxed a bit then, and she seemed more calm, just lying there, watching the dogs. That was all, and we left.

I could not get Eva out of my mind, and we kept going back. Strut in particular, continued to give me the sense that he had a special mission on the second floor of that building. When next he pushed Eva's arm, her eyes flew open with the first nudge, and I saw a hint of a smile. Eva's restraints came off this time, and her mittens as well, as long as I promised to make sure that she did not begin tearing at herself. No sooner was the mitten off than Strut eagerly pushed his head under Eva's hand. He had obviously been waiting for this moment. Eva began to slowly stroke him, and Strut stood there enjoying her caresses. Amy moved closer to the bed, but still kept a respectful distance, perhaps understanding the importance of the interaction. After several minutes, almost as if she had soothed herself to sleep, Eva dozed off. The nurse began reattaching her restraints as we left.

Eva was again unbound and reaching for Strut the following week, while I tried to make conversation. I was telling her about my work, more about the animals in my care, when all of a sudden, her eyes got very bright and piercing, she took her hand and brought it to her heart, saying, "Saluki!" in a ragged voice.

"No, they are greyhounds," I corrected her. I just didn't get it.

Her gaze sharpened for a moment and I had never seen a look so acute. Then she smiled and said, again pressing her hand to her heart, "Eva. Saluki." Another smile.

I shrugged to myself. She could call Strut and Amy whatever she liked. It just made me happy to see her come alive. As we left, the nurse touched my arm and said in a low voice that she was amazed. Those were the first words Eva had spoken since her arrival.

Eva's niece, who was her only living relative, was visiting the following week and when I asked about her aunt, she told me Eva had been a breeder of Salukis when the dogs were barely known as a breed in this country. She had also been a judge. I thought again of Eva's look when I had tried to teach her that Strut was a greyhound. Beneath her fragile exterior, there was obviously someone of formidable intelligence and experience.

Eva did not speak again during our visit, but continued to caress Strut over and over. He leaned against the bed, and her hand, and radiated love.

Eva was happier than I had ever seen her the next time we came. She sensed our approach, opening her eyes and turning her head in our direction, even before Strut gave her his welcoming nudge. Once again freed of her restraints, she again stroked him over and over, and finally dozed off, but not before giving me a look of serenity and peace. I remained sitting in the chair

I had taken near the door and allowed the dogs to have freedom of the room. Strut remained motionless, his sleek, muscular body pressing gently against the bed, and his head under Eva's hand. I remember thinking that it somehow reminded me of a knight keeping a sacred vigil. He seemed so full of calm intent, as if he willingly would have stood there forever if need be.

"Strut and Eva"

We arrived the following week. There was a different person in Eva's bed. I went to find the nurse, already dreading the answer.

"Eva died about a half hour after you left last week," she said.

"I'll miss her," was all I could manage in the moment, thinking of her piercing blue eyes and the way she had held her hand on Strut, and how Strut had so insistently led us to her.

"You're probably the only one who will," the nurse responded, remembering Eva's yelling. "Although," she went on, "it was rather amazing, when I went in and found that she was dead, to see the anger gone. There was actually a peaceful smile on her face."

With tears in my eyes, I walked out with the dogs. In my heart I knew it was Strut who had known how to liberate Eva. It was an incredible feeling to know that the gentle push of Strut's nose under her arm had brought Eva back to herself, even briefly. Strut was able to sense something in Eva that was still alive, that could still give and receive love. The first time he indicated that he needed to enter her room, I could not have guessed that I would be given one of my most powerful lessons in the healing energy of the heart.

Heart energy is in a constant state of flow. If people experience a lack of love, it is because they have in some way interrupted the flow by being unwilling to accept love or unable to give it. By its own nature, love is a beautiful harmony of both. The way to get things moving again, which Strut could do so very well, is to send heart energy out. It always wants to flow both ways; it will always come back.

It is not uncommon for clients whose dogs have died to tell me that they feel shame because their sense of loss is far deeper and more painful than what they felt upon losing a human loved one. I believe this happens because the love between dogs and humans is in a very pure form. I believe our strongest attachments to animals occur because they have been given unconditional love—love without an agenda. We are all born with the ability to be unconditionally loving, but somehow humans lose it, whereas animals never do.

If the concept of working with heart energy is new to you, the following exercise may be of help. Practice with visualization will already have given you some familiarity with inner guidance. This particular exercise focuses more on "sending" positive energy than on using your mind and emotions.

- Choose a subject with which you have a strong heart connection. It can be a person you care about, a place you enjoy, or even a beautiful plant—anything that automatically evokes a good feeling in you.

- Sit comfortably and relax your body. Take a few deep breaths and clear your mind. Allow an image of a person, place, or thing to come into your mind, and as you visualize, get in touch with your positive feelings for the subject of your visualization. Notice how your body feels; you may tingle with happiness, your heart may feel full of joy, you may feel light and buoyant. Notice all of these feelings very specifically and how they resonate in you.

- While maintaining your focus on the sensations of love, happiness, joy, pleasure, laughter, or any other positive feelings, imagine that you are sending those feelings like a gift to the object of your visualization. It doesn't matter whether the subject is near or far, or whether you have seen this person, place, or thing recently or long ago. Picture the subject in your mind and imagine that the subject is receiving your powerful emotions. You may see the subject transformed by this; a person could begin to smile, a lake could begin to shimmer, a plant could grow a new flower.

This is the essence of sending positive energy. It is a crucial tool in training your dog. If you are having a problem feeling positive about your dog, or any other subject that you wish to send positive energy to, then you begin by focusing on something that you do feel good about. Once you have raised the energy of your feelings to a positive, affirming place, take those feelings and send them where you want them to have an effect. For example, you could get in touch with the experience of buoyancy and pleasure that you receive when you see an old friend, then take those same feelings and send them where good energy is needed to bring harmony and balance.

The more familiar you become with the feelings and sensations of good energy, the more easily you will be able to automatically call them up when dealing with people and dogs and even in situations that do not necessarily evoke the good feelings. The goal of Awareness Training is to be able to instantly send your dog positive energy whenever you want to reinforce a behavioral cue, after you have given a correction, or, best of all, in the moment before you perceive that your dog is going to do something inappropriate and put your mutual energy out of balance.

A very powerful way to send energy is to visualize and energize a symbol. It can be a color, a light, a geometric shape, a golden heart, or anything that has personal significance. Whenever you want to heighten your acknowledgment of a job well done, you activate this symbol in your mind while you are praising your dog and anytime you wish to express love and a sense of communion.

My discovery of the use of a symbol with the Vermont dogs marked the beginning of a real quantum leap in my development of Awareness Training; a whole different dimension in communication had been revealed to me. I had discovered that if a picture is worth a thousand words, a mental image is worth a thousand thoughts. When I visualize my symbol in combination with all of the other ways that I am meeting a dog in a given moment, I am telling that dog that I honor him and the relationship we are creating together; I bypass all of the conditional praising that humans tend to do, and I give something that is a pure acknowledgment of who he is rather than an assessment of his performance as a dog.

A GUIDED MEDITATION FOR CREATING
YOUR SYMBOL

Our culture is filled with potent political, religious, and cultural symbols, like the American flag, the Christian cross, and the Pepsi sign. These symbols can evoke all sorts of emotions, but few people know how to create personal symbols to use as a source of strength and focus in challenging situations. The symbol I will help you create can be anything you want. Even if you have more than one dog, you only need one symbol. Each member of your family, however, should create his or her own symbol, which will generate a unique energy that the dog will recognize.

Read the following steps into a tape recorder and then play the tape back or take turns reading and doing the exercise with a friend.

- Pick a time when you can be relaxed and focused and will not be interrupted. Unplug your phone. You may want to burn some

incense or play soothing music—meditation music or music
without words—to enhance the atmosphere.

- Get comfortable, either sitting or lying down. Allow yourself to
  fully relax.

- Begin to visualize a place where you feel very happy and safe. It
  can be a real place that you enjoy or a place where you would
  like to be, one that you create in your mind. And it can be anywhere that you want to be—on a mountain top with beautiful
  views, by the ocean, in a meadow full of wildflowers, a beautiful
  forest, or in a quiet, secluded spot by a stream or a lake.

- When you have chosen your special place, add as many details
  as possible to the picture. Can you feel the warmth of the sun
  on your skin? Can you smell the damp earth if you are in the
  forest, or the smell of salt water if you are at the ocean? Are
  there fragrant flowers blooming in the meadow? How does the
  breeze feel on your skin or as it blows through your hair? Are
  there birds singing or other beautiful sounds like the rush of
  a stream?

- Take a minute to make your place as real and as beautiful as possible. Take a few deep breaths and fully relax and enjoy all the
  peace and beauty that surrounds you.

- Now see yourself walking along through that place as if you
  were watching yourself in a movie. As you walk along, see that
  your dog is bounding along happily beside you.

- Notice how happy your dog is as he sniffs the breeze and explores
  the surrounding area, tail wagging and tongue lolling. Notice the
  sunlight shining on his coat, making it glisten in the sun.

- Continue to walk, with your dog beginning to move happily
  along ahead of you. When he is several yards in front of you, see
  yourself coming to a stop. Take a second to just look at your
  dog; notice how truly wonderful he is as he revels in the
  moment of each new smell and discovery. See how vibrant and
  joyful he is.

- As you look at him, begin to get in touch with all of the wonderful feelings you have for him and how much he means to
  you. Begin to feel and see a warm glowing light start to emanate
  from your heart, which begins as only a small pin prick of light
  but rapidly expands and grows in strength and intensity as you
  send it from your heart toward your dog.

- As this beam of light travels toward your dog, see your dog become aware of it. See him stop what he was doing and turn to look in your direction. As he turns to face you, begin to see the same radiant beam of light coming from his heart and moving toward you.

- See the two beams of light converge and become one, until there is a beautiful, golden gossamer beam that connects the two of you heart to heart.

- See yourself and your dog beginning to move joyfully toward each other, as if drawn along the beam of light.

- As you meet, see yourself bending down and embracing him. See your dog leaning his body into you as he moves closer into your arms and gazes deeply and lovingly into your eyes.

- Take some time to be in that moment, to be one with that feeling. Be one with your dog.

- Now think of a symbol that represents all of the love you have for your dog. It can be anything you want: a geometric shape, a color, a tone, a star, anything at all.

- Take a few moments to energize your symbol with all of the beautiful, loving feelings that you and your dog have for one another. Send those feelings into your symbol until it is glowing and radiant with unconditional love.

- Watch as your symbol duplicates. Instead of one, there are two that are identical.

- See one symbol move into your heart center and the other into your dog's heart center.

- Take a moment to just be with that image and feeling.

- Now that you have created and energized your symbol, it will be there for as long as you want it to be. You can connect with it at any time by merely holding it in your mind. In the fraction of a second that it takes to think of your symbol, you will be activating it and sending it to your dog.

- See yourself standing up and walking along once more, back in the direction from which you came, moving along freely and happily with your dog bounding joyfully along beside you.

- As you leave your special place, come back into the present time, into the place where you are sitting or lying. When you are ready, open your eyes and, if you would like, stretch your body and come fully and completely back into the present.

You have just created and energized your symbol. Remember, you can use it anytime simply by thinking of it and it will automatically connect with your dog's energy. Your dog does not even have to be with you. You can be at work and activate your symbol to send positive thoughts and energy to your dog at home.

I once had a woman named Marilyn and her feisty young Pekingese, Tarin, in a group training class. Tarin was giving Marilyn a lot of trouble and was particularly aggressive toward other dogs. One night Marilyn walked in with Tarin trotting along beside her, just as good as gold. "It works!" she called out to me, alternating between laughing and heaping praise on her model puppy as they paraded in my direction. "I can't believe it," she said. "I pictured him being good. Then I took that symbol and put it right on top of his forehead before he even got out of the car! He stopped growling at the other dogs and pulling on the lead! It's incredible!"

"Creating Your Symbol"

Now that Marilyn's focus came clearly from her heart, on seeing what her dog was going to do right, rather than on worrying and and thinking, "Omigod, he's going to go after the other dogs," her awareness and energy changed. And Tarin was able to stop reacting in part to his owner's fears and was also able to pay better attention.

Another way you can maintain your focus and increase the emotional energy in your intentions is by creating an affirmation for yourself. An affirmation is a strong, positive statement—spoken, written, or mentally recorded—that something you desire is already manifest in the present. Here are examples of affirmations you can use for your relationship with your dog: "I am learning more about love every day from my dog," and "I am open and receptive to the lessons I can learn from my dog," or "The love I receive from and give to my dog enriches my whole life."

Affirmations should always make you feel expanded, free, and energized with positive feelings. Rather than giving energy to any fears, fill yourself with the joy of knowing that love and focused attention can bring about the changes that you desire. Your dog can sense your power of positive conviction.

As you become more confident in your capacity to give and receive the abundant energy of the universe, you will become conscious that there will be some moments in your relationship with your dog that will call for you to be active, and others where you will need to be receptive. When you are active, you will be creating and directing your energy through visualizing and affirming. For example, if you want your dog to do a certain behavior, you will visualize your dog already being able to understand and accomplish the behavior. If you need to address an area of conflict with your dog in the right way, you will see in your mind and positively affirm that you are already handling the situation successfully.

A moment that calls for receptivity will be a time when you need inner guidance from your higher self. Quiet your mind, ask questions, and become open to receiving answers through your intuitive sense. You may receive words, a mental image, or simply a feeling about what to do. This was the state I used when I felt at a loss about the Vermont dogs. At the end of the first week I asked for guidance. "Love" was the simple answer that I was given.

Teaching Awareness Training has had wonderful, far-reaching consequences. Many people have learned lessons that have had numerous important applications in other areas of their lives. For example, two women in one of my classes were coaches of their lacrosse team at Dartmouth College in New Hampshire. They were fascinated by Awareness Training and practiced it with their dogs and one another. Then one of them called up and said, "You know that energy stuff you do on the first night of class? Could you do a whole separate workshop for the women's lacrosse team? We're not playing together very well. We think this could help."

They came, and we went through the exercises. A number of the team members were less than thrilled to be spending their afternoon with a dog trainer. However, they got very interested when it was clearly demonstrated through kinesiology that they were canceling each other out. They did not realize how they had been affecting one another, nor did they understand how much help they could give each other with the support of positive energy. By the end of the session, everyone was beaming. They went out, had an incredible winning season, and enjoyed every minute of play. Instead of meeting their competition with fear and aggression, they moved onto the playing field with smiles, reminding one another to "Remember love and light!" There was so much joy in the pure experience of working together that it became even more fulfilling than the game itself. Whether they won or lost became a secondary factor.

This chapter ends with the story of Jessica, the guiding light of all of the animals at Hearthside, and the most highly evolved dog I have ever been privileged to know. It may inspire you to read how our bond has grown over the years and to know that bonds like this are possible.

The first time I saw Jessica, her human companion, a tense middle-aged woman named Karen, led her into the training hall for a private counseling session. I noted the dog was a female blue merle Australian shepherd with a big white blaze and one blue and one brown eye. She was in her early adolescence and full of energy and intelligence. I liked her immediately, and she seemed pretty responsive when I worked with her. Karen however, was upset with her and found her too hyperactive. I asked for details and found out that the dog was spending most of her day in a crate while everyone in the household was away. When she was let out at the end of the day, it was like letting a tornado out of a jar. She was, after all, a working dog with tons of energy, not a lie-by-the-fire type by any means.

When I outlined what needed to be done to remedy the situation—spending time with the dog, changing her diet, practicing training exercises on a daily basis, making sure she got exercise—the woman exploded. "I don't have time for that!" she exclaimed. "I'm going through a divorce! I have two teenage sons. I got the dog when I left their father so that they would have something else to focus on!"

She may have meant well, but unfortunately the two boys had no interest whatsoever in Jessica, and there seemed to be a lot of turmoil and anger in the family. Karen finally asked if she could leave the dog with me to be trained.

"Yes," I replied, "but you will have to follow through and reinforce what she learns from me, or else you will be wasting my time and your money." Karen agreed readily and left the dog with me for two weeks. At the end of that time, the whole family came to get her, and they were very impressed to see her so alert and willing to follow my directions. I showed them some basic communication skills and with mixed feelings, watched them drive away. The dog was so smart, and they all seemed so distracted; would she really get what she needed?

I called a few days later to see how things were going. They said Jessica was wonderful; everything was fine. Several months went by. Then Karen called in desperation, saying, "Do you know of anyone who would take our dog? Otherwise I'll have to have her euthanized."

"Why?"

"She bit someone," said Karen, "and they have threatened to sue me if I don't get rid of her."

"And is this the first time this has happened?" I asked.

"Well, no, she's bitten five people, but this is the first person who needed stitches!" protested Karen.

I sighed. I hate hearing these kinds of stories. Why couldn't she have called me sooner? Dogs don't get over things like this; you have to take any kind of biting incident very seriously right away and make sure that, with proper training, it will not happen again.

So I ended up taking the dog, since it was pretty certain she was doomed without proper attention. When they brought her to me that night, I was sad to see the change in her. Jessica had been a highly energetic and not aggressive animal, but she had been changed into a dominant, territorial dog who had no respect for anyone. She was tense, anxious, and ready to assert herself at any moment.

Nevertheless, she obviously remembered me and came right up to me, which surprised Karen. And she showed no emotion when her people were getting ready to leave, even though she undoubtedly sensed that a major shift in her life was under way.

At that moment another client came into the house to talk to me over the half-door that separated the living room from the hall. Immediately Jessica gave a deep growl and leaped at the door, every tooth in her head showing, nearly causing the newcomer to have a heart attack.

"Leave it!" I thundered, and Jessica dropped to the floor and looked at me with surprise. "Sit!" I said firmly, and she did.

Karen leaned over the dog and spoke to her in a whiny kind of baby talk, "Oh, now, you see that? If you would listen to me like that, Jessica, Mommy wouldn't have to get rid of you."

If Karen had been willing to take responsibility for her actions, Jessica's behavioral problems would never have developed. In any case, I now had a new challenge, and I had my work cut out for me in the first week! During mealtimes, Jessica would actually leap with all four feet onto the table and start eating off any nearby plate. If anyone went to push her off, she would bare her teeth and growl, insisting no one was going to tell her what to do. Despite her attempts at intimidation, I knew from working with her earlier that she wasn't fundamentally an aggressive dog, just a very dominant dog who had learned that this kind of behavior worked. She had been allowed to do anything she wanted, and she got a kick out of scaring people. I finally attached her to me by a leash, and she had to follow me everywhere while we put things back into a balanced perspective.

Jessica was, from the first, an extremely protective dog who needed to learn that it was all right for people to come and go from my place. I was eventually able to get her to listen to me but not before she made an indelible impression on a few people!

An unfortunate UPS driver was one visitor who had Jessica's memory burned into his brain. As soon as she heard his truck in the driveway she turned into an enraged beast. I asked her to sit, but she was in such a frenzy that she couldn't hear me. The guy opened the door and froze, turning as white as a sheet with his mouth open and his eyes popping. I gave Jessica repeated corrections with the leash, telling her to be quiet and sit, but she barked and lunged and snarled at the driver. If she had gotten away from me, he would have been seriously bitten.

I finally reached down to make her look at me, since she was beyond being able to pay attention to what I was saying. She wheeled around and latched on to my arm. She was so agitated that she just had to bite someone. She must have known me well enough by that time to do some quick rethinking, though, because she quickly let go. I grabbed her by the fur on the sides of her head and, glaring right into her eyes, blasted her at full volume: "Stop it! That is absolutely *not acceptable* behavior here!" Meanwhile, my package was disappearing with great speed down the driveway, and who knows which of the two of us the poor man feared the most!

Jessica finally gave in and sat, and as soon as the sound of the truck died away, she was fine.

It took the better part of six months to get her to come around. During this time I was doing a lot of professional showing of miniature horses, which took me to various parts of the country. Jessica always came along and, by that time, had learned to help out by carrying brushes or pails and by retrieving lead ropes and halters for me. One time, when we had just arrived in Kentucky, I was walking to find our stall area with Jessica ambling out in front of me on a lead. I heard someone up ahead say even before she saw me, "Well, April must be here, because here's Jessica!" Everyone knew me by the dog that was constantly at my side. By that time, we were becoming inseparable and were well known as a team.

Jessica would stay in the tack stall while I was showing, and I never had to worry about theft. One competitor told me he needed to borrow my leather punch, had opened the tack room door, and had seen nothing but teeth! He'd tried to negotiate, but Jessica wasn't buying any of it. As soon as I went back and told him to go ahead, Jessica just yawned and was totally uninterested.

She eventually began to teach me about extrasensory perception. At first I thought she was picking up on physical signals. For example, I would be working at the computer and when I turned it off, she would come to me. I figured that that was her signal that it was four o'clock and time to feed the menagerie. Nevertheless, I was intrigued to see how magically she would appear whenever my energy changed, so I started experimenting. I found that no matter what time of day it was or what I was think about—heading to town, going to do chores, or ending a project—when I turned around she would be at the appropriate door waiting for me, even though she had been asleep moments before. I had not even given her a visible clue. All I had to do was think about getting up and she would be next to me, looking up into my face, wiggling all over, and saying, "Okay, I'm ready; let's go!"

Jessica assigned herself the role of helper and protector of everything on my property. When I was first reawakening to my knowledge of animal communication, I attended a workshop to be with other people who'd had similar experiences. In it, we did an exercise where each participant had to connect with an animal other than his or her own. A couple of people came up to me afterward and said they had picked Jessica and gotten the strangest message; Jessica had reported that her job was to take care of me and keep all of the other animals in line. I burst out laughing and said, "That's exactly what she does." She was simple, direct, and to the point. Unlike me, she has always been clear about her purpose in life and has never wavered from it.

Even though she and I are very close, she rarely shows affection by licking me, which in many dogs is a sign of submission. She has done this on only a few occasions, when I was having a very bad time and crying. She came up and nuzzled me and licked the tears off my face. She goes around and cleans the ears, eyes, and scrapes or bumps of the other dogs and takes care of them. She is a presence: very nurturing, intensely loyal, yet discerning. She maintains her dignity and her space except in unusual circumstances.

One time I was traveling alone with her, and we were staying in a motel. Right before bed, I took her outside for a last chance to relieve herself. We

went around the back of the building into a wooded area. As we were returning moments later, all of a sudden she froze in place, the hair rose on her
back, and a deep, ominous growl came out of her gut. I felt a shiver go down
my spine, and I froze also, mystified. Then a man stepped out from the darkness under the motel fire escape and just stood there motionless, looking at
us. I felt he was sizing her up, and after her, there was me. Jessica growled
again, a chilling sound with a high-pitched whine in it that I have heard her
make only one other time. I could feel her muscles tensed. She was ready to
spring, and I knew that nothing I could do or say would stop her if she chose
to attack. The seconds ticked by, and then the man abruptly turned around
and she let him go. You can be sure that we slept close together that night!

These days Jessica is my top public relations dog. She comes to my training classes to demonstrate some of the wonderful things that dogs can be
trained to do. She happily holds still while kids hug her and pat her, but if
any strange dog acts disrespectful, she wastes no time in setting it straight.

A few years ago there was a small-sized man in class with a very big Bouvier des Flandres, a nice dog, but very powerful and intimidating-looking.
This breed originated in Belgium and was bred to pull carts, but today they
are frequently used as formidable guard dogs. We were working with distractions, and I had put one of my chickens in a cage so that people could test
their work with their dogs' motivation response levels. All of a sudden the
Bouvier yanked the leash out of his owner's hand and rushed up to the cage,
knocking it over. I was occupied elsewhere with another dog, but instantly,
Jessica broke her down-stay position, hit that Bouvier so hard she knocked
him right off his feet, and stood right over him, even though he was three
times her size. Her message was crystal clear: "Don't even *think* about mess-
ing with that chicken!" He immediately recognized the error of his ways.
When the Bouvier's human said, "What do I do now?" I replied, "Nothing! I
think he's already got the message." Jessica kept the dog pinned there until I
came and said, "That'll do."

Another time, a client's small terrier got loose while its owner was getting
out of her car. It headed straight for the horses, anticipating a good chase. Even
from a distance, I could see how ears were starting to flatten and hooves to flash
and knew I couldn't move fast enough to keep the dog from being trampled.
But Jessica went full speed ahead, hit the little terrier and pinned it until I got
there to rescue it. She just gets in and does the job when a job needs to be done.

Jessica also comes to puppy kindergarten classes. If people need a lesson
in eye contact and body posture, I tell them to watch her. She puts the puppies in their place, never hurting them but just letting them know who's in
charge. If the puppies are passive, she'll lick them. If they are too aggressive,
she'll give a warning. I've seen her stop a whole group of puppies from play-

ing when she found them too raucous.

I don't assign the roles that my dogs assume with me; they just evolve, and it is different with each one. Each finds its own way of being according to personality. For example, my greyhound, Amy, is my heart dog, who reminds me to be playful and lighthearted. Tawny is my court jester. And Jessica is my partner, the one who shares the work of maintaining the center and all the other

animals. Rainbow is the only other dog who connects with me in this way.

I remember another hard, lonely time when I couldn't sleep. I got up and went for a swim in the pond, and the dogs joined me. It was cool when I got out, so I started a small fire, and we all lay together in the circle of light. I looked at Jessica sitting by the fire, and she was both looking at me and looking through me. I've been told that dogs with odd-colored eyes can see the wind. Did Jessica also see my spirit in the light, on the edge of darkness?

All of a sudden I had an incredible perception, a déjà vu, that these animals and I had been like this before but they weren't dogs then; they were wolves. I felt I had been a medicine woman, alone in a wilderness with these powerful spirits. We spoke each other's language. We lived then, as we live now, heart to heart.

7

THE PHYSICAL CONNECTION: YOUR COMMUNICATION TOOLS

This chapter will give you information about the physical tools that you use to establish communication with your dog. The first tool, through which the energy of your intention flows, is your own body. This is more important than any other physical tool that you use. The collar and leash will also assist you in communicating with your dog, but I have seen too many cases where the dog respects the fact that these devices can restrain and control him but does not respect the person. As soon as the physical controls are removed, the connection between the dog and her human will vanish. The ultimate goal, whether the dog is wearing a collar and leash or not, is to reach a point where the dog will respond to you because she loves and respects you. This means that the two of you are on the same wavelength and the clarity of your communication is mutually beneficial.

Using your body to communicate with your dog is a skill that takes practice but a lot of communication will develop naturally as a bond between you is created. For example, no one needs to teach you how to look lovingly at a dog; your dog will teach you that herself.

When you use your body, whether you are crouching down to invite your dog to come, speaking emphatically to get her attention, or giving her a look that reminds her to stay off the furniture, it is important to be objective and somewhat theatrical. When you are a visitor in a foreign country struggling with the language, you want the native speaker to talk slowly and clearly and to use a tone of voice and gestures that will help you understand. Dogs need this same consideration when they are learning from us; they are expert readers of body language, but they need help isolating those cues that are important at the moment.

What follows is a summary of ways your body can be an instrument through which you project the energy of your intentions to your dog.

YOUR VOICE

The emotional energy in your voice has tremendous power to evoke all kinds of emotional responses. It is one of your most important tools. Try this simple exercise to experience how tone of voice can affect your feelings. Read the words into a tape recorder, or ask a friend to read them to you:

- Close your eyes and listen to someone read the word "sit" in different voices—questioning, angry, pleading, coaxing, teasing, demanding, outraged, flat and definite, hopeful, nervous, and pleasant but emphatic.

- Wait for a count of ten after each read before saying "sit" in a different tone of voice. Allow time to feel your emotional response to the different tones and the emphasis of the voice. In the silence, imagine that you are your dog, listening to that tone of voice. Did you notice that the different tones of voice evoked different emotions in you?

I often see clients who respond to their puppy's teeth breaking the skin on their hands with, "Oh, you naughty boy. You shouldn't have done that to me," in a light, singsong voice. How is the puppy supposed to know that he has done something inappropriate? If a puppy nips me, she is instantly met with a sudden change in my energy, transmitted through tone of voice, eye contact, and body posture so that she is sent reeling right over backwards with surprise. I don't even have to touch her to give an emphatic message.

When puppies grow up in a natural pack environment, they learn very early to develop an inhibited bite. If a puppy exerts too much pressure when playing with his littermates or adult members of the pack, the adults will instantly reprimand her. Dogs have no problem establishing limits and teaching lessons in respect and appropriate behavior. If people do not respond with the same swift reprimand when it happens with them, the puppy assumes that this kind of behavior is acceptable. If you give an honest reaction to inappropriate behavior, the puppy won't have to guess whether she's done something incorrect; she'll know it!

When you speak sharply to a dog—and sometimes it is necessary to do this—you can sound severe, but you need to indicate strong disapproval without really feeling angry. Remember, you are only being theatrical; do not get sucked into feeling negative. Remain objective. Your aim is to indicate enough disapproval so that your dog will clearly understand right away. If you learn to do this effectively, you will avoid the possibility that the behavior will escalate until you get angry, which is unproductive and emotionally draining.

YOUR EYES AND FACIAL EXPRESSION

Dogs are masters of subtlety; they pay attention to the tiniest details in an encounter and use their eyes to indicate a range of attitudes from aggression to acceptance. Therefore, they are extremely sensitive to the energy that you send when you look at them. A prolonged intense stare is considered very aggressive and dominant in dog language. A neutral look is a soft gaze at the whole body. In a submissive look, the eyes are averted.

Some dogs consider anything more than a few seconds' eye contact a reprimand, and they will quickly look away if you persist. If someone brings a dog for private counseling, I relax my eyes and look softly at the whole dog in the beginning. A very shy dog can be nervous, and an aggressive one can sometimes feel threatened even with this minimal eye contact. When the dog begins to feel comfortable with me, I shift my gaze, still very relaxed so I can better understand her personality.

I approach any new dog in my household the same way. Once a bond is established, I can look lovingly right into the dog's eyes, and she will reciprocate.

I can look at my dogs from all the way across a room in such a way that they say, "Uh-oh!" or, I can start their tails wagging and cause them come over to me without my saying a word.

Practice facial expressions and eye contact with your dog to test your ability to elicit a response:

- First make a sound to get her attention.
- If you keep your eyes open and relaxed and send love, how does she respond?
- If you raise your eyebrows, smile widely, or open your mouth at the same time, does her response change?

If you see your dog is about to do something inappropriate, try to prevent it by narrowing your eyes, staring a little, and projecting disapproval. If this does not stop her, try increasing the severity of the stare and frowning. Or pull down the corners of your mouth and scowl fiercely. Remember, be a little theatrical. You will learn how much drama you need to cause a reaction. In the case of eye contact, it is the intensity and the duration of the stare that are the most effective. (*Caution:* Do *not* do this with a dominant dog who has a tendency to growl or bite.)

YOUR BODY ENERGY AND POSTURE

If you see a dog walking tensely, up on his toes with his tail stiff and elevated, it is not too hard to guess his intentions; he looks as if he is ready to explode.

Dogs are masters at posturing to one another, so you can learn a lot by watching them do this.

If I need to reprimand a dog, I pull myself to full body height and tighten my muscles so that I look as if I am ready to react instantly. This is different from my normal communication posture, which is a relaxed, confident stance.

Try acting out different body postures with your dog. Notice how changing your posture affects your own energy and emotions; it will show you the kind of energy you are sending out. A relaxed, confident stance not only puts your dog at ease but also helps you, because keeping your muscles loose sends a signal to your brain to relax and stay calm. However, if you allow yourself to slouch and reduce your body posture as a result of insecurity, you are indicating submission. This is detrimental, because the dog will pick up on your hesitancy and wonder if he needs to comply with your wishes. An insecure dog can become more insecure, and a more assertive dog can feel that he needs to assume control of the situation, since you aren't able to. Both will have more difficulty responding positively to you, because of your mixed signals.

Other body posture issues concern the size of our bodies as well as the way we move. Because dogs watch human body language so closely, those that have not been properly socialized with children early in life can sometimes be fearful of them. To a large extent, this is so because children move differently and more unpredictably than adults. Dogs can also be more fearful of men than of women because men are frequently larger, their voices are deeper, and their gestures are bolder, which usually makes them look more dominant.

YOUR BODY LANGUAGE AND YOUR DOG'S TEMPERAMENT

Use your body as an instrument of communication will vary according to a dog's temperament. If you have an inhibited dog, you will need to keep lots of lightness, warmth, and encouragement in your eyes and voice as well as maintain a casual, relaxed posture to help convince her that life isn't as bad as she thinks it is.

If you use bubbling, happy talk with an excitable dog, however, it will be like grabbing the tail of Halley's comet! That's too much sensory input; you will need to keep your voice calm, low, and steady and your energy centered. When you look at him, make your gaze loving but clear, expressing a sense of being calm.

If you have an overreactive dog, you may sometimes find yourself dealing with temper tantrums, which can take different forms. He may rear up and pull on the leash or do a lot of vocalizing. This can occur for different reasons; you will need to find the cause of this, so you can best determine how to solve the problem quickly. Some dogs act this way if they simply feel reluctant to follow your lead. Others put up a fuss because they are frustrated and don't understand what you want. You will have to keep your energy very calm, steady, and clear in either case, so that your clarity cuts through the storm he's trying to create. At the same time, you avoid getting sucked into his disruptive energy pattern.

And what if you have a huge Newfoundland who is totally unresponsive and refuses to budge and you can't move him because he outweighs you by fifty pounds? That is how some dogs resist or show frustration. There are any number of ways to work with this, but they all depend on what motivates the dog, so you need to know your dog well. If he loves food, you can use treats. If his spirits lift when he sees you use a ball, be sure that a ball is part of your tool kit. Most important, you will have to be ready to expend energy that is joyful and exuberant. You can let your body move in a light, happy, and encouraging way that becomes contagious. His brain is the only way to reach him since he is too big for you to move, so you have to know your dog very well and be prepared to make the necessary adjustments to gain the desired response.

Your Vocabulary

Dogs are capable of learning to understand more than two hundred words, and you will, without doubt, develop your own way of carrying on a conversation.

In addition to the importance of the tone of your voice and the use of your body language, you will need to create a vocabulary of signals for cuing your dog. I use a combination of oral directions and hand signals.

Notice that I use words like "direct," "signal," "request," and "cue" instead of "command" when I refer to training vocabulary for your dog. It's a challenge to come up with words expressing a more enlightened relationship without the old master-servant connotation. Language is powerful, and I think it makes a real difference on a deep psychological level whether you give orders or directions to your dog. The outcome can be the same, but how you get there says everything about your intentions.

It's not merely a matter of the difference between teaching and training. We potty-train our children, but in our culture raising children has gone beyond the concept of domination and harsh discipline. We don't think in terms of commanding them to learn different types of behavior. We help them learn skills and rules by either teaching or giving directions.

You may have already established a vocabulary of signals with your dog. Any words you use are fine, as long as they get the message across. Be sure that each signal has only one meaning and one expected response. Two common mistakes are the way many people use "come" and "down." People often yell "Down!" when the dog is jumping up on someone. Then when they want him to lie down, they say the same thing. "Off" is effective for directing the dog not to jump while "Down" means "Lie down."

"Come" is even more problematical. It can mean "Come on, we are going somewhere together," or "Come here," "Come on, do it, cooperate—as in right now" or "Come on, cut it out." It is confusing for dogs to grasp the importance of coming to you when the word also means so many other things and encourages a selective response. To humorously encourage my clients to pay better attention to their speech in my training classes, I have a fine jar. People often have no idea what they have said or how many times in a row they have said it. If they have to pay a fine, however, they become more attentive. I also recommend that people keep a jar at home to remind the whole family to pay up every time they use "Come" to mean anything other than "Come to me." At the end of the week, there is usually enough money in the jar to buy the dog a treat as a reward for putting up with all of the bloopers!

Make sure each of the words in your teaching vocabulary refers to only one specific action you want the dog to accomplish. Be consistent! My suggestions for directive vocabulary are as follows:

- **Let's go.** Use this phrase when you and the dog are going somewhere together, usually on a leash. Do not use "Come on" because you need to save "Come" for times when the dog is at a distance from you and you want him to come quickly to you.

- **Sit.** This directs your dog to assume a sitting position. Do not allow any other position if this is what you are asking for.

- **Down.** Use this to mean "Lie down." Lying quietly on the side is all right, but the dog should not be rolling around and out of control.

- **Come.** This means the dog is to come to you as fast as possible. *Only use this word for this signal!*

- **Heel.** With this, you ask the dog to walk with her neck and shoulder even with your leg at all times, to maintain that position regardless of your pace or direction, and to sit automatically when you stop.

- **Stay.** The dog is to remain exactly in the spot and body position you ask for and to hold that position until you release her or direct her to another action.

- **Wait.** This means she is not to proceed any farther forward. This is different from "Stay," which means "Freeze," "Wait" means "Stop all forward motion." This is especially beneficial to use at car and house doors.

- **Free.** This is a release cue that tells the dog she can relax. It's like saying, "All done." I do not recommend using "Okay" as a release word because we use the word constantly in conversation—often with the same voice inflection—which could cause confusion if you need your dog to stay in one place while you talk to someone.

CONSTRUCTIVE CORRECTION VOCABULARY

The following are my suggestions for constructive correction vocabulary to use when you want your dog to stop doing whatever she's doing. Because you want to keep your emphasis on the positive, use directions that tell the dog what to do instead of what not to do. This is especially important when the dog may not know what is allowed or desired in the first place. Get into the habit of using constructive reprimands that direct the dog to the right behavior, which you can immediately acknowledge with praise.

First of all, get rid of the word "no." The word "no" is best avoided for a number of reasons. The fastest and most effective training will happen if you avoid using negatives. "No" gets used for everything; therefore it means nothing! It doesn't tell the dog how to fix her mistake or what you want her to do, and it makes even less sense to the dog when it's being used constantly for punishment and then gets coupled with a direction, such as "No! Sit!"

CONSTRUCTIVE CORRECTION VOCABULARY

- **Off** means the dog is not to put any part of her anatomy in contact with something or someone.

- **Outside** means to go outdoors. This is useful if you catch the dog in the act of house-soiling, and it's also used for other purposes.

- **Inside** is useful when you want the dog to enter the house or a vehicle. It is especially useful when you know the dog would rather be outside, because it allows you to avoid negative associations with "Come."

- **Leave it** means "Don't go near something, don't touch it." Use this phrase if you drop something on the floor and you don't want the dog to make a grab for it, or if you don't want her to approach or harass the cat.

- **Stop it** tells your dog to cease a particular behavior, such as racing wildly about the house.

It is also useful to have a word or words that tell your dog it's time to relieve herself, such as "Get busy" or "Go potty," Make sure that all members of the family use the words consistently. This cue is very helpful while traveling when your dog is not in her normal place of elimination.

VOICE INFLECTION

Put enthusiasm and lightheartedness in your voice when you are releasing your dog: "Free!" The inflection in your voice should indicate clearly, "All done! That's it!" Directive cues are given in a pleasant but emphatic tone of voice, and corrective cues are given in a firm tone of voice that indicates strong disapproval.

HAND SIGNALS

Because dogs are so sensitive to motion and can read body language so well, I combine oral directions with a hand signal for added clarity. Later on, I use only gestures to give directions if I choose. I'll explain the specific hand signals in the actual training chapters.

EQUIPMENT AND AIDS: THE COLLAR AND LEASH

Training equipment is the means to the end. I never want people to become dependent on the equipment to control the dog, instead of attaining respect and communication.

Snap-Backs™ is a new training device that is used with a regular collar. It minimizes impact during corrections to both dog and handler. I have found it to be effective enough with most dogs that we could use it instead of a training collar.

Types of dog collars that I use range from flat cloth to nylon or leather for everyday use to chain collars, commonly referred to as training collars, which enable you to use the element of surprise to interrupt your dog's behavior when you give a quick pop on the leash.

Training collars are made out of a length of chain (or fabric or leather) with a ring on either end. They are created by holding one ring and dropping the chain through it, until the other ring meets the first ring and makes a

loop that will fit over the dog's head. If you do this, you will see that it is possible to hold one ring and the chain will slide back and forth along it when
you pull. This is the slide-and-release feature that makes training collars so
effective. Because it can be tightened and released quickly around the dog's
neck, this collar is frequently called a choke collar. People who do not understand its proper use, allow their dogs to drag them around while the collar
tightens around the dog's neck and causes her to choke. Never leave a training collar on your dog after you're through with a training exercise. They are
very dangerous, especially the chain collars.

If you have a dog who is responsive to a regular buckle collar, whether
fabric or leather, then use that. If your dog doesn't need anything more, that's
great. I don't like or use nylon training collars because they don't release well
and they get tangled in the fur of dogs with thick, long coats.

Some trainers advocate cloth collars. I don't use these; I find they don't
release as fast, and I prefer the "warning bell" sound made by the chain. Also,
on long-haired breeds, cloth collars get all tangled up in the dog's coat.

When you purchase a training collar, look for one with flat, smooth-
running link, because it will close and release faster than an open, bumpier
link.

The fit of the collar is also very important. It should just barely slide
comfortably over the dog's head when you put it on, and there should ideally

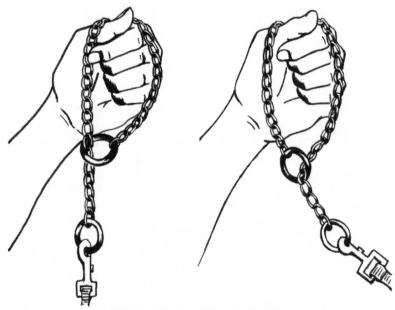

" 'P' is for Perfect, 'Q' is for Quit"

only be 2 inches of chain beyond the ring when the collar is drawn up snug to the dog's neck.

Putting the training collar on your dog: It's important to know that there is a right way and a wrong way to put the collar on. Before you slide it over your dog's head, hold it up so that it forms the letter *P* when you are facing the dog. This is the correct way for it to look before you slide it on. It will release every time the leash pulls on the ring. *P* is for perfect! Now, slide the collar over the dog's head, and attach the leash to the free ring.

If the collar is on backwards and is forming a *Q* as you face your dog, it will not release after you put it on and pull on the chain. *Q* is for quit! (See the illustration.)

Removing the training collar: Avoid jamming your fingers in between your dog's neck and the collar and trying to pull the collar over her ears and lots of loose skin in the opposite direction of the hair. This makes removal uncomfortable for her. Instead, get the collar up high underneath the chin and high up on the neck behind the ears. Gently fold down one ear and lift the collar over it; then do the same with the other ear, and the collar will come off easily.

Use the chain collar only for training: The training collar is meant to be used only for training under your immediate supervision; otherwise, take it off. When your dog is wearing a training collar, it should be the only collar she has on at the time, because other collars can interfere with the quick release feature. Never put tags on the rings because they can flip up and get between the skin and the collar, and if you make a correction, you will drive the tag into the dog's neck and cause pain.

I never use training collars on young puppies because they usually do not need them, and I don't like starting dogs out that way. I prefer to use a flat-buckle collar, because most puppies are so responsive that, if people use their other tools, namely themselves, nothing else is needed. Why use more if you can get away with less?

Training collars are a very effective means of communication, but do not assume that you have to use one. I have dogs who have gone up through some of the highest levels of competition and have never worn one in their lives. It depends on the sensitivity of the dog, your own skills as a communicator, and the depth of your connection.

For regular use, and for puppies, use a fabric, or leather buckle collar. I strongly suggest that you use the newer-style collars with

"The Right Way to Wear the Collar"

the safety release buckle, because no matter how much pressure is on them, you can squeeze and the buckle releases. The modern styles are very expandable—I have one that can go from 14 to 20 inches—and they also last longer than the old buckle-and-pin collars, which have a limited number of holes. This is very helpful if you have a big, fast-growing puppy; otherwise you'll need to join the collar of the week club! The old buckle-and-pin collars have another problem: you have to pull them tighter before you can take them off.

Collars can be hazardous: A chain collar that is far too large can cause a number of problems. A dangling end, for example, can allow the buckle of the leash to fly up and hit the dog in the face or eye. Dogs can also get a foot caught in a collar that hangs down low on the neck and shoulders.

An even more important point about collars is that they can cause serious injury and sometimes kill if used incorrectly. If I had my way, every collar would carry warning instructions for proper, knowledgeable use. You can collapse a dog's trachea, even with a regular collar, if the dog is pulling incessantly. A training collar that has been put on the wrong way can be the cause of a tragic accident. Many dogs are killed because they are put on a tie-out chain in the backyard with a training collar on backwards. When a squirrel or the neighbor's cat comes zipping under his nose, the dog chases it to the end of his chain, which she hits at about 25 miles per hour. This shock can break her neck—and this can happen, no matter what kind of collar she is wearing—or she can be strangled because her collar is on incorrectly and won't release.

When I am out in public, I frequently encounter dogs running around loose with training collars on. Usually the collars are many sizes too big and their rings have multiple tags dangling down, waiting to get caught on something. I call the dog over to me (I always have a slip lead in my pocket), remove the collar, and put the chain through both rings at the same time, which locks it so neither ring can pull. Then I put it back over the dog's head. I always wish I could attach a note of admonition as well, but I can only give the dog a caress, release her, and say, "Blessings," with a prayer for her future health and safety.

One of the biggest hazards that collars can present—and this particularly applies to chain training collars—occurs when dogs wear them while playing together. Never let them do this, because dogs play mouth games around the neck and shoulder area. If one dog gets his lower jaw caught inside the collar, and either dog turns, causing the collar to become twisted, the dog wearing the collar panics because she is strangling and will usually begin attacking the other dog. The dog who has her mouth caught will be defenseless and hysterical because her jaw is being torn off and she can't get loose. Each dog will think the other dog is trying to kill her.

This very accident occurred with two shepherds who were the best of friends and who lived with a couple named Bill and Sharon. Fortunately, both Bill and Sharon were home when the dogs, who were playing in the living room, got hung up. However, when Bill tried to get the buckle-and-pin type collar off the dog that was wearing it, he could not pull it tight enough to get it to release. The terrified dogs attacked him and chewed up his hands, which put Bill, a surgeon, out of work for a month.

Bill didn't dare use a knife to cut the collar off, because the dogs were thrashing so much. He and Sharon had to stand there and watch helplessly until the dog wearing the collar passed out from lack of oxygen. After long, agonizing minutes, Bill was able to lie on top of the other dog to hold him absolutely still. Then Sharon used a knife to cut the collar and free the dog's jaw and also to restore his playmate to consciousness. What if Bill and Sharon hadn't been home? What if the dogs had been wearing metal training collars?

Other restraints: There are many training devices out there, and some of them are cruel and completely unnecessary. I have absolutely no use for those that control through pain. If you have a sweet, passive, sensitive dog like a Sheltie or a greyhound and you use harsh training equipment, you will shatter that dog's confidence in herself and you. When people choose equipment that works by using pain to control a dog, this basically tells me that person is looking for a quick fix or that he has been badly misinformed.

If you have a large, very powerful dog, and a child or an elderly person or someone with a physical disability will be working it, use what is known as a Halti, which goes on the dog's head. It functions like a horse's halter and allows someone without much body strength a good amount of control. I tell my classes that the training collar is like standard steering in a car, and a Halti is power steering.

Haltis are not muzzles; the dog can open her mouth, but when she pulls on the lead, the device closes down a little bit so you can direct the head and she isn't able to use her whole body to overpower you physically. Although the dog has to get used to having a band over her nose, there is no discomfort in wearing a Halti.

Leashes and long lines: I like cotton leashes because they are very easy on your hands. I have had my hands laid open down to the bone by a nylon leash when a dog made a lunge and I wasn't expecting it. Six feet is a good working length for a leash.

I find that retractable leashes are not effective as a training tool, because they don't give you directional control, but they are fine, especially in urban settings, for walking a dog who is trained, when you want to give her more space to move around without getting tangled in a line.

Long lines are used in communicating to teach the dog to come, and later in training for more direction at a distance. They come in various lengths; I like to work with a 30-foot line. Nylon is the preferred material in this instance, because the line drags on the ground and can get wet and heavy if it is absorbent, like cotton or hemp. Use leather gloves for traction and protection. Look for brass snaps, which are strong and lightweight and do not freeze up in winter if it is wet or icy outside.

USING THE TRAINING COLLAR AND LEASH AS CUES

Many people who use training collars and leashes do so incorrectly. A training collar should be used *only* as an interruption device, and the way you use the leash creates this interruption. It is a communication tool, not a weapon. Think of the leash like a telephone wire; it transmits your signals through the collar to your dog. When you use it to give a correction—meaning to correct the dog's understanding of what is appropriate behavior in a given moment— you give it a quick pop and release, a sharp down-and-up jerk with your hands, a gesture that is somewhat like snapping a wet towel at someone, shaking out a heavy, wet towel, or cracking a small whip. When you do this correctly, the training collar will close briefly on the dog's neck and release instantly.

Popping the leash works with the element of surprise; it's sort of like sneaking up behind someone who is not paying attention and saying "Boo!" A correction is *not* painful; it is mildly unpleasant. Dogs react to this in different ways; some merely turn around and look at you, while others jump and go "Whoops!" The dog is momentarily startled. It is a very effective way to immediately change the dog's focus, which for some, takes a lot of doing, and for others, very little. It is important for the motion to be quick, so that she thinks that, from out of nowhere, something "got" her. She will look at you then for reassurance, and now that you have her attention again, you can remind her with praise and affection to pay attention while you show her what you want her to do.

Practice the pop and release: Before you try the pop and release with the collar and leash on your dog, try it a few times yourself, in order to experience what your dog feels if you give her a correction. Put the collar over one hand and, holding the ring that the leash would be attached to, give it a couple of quick pops. You will see that it is not painful when the collar closes briefly on your hand but it does create a mildly unpleasant sensation. Your only goal is surprise. After you have done this exercise a few times, look at your hand. You will see there are no marks.

Test the difference between pulling and the pop and release: When you allow your dog to pull, she immediately braces herself. You set up an area of physical and mental resistance and end up in a test of wills before you even start to train. To see how a dog feels when the collar is choking her, put it on your hand again, hold one ring, pull hard, and keep the pressure on while you count to fifty. Notice the difference in sensation. Your fingers will begin to throb and ache.

I have seen dogs who know how to get beyond this feeling; unable to take the pressure off themselves, they do the opposite and hit that lead so hard and so fast that it's quite painful for a few minutes. Then everything goes numb and the dog can drag its owner around and be in control.

Look at your hand again and remember the painful sensation that was in your fingers from the pressure. This is what happens if you do not release instantly. Furthermore, because the pulling puts you in a clench, tensing your muscles, you are not as able to respond quickly. Coming out of a contracted state takes more reaction time than when you are relaxed.

After a correction, there should not be any lingering pressure on the collar; you want a complete loop of slack in the lead.

Keep your hands down: Take your hand, palm up, and pretend that you are making a correction, a quick downward pop. Notice that in this position, the whole corrective action stops at the elbow. It makes your arm sore and jars your whole body. If you have a big dog and pop the leash while using your arm like a hinge, you could end up with some badly damaged muscles.

Now turn your hands over so that both are palms down and pretend you are making the correction again. Notice that if you need to make only a light correction, you can just move your hands slightly. If you need a stronger one, you can let the energy of the movement flow up your arms and through your whole body.

Pop the lead when your dog pulls: When you hold the leash, keep your arms in close to your body in a relaxed way, and your hands close together so that both carry equal energy. If you have a large dog, use both hands for corrective pops in the beginning, and later, depending on the dog, you will be using your leash only as a light communication device.

To give a correction when the dog is pulling, break the tension on the leash by moving your hands quickly in the direction of the pull, and then pop down. *Unless you can put slack in the lead by moving your hand toward the resistance, your correction will be ineffective because it will result in a pull rather than a pop.*

Practice first with friends: Practice this technique initially with other people. Take the leash and walk around with a friend holding one end, and you the other. Be sure that one of you is holding the buckle of the leash so that it doesn't swing up and hit anyone. Ask her to pull on the leash at random, and to not relax the tension at those times. It will be up to you to create the slack so you can give the correction. You will be teaching yourself to respond instantly when you feel the slightest tension, until your reaction becomes automatic. Remember: you always have to move your hands quickly.

Listen and you will hear the leash make a "pop" sound. If you don't hear this, you are not giving a fast enough movement with your hands.

USING FOOD IN TRAINING

Although praise in various forms from you alone is the best and most effective reward for appropriate behavior, some dogs also respond very well to the use of food as a motivator. Food can be used in four important ways: to help motivate the dog, to maintain her attention, as a lure to teach a behavior, and as a reward to reinforce a correct response.

I use food on and off all the time with my dogs, not just in the initial stages of communication. When you use it as a motivation tool, you need to use it wisely and especially not as your primary means of expressing affection. It is important to realize that food is not synonymous with love. A dog who is used to treats all the time for no reason may not be particularly motivated when you also include them in training.

Food as a lure is used very effectively with little puppies and older dogs who are food-motivated. Some dogs, however, are simply not interested in following a piece of food around, and others get too excited and lose their ability to concentrate. If you are interested in using a food lure with your dog, it is best if you try a few simple things, like teaching the sit, in order to see whether it is likely to be a successful approach for you. If it is, your long-term goal will be to turn a food lure gesture into a hand signal, so that ultimately you will not need to use a food reward to elicit a response.

Once the dog can successfully accomplish whatever you are asking for, the wise choice is to use food only for the best, most accurate, and fastest response. Many people get into problems in their training when food rewards are given whether the dog performs really well, very poorly, or hardly at all. Quickly the dog realizes that she can give any kind of performance and she will still get the treat. This seriously undermines your progress, because your intentions are not being clearly expressed.

Food rewards can be given both to your dog and to you! Training should be fun, and sharing rewards with your dog helps keep you on track of your mutual progress. Choose a treat that both you and your dog enjoy. If all goes well with each phase of the practice, celebrate together. If either half of the team messes up, no treat for that half. This method helps maintain the focus all the way around! It is interesting to watch a dog's expression when you eat *your* treat in front of her because you did your part and she doesn't get one because she didn't. This is a real attention-getter and very effective.

Food used during a training session generally consists of about a dozen pieces of something your dog loves and that she can chew and swallow quickly. Biscuits generally don't work well in these situations because the dog drops crumbs and then shifts her attention from you to looking for them. A tiny piece of meat or cheese often works best.

When I say a tiny piece, I mean a nugget about the size of a pea. For a toy breed or a puppy, it can be even smaller. If I am working a Great Dane and she does something well, I still only give her a teensy morsel as a reward. The purpose of the food is not to feed her, but to acknowledge and reward her effort or, when used as a lure, to show her a direction.

Vary your motivators; don't always give the same treat, or the dog may lose interest. I generally use meat, cheese, popcorn, organic raisins, or pieces of carrot. *Never* use chocolate, which is highly toxic to dogs. Find out ahead of time what your dog really likes.

Keep your food treats easily accessible during training sessions. We wear carpenters' aprons with the big easy-access pockets. Be very careful not to release your dog from what you have asked her to do as soon as she finishes eating the treat or she will soon associate getting the treat with being released from your request. Keep her holding the position longer by giving several small pieces instead of just one and/or by giving her more praise and attention. Then release her.

The most important thing to remember about collars, leashes, lines, and food is that they are all used to transmit your intentions to your dog. They are not useful in and of themselves. This is also, in a lesser way, true of the verbal and hand signals and even your body. All of these are instruments for the energy of your mind and heart to flow through. *You* are absolutely the most important training tool of all.

8

PUTTING IT ALL TOGETHER: THE HOLISTIC PRACTICE OF AWARENESS TRAINING

Working with your dog simultaneously on a mental, emotional, and physical level creates wholeness and re-creates the spirit of a time when animals and humans understood the same language and recognized and respected one another's unique gifts. This chapter offers guidelines in how to apply the principles of working with energy in Awareness Training, both in your everyday relationship with your dog, and in structured communication exercises.

You use your energy and communication tools in three basic ways—through directions, corrections, and rewards.

Directions: You can give directions (also called cues, requests, or signals) with your voice, hands, eyes, body posture, and aids like the collar and leash or long line. You will use these directions to guide, or cue, the dog so she can more easily understand what you are asking her to do. You will also use visualization and send loving energy to keep your signal clear and to give your dog emotional support by affirming that you can already envision her ability to understand and accomplish what you are asking of her.

Corrections: You will give corrections to interrupt any behavior other than the behavior that you are looking for. You give corrections by using your voice, eyes, and posture, and if needed, you will also get your dog's attention by giving a quick pop on her leash, as described in Chapter 7. Be sure that you do only what it takes to change the behavior and nothing more, because nothing more is needed or warranted.

It is important that you do not apply corrections unless you know your dog is capable of understanding and accomplishing what you are asking her to do. As you get to know your dog and increase your understanding of what is involved in training by practicing the training chapters, you will learn what specifically works to get your dog's attention.

Rewards: You will use rewards to reinforce the dog's understanding of the behavior you are asking for, and to motivate her to continue to pay attention and try to give you the response you are looking for. Rewards include sending loving energy with your eyes, through the warmth of your voice, and through the relaxed posture of your body; using your positive energy symbol; and giving physical caresses and/or food.

After you give a direction, you immediately reward your dog if she gives you the response you are looking for. If she does not, you give her a corrective signal with the leash to interrupt any inappropriate behavior and encourage her to give you her attention. Then you repeat the cue. You repeat this sequence of directing (including visualization) and correcting *only* until the dog gives you the right response, and then you immediately shower her with praise and other forms of reinforcement.

HARMONIZING ENERGY THROUGH WORKING WITH YOUR DOG'S POINT OF MOTIVATION

Behavior is a flow of energy that is manifested in the physical world. Your energy flows through your own behavior as you direct, correct and reward in such a way as to balance and harmonize with your dog's flow of energy. The balance in energy that you are seeking is achieved by working with your dog's point of motivation. In earlier chapters, I said that each dog has its individual trigger, or point of motivation, which will awaken her desire to respond. When you are working at your dog's point of motivation, you have found the right expression of your energy through eye contact, body posture, tone of voice and, if necessary, physical correction that will immediately gain the desired response from your dog. The amount of energy you have to put into getting a dog's attention has nothing to do with her size. The level of your dog's desire to please and her degree of touch sensitivity are the determining factors.

It is important to remember that a dog's point of motivation has nothing to do with whether the dog is considered good, bad, smart, or dumb. I am only talking about basic differences in dogs and how they need to be handled.

If you have to keep cuing your dog over and over, you are functioning below the dog's point of motivation, and you are nagging her. This results in your dog receiving a lot more corrections and a lot less praise. The dog will find this very frustrating, and so will you, with the result that the whole training program will become an exercise in negativity. Instead of wanting to listen to you, your dog will choose to ignore you.

You must attain the point of motivation immediately to be an effective trainer; the challenge for you, however, is to learn to read the energy of your dog's behavior so well that you will be able to predict what that point will be, given the circumstances. Sometimes it will take a little and sometimes it will take more of your energy in your cues to get his attention.

Dogs always do best when they are self-motivated and when they understand the relevance of responding to your directions. For example, when I ask a dog to lie down, I do not force her into a down position. Instead, I hold the leash in such a way that she sees that if she does go down, she will be more comfortable. She is the one who chooses when to do it. This gives her a sense of control and is therefore more self-rewarding. In this way, my relationship to the direction makes more sense to her, because my role has only been to show her something and encourage her rather than to force her.

This also applies to corrections. One objective of every lesson is to help the dog learn that she is in control of whether or not she receives a quick attention-getting pop from the lead. She can avoid doing this to herself by choosing to give you part of her attention all of the time. By being aware of where you are and what you are doing, and by remembering the behavior patterns you have taught her, she is constantly able to keep herself feeling very good mentally (she made the right choice), emotionally (she is receiving praise and acknowledgment from you), and physically (she avoids the mildly unpleasant correction).

Remember always to make sure that the desired behavior is pleasant, easy to accomplish, and rewarding, so that it quickly becomes self-rewarding for the dog to make that choice. Make the undesirable behavior difficult or impossible to accomplish (by interrupting incorrect responses), mildly unpleasant (also by using some kind of correction, usually through the leash, although in many cases, your voice can be enough), and unrewarding (by offering no praise or acknowledgment). Very quickly the undesired behavior becomes unsatisfying, so the dog herself chooses not to continue it.

TIMING IS THE KEY TO EFFECTIVE COMMUNICATION

In effective communication, and in effective training, timing is crucial. If you want to have a conversation with someone, it is a give-and-take. You give your response at the appropriate time in order to help the conversation progress. It is the same when you communicate your needs to your dog. All dogs are born knowing how to sit and lie down, so you don't have to teach them how to do it, just when and where.

Do you remember that old game called hot-and-cold? It was played by hiding an object, and then asking someone to try to find it by listening to your cues. If you said "Hot" the person was getting close. If you said "Cold," the player was heading in the wrong direction. Timing was important in that game, because, if you didn't watch the searcher closely to monitor her responses, and if you forgot to say "Hot" at the correct moment, the person wouldn't have a clue as to how to find the object.

This is a good example of what you have to pay attention to when you are communicating with your dog, no matter whether you are praising, dispensing food, caressing, giving some kind of direction, or effecting a correction. You have to be very careful not to send mixed signals and end up rewarding the wrong behavior. For example, if you give your dog a food reward because she sat when you asked her to, and then verbally praise her while she is eating the food, she will think you are telling her she is a good dog for eating, instead of sitting! The praise for the accomplishment of the behavior belongs *with* the actual act, not after it. By the same token, if you correct your dog after she has done something inappropriate, she also will get the wrong message. The correction must come at the moment that the behavior is taking place in order for the dog to understand its relevance.

A game to practice your timing: Try this game to practice your timing skill; it can also be great fun at a party. Two people play; one is "the dog," and the other is "the trainer." Other people can have a good time watching; it's educational for everyone. You will need a way to give sound cues. You can use a squeaky toy, a whistle, a clap of your hands, or whatever appeals to you.

- The person who is playing the part of the dog leaves the room, and those remaining pick a simple behavior to have the person accomplish when he or she returns. It can be something like sitting in a specific chair, opening a door, kneeling on the floor, or hugging someone. Later on, it can be more complicated, like taking an object off a table and putting it in someone's hands. The goal is written on a piece of paper and held by the "trainer," to be checked at the end of the game.

- The "dog" reenters the room and is instructed to start moving randomly around while listening for the sound cue. The only thing the "dog" cannot do is stop moving.

- The sound cue is given whenever the "trainer" wants the "dog" to do more of what he or she is doing. For example, if the goal is to send the "dog" to the window, the "trainer" should make the sound as a reinforcement of that behavior whenever the "dog" moves in the direction of the window.

- There can be no other clues—no pointing, nodding, or facial expressions.

It will become obvious as the game goes on, that the timing of the trainer is everything. If the sound is not given at the appropriate time, the person who is trying to figure out the goal will become frustrated and confused. This is the wonderful aspect of this game; it shows you so beautifully what you need to do to help your dog understand you.

There is another reason why the use of praise is so important during your practices in communication with your dog. Imagine how you would feel if you ended up in a different culture, where a different language is spoken. One of the inhabitants of the culture is trying to get you to do something, but you haven't a clue what that something is. The person physically manipulates you, moves you into certain positions, and glares at you the whole time to make sure you don't resist. All of a sudden, for no reason that you can figure out, the person makes a certain sound. You sense that you can move again, and the person acts relieved and happy. All you know is that something unpleasant was going on while the person was controlling you, and now that it is over, you can both relax and enjoy yourselves.

The only message that the dog receives in this kind of scenario is that close interactions with you are unpleasant. This misplaced focus is the reason I stress that it is very important to stay relaxed and joyful while you are in the midst of a practice. The praise, eye contact, relaxed body posture, and reassuring tone of voice all combine to give the dog a memorable and happy experience. When the exercise is over and the dog is released, *stop the praise*. Always leave the dog with a good memory of the experience. The accuracy of your timing is again an important issue. From the dog's point of view, it makes no sense to receive more praise when the exercise is over than she received while you were working together.

MAINTAINING YOUR RELATIONSHIP WITH YOUR DOG IN TRAINING AND IN EVERYDAY INTERACTIONS

The discussion of directing, correcting, and rewarding your dog applies to both the formal and the informal aspects of your relationship. The formal aspects are those practices of certain lessons in specific directions such as sit, stay, down, and so forth. The informal aspects have to do with the way you relate to each other on a daily basis, while your dog is learning your expectations. Informal learning covers things like how you want your dog to conduct herself in general around issues like jumping on the couch, raiding the trash, begging at the table, and scratching at the door. All of us have our own preferences around these issues, but it is important to realize that you have to be consistent, and everyone in the household needs to agree on the guidelines. You cannot allow your dog to beg at the table every day—but not when you are entertaining.

There is one key training concept that I cannot emphasize enough: *always be clear exactly what you are asking for and why*. For example, if you ask your dog to lie down when sitting could work as well in a certain situation, be clear about your reason for asking. Don't say "Down," and then, if your dog ignores you say, "Oh, never mind. I don't really care if you want to just sit."

If your intentions are not clear, if your timing is off, and if your expectations are inconsistent, your dog will try to figure out the most self-rewarding behavior on her own. And pretty quickly, she will get locked into one behavioral response whether it is the right one or not; soon she doesn't know a different way to deal with that situation.

You probably know this drama well: someone comes to the door of a guy named Sam, and his dog, Fidel, jumps all over the visitor. Sam goes over, grabs the dog by the collar, holds her down, yells "Stop it, bad dog! No!" and drags her away. Five minutes later somebody else comes to the door, and the whole scene is repeated. Why? Because the visitor is probably smiling down at his rambunctious welcomer and saying, "Oh, that's okay. I don't mind. I like dogs." Fidel is therefore being rewarded by receiving praise and recognition for her out-of-control behavior.

Sam can punish after the fact, but he will not change a thing because the dog hasn't learned a different way to behave in that situation. Until Sam teaches Fidel the right way to greet visitors at the door, everyone will have to put up with the dog's lack of understanding. Inappropriate behavior is like sparks. If you put out the sparks by changing the energy, you won't have to deal with an out-of-control fire.

HARMONIOUS ENERGY AND THE THREE LEVELS OF CONSCIOUSNESS

Your goal should be to achieve a harmonious exchange of energy between you and your dog, who will be doing things *with* you, not just *for* you. If you work to understand your dog's natural tendencies and behavior, you will have the opportunity to adjust your own in order to find a point of balance between you.

I learned this lesson from my first horse, whose name was Warlock. He was almost as wide as he was tall when I got him, because he had been turned out to pasture for a couple of years. I had no money for a saddle or bridle, so I rode him bareback with a halter and a lead rope, and he was so round that I could hardly get my legs around him to get a good purchase. He knew this! He would shy or duck his head and stop fast, and I would be airborne. This was a lesson for me: I learned that I had to be totally aware of his every intention if I wanted to stay on. If I wasn't watching his ears every second, and feeling for the tightening of his muscles that signaled a shift in his intentions, I would end up on the ground again.

My mother had paid for a few riding lessons when I was a kid, but I hadn't really learned a lot. My best teachers have always been the animals themselves. If I studied them and learned what types of things upset them and what they liked, I became aware of what would cause problems or get good results. From the very beginning I was giving Warlock equal status. I was working with his intelligence, not watching for things to overcome or to punish him for. I learned it was easier to divert the program from something he didn't want to do than it was to pick myself up off the ground! To punish him for bucking, after he had already bucked, didn't make sense. It was better to figure out just when I was about to be a human missile, and to avoid it.

As I became a better rider, and as Warlock lost weight, I found that I could stay on, even through the bucks, but it still didn't make sense to punish him after the fact. He was learning things that were new to him, and he was resistant because he was unsure. I could interrupt and divert his attention, for example, by suddenly asking him to stop, by making him do some circles, or by turning around on the trail and going back for a while. Eventually he would forget what he had been planning, and I wouldn't get catapulted into the trees. With time and repetition, he grew more confident of himself and of me, and the undesirable behavior disappeared.

Being proactive with your dog, as I was with Warlock, is similar to a common dog training practice in which you distract the dog from unwanted behavior and reward her for behavior that is pleasing. With my approach, however, your goal is not only to prevent unwanted behavior but to bring your dog to a level of awareness where she also puts the brakes on before things get out of hand, because she understands and respects you.

Consider the different levels of awareness that can exist between you and your dog:

Consciousness level one: Your dog does something you don't like; you yell or punish or both. You react after the fact, saying "It happened again," and pretty soon your relationship becomes very predictable. You go around worrying about your dog misbehaving; your dog gets into the habit of cringing and acting guilty because she knows you always yell after she does that thing you hate. But neither of you ever figures out how to get past this point.

Consciousness level two: You become aware that something you don't like is happening while it is occurring. Your dog also becomes aware while she is engaged in the behavior, but she does not yet know what to do about it. And both of you are thinking, "It's happening again." You still have a chance to shift the outcome of the behavior, so you interrupt and divert it to something positive.

Consciousness level three: At this level, both you and your dog say, "It's *about to happen!*" And you can both consciously decide to take steps to prevent the behavior, or you yourself can decide to go ahead and allow it. You can observe the decision-making process going on in your dog's mind; she will start to do the wrong thing, and then catch herself and consciously change her behavior. Why? Because she has learned that she can absolutely count on one consistent response from you. This degree of mutual sensitivity is the ultimate goal in human and animal communication.

MAINTAINING THE ENERGY OF RESPECT
Often dogs (and children) fall into the same behavior trap: when they are being good, everyone takes the behavior for granted, but when they do something wrong, they have everybody's undivided attention.

Dogs can take their human companions for granted too, so if you want to create mutual respect, remember food, praise, and attention. If your dog does not have to earn privileges because she gets them for free or, even worse, because she demands them, you have devalued them and lost your most powerful means of having a happy, self-motivated dog.

When the dog is soliciting something from you, whether it is attention in the form of caresses, being noticed, or wanting to go out, come in, or go for a walk or a ride, it is very important that you offer an exchange, instead of simply acquiescing to whatever the dog wants from you. The exchange can be something as simple as a "sit," which is a polite way for the dog to say "please." If he immediately complies with your first request, instantly praise him and use your symbol. Let him know that you accept his offering in exchange for also responding to his request. If he does not respond when you ask him to, you can give this message to him: "You must not have wanted it very much, because you weren't willing to give something in exchange for it."

Be clear that this is a general approach for those times when the dog is soliciting something. It is different if you ask your dog to do something because you need him to do it. If he does not comply at those times, then he can receive a correction, if needed, immediately followed by praise as soon as he follows through on your request.

There was an incident in my house recently. I was on my way out the door to go to town, and five dogs wanted to go along with me. I asked them to sit while I opened the door, and four of them did, but Hawk just kept wiggling all over and waiting for me to get on with it. "Okay," I said, "Jessie, Rainbow, Tawny, Shaman, let's go! Guess you didn't really want to go, Hawk, or you would have sat when I asked." Hawk watched us through the window with an expression of total disbelief as we drove off. Did he get the point? Yes. The next time I was heading for town, I had to laugh, because he was sitting by the door before I even gave the cue.

Your dog needs to learn that the faster she responds, the sooner she gets what she wants, which actually creates the belief that she has trained you not to waste her time! This may sound manipulative, but it is not. Manipulation is based on a lack of respect and selfish reasons. Your motivation is always to teach your dog the rules that will keep her safe and in harmony with you. Awareness Training respects how the dog's mind works, celebrates her uniqueness, and above all, teaches her how to control her energy so that her life is pleasant and rewarding.

An Outline of Awareness Training

The basic elements of Awareness Training are incorporated into formal training practices in the following chapters. This is the specific sequence outlined in the chapters, which I strongly encourage you to follow:

PREPARE YOURSELF AHEAD OF TIME

- Clarify your goal for the practice—for example, teaching your dog to sit on cue.

- Read the steps and explanations of the practice *all of the way through*, so that you will fully understand where your energy will be needed and how to direct it. Every time you communicate, there are numerous levels of give-and-take, process and exchange, all occurring almost simultaneously. Because so much happens so fast, you need to clarify and practice your intent, so that it becomes automatic and consistent.

- Have all of the physical components of the practice ready: the collar, leash, long lines if needed, food rewards, a partner if needed, and so forth.

- Practice anything that you do not understand—for example, how to give a correction with the leash—ahead of time with another person, so that your energy will be clear. Practice using the correct posture, tone of voice, eye contact, and timing ahead of time in your mind or, for even better results, with a human partner.

- Decide how long you will work (refer to notes in the training lesson) and where the practice should take place.

- Prepare yourself mentally and emotionally. Take a moment to get yourself calm and relaxed. Relaxation is essential for both you and your dog during the learning process! Dogs interpret tension as something unpleasant, and that energy can make them nervous and apprehensive, instead of calm and responsive.

OPEN AND HONOR THE PRACTICE
Before you begin, take a moment to just *be* with your dog. Send her your symbol and visualize the pleasure that you will have working together.

PRACTICE WITH YOUR DOG
- Working with your dog's point of motivation, ask for the intended behavioral response with well-timed physical and verbal cues. Simultaneously hold in your mind the emotionally charged positive image of the appropriate response.

- The moment your dog shows you that her energy is moving toward accomplishing your goal, smile and begin to encourage her with praise.

- When your dog fully accomplishes the behavior, immediately reinforce her understanding with well-timed praise; use your symbol, and send the energy of love and appreciation through your eyes and voice.

- If desired, give a food reward. Remember not to offer verbal praise while the dog is eating the food so that your timing of praise is for the right behavior.

- Whenever you see that your dog is thinking about doing something other than what you have asked her to do, anticipate the shift in her energy, redirect it with a quick, well-timed correction, and then immediately repeat the cue and send the energy of your intentions again.

CLOSE AND HONOR THE PRACTICE
Whenever I end a practice session, I take a moment simply to *be* with the dog. I reflect on all of the little successes we have had during the exercise, and express gratitude for the effort she has made. Once again I use my symbol and honor our shared learning process and the mutual respect and level of communication that is growing between us.

When you want to let your dog know that she can relax her focus say, "Free!" with a big smile and an animated tone in your voice.

Once I release a dog, she understands that for the time being, nothing more is needed of her. Our interactions become more casual. She can go her way while I go mine. When our paths cross later on, we exchange affection, but without the same level of intensity that I use in a lesson. This is because I want the praise, attention, and recognition to be part of our sharing and learning. I don't want to give the impression that things are more pleasant once we stop a practice session. It is in doing the exercises that we have a special connection with each other; it is the way that we heighten our awareness and sensitivity.

After the lesson is over, review each section to see if you are forgetting anything.

COMMUNICATION PROBLEMS

Recognize that at times your dog may try to avoid having to listen to you, especially when she is in her adolescent rebellion phase. She can ignore you, refuse to look at you, and basically defy you. She can throw a tantrum. She can act helpless, lie down, roll on her back and refuse to move, paw at, tangle, or chew innocently on the leash, jump up on you and try to distract you with kisses, or snap at your fingers. She may do these things because she feels confused and stressed, or she may be testing you. She may be feeling an excess of energy and be wondering how you will respond. If you decide that it is better to wait to train her when she is in a more receptive mood, you may teach her that it is all right with you if her energy dominates your relationship. This will only cause problems in the future.

There are two helpful ways to work with your dog when you have a communication problem: by using your dog as a mirror, and by becoming a detached observer.

Dogs can be wonderful mirrors of the state of your mental and emotional well-being. If I'm having a bad day, my dogs will be restless and agitated. When I walk through the house feeling tense and irritable and notice that my mood has been absorbed and reflected back to me by my dogs, I become aware of my emotional state and the need to take some time to meditate and shift my energy.

If I'm having a good day, everybody in the house is happy and calm. This takes compromise on everyone's part, because I have thirty dogs that live with me, plus clients' dogs and an occasional rescued dog.

Since a dog will mirror your inner state, the big lesson is that if you want to take really good care of your dog, you have to take good care of yourself. Dogs feel our emotions intensely, and their impulse is to try to help heal us because that will help them feel better too. A dog will comfort you if you are sad: lick your face, wag her tail, ask to play, gaze anxiously into your eyes, or simply try to press her body against you to help hold you together. By the same token if you don't get better, your dog will frequently begin to mirror your illness and stress as well, because she is so tuned in to your energy.

Using your dog as a mirror can be a valuable training tool. It's a wonderful way to learn a few things about yourself. When you ask for your dog's attention but the tone in your voice says, "I doubt that you are going to do what I ask because you probably have no respect for me," or "I doubt that you can really understand me, because I'm doing this all wrong," your dog will mirror your lack of conviction by not responding. Dogs can help you become who you want to be. As you two practice working with energy, your dog will give you frequent reality checks, because you usually get back just what you have put in.

Donald's relationship with his dog, Misty, was another example of a way a dog can mirror your inner state. Misty had developed an aggression problem with other animals, but things were absolutely fine when he and Donald were home alone. When he took Misty out for a walk, however, Donald immediately became very nervous whenever another dog approached. He was afraid that Misty would get out of control. Misty instantly sensed that Donald's energy had changed. The dog decided that the approaching dog was making Donald anxious, and this made sense to him, because at home, Donald was relaxed in Misty's presence. Therefore, Misty went on red alert because Donald's energy sent him a signal.

Using your dog as a mirror will teach you a lot about the way your emotions can be either a contribution or a detriment to achieving your goals. You will recognize that they can be all over the place, particularly when you and your dog are struggling to come to an understanding.

Whenever I hit a speed bump in my relationship with a dog, I stop everything, take a deep breath, close my eyes, and mentally disengage from the present situation. I take a moment to re-create our interaction in my mind's eye, as if I were watching an instant replay. This allows me to observe without any ego or emotional attachment to the situation. I analyze my actions, remembering my tone of voice, posture, use of the leash, and the dog's reactions to my cues. I refresh my memory about his point of motivation. Usually I can figure out what I need to do next. This is the principle of detachment, which is well known in meditation. Make it a habit to do this whenever you find yourself becoming upset or confused about the way the communication is going. It is especially helpful if you are having a problem during a specific training session.

When you detach your energy from an unproductive situation, you give yourself a chance to start afresh. You also detach from the worry that your dog won't love you, from anger and frustration that you aren't getting what you want, from self-criticism, impatience, and any other negative emotion that usually arises when you find yourself performing in unfamiliar territory.

If your dog's behavior is causing a strong, negative emotional reaction in you, switch your focus away from the dog; detach and observe yourself. A negative emotional response is often caused by painful unresolved issues about control, victimization, or manipulation in your past. You have emotions, but you need to remember that *you* are *not* your emotions. You can always step back, take a deep breath, and repeat again, making any necessary adjustments. If your dog is expressing a lot of confused emotion, do not get sucked into his energy. It is imperative that you stay positive, clear, loving, encouraging, and keep your energy moving toward your goal so that you can give the appropriate response. Flood the situation with loving energy; visualize and use your symbol. Instead of drawing away in frustration, go into the exercise with loving energy.

If you think about it, this is really a practice of unconditional love. By freeing your ego self from hurt or anger when you don't get the response you are looking for, you are able to stay in a place of instant forgiveness and love, both for yourself and for your dog. A mistake or an inappropriate response is not the end of the world. It is merely one thing that didn't work. Acknowledge the lesson, move on, and keep your focus on the next step of your learning adventure.

Here are a few important reminders in frustrating circumstances:

- Mistakes are part of the learning process. Do not judge yourself or your dog too harshly. Acknowledge the fact that you have doubts and fears, but do not get hung up on them. Fears and regrets are another block to finding joy in the learning process. Give your doubts and fears new energy and new jobs, so that they can work for you.

- If you experience doubts about your ability to communicate with your dog, use your imagination and *pretend* that you can already do these things. Perhaps as a child, you had an imaginary playmate with whom you communicated freely. Pretend that your imaginary playmate has come back to visit you in the form of your dog. Play with these new ideas; have fun!

- As you progress in your training, let go of past problems and stay in the now. Remember that all thoughts and beliefs can be changed and that resistance is merely the beginning of the possibility of change.

- If you still are not able to make the progress that you are hoping for, perhaps you are trying to push your dog to learn too quickly. Watch for the subtle changes in the energy between you, and detach yourself from a need to achieve instantaneous dramatic results. You can also bring more objectivity into the situation by seeking professional advice. You may also want to try some of the suggested supports for learning given in Chapter 13, such as flower essences or massage.

- Do not confuse love and respect. You do not have to earn love; it is a universal state into which all beings are born. You do have to earn respect, which comes from the energy of your love, understanding, and compassion. If your dog respects you, she recognizes you and your unique energy. And you give the same to her. Fear and intimidation destroy respect and inhibit the ability to express love.

  It is common to be reluctant to stand in our own power because we are afraid that if we do, we will disappoint another person and lose that person's love. It is also common to do this in a relationship with a dog. It is *necessary* to set your own limits and guidelines to honor yourself. Even if you are afraid to stand up for yourself with your human friends, your dog will help you discover that you do have the strength to do this. She will quickly show you that setting limits for her makes her respect, love, and trust you all the more.

- Don't forget to separate the pattern from the pup. If your dog is locked into a behavior pattern, remember to separate who she is from what she did. She is a dog who wants to please you. When she does something inappropriate, she doesn't do it deliberately to annoy you or to make you angry; she does it because that's all she knows how to do at that point in time. When you antici-pate, or interrupt and redirect her inappropriate behavior, when you visualize her behaving correctly and give her lots of praise when she complies, you are saying, "I love you. I don't like what you just did, but I still love you."

- If you have given your best, whatever evolves is as it should be. Dogs, like people, have different reasons for coming to the earth; some are here just to experience being a dog without any intention of engaging in a deep relationship with people. If, despite all of your love and dedication your relationship with the dog does not become all that you wish, you still owe it to yourself to look at what you have learned from the experience.

I once worked with Tim and Sue, a young couple who were studying to be veterinarians. They had a beautiful dog named Kyle who, before they acquired him, had had a traumatic and violent puppyhood that was devoid of any socialization. They had taken him on because they felt sorry for him. He grew to somewhat trust them, but if he felt threatened—for example, if his foot got tangled in the leash and one of them reached down to untangle it—he would panic, become aggressive, and bite. When he felt safe, he was very affectionate with them, which ultimately made the decision to euthanize even more difficult for them. He was a large dog who looked very appealing and cuddly, which increased the danger of a biting incident, since whenever they had him out in public, someone would inevitably try to pat or hug him. His response was lightning-fast and ferocious, and his ferocity was even greater when he was taken to a boarding kennel or to the vet.

We worked diligently with him. I employed every healing and communication and repatterning technique I knew, and Tim and Sue were totally dedicated and committed to following through on my suggestions, despite the burden it put on their time. I became as emotionally involved with Kyle as they were, because he accepted me and was always calm and friendly with me. Things would go really well for a while, and then there would be another serious incident. When I had exhausted all my knowledge and methods, we even discussed the option of trying him on traditional medications like Prozac, but Tim and Sue both felt very strongly that they didn't want to do that. That's when the tough decision was finally made.

It was important to me to convey to Tim and Sue that they had not failed Kyle in any way. I told them that they had done more than most people would have in that situation, had given him every opportunity to change and respond, but that he just wasn't capable of it, even though he loved them as much as they loved him.

A couple of weeks went by and they stopped in one day to share their feelings with me about the whole experience. They said that working with Kyle had taught them so much about patience, commitment, understanding, and love. I reminded them that, in spite of their love for Kyle, he was never really happy in our world. Knowing that they had done everything possible and still had to let him go became a very important lesson for them, especially in light of the profession they had chosen. They agreed that it is important to remember that, once you have done everything that you can, it is enough. You can neither take credit for the successes nor assume the blame for the failures, because frequently the outcome is not under your control. Even a dog like Kyle offered a meaningful and beautiful lesson; I was impressed that Tim and Sue were so open to seeing that was so. They related that they had decided to become holistic veterinarians, partly because of everything they had learned during the work we did together with Kyle. I know that they will be dedicated healers and that their clients will be very fortunate.

There is a lot to absorb when you embark on this joyful adventure. Always be sure that you are having fun. By communicating with your dog and teaching her to accomplish certain actions when needed, you can establish a wonderful structure for your relationship. It should be an inspiring and deeply rewarding experience for both of you. Keep your praise abundant and your energy high while you are both learning.

KEEP A RECORD OF YOUR PROGRESS

You can review the progress of your training by audiotaping yourself during a training session so that you can hear your tone of voice, evaluate the clarity and timing of your cues, and check the level of positive energy when you review the tape. You might instead have a friend videotape your sessions so that you can pinpoint any areas that need to be changed or fine-tuned.

It can also be helpful to photocopy a specific exercise and keep it in a weatherproof training notebook, which you can refer to for practice ahead of time, as well as during the actual session.

I strongly suggest that you keep a daily log as a record of your progress. Write down your goals, both for yourself and for your dog. Note any areas that need work, and be very specific. It will not be helpful to write, "I want to have a dog that behaves well." Instead, record somethings like this: "I need the dog to come when she's called. I need her to stop jumping on people. I need her to walk on a leash without pulling." Target the behavior problem and your goals for your dog's future.

Make a list of any and all undesirable behaviors that need to be addressed and any directions that the dog does not respond to consistently.

Your goals for yourself could include the following: "I need to learn how my dog is thinking," "I need to be more consistent," "I have to be honest about what I need to change," "I need to develop a faster response"—or be proactive, have better timing, or use a more flexible tone of voice.

Remember that you are the only one who is empowered to make changes in your dog's behavior. Your dog has no way of getting there by herself, because she has minimal, or no, control over how people interact with her, or over the effects of her environment. When you set training goals for your dog, realize that they are predominantly *your* goals.

Fill in the worksheet below. As you proceed week by week, you should be able to take everything in the left-hand column and move it to the right. The amount of time it takes to progress does not matter. It is better to achieve slow, steady progress than to make a big leap forward and then regress. Watch for the subtleties. You do not have to be perfect to experience success.

WORKSHEET

MY DOG *Problem Behavior and Directions Dog Is Not Responding to Immediately and Consistently:*	MY DOG *Solutions and Accomplishments:*
MYSELF *Attitudes and Skills I Want to Improve:*	MYSELF *Solutions and Accomplishments:*

THE THREE *T*'S OF TRAINING

When you are training your dog, it is better not to overwhelm her with too many lessons. This also should be recorded on your worksheet. Always keep the three *T*'s in mind:

Teach. Teach one thing at a time and make sure the dog thoroughly understands it.

Train. Repeat with appropriate praise and corrections until there is a consistently correct response without the need for constant corrections.

Test. Proof the dog out in controlled situations (on a leash or long line) with all kinds of distractions until you are sure she will respond to you, no matter what the situation.

Training is something you do *for* the dog, not *to* the dog, because you want your dog to experience love, realize her own potential as a loving being, and have as expansive a life as possible. No dog can have too many human friends who want to include her in the fun! The better your dog's manners are, the more people will welcome her arrival, from friends, relatives, and neighbors to professionals like the groomer, the kennel boarder, and the veterinarian. If your dog is easy to work with, polite, friendly, well behaved, and responsive to directions, she is more apt to get special attention. An untrained dog with poor manners has a limited life, often gets left at home, often is confined to a crate or put on a tie-out chain because of destructive behavior, and leads a lonely life through no fault of her own.

My Sheltie Tarl was a perfect example of a dog whose life was enhanced as a result of the development of his interactive skills and who enhanced the lives of those around him. He was the ring bearer at my wedding to my second husband, and he carefully, and with great dignity, carried a pillow with the rings on it, holding it in his mouth by a ribbon handle while he walked down the aisle beside my daughter Lara, who carried flowers. Then he sat quietly and respectfully beside her until the ceremony was over. Tarl's contribution so impressed a friend in the audience that he was invited to do the same thing all over again at her wedding.

A well-trained dog is a great ambassador for the whole dog kingdom. If for any reason you have to find a different home for your dog, you will have a much better chance of doing so if she is well mannered. There are not enough homes for dogs to begin with, and those dogs who have not been taught the basics of living with humans are less likely to survive if they end up at a humane society. Furthermore, if you give your dog the gift of knowing how to behave in our world, you will never have to worry whether she will lack for caretakers should something happen to you.

"*Tarl as Ringbearer at My Wedding*"

9

BUILDING THE BOND: COMMUNICATION AND SAFETY WITH WALK, COME, AND WAIT

The three practices in this chapter are the most important of all behaviors you will teach your dog. They will help you establish communication and keep your dog safe. First you will teach your dog to walk on a lead, giving you part of his attention all of the time. Then you will teach him to come and to wait. If your dog learns to respond immediately when you give him either of these two directions, you will have the tools to prevent him from walking into unpleasant or dangerous situations, like a skunk on your back porch or a heavily loaded semi coming around a corner out of nowhere when he is on the other side of the road wanting to cross.

THE FIRST PRACTICE: ATTENTION AND COMMUNICATION

Teaching your dog to walk on a lead without pulling is fundamentally an attention-and-communication exercise. It will help you learn how to attain the third level of consciousness, which is to be proactive, thinking ahead of your dog.

Your objective in this practice is to achieve a constant flow of understanding and energy, like the movement of the figure-eight symbol that skaters trace on the ice: one loop is your energy; the other is that of your dog. This is also the symbol for infinity; it is a perfectly balanced, endless exchange. If the two of you are feeling relaxed and attuned to each other, this exchange should feel equally as balanced as those times when you are feeling high-spirited and energetic.

It is quite typical to see people struggle with this first communication exercise. I am often reminded of an elderly woman who was referred to me by a veterinary clinic because her dog, Corfu, had a very bizarre behavior pattern. Every time she took him for a stroll, they would only get so far, and then the dog would suddenly collapse, flop over on his side, and begin shaking and trembling. After a moment he would come out of the "seizure" and get up. The walk would proceed for a time until the same thing happened again. The woman, whom I'll call Evelyn, was sure that the problem was caused by the dog ingesting her neighbor's pesticide-laced grass. She could not imagine why the vet had referred her to me, after saying that he could find nothing physically wrong and that the problem had to be behavioral.

When Evelyn arrived, I happened to be standing just outside of the training area, some distance away from her. I watched her get out of her car with the dog on a leash, and begin to head downhill toward me. The lead was quickly taken over by Corfu, an overweight miniature schnauzer. A nervous little dog with an excitable temperament, he came straining and plowing down the hill with his gentle companion gamely in tow. The dog was so overzealous he looked like a turtle trying to crawl out of its shell, head down with determination, legs clawing frantically sidewise at the dirt driveway.

I had the problem solved before Evelyn even reached me, her face pink with the effort of hanging on to her end of the leash, while Corfu's tongue was three-quarters of the way out of his mouth and turning black from the lack of oxygen in his system. It was obvious to me that his walks with Evelyn consisted partly of taking in the fresh air and partly of passing out from a lack of it! After a faint, it only took a minute or two of lying on his side, while Evelyn bent over him in concern (with the collar and leash slack), for Corfu to begin to breathe again, whereupon the two of them would resume their unorthodox progress down the street!

I gave examples, I lectured, I demonstrated, I did everything in my power to show Evelyn how to give Corfu a correction with the leash that would help him understand how to balance his energy with hers. Because he had a nervous temperament, it took a strong pop on the leash to get his attention at first. This was Evelyn's main problem—and it is a common one. She was too afraid of hurting him and could not bring herself to do it. I finally took the dog for a day, and he caught on quickly. He and Evelyn lived happily ever after, once the communication barrier was overcome.

In sum, your main challenge in this practice will be to learn how to use the leash to give an effective correction. Remember, a "pop" with the leash is not painful. Only do what is required and nothing more. This is a test of your knowledge of your dog's point of motivation. You can do it!

Goal: Your goal will be to move about effortlessly with your dog on a leash, while he gives you part of his attention at all times, in order to establish mutual respect and communication.

Practice guidelines: The length of time required for practice will depend on your dog; use your best judgment. This exercise needs to be done for a long enough period of time to help your dog learn to focus on you. Future lessons will need to be brief and intermittent, or else you will bore your dog.

- A minimum of two 10- to 15-minute sessions a day for dogs four months of age and over. If you do more, there should be a minimum two-hour break between the sessions.

- Five to eight minutes several times a day for puppies eight to sixteen weeks of age.

- Practice in a variety of locations.

- After teaching your dog how to walk on a lead without pulling, which you should be able to do in one session, you should never allow him to pull again. Otherwise you are being inconsistent, which is confusing and unfair to the dog. Do this exercise inside your home and also out-of-doors. He needs to know that he can count on the same signals in the same situation, all of the time.

Things to check before you begin: Read this section all the way through and underline any points that you think will be especially important for you to remember. I strongly suggest that you photocopy the section that you are working on, so that it will be handy for reference.

- If you are giving a food reward, have a dozen pea-size pieces at hand in an apron or easy-access pocket. Remember to have treats for yourself too, but don't choose chocolate; it's toxic to dogs!

- Be sure that you have taught yourself beforehand how to give a corrective pop with the leash.

- Be sure your dog's training equipment is on correctly.

- Adjust the leash to a comfortable length.

- Hold the leash with both hands together, palms down. A common mistake is to separate the hands, resulting in the use of only one hand for giving corrections. This could give you a wrenched arm or shoulder if your dog makes a sudden move.

Mental and emotional preparation: It is very important to think each exercise through from beginning to end before you start. Be methodical; make your visualization very clear, or systematically review the sequence. If you run into problems, it can often be because you are pushing the dog too fast and he

doesn't have time to mentally process
the full scope of the exercise. I strongly
suggest that you tape-record this exercise ahead of time and listen to the tape
while doing a practice visualization.

- Get yourself quiet and focused
  by taking a few deep breaths.
  Clarify your intent.

*Open and honor the practice as
described in Chapter 8:* Energize your
symbol.
Technique:

- When you are ready to begin,
  remember to visualize, and use
  the cue "Let's go" in a cheerful
  and emphatic tone of voice.
  Begin moving forward with
  purpose and confidence.

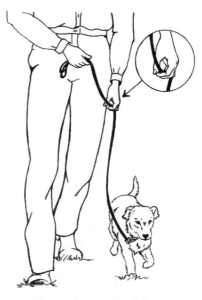

*"Holding the Lead with Puppies
and Small Dogs"*

- Imagine that the leash has become a golden cord: light, delicate,
  and strong. This is a magical line of communication that will
  maintain a connection between the two of you.

- The slightest pull from the dog will immediately cue you to give
  a corrective downward pop on the leash, and you will come to a
  complete halt. He will learn that when he pulls, he effectively
  causes you to put on the brakes. Take care not to pull or drag at
  the leash instead of giving it a pop. Remember, the pop is a
  quick, sharp move. The pop may need to be more energetic for
  a very big, strong dog than with a smaller dog. However, take
  your dog's sensitivity, temperament, and personality into
  account. Watch your dog to see how much pop makes him stop
  and focus on you. You don't want to hurt or frighten him; this
  practice should be completely nonconfrontational. You just
  want to interrupt the direction of his energy and get it moving
  into an exchange and flow with yours.

- Continue to visualize the desired outcome even if you need to
  make frequent corrections.

- Change your pace and direction frequently to keep your dog's
  attention and interest. Do not worry about whether your dog is

heeling. The primary goal at this point is only to teach your dog to pay attention and move on a loose leash without pulling.

- *Say nothing* when you correct! Except for giving the signal and verbal praise, you should communicate through your body, your hands, and the leash. Resist saying "No if the dog pulls or "Come on" if you want him to listen to you and start moving again. Fine yourself a nickel each time you forget!

- When your dog takes the pressure off the leash, smile, praise him, and use your symbol. Repeat the signal "Let's go" in a cheerful but emphatic tone of voice and move forward with confidence and purpose. Repeat this as often as necessary.

- Limit your verbal directions to the basic "Let's go!" or "Off!" if he is jumping up on you, and "Leave it!" if he is chewing on the lead or trying to play tug-of-war with it. Research shows that dogs can understand hundreds of different words. Like all of us, however, they have to be presented with concise and consistent information in a learning situation.

- Whenever your dog is moving with you on a loose leash and consistently giving you part of his attention, honor his effort to understand you by smiling every now and then, praising him, using your symbol, and sending out lots of positive energy. I say things like, "That's it! Thank you. You've got it! Very good. Yes, good boy! Good girl." This is also the appropriate time to give a food reward.

- If you are having a problem, *stop immediately*, and refer to the end of this section to see how to solve the problem before you establish a bad habit that will be difficult to unlearn.

Close and honor the practice as described in Chapter 8: Let your dog know that he can relax his focus say, "Free!" with a big smile and an animated tone in your voice.

If you are not communicating well during training: If you are not getting the expected results, you need to become the detached observer and analyze the situation. This means you must stop, look, and listen.

- *Stop* everything. There is no point in repeating something that is not working.

- *Look.* Step out of the situation and review how the two of you looked together as if on a movie screen inside your head.

- *Listen*. Recall the tone of voice you were using, both for praise and for corrections.

- Determine the emotion you sent to your dog during corrections.

- Decide what needs to be changed or adjusted to bring about the desired response.

- Check your eye contact and body posture, and dog's point of motivation and focus of attention. You cannot teach him anything if he is not paying attention to you.

Points to review: Here are some questions to ask yourself both during and after a session.

- How did you sound? When you were praising your dog, were you so enthusiastic that he got too excited?

- If your dog was very boisterous or excitable, did you get pulled into his energy pattern and become frustrated instead of staying calm and centered?

- If he was unresponsive, did you need to be more animated, enthusiastic, give more praise?

- Were you consistent about stopping the instant he thought about pulling or began to pull on the leash?

- Did you go on too long and find that your dog's performance began to diminish because he was bored?

- Did you use too many unnecessary words?

- Have you learned the right way to pop the lead? Perhaps you need to practice snapping it without your dog.

- Did you use the type of energy you were visualizing?

- Did you remember to focus on everything your dog did correctly, even if it was not perfect?

- Did you two match your inner picture from before? Did you remember to keep that picture and that positive feeling present while you trained, so that you were sending him the physical, emotional, and mental messages all at the same time?

If you were able to do all of this, congratulations! You were *training with awareness*.

SPECIFICS

If your dog continues to pull on the leash:

- Immediately pop the leash and *stop* all forward movement.

- Check to see if you are under the dog's point of motivation with your correction. Popping the leash should make him stop and look at you while he tries to figure out what happened. If he ignores you completely, you probably are not giving a strong enough pop, or perhaps your timing was off and your interruption came too late.

If he is lagging and refusing to move forward with you:

- Pop and release the leash and move briskly forward. Be sure there is no pressure on the collar when the dog moves ahead. Keep a loop of slack in the lead.

- Be sure to praise instantly with a lot of happy talk and encouragement.

- Pat your leg to encourage the dog to keep up with you.

- If necessary, use a food lure.

If he is jumping on you:

- Say "Off" emphatically, with strong disapproval in your voice. Sounding angry is like a warning growl in dog language; be theatrical, but don't get caught up in negative emotions. Send positive energy at all times and remain calm, centered, and focused on doing the exercise correctly.

- If necessary, give a downward pop on the leash.

- Stop all forward motion.

- When your dog has settled, start up again, as if nothing has happened.

If your dog is grabbing the leash in his mouth:

- Stop all forward motion.

- Say "Off" or "Leave it" with strong disapproval in your voice.

- If the dog persists, repeat the reprimand after making sure that nothing metal, like a buckle, is in your dog's mouth, and give a firm pop on the leash.

- Remain calm, centered, and focused on doing the exercise correctly.

- As soon as the dog has released the leash from his mouth, say "Let's go" in a cheerful, emphatic voice.

- Begin moving forward with purpose and confidence, as if nothing has happened.

As you improve: After only a few successful practices of this exercise, you will be able to walk your dog with a new sense of enjoyment for both of you. Because of this practice, walks can be comfortable and pleasant, since mutual respect and a harmonious exchange of energy has now been attained.

Of course, part of the pleasure of adventuring is that there are a lot of stimulating smells, sights, and sounds out there beyond your door. Keep part of your attention on your dog at all times as well, so that you can be instantly aware of any major shifts in his energy. Allow him to figure out that in spite of any extra stimuli, if he keeps one eye on you all the time and stays reasonably close to you, he can avoid giving himself a correction and bringing the walk to a halt. Then he is in control of his own physical and mental comfort.

Be sure to keep up the encouragement during your walks. Smile, praise, open up your heart center and feel the power and energy of love. Send that energy to your dog while you visualize your symbol. The better your dog's response, the more extravagantly you should praise.

As you walk along, you will have to decide what your tolerance level is for your dog's interests versus your own. What if he sees something fascinating along the trail? If the object of his interest is something safe and acceptable, of course you can allow him to investigate it. Dogs enjoy sniffing lots of things, and you may want yours to have a good time checking things out. However, he should not be allowed to drag you from place to place, oblivious of whether it causes you discomfort.

THE SECOND PRACTICE: COME

"Come!" It's a powerful, magical word. When your dog responds instantly and joyously to your call, it is a wonderful proof of the love and respect between you.

You have to be very careful though, about how and when to use this signal with your dog. If he comes when you call, and the immediate result is that something negative, unrewarding, or unpleasant happens, you are teaching him that coming to you feels like punishment!

Here is a typical scenario: Your dog disappears somewhere in the neighborhood, and you spend hours looking for her. You finally give up and go home, and eventually she shows up on the back porch. Now suppose that, like many people, you react in the following way: "Sara! Come here! Where have you been? You are a bad dog!"

Puppies

When you are teaching your puppy to walk on a lead, it is important to understand why he may be reluctant to do certain things, like leaving the security of his house, which is his den area. It is normal for young puppies to stay close to their den, since that is where they feel safe and protected.

Although it will depend somewhat on temperament and personality, generally the puppy is inclined to avoid strange situations and territories, so it is not uncommon for a very young one to resist strongly if you try to walk him down the street. You are asking him to do something unnatural, and he is picking up the scent markers of bigger, more dominant dogs who have already established their territory in the neighborhood. To him, all of those markers say "No trespassing!" His nose tells him he is in the wrong place and that he had better head for home.

All of this means that, rather than dragging the puppy on leash out of the house or across the yard, it is better to pick him up and carry him to the edge of the yard, set him down, and let him walk back toward the safety and security of the house. This avoids the problem of teaching the puppy to associate the leash with something fearful and traumatic, like being taken away from safety.

Carry him until you are far enough away so that he realizes that you, and not his den, are his security. You can also take him somewhere in the car before you start your walk. Then he will be more able to pay attention to you. As he grows older, his own maturity and curiosity will overcome his reluctance. Once a puppy has learned to walk on the lead and feels secure in your presence and in following you about, you can take him for longer walks and expose him to a greater variety of surroundings to help him develop confidence.

The dog has no idea that she is being reprimanded because she left; she thinks she's being scolded for coming home. If your dog runs off, the correction has to accompany the act of leaving, not the act of coming back.

Here's another common scenario: Your dog is playing outside, running around, and having a wonderful time. You call her to come. She does, you praise her and then take her inside for eight or ten hours of solitary confinement while you go off for the day. Since your dog may prefer to stay outside, you need a word that tells her you expect a certain response. I say "Inside!" when I want a dog in the house. *Save the word "Come" for positive experiences only and for coming directly to you.*

A dog may feel punished if you call her to you to give her a pill, give her a bath, trim her nails, or take her to the vet. If you have to give your dog a pill, just go to her, open her mouth, and pop it in. If you need to give her a bath or trim her nails, don't call her to you first; just go to her and do it. If you are going to take her to the vet, just go to her, snap the lead on, and say "Let's go!" Under no circumstances should you have your dog associate the word "Come" with anything unpleasant or unrewarding.

It's important to use "Let's go" rather than "Come on" when the dog is on a leash, because you don't want her to think that the leash and "Come" mean that you two are going to go somewhere together.

I never teach sit-stay-come, especially in the beginning stages. In my experience, the times when I need a dog to come are not when she is already doing a sit-stay; they are usually when the dog is off leash, out of control, and heading for trouble. If you teach "Come" from a sit-stay, the dog looks at it as a two-part exercise. If you yell "Come" when she is disappearing over the hill, she doesn't know how to do it because she has not done the first part of the sequence.

It is bad planning to link a nonmotivational exercise like "Stay," which is boring and requires patience, with a motivational one. Dogs tend to break the stay position because they want to please you and show you how well they understand what is coming next. If you reprimand the dog for not staying at this point, she thinks she is being reprimanded for trying to please you, since she knows you are going to ask her to come next. Therefore, she will think she is being reprimanded for doing come. If this happens over and over, the dog loses her trust in you because of the inconsistencies. Now she anticipates being punished when told to stay, and she may run away or refuse to respond when you call.

Training is nothing more than establishing habits. In the following exercise you will establish the correct habitual response to the word "Come," so that it is there for you when you need it.

Goal: Your goal for this exercise is to have your dog come to you immediately when you call. This will help you to keep her safe in an emergency situation.

Practice guidelines:

- Practice three to five times in a row at each session, but never more than five, so that you will not bore your dog. Always stop while the energy is still high. If you are getting perfect responses after three repetitions, praise lavishly and stop.

- Practice two or three times in a row per session for puppies eight to sixteen weeks of age.

- Vary the number of times in each session, and practice several times a day if possible.

- Practice in a variety of locations.

Things to check before you begin:

- You will need a partner for this exercise. Initially, your partner will serve as a post to which you have temporarily attached your dog. He will not look at, talk to, or pat the dog. The dog's attention needs to be on the person who is calling her, instead of the person restraining her.

- Your dog will have her training equipment on and be attached to a 30-foot-long line, which your partner will control. If you are working a large dog, I recommend that the person wear gloves to avoid rope burns. Leather gloves rather than cloth are best because they won't slip.

- Measure the length of the line ahead of time and make a mark on the ground at both ends. When you do the exercise, make sure that you and your partner stay within those boundaries. Otherwise, the dog might be accidentally stopped short by the line, and think she is being corrected.

- Practice your voice cues by yourself ahead of time. It is very important that you remember to say your dog's name first, followed by "Come" in a clear, emphatic voice, rather than saying, for example, "Come on, Taffy." This sounds wishy-washy, as if the dog can do it if she wants to. Try out the difference around your dog without doing the rest of the exercise. As if you were including the information in a conversation, say, "Come on, Taffy," and you will see that you get little or no reaction from your dog. Now, say, "Taffy, Come! in an animated, enthusiastic voice, and you will see your dog's ears prick up immediately. This is the reaction you are looking for.

- Also practice alternating the tone of your voice from enthusiasm to reprimand and back again. You may have to make a rapid switch in energy in the middle of the exercise, and it helps to feel the difference ahead of time. Your dog may be headed toward you when you say, "Taffy, come," and then get distracted by something like a great smell, so that you will have to immediately drop your voice deep in your chest, make the energy sharp and disapproving, say, "Leave it!" and then switch the energy up high to enthusiasm again and repeat "Taffy, come!"

Mental and emotional preparation: Get yourself centered and focused. Clarify your intent.

Open and honor the practice: Energize your symbol.

Technique:

- Your partner will allow the dog about 6 feet of line in the beginning. The rest of the line should be thrown out straight behind him on the ground in order to avoid knots and tangles, which could interrupt the practice.

- Show your dog that you have a treat. Allow her to smell it and lick it, but do not let her have it. If your dog is not motivated by food, use a favorite toy instead.

- Now turn your back and run away from her as fast as you can, because anything moving rapidly away from a dog will get her undivided attention. This is why dogs often pursue cyclists and joggers. The faster and more enthusiastically that you go away from your dog, the better she will keep her focus, so you need to put a lot of energy into this exercise.

- Be sure that your dog is not sitting when you show her the treat and run away. She needs to be excited and moving around, because that is more likely what she will be doing when you will need her to come in an emergency situation.

- Your partner will be standing inside the marks that you have made on the ground. He will be restraining your dog with the long line while you run away. This will intensify the dog's desire to follow you.

- Stop inside of the other mark on the ground. Turn, face your dog, and reduce your body posture. Get right down on eye level with little dogs; with bigger dogs, you can just bend over. This is an imitation of the play bow, which dogs do with one another to initiate play. By reducing your size, you are not holding your body in an aggressive or dominant posture; your low position is more inviting for your dog to come and join you.

- While in this posture, spread your arms wide or tap the ground with your hands.

- Say the dog's name first, followed instantly by the word "Come" in an animated, inviting, and emphatic tone of voice. The order is important: "Susie, *come!*" Do not say "Come on" over and over! Keep your cue *simple and emphatic*.

- At the same time, visualize to your dog what you want her to do. Use your energy like a homing beacon. Imagine that you are creating an energy field lined with lights like those on a landing strip. Or imagine that you have established that fine gossamer cord between your heart and the dog's heart. When you run, that cord between you stretches, and when you call your dog, that cord brings the dog to you.

- The instant that you've said "Come," your partner should loosen his grip on the line, allowing the dog to move forward freely. If the dog takes off toward you—and most dogs will—your partner should allow the line to pay out through his hands, and run along behind the dog, maintaining a distance of 15 to 20 feet. He should remain prepared to tighten his grip again and give a correction if needed.

Note: *Your partner should never allow the dog to go forward until you say "Come."* Also, he should *never* correct if the dog is jumping up and down, barking, or pulling on the line. This is the *one* time when the dog is allowed to pull on the lead and get excited, because you are using that restraint to

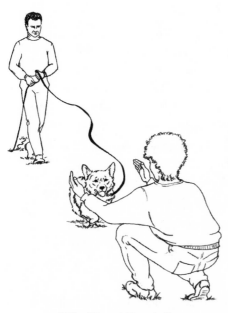

"The 'Come' Practice"

heighten her desire to come to you. If the dog seems apprehensive of the line because she isn't used to it, your partner should start the dog moving forward by moving forward himself. (This person should still not say anything.) He should also shorten the distance to a few feet until the dog is more confident. The line should always be held at an elevated angle to ensure that the dog does not step on it and inadvertently give herself a correction.

- If your dog is headed straight toward you, give lots and lots of praise: "Yes! Good dog! That's it! Good job!" Your praise should be high-energy and enthusiastic. If your dog is slow to respond or lacks enthusiasm, you will have to double or triple the energy of warmth, excitement, and invitation that you are putting into your voice. Don't keep repeating "Come" if she is already coming toward you, just praise her. This will heighten her confidence that she is giving you what you want.

- If the dog goes off-course, stops, loses her focus, or does anything other than coming straight toward you, instantly give an appropriate verbal reprimand such as "Hey!" "Leave it!" or "Off!" to indicate sharp disapproval.

- If your dog heads toward you and then shoots right on past, do not grab for her collar, try to tackle her, or pursue her as she goes by, because you might start a game of catch-me. Stay where you are! Limit your reaction to a sharp, disapproving "Wait!" or "Stop!" or "Hey!" or any sharp, disapproving word you can get out in the moment, while your partner instantly makes a correction at the sound of your voice.

- As soon as the dog has been corrected, repeat the dog's name and "Come" in an inviting tone of voice.

- Timing is crucial. The dog must receive the correction *the very moment* you see her attention wander. At the same time, your partner needs to stop running and give a correction with the long line. As soon as the dog has been corrected, repeat her name and "Come," in a cheerful, inviting tone of voice and resume enthusiastic praising immediately when she starts toward you again: "That's it! Good girl! Yes, you've got it!"

    Note: It takes good mental and emotional discipline to be ready to shift the sound of your voice from inviting warmth to sharp reprimand. You might want to practice doing this by yourself first. I find that people often begin by enthusiastically calling "Come!" and then, if the dog runs the other way, they switch to yelling "Come" in an angry voice. Any time you want the dog to approach you, your voice needs to be pleasant and inviting, not angry. Sharpen your tone and use reprimands that are specific to the distraction when your dog is not moving toward you and has lost her focus.

- As your dog gets closer to you, extend the hand with the treat in it straight out in front of you.

- When your dog reaches the treat, do not let her have it, but allow her nose to follow it, while you retract your arm and bring it all the way in so that your arm is touching your body. Now you can easily take hold of your dog's collar without having to reach for it.

  Note: Get into the habit of taking your dog's collar every time she comes to you, so that, in an emergency, she will automatically come in close to you and expect you to take her collar. It is absolutely crucial that you remember to bring your arm all the way in to touch your body every time, which brings your dog securely within your reach so that you can be sure of getting a grip on the collar. Many people make the mistake of leaving their arm extended and then giving the treat once the dog reaches it. This trains her to stop beyond your reach and you might scare her if you then are forced to make a lunge for her, since dogs' reflexes are 500 times faster than those of humans. You don't want her to know that she can evade you. She also could be inclined to think that you want to play "catch me if you can."

- Once you have taken hold of the collar, take a minute or two to praise your dog and send your symbol. This is very important! Do not be cursory!

- Now you can give your dog the treat. Be sure not to praise her while she is eating, or she will think that is why you are praising her. The food is reward enough. Give yourself a treat too, and congratulate yourself; it makes the learning more fun.

- You can release your dog. Let go of the collar and say "Free!" Some people allow the dog to run to them, receive the treat, and then run away again without being released. This increases the possibility that, in an emergency, you will have less control. Always *consciously* release your dog by letting go of the collar and saying your release cue.

I like this method because, right from the beginning, we help the dog make the choice to come. Another common approach is to teach "Sit-Stay" and then do "Come" by reeling the dog in like a fish on a line. That method, however, only teaches the dog that pulling makes her come to you. Then you have no idea whether she has decided to do it correctly or not. The method I teach offers the chance to correct the dog's understanding of your cue, and gives her freedom of choice and dealing with the consequences of her decisions. By her responses, you can tell from the very first whether she has a working understanding of the exercise.

Extra notes:

- From now on, reinforce the training by using the dog's name and "Come" just prior to any activity that the dog especially enjoys. Make a list of things that your dog enjoys to help you remember. If, for example, your dog loves to ride in the car, always say the dog's name and "Come" before you take her for a drive.

- Different members of the family can take turns restraining and calling your dog, but at this level of training, the dog needs the visual stimulation of someone running away from her. Therefore, do not have her run back and forth between two people like a Ping-Pong ball.

Let your dog know that she can relax her focus. *Close and honor the practice.* Say, "Free!" with a big smile, and an animated tone in your voice.

If you are not communicating well during training: When you are not getting the expected results, stop, detach from the situation, and analyze everything. Decide what you need to change, get centered and refocused, and then try again.

SPECIFICS

If your dog is circling, getting distracted, or ignoring you, ask yourself these questions:

- Are you remembering to be proactive? As soon as you see her lose her focus, you need to immediately use a reprimand word like "Stop," "Leave it," or "Off!" Suppose, for example, that you called her to come, she started toward you, and then she found something wonderful to sniff instead. In this case, make your voice abrupt and very emphatic so she will understand your disapproval: *"Leave it!"*

- Did whoever was handling the line give the correction the moment he heard you give the reprimand?

- When you had your dog's attention again, did you immediately repeat your call with warmth and enthusiasm—"Taffy!

Come!"—and begin to praise her again, using your arms and body energy to welcome her in? This approach usually works. However, if you are having problems, try using a ball or a favorite toy instead of food as a motivator.

Puppies

This same exercise should be done with puppies who are at least eight weeks old, but you can start earlier in other ways. As soon as I start feeding solid food, I call "Puppy, come!" and allow the puppies to approach me. I praise them and put the food down so that they can eat. Therefore they associate "Come" with pleasant and rewarding experiences right from the beginning.

THE THIRD PRACTICE: WAIT

One brilliant fall afternoon I was walking with ten of my dogs up behind my house. It was the kind of day with lots of shadows; the sun was low in the sky, and there were dark, mottled patches under the trees. My dogs were romping around me, eagerly sniffing all kinds of intriguing smells, so that I felt a little like a mother hen with all of her chicks. This was just as it should be; I had taught my dogs not to go too far ahead of me, in order to avoid running into unpleasant surprises.

We came to a place where the dirt trail does a dip and then bends and rises to higher ground. As we came around the bend, there in the deep, black shadows, I saw what looked like an enormous rock—except that it moved!

I stopped abruptly; it was a huge porcupine! The moment I realized what it was, the dogs went on alert and headed up the track to check it out. I immediately called out, "Wait!" in my most authoritative voice, gave a piercing whistle to get their attention and then turned and ran as fast as I could go, wondering if one of my companions was going to go to the vet with a noseful of quills on that Sunday afternoon. But every dog stopped, turned, and followed me back down the trail.

This signal can also be used before crossing a road, at the door when there are visitors, on leaving the house, getting in or out of a car, or whenever you need your dog to stop. I use "Wait" when I am out backpacking. I especially do not want my dogs to venture too far ahead if we are in public areas. I don't care if they follow up this direction by sitting, standing, or lying down; I just want to be sure that they stop moving forward. It gives me a way to put some brakes on them.

"Wait" also helps in a subtle way to establish that you are the captain of the team and that people go through doors first, and not dogs. Dogs go when and if they are given permission, both for safety reasons, and because it makes sense to them in terms of pack behavior. In a pack, the higher-ranking dogs always go first; if any lower-ranking dog attempts to go ahead, he is immediately corrected.

For this reason, "Wait" is an easy direction to teach; dogs can quickly grasp the meaning if you are sending a lot of intentional energy through your eyes, body posture, and tone of voice, because the meaning is already there in dog language.

Do not confuse this directive with "Stay." "Wait" means "Stop moving." "Stay" means "Remain in one place until you are released and asked to do something different."

Goal: In the "Wait" exercise your goal will be to have your dog stop all forward motion in response to your signal.

Practice guidelines:

- Repeat this exercise as many times as it takes until your dog understands it.

- Practice in a variety of locations, especially whenever you go outside with your dog.

Things to check before you begin:

- Your dog should be wearing a 6-foot lead and an appropriate collar.

- Practice the hand signal: With the dog on your left, hold the leash in your right hand with a short loop of slack in it. Bend forward slightly, put your left hand in front of your left knee, swing it to your left like a pendulum, and stop it abruptly, palm open, in front of the dog's face. Visualize this signal also.

- To understand the difference between a clear signal and a vague one, do the following exercise so you can experience things from the dog's perspective. Move your hand quickly in front of your face and past it. You will see that this motion is distracting and vague. Now make a fist, and bring in front of your face as if you were closing a door; the moment your hand stops, spread your fingers wide open, so that there is an added emphasis in the gesture. You will see that this makes a powerful impression on your energy field. In the same way, you will create a force field in front of the dog that says "Stop!"

- You will be using your eyes and your posture and projecting extra energy from your solar plexus to keep your dog in position. To do this, put your attention on your solar plexus and imagine that you are sending out an energy force field to prevent your dog from moving forward.

Mental and emotional preparation: Get yourself centered and focused by taking a few deep breaths. Clarify your intent.

Open and honor the practice: Energize your symbol.

Technique, part one:

- Teach this exercise using a visual barrier like a doorway or a gateway, because it is easier for the dog to process your directions in terms of a boundary.

- Approach the barrier with the dog on lead by your side.

- While you are still a few paces away from the barrier, give the verbal cue and hand signal simultaneously. This timing will give the dog a chance to respond before you actually reach the threshold. Say "Wait" in a pleasant and emphatic tone of voice while simultaneously using the hand signal: sweep your open

"The Hand Signal for 'Wait' "

hand to your left and stop it abruptly in front of your dog's face as you halt just at the edge of the boundary. Use a very clear, concise gesture.

- If your dog moves forward, correct with the collar and leash while you emphatically repeat "Wait." Visualize your dog not moving forward. As soon as your dog stops, praise him and use your symbol.

- Repeat the exercise by turning your dog away from the boundary. Do not let him proceed through it. If you do, he might think you are only asking him to hesitate for a second before proceeding.

- Praise your dog and use your symbol when he stops all forward motion and you see that he comprehends what you are asking. This is the time to give a food reward if you are using one.

Technique, part two:

- When you have successfully completed part one, approach the boundary with your dog again.

- Say "Wait" pleasantly and emphatically. Now step across the barrier and immediately turn and face the dog so you are blocking his forward motion.

- If the dog begins to move forward, do *not* attempt to push him back with your hands. Instead, immediately lower and sharpen your tone of voice as you say "Wait!" Bring your hand up, with your palm facing the dog, like a traffic cop. Project an energy force field from your solar plexis to hold the dog back, and at the same time tighten your body so that you are very stiff and erect, and walk forward into your dog to make him back up. Project your intent

"Projecting Your Force Field in Wait"

by looking directly into his eyes. Imagine that you are holding him back with a barrier of energy coming from your solar plexus. When you see that your dog has settled, smile and praise him quietly.

- If your dog bolts past you, give a correction with the leash, and go back to the beginning of Technique, part two.

- If he remains where you directed him to wait, feel how pleased you are with his response, and send that emotion to your dog while you activate your symbol, smile, and praise him quietly and very sincerely. If you are using food rewards, be sure to give them while your dog is holding the Wait position. Remember to save verbal praise for responding to the cue only. Now return to him and take him back away from the barrier. Walk a short distance with your dog, turn around, approach the door again, and repeat the exercise.

- Once you are sure the dog understands your signal, move to his side again, say "Let's go," and proceed with him through the opening.

Practice guidelines for "Wait" with cars: Practice in a variety of locations, and especially whenever you approach an exterior door. Be sure that your dog is always on a leash at these times, whenever you are heading outside.

"Wait" before getting in or out of a car: It is especially important to practice this exercise with your dog while you two are getting in and out of your car. Sometimes you may want him to wait before he enters, while you deal with packages or an infant in a car seat, or the dog may have muddy feet, and you may want to clean him off first. This signal is even more important when your dog is leaving the car. Tragically, many dogs are killed every year because they bolt out into traffic when a car door is opened.

Technique:

- Walk your dog on a leash to the door of the car and tell him to wait while you open the door.

- If he tries to leap in, correct him with a stern "Wait!" and a pop on the leash. Practice this as often as needed until he responds correctly. Praise immediately and use your symbol as soon as your dog gives the correct response.

- When you are ready to have the dog enter the car, tell him "Get in." (I suggest that you use "Inside" only when you want him in your house.)

Waiting in the car while the door is open and you get out: This is a training exercise only! Never leave your dog alone in your car. The leash could get tangled, and he could jump over the seat and get hung up, or else he could chew up the leash.

- To practice "Wait" while your dog is in the car, attach the leash to his collar before you open the door. Say, "Wait!" and send him a powerful visualized message that you need him to remain inside while you open the door and get completely out.

- Once you are outside and the dog is still inside the car, hold the leash in your hand and move back and forth outside while the dog remains seated inside. If he jumps out, correct him and repeat the exercise. As soon as he gives you the behavior you are looking for, praise him quietly and with warmth and send your symbol.

- Once you are getting consistent responses from your dog, get out of the car with the leash in your hand and shut it in the car door so that the leash handle is outside.

- Go out of sight for a few moments so that the dog can't see you, but you can see him. (For safety reasons, it's important to keep your dog under observation at all times!) This will increase his excitement on your return, which will make the exercise a better test of your communication skills. Tell the dog "Wait," and use the hand signal, which you will make this time by bringing it up in front of the dog's face through the window. Take hold of the leash, and open the car door. Use your body and the leash to block the dog from jumping out. If he does get past you, you will have control of him and be able to correct him.

- Be sure that the amount of leash you give him is either short enough so he can't jump over the seat or long enough for him to get all the way over.

Waiting in a hatchback vehicle: Eventually you may need to experiment with variations on this exercise. This is a particularly important if you have a van or a car with a hatchback, because this kind of door creates a barrier when you lift it, making it impossible for you to catch your dog if he bolts out from underneath.

- You will need a leash at least 6 feet long. Leave a piece of it sticking out of the hatch after you close it. Go away out of sight for a few minutes, but make sure you can see your dog. When you return, take hold of the leash before you lift the hatch. If your dog jumps out, you will be able to give him a correction. Time this for the moment when you see that he is about to reach the end of the lead. Say "Wait!" very sternly to coincide with him being stopped abruptly. Then put him back in the car. When you are both calm and refocused, try the exercise again.

- Practice consistently until you can walk away and your dog will remain inside, even when you leave the door open.
- Give the cue, "Outside" when you want the dog to get out of the car

Wait at doors and at stairs: For the sake of safety and good manners, and to establish respect for you as the captain of the team, do not allow your dog to push past you when you walk through narrow spaces or up and down stairs. He should understand that you will go ahead of him whenever there is a door, gateway, or obstacle. Many people have been injured when their pets have knocked them over unexpectedly, particularly on stairways. You need to protect yourself by establishing clear boundaries in these situations.

Begin to teach your dog to wait at stairs after he is responding reliably to your cue. Start with just a few steps, and then increase the distance as your dog learns the application. Your goal will be to have him wait until you are off the stairs and give him a signal to join you. As he comes toward you, he should move at a moderate, controlled speed.

Things to check before you begin: You will need a leash or long line that is equal to the length of the stairway, and you must remember to visualize the whole exercise from beginning to end, ahead of time.

Technique: It is easier and safer to teach this behavior while you head upstairs rather than down.

- Bring your dog on a leash to the bottom of the steps. Have the rings of the collar under the dog's chin.
- Give the hand signal for "Wait." Move past your dog and head up the stairs next to the handrail or wall. In this way, if the dog tries to shoot past you, he will not be able to wrap the leash behind you or tangle you in it, because he will not be able to get past you on that side.
- Climb a few steps, praise him if he waits, and immediately return to him. Give more praise and then a food reward if you are using one.
- If your dog starts to move up the steps, immediately turn around, hold your hand out in front of you like a traffic cop, and

repeat "Wait!" Project energy from your solar plexus to push him back as you walk back down the steps. Refocus, and start the exercise again.

- If your dog shoots past you, lead him back down, and start again. Do not give a correction with the leash while working on the stairs, as your dog could fall and be injured.

- Repeat the exercise in small increments, adding only one or two steps at a time. Do not try to cover the whole flight of stairs in one session.

- When you are ready to release him, do a half-turn as if to move on, and say, "Let's go." Keep your voice very calm and low, so that your dog does not scramble up the stairs. Say "Easy" or "Slooooww" to help him understand that you want him to move slowly.

- Wait at the top for him to join you, so that he does not think he has to hurry to catch up with you. Praise again before releasing him.

Extra notes:

- Whenever you are practicing with an opening that leads into an unsafe situation, such as a car door or the front door of a house, *always* be sure that your dog has his leash on before you open the door.

- Your dog can be standing, sitting, or lying down while he is waiting, as long as he is not moving forward.

- Once your dog understands this exercise, continue to practice in the house when he is off leash, practicing "Wait" frequently whenever you go through a door or up and down a hallway as well as on stairs.

Close and honor the practice.

If you are not communicating well during training: If you are not getting the expected results, stop, detach from the situation, and analyze everything. Decide what you need to change, get centered and refocused, and then try again.

Points to review: Were you using an inappropriate or ineffective tone of voice? Were you praising or patting your dog so enthusiastically that it was overstimulating, so that your dog jumped out of position? Were you sure not to overpractice and bore your dog?

SPECIFICS

If your dog still tries to approach, immediately lower and strengthen the tone of your voice. Use the hand gesture, strong eye contact, and walk forward, right into him to send him back, saying, *"Wait!"* Now focus on your solar plexus and feel that there is a force field of energy coming out from it to a distance of two to three feet. Fill that space with your energy; project a thick wall of resistance to keep the dog back. Keep your body posture erect and call up your energy; do not bend over and push the dog back. That movement will collapse your force field!

Puppies

Remember that puppies have a short attention span and will be easily distracted. Do short practices, but repeat them several times a day. As the puppy grows, you can extend the length of time he waits. Don't feel that you have to correct him harshly; pay attention to his struggles to understand within the limits of his age.

Depending on the size and age of your puppy, it may not be a good idea to practice "Wait" on stairs until he is older.

Remember also that small puppies may not be able to safely jump in and out of cars. Use common sense in all cases. Lift or carry your puppy until he is older.

10

MUTUAL RESPECT: SIT, DOWN, AND STAY

In this chapter, you will be learning how to teach your dog to do the basic behaviors: Sit, Down, and Stay. These behaviors are good manners. Sit is an easy exercise for all dogs to learn. One of the nicest things about the Sit is that it quickly becomes the dog's way of saying "please." He learns to use it, for example, when he wants attention or when he wants to go out. This becomes an orderly, respectful way to ask you to focus on him, instead of jumping up on you or scratching at the door. It is a moment of communication that has mutual recognition, trust, and affection.

It is quite common to encounter people in my classes who struggle with the whole issue of establishing respect. Jerry was an example. He came to class with an adorable mop of a terrier named Sugar who was both the apple of his eye and the bane of his existence, a spoiled brat so needy of his attention that she never gave him a moment's peace. Jerry was an older man, who lived alone and worked long hours five days a week as the manager of a hardware store. When he got home, he and Sugar always went for a long walk or played in the backyard, and then, when they came back to the house, Jerry loved to put his feet up and read the paper while his supper warmed on the stove.

Sugar, however, still had many miles of running in her, and she tore around the house, nipped at Jerry's ankles, and grabbed and shredded the edges of his paper. When he got a box of treats and sought to buy her off, she jumped all over him and bit his fingertips in her eagerness to get the food. When he shut her in the kitchen, she yipped and howled and scratched frantically on the linoleum under the door.

This was not a case of mutual respect; Jerry was totally at Sugar's mercy. And he couldn't be angry at her because whenever he looked at her black-button eyes peeking innocently out from under a shaggy fringe of hair, his heart would melt. His brain was constantly making excuses for her because his heart was so invested in keeping her love and affection. He kept telling himself that she didn't know any better and that it wasn't her fault that she loved him so desperately. After all, she had been alone all day, and she craved his attention.

Jerry did a fair job of teaching Sugar to walk on a lead, and he had no trouble getting her to come when he called. Getting her to wait was a different matter, because that called for him to be very definite with her when she wanted to follow him through the door. It was hard for him to create a force field of his own, because he was constantly melting into hers. Training felt like punishment to him, and when I took her leash and showed him how to correct her, I had to resist laughing to see the look of utter abandonment she gave him from under her long lashes.

Many dog owners have difficulty with the three exercises in this chapter because, like Wait, the teaching involves emotional discipline and follow-through. You have to maintain a calm, loving focus, no matter how your dog reacts.

Remember, some dogs resist training by trying to change the subject. They jump on you, pull away, lick your hands, mouth the leash, roll on their backs and ask for belly rubs, or yelp and carry on miserably whenever you give a correction. Other dogs try intimidation or simply gaze off into space and wait for you to give up.

Many times, this behavior is repeated because it has worked for the dog in the past. At other times your dog may be simply trying to avoid the issue, or he may be confused and anxious because he doesn't know what you want. This is why it is so important for you to know your dog and be clear about what you are going to do before you ask the dog to do it.

Jerry did learn how to stick up for himself. When he learned to send Sugar positive energy, he began to connect with the power of his heart. Because this made him feel less lonely, he gained the courage to set limits and stop spoiling his dog. He now reads his paper in peace while Sugar happily plays with her toys or chews a bone.

Jerry began by practicing the Sit exercise with Sugar.

THE FOURTH PRACTICE: SIT

Goal: Your goal will be to have your dog sit immediately in response to your cues.

Practice guidelines:

- Practice on and off at random throughout the day. Start with up to 30-second sessions with dogs four months of age and older. Over the next several days, work up to 2 or 3 minutes.

- Begin with 30-second practices for puppies eight to sixteen weeks of age, and gradually increase the time to a minute or whatever seems reasonable, depending on the dog's personality and age. Build on small successes rather than pushing your dog too fast.

- Practice in a variety of locations.

Things to check before you begin:

- Be sure your dog's training equipment is on correctly.

- If you are using food rewards or lures, have a few dozen pea-sized pieces handy in an easy-access pocket. Have some rewards for yourself also!

- Choose a quiet place to work without distractions.

Mental and emotional preparation:

- Get yourself quiet and focused by taking a few deep breaths.

- Clarify your intent.

Open and honor the practice: Before you begin to work, take a moment to appreciate your dog and align your energies. Energize your symbol to open your practice session with positive, connected energy to your dog.

Technique #1—pressure point method:

- Position the collar high on the dog's neck with the rings on top. Hold the

" 'Sit' Using Pressure Point"

leash above the dog's head, just above the collar ring, with the excess leash folded in your hand so it is not dangling down. You can slip your finger lightly under the collar for added control. Your hold on the leash is to prevent the dog from moving forward or spinning around. There is *no* pressure on the collar.

- To find the pressure point: with the hand that is not holding the leash, start at top of your dog's hips and run your thumb and a finger lightly down in a V toward the base of the tail. Midway between, there is a slight indentation. If you put gentle pressure forward and down at this point, the dog's knees will start to bend. This causes the muscles to give, just as if someone came up behind you and pressed behind both of your knees at the same time.

- Now gently tip the dog's weight slightly backward off his front quarters onto the hindquarters by putting a little backward pressure on the collar.

- Say the dog's name to get his attention and "Sit," just before activating the pressure point.

- When he responds and begins to sit, immediately release all pressure on his collar and hips and allow him to finish the move on his own.

- As soon as your dog moves into the correct position, use your symbol, smile, and praise him quietly and very sincerely. If you are patting your dog, use a calm, soothing, caress. Continue to give positive reinforcement off and on as long as your dog is sitting.

- If you are using a food reward, be sure to give it to the dog while he is still sitting, not after he has been released. Give yourself one as well!

- Keep your dog in the sit position with more praise after the food reward.

- After a short time, use your release word.

- After your dog is released, your praise and focused attention ends.

Technique #2—food lure method:

- Hold one morsel of food under your dog's chin, eliminating his tendency to jump up for it, bring it up and hold it right in front of his nose so he gets a good sniff.

- Remember to visualize and continue upward, bring the treat slowly along the top of his nose and right up over his head, shoulders, and back toward his tail. The dog will attempt to follow with his nose, which will put his weight on his hindquarters and cause him to sit down.

- A split second before the dog's rear comes in contact with the ground, say, "Sit."

- As soon as the dog is sitting, energize your symbol, smile, and praise him quietly and very sincerely. If you are petting your dog, use a calm, soothing, caress. Continue to give positive reinforcement off and on, as long as the dog is sitting.

- After a short time, use your release signal; your praise and focused attention stops.

Technique—sit with the hand signal: Once your dog understands what "Sit" means, you can teach him to respond to your hand signal:

- Stand in front of your dog, with one hand holding the leash and the other holding a treat between your thumb and the palm of your hand, down by your side.

- Stand very erect, bend your arm—the one holding the treat—slightly at the elbow, and gesture straight up in the air and just slightly toward the dog with a crisp, sweeping motion. Say your dog's name and "Sit."

- Your dog's head will tilt back to look up at you and the treat, and this will help him to attain a sitting position.

- Praise him if he follows your signal, and give him the treat. If he doesn't respond, repeat the sequence. You may need to go more slowly so that your dog can really follow the lure. When you slow the motion, fill the intent of your hand with energy and presence.

- Since by this time your dog should thoroughly understand the Sit signal, do not give him a treat if he does not respond.

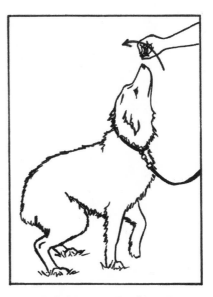

" 'Sit' Using a Food Lure"

- When your dog is responding every time you use the verbal and hand signals alone, you no longer need the treat in your hand. Keep the treat in your pocket, and give the verbal and hand signal together. If your dog responds immediately, reach into your pocket and give him the treat. If he does not respond (and you are sure that he understands what you are looking for), correct him immediately with a quick *upward* pop on the lead, and praise him as soon as he complies, but do not give him the treat.

- Gradually move to giving the food reward at random. In the future, give treats only for your dog's best performances.

Extra notes:

- Once your dog learns to respond to your signal, keep him sitting long enough and for random time periods so that he doesn't get the idea that a sit is a curtsy before a treat.

- Be sure to praise your dog *while* he is doing what you wanted him to do and not after you have released him.

"The Hand Correction for Gaining Distance with 'Sit' "

- As you practice over the next several days, begin to give food rewards randomly to teach your dog that the longer he sits, the greater the chance he will receive another treat. Eventually you should save your food rewards for your dog's best responses.

Gaining distance with Sit: Stand facing your dog with him in the sit position.

- Make sure the collar is up high on the dog's neck, positioned so that the leash is directly under his chin.
- Hold the leash in one hand.
- Drape the leash over the other hand.
- Step slowly back to a distance of 3 feet and see if your dog will remain in place.
- If he does not, emphatically repeat "Sit" and quickly separate your hands straight up and down on the leash. This will cause the leash to make a wave motion, which will tap him under the chin and give a correction. You may need to step quickly forward at the same time, depending on the distance. Use your energy field to hold him in place and keep him from coming to you.
- Be proactive—watch your dog's body language to catch the moment when he *thinks* of changing position so you can interrupt the thought and redirect him toward the goal.
- Gradually increase the distance to 6 feet as your dog gains confidence.

Close and honor the practice: Take a few minutes to just be together and honor all of the ways that you and your dog have improved in understanding and communication.

If you are not communicating well during training: If you are not getting the expected results, stop, detach from the situation, and analyze everything. Decide what you need to change, get centered and refocused, and then try again.

SPECIFICS

- If your dog gets up before you release him, instantly repeat the exercise and keep repeating it until he holds the Sit. You will have to use your knowledge of your dog to see if he is getting overtired. He may be too young for the length of time you are practicing, or he may be testing and defiant. You may need to take a break for a few minutes and just walk your dog around to help you both refocus.

- If your dog lies down instead of sitting, bring him back into position with a collar correction the *instant* you see him begin to consider the move. Using your body space, walk into him, which will crowd him back into sitting. Or put the food lure on his nose and then over his head to cause him to rise into position again. If he is faster than you are, you may have to walk a few steps to get the dog standing again, and begin the exercise again.

- If your dog is hyperactive and cannot focus, go back to the attention and communication exercise. Maybe you need to be more assertive. Perhaps your signals are too fast for the dog to follow. Detach and analyze.

THE FIFTH PRACTICE: DOWN

Teaching your dog the cue to lie down is not hard, but it can be an exercise in patience. Learning how to communicate this exercise will offer you new challenges in working with your body energy and visualization. Do not rush the training or allow yourself to lose your focus. Stay clear and centered in your intent. The following story about one person in my class is a good example of how doubts turned to triumph. It may give you inspiration.

A woman in her mid-thirties named Sandra came to training class with Robby, a squirmy young golden retriever in his adolescent rebellion stage. He was a replacement for her first dog, who had died a year before. Although she adored Robby, he was a very excitable dog with a mind of his own, and it took a lot of focused attention to get him to listen.

Robby also had developed an avoidance behavior: as soon as Sandra would ask for his attention by popping the leash, he would either whimper or yelp as if she had knifed him. He was a marvelous actor who had learned his lines from Sandra the first time they had gone home after a training class and practiced

Puppies

Remember that puppies have a short attention span. Keep your sessions brief, and practice often.

together. When she popped the leash, Robby had yelped with surprise, and Sandra had immediately fallen all over him with apologies and caresses. She thought she had hurt him, had destroyed his trust, and made him afraid. She ended the lesson, not knowing that she had taught him a new trick.

When Sandra and Robby returned to class the next session, it was time to learn how to signal a dog to lie down. Sandra held the leash correctly, gave the hand signal perfectly, but when she gave the verbal signal, her voice was very tentative, as if asking whether Robby was willing. He was not. When she applied downward pressure on the leash, he whimpered constantly while bracing his four legs as if she was trying to drag him off a cliff.

"Just hold and wait him out," I said, showing Sandra again how to keep a mild tension on the leash under his neck until Robby got tired of being braced in that fashion and decided to make himself more comfortable.

The minutes ticked by, and Robby whimpered away, digging in his toenails. Sandra began to weep, her feelings a mixture of frustration, loss of conviction, and fear that she was betraying her beloved pet by being so "mean" to him.

I turned to the class: "Okay, everyone," I said. "These two need some support. I want everyone to focus on Robby and see him lying down calmly and happily. Send him a mental message of encouragement; tell him you know he can do it."

I turned back to Sandra: "And, Sandra, start sending Robby love instead of fear."

The training room became utterly silent and electric with intent. Sandra pulled herself together and returned to holding the leash in the correct position. It took another minute, but then Robby visibly relaxed. As soon as I saw that he had the right idea, I began quietly murmuring encouragement: "That's right. You've got it. You can do it. That's a good dog."

Robby lay down, heaved a big sigh, and I began to praise him: "Good job. That's it. I'm proud of you. I knew you could do it." Sandra buried her face on the nape of his neck and then raised her head to smile at everyone and said, "Okay, one more time!"

It still took some doing the second time around, but by the third time, Robby was immediately going down himself in response to her verbal cue and hand signal. By the next class, it was a piece of cake, Robby had stopped whining and started following Sandra's every move with an eager look as if to say, "Well, that wasn't so bad after all. What's next?"

Goal: Your goal in this exercise is to have your dog calmly and happily lie down in an immediate response to your signal.

Practice guidelines: Practice for a few minutes at a time several times a day. Then gradually increase your time to 4 or 5 minutes for dogs four months of age and over. Practice only 1 or 2 minutes with puppies eight to sixteen weeks of age.

Practice in a variety of locations, and remember that frequent short practices will be more effective than one long session.

Things to check before you begin:

- Be sure the training equipment is on correctly.
- If you are using food rewards or lures, have about a dozen pea-size pieces handy in an easy-access pocket.
- Choose a quiet place to work without distractions.
- Practice your hand signal and body positions for the Down: hold your hand out straight, palm facing down. You will move it from in front of the dog's face, past his field of vision, and down to the ground. At the same time, you will go from standing into a crouch or down on one knee.

Mental and emotional preparation:

- Get yourself quiet and focused by taking a few deep breaths. Clarify your intent.

Open and honor the practice: Energize your symbol.
Technique #1—collar pressure method:

- Put your dog in the Sit position. This makes him stationary with half of him already down. Once he understands the exercise, he can practice it from a standing position.
- As soon as the dog is sitting and you have praised him for doing as you asked, focus your intent on your goal and visualize him already lying down.
- Position the collar high up on the neck, right behind the back of the skull, with the rings underneath the dog's chin. This is important because it will help you encourage and draw your dog's head down toward the ground. If the collar is sitting low on the neck, the dog can just brace his shoulders and strongly resist going down, which will make the exercise more difficult than it should be for both of you.
- Fold the leash, and hold it in one hand, close to the collar under the dog's chin.
- Say the dog's name to get his attention.

- At the same time, give both the verbal cue and the hand signal for Down.

- Initiate a mild vertical pressure *straight* downward on the leash, while bending and going down on one knee to help your dog understand that you want him to lower his body to the ground. Be sure the collar pressure is straight downwards; if you pull toward you, the dog will want to stand up to catch his balance.

- Take care not to use too much force. That could cause an adverse response of fear or determined resistance. This exercise is *not* about force; it is about gentle pressure and patience. You are making the dog mildly uncomfortable, and waiting until he figures out what will feel better. Put your energy into your intent and wait him out with a feeling of calm, grounded energy. Remember, you have the power of the universe on your side— it's called gravity!

- Tap the ground with your fingers to let your dog know the answer is down there. If he looks down, acknowledge and encourage the thought. If you feel him relax away from the collar pressure, gently let up on it. If he braces again, gently increase the pressure to help him discover that, if he goes with the pressure, it stops and if he resists, it resumes. You are coaxing, not forcing, the dog down.

- Once you have given the verbal cue and begun to apply the pressure, do not keep repeating "Down"—especially not in a

" 'Down' with the Hand Signal and Collar Pressure"

pleading or angry voice. Just let your dog figure out that it is up to him how long he chooses to make himself uncomfortable. It is pointless to keep saying "Down" while he is still sitting. Hold the *visualization* of your dog already lying down and send calm, positive energy. Repeat "Down" only at the moment when he actually does it, and then praise him immediately.

- *Stop the collar pressure immediately* as soon as the dog goes down, and repeat the word "Down" at the moment your dog achieves the position. Timing is important: be sure to give the verbal cue just as the dog moves into position.

- As soon as your dog is lying down, send your symbol. smile, and praise him quietly and very sincerely. If you are petting your dog, be sure to use a calm, soothing caress. If you are using a food reward, be sure to give it to the dog while he is still lying down, not after he has been released. Receiving the food is a reward in itself, so save verbal praise when your dog responds to the signal rather than when he eats the food.

- Continue to give positive reinforcement off and on as long as the dog is lying down. Keep your praise sincere, encouraging, calm, and steady while your dog maintains his position. Be sure to praise him while he is doing what you wanted him to do and not after you have released him.

- After a short time, use your release signal.

Extra notes: Vary the length of time your dog is lying down and vary the frequency of food rewards.

Technique #2—food lure method:

- Put your dog in a sitting position.

- Hold the food lure just in front of the dog's nose so that he gets a good sniff.

- Remembering to visualize, slowly bring the food straight down under the dog's chin, down his chest, and all the way to the ground between his legs. Then move it *very slowly* forward along the ground so that the dog follows it with his nose. This will cause him to want to lie down so that he can better reach the food.

- Just as he is about to attain the full down position, put the word on the action: "Down."

- As soon as your dog moves into the correct position, send your symbol, smile, and praise him quietly and very sincerely. If you are petting your dog, use a calm, soothing caress. Be sure to give any food rewards to the dog while he is still down, not after he has been released.

" 'Down' with a Food Lure"

- Continue to give positive reinforcement and food rewards off and on as long as the dog remains in position.

- When you are teaching this behavior, give the food reward as soon as the dog does what you are asking for. Then begin to wait a little longer before you give the food reward. This will get him to hold his position longer.

- After a short time, use your release signal; your praise and focused attention stops.

Extra notes:

- Vary the sequence of behavior cues so that your dog doesn't start to think that "Sit" is always followed by "Down." This is not a two-part exercise; they are separate behaviors. Also, do not ask your dog to "Sit down," because your dog's understanding is very literal and you will confuse him. Do "Sit" and then "Free," several times during the course of the practice to establish that Sit is a distinct behavior.

- As soon as your dog understands "Down" from the Sit position, you may begin practicing it from a standing position, using the same techniques.

- As the exercise proceeds, wait longer before giving the dog treats, and vary the frequency of food rewards.

Close and honor the practice.

If you are not communicating well during training: If you are not getting the expected results, stop, detach from the situation, and analyze everything. Decide what you need to change, refocus, and then try again.

SPECIFICS

If your dog starts to stand up when you have him in a sitting position and are asking that he go down, it's his only way of asking, "Does this work?" If you let up on the collar pressure in response to his action, your dog thinks "Yes, standing up works." He also thinks that when you say "Down," you really mean "Stand up," and he becomes thoroughly confused.

Instead, do not increase or decrease the collar pressure, but reach over with your hand, activate the pressure point for sit, and clearly visualize that you are asking for the Down. Your response to your dog's question is "Nope, wrong answer. Try again." Be patient and do not let up until he gets the message.

It is all right if the dog lies down on his side, as long as he is not thrashing around and wanting to play. If he is getting excited, stop interacting with him. Don't pat or touch him until he calms down and lies there quietly or else rolls back onto his stomach again. When he is calm, resume praising.

If your dog jumps up before the release cue, repeat the exercise until he waits for the cue.

THE SIXTH PRACTICE: STAY

People tend to oversimplify this exercise and push for too much too fast. They don't look at it from the dog's point of view. When this happens, the bonds of communication and trust can quickly break down.

When you tell your dog to stay and then walk away, it triggers a certain amount of stress and anxiety that you are going to leave him. His natural reaction is to follow you. If you turn around and reprimand him, especially if he doesn't clearly understand what you want, he thinks that he is being punished for trying to be with you.

At this stage of training it is not advisable to put "Stay" and "Come" together. Be very careful not to push for too much too fast. You are building a foundation and you need a solid one. You want to build confidence in your dog and have him totally trust you.

Practice guidelines: This exercise will be taught in three progressive levels so it will be easy for your dog to understand what is expected of him. Since there are several steps to the exercise, I highly recommend that you read it aloud into a tape recorder, so that you can talk yourself through the exercise. I also suggest that you practice the various steps alone several times using only a stuffed toy, or a pillow with a rope tied around it. You can also practice with a person who is substituting for the dog. This will help the dog considerably later, because you will be more confident and smoother in your actions and directions. You will be smoothly and gradually moving away from the dog instead of just walking away from him in a straight line and you will be returning to him so quickly that he won't have a chance to become anxious. Correctly positioning your body minimizes any opportunity for the dog to break from position. By frequently praising him because he is successful, he will associate not moving with being praised.

The "Stay" exercise should be practiced in a variety of locations starting with few or no distractions and then gradually increasing the distraction level.

- When you begin this exercise, the dog should be sitting on your left. (If you would prefer to have him on your right simply reverse the directions.)

- When teaching the "Stay" exercise it is important to watch the dog's eyes and ears. If you see him think about breaking from position, you can quickly interrupt the thought *before* he has an opportunity to move out of position.

This exercise will be taught utilizing three different body positions:

1. Moving in front of the dog and then back to your starting point.
2. Moving half-way around the dog and then back to the starting point.
3. Moving all the way around the dog and then returning to the starting point.

[Start from here to read the exercise into a tape deck.]

- Before you start, take a moment to get centered and focused. Take a couple of deep breaths and relax your body. Visualize bringing energy up from the earth through the bottom of your feet, letting it travel up your legs into your abdomen, up into your chest and send it out through your left arm, down the leash, down the dog's spine and back into the earth. You have now created an arc of grounded energy to help stabilize the dog.

- Hold in your mind an image of your dog sitting and staying exactly where you ask him to and being very happy and confident about doing so.

LEVEL 1

- Your dog should be sitting on your left, facing the same direction that you are.

- Position the collar high on his neck, near the base of the skull, so that the leash ring attachment is on top of the neck.

- Hold the entire leash in your left hand, at a comfortable level (ideally it should be aligned with the level of your hip). The excess leash is folded in your left hand, so there is nothing dangling down that will distract or annoy the dog.

- Raise your left hand vertically so that the leash is in a vertical position. You want just enough contact to be able to feel the dog's body through the leash, but you don't want to exert pressure. You want to be able to feel the slightest movement through the leash, but you don't want it to be so tight that he is uncomfortable in any way.

- If at any point during this exercise, the dog starts to get up or lie down, immediately correct him with an upward pop on the leash. *This is the reason for the contact on the leash, so you can tell when the dog is going to move.*

Contact is maintained on the leash *throughout* Level 1 of this exercise. You are using your energy and the leash to stabilize the dog.

- Bring your right hand in front of and toward the dog's face, as if you were closing a gate or door (bend over if you have a small dog to be sure the hand signal happens in front of their face, not over their head).

- As your hand stops in front of the dog's face, extend your fingers stiffly while simultaneously saying "STAY." Be sure to give the verbal and hand signals simultaneously, before you move from the dog's side.

Body Position One: From the starting position, step forward with your right foot and swing immediately in front of the dog (about 6 inches from the dog's body) and then immediately swing back to the starting position.

- Activate your symbol.
- Smile at the dog to show your approval.

- Praise quietly and sincerely for a moment.
- It's best to refrain from touching the dog when you are praising. This is often too much stimuli. It tends to distract or excite the dog, causing him to move from position and lose his concentration. It also causes you to break the contact on the leash.
- Simultaneously repeat the verbal and hand signal to "Stay" before you move.
- Immediately proceed to Body Position Two.

Body Position Two: From the starting position, move in an arc, maintaining a distance of about 6 inches from the dog's body, go half-way around the dog and immediately return to the starting position. Be sure to keep your body upright and walk normally.

- Activate your symbol.
- Smile at the dog to show your approval.
- Praise quietly and sincerely for a moment.
- Simultaneously repeat the verbal and hand signal to "Stay" before you move.
- Immediately proceed to Body Position Three.

Body Position Three: From the starting position, walk an entire circle around the dog, maintaining a distance of about 6 inches from the dog's body. Return to the starting position. Remember to keep your body upright and walk normally and smoothly, being very careful not to step on the dog's tail as you move behind him.

- Activate your symbol.
- Smile at the dog to show your approval.
- Praise quietly and sincerely for a moment.
- Gently relax all contact on the leash.
- At this point, it is okay to gently touch the dog while praising him.
- If your dog remains stationary through all three body positions, give him a food reward while he is still honoring the Sit/Stay position and before you release him.
- Be sure to take several moments at this stage to praise your dog and honor his efforts to understand and comply with what you are asking.

- Using your release command, allow him to move out of that position.
- This completes Level 1 of the "Stay" exercise.
- Repeat Level 1 for 1–2 days so that you are sure your dog understands what you are asking him to do and has been praised many, many times for remaining in the "Sit/Stay" position.

Note:

- If the dog breaks from the "Sit/Stay" position at any point during the exercise, correct him immediately by using a quick upward pop on the leash as you repeat "Sit/Stay." If necessary, go back and start the exercise over again.
- Wait until the dog is successfully holding his position throughout the entire exercise before using a food reward.
- It is also important to get in the habit of sincerely praising the dog before you release him. If you release the dog as soon as you have given him the food reward or as soon as you return to the starting position, he will quickly take this as a cue that the exercise is over and that he should not wait for your release signal.

Level 2

- Your dog should be sitting on your left, facing the same direction that you are.
- Position the collar so that the leash is hanging directly under the dog's chin.
- Hold the leash in your left hand at half its length, creating a 3-foot loop of slack.
- Simultaneously give the verbal and hand signal to "Stay" before you move.
- Immediately position your hands on the leash the same way you were holding it as in the correction for "Sit." (Refer to Illustration on page 196.) This enables you to immediately interrupt an incorrect response from the dog. As you make the correction, you need to simultaneously repeat "Sit/Stay," so the dog understands why he is receiving the correction.

Body Position One: From the starting position, walk forward approximately three feet, being very careful not to pull on the leash, then immediately turn and face the dog and return to the starting position.

- Activate your symbol.
- Smile at your dog to show your approval.
- Praise him quietly and sincerely for a moment.
- It's best to refrain from touching your dog when you are praising him. This is too much stimuli. It tends to distract or excite your dog, causing him to move from position and lose his concentration. It also causes you to break the contact on the leash.
- Proceed, then do something before the next thing.
- Immediately position your hands on the leash, as in the correction for "Sit."

Body Position Two: From the starting position, walk to the opposite side of the dog, maintaining a three-foot distance from him. Immediately return to the starting position. Keep your body upright and walk normally. Do not stop or get stuck anywhere. Strive to maintain a smooth and fluid rhythm.

- Activate your symbol.
- Smile at your dog to show your approval.
- Praise him quietly and sincerely for a moment.
- Immediately proceed to Body Position Three.
- Simultaneously repeat the verbal and hand signal for "Stay" before you proceed.
- Immediately position your hands on the leash as in the correction for "Sit."

Body Position Three: From the starting position, walk around the dog, being very sure that the leash stays in front of the dog's face as you move behind him and return to the starting position. Remember to keep your body upright and walk normally and smoothly, being very careful not to step on the dog's tail as you walk behind him.

- Activate your symbol.
- Smile at your dog to show your approval.
- Praise him quietly and sincerely for a moment.

- Gently relax all contact on the leash.

- At this point it is okay to gently touch your dog while praising him.

- If your dog remains stationary through all three body positions, give him a food reward, while he is still honoring the "Sit/Stay" position and before you release him.

- Be sure to take several moments at this stage to praise your dog and honor his effort to understand and comply with what you are asking.

- Using your release command, allow him to move out of that position.

- This completes Level 2 of the Stay Exercise.

- Repeat Level 2 for 1–2 days so you are sure your dog understands what you are asking him to do. Praise him many, many times when he remains in the "Sit/Stay" position.

Note:

- If the dog breaks from this position at any point during the exercise, quickly make a correction with your leash as you repeat "Sit/Stay." Immediately move toward the dog to prevent him from coming to you. If necessary, reposition the dog and repeat that part of the exercise again.

- Do not use a food reward until the dog is successfully holding his position throughout the entire exercise.

- It is important to get in the habit of sincerely praising the dog before you release him. If you release him as soon as you have given him the food reward, or as soon as you return to the starting position, he will quickly take this as a cue that the exercise is over and he will not wait for your release signal.

LEVEL 3

- Your dog should be sitting on your left, facing the same direction that you are.

- Position the collar, so that the leash is hanging directly under the dog's chin.

- Hold the end of the leash in your left hand, creating a six-foot loop of slack in the leash.

- Simultaneously give the verbal and hand signal to "Stay" before you move.

- Immediately position your hands on the leash the same way you were holding it to make the correction for "Sit." (Refer to Illustration on page 196.) This enables you to immediately interrupt an incorrect response from the dog. As you make the correction, you need to simultaneously repeat "Sit/Stay," so the dog understands why he is receiving the correction.

Body Position One: From the starting position, walk forward approximately six feet, being very careful not to pull on the leash, then immediately turn and face the dog and return to the starting position.

- Activate your symbol.

- Smile at your dog to show your approval.

- Praise him quietly and sincerely for a moment.

- It's best to refrain from touching the dog when you are praising him. This tends to distract or excite the dog, causing him to move from position and lose his concentration. It also causes you to break the contact on the leash.

- Simultaneously repeat the verbal and hand signal to "Stay" before you move.

- Immediately proceed to Body Position Two.

- Position your hands on the leash the same way you were holding it to make the correction for "Sit."

Body Position Two: From the starting position, walk to the opposite side of the dog, maintaining a 6-foot distance from him. Immediately turn and return to the starting position. Keep your body upright and walk normally. Do not stop or get stuck anywhere. Strive to maintain a smooth and fluid rhythm.

- Activate your symbol.

- Smile at the dog to show your approval.

- Praise him quietly and sincerely for a moment.

- Simultaneously repeat the verbal and hand signal for "Stay" before you move.

- Immediately proceed to Body Position Three.

- Immediately position your hands on the leash as in the correction for "Sit."

Body Position Three: From the starting position, walk around your dog, being very sure that the leash stays in front of the dog's face as you move behind him and return to the starting position. Remember to keep your body upright and walk normally and smoothly, being very careful not to step on the dog's tail as you go behind him.

- Activate your symbol.
- Smile at the dog to show your approval.
- Praise him quietly and sincerely for a moment.
- Gently relax all contact on the leash.
- At this point it is okay to gently touch your dog while praising him.
- If he remains stationary through all three body positions, give him a food reward, while he is still honoring the "Sit/Stay" position and before you release him.
- Be sure to take several moments at this stage to praise your dog and honor his efforts to understand and comply with what you are asking.
- Use your release command.
- This completes Level 3 of the "Stay" exercise.
- Repeat Level 3 for 1–2 days so you are sure your dog understands what you are asking him to do. Praise him repeatedly when he remains in the "Sit/Stay" position.

Note:

- If your dog breaks from position at any point during the exercise, correct him immediately with your leash as you repeat "Sit/Stay." Quickly move toward your dog to prevent him from coming to you. If necessary, reposition your dog and repeat that part of the exercise.
- Do not use a food reward until the dog is successfully holding his position throughout the entire exercise.
- It is important to get in the habit of sincerely praising the dog before you release him. If you release the dog as soon as you have given him the food reward or as soon as you return to the

starting position, he will take this as a cue that the exercise is over and will not wait for your release signal.

"Holding the Leash Vertical with 'Stay' "

- When the dog is consistently maintaining the "Sit/Stay" position you can then ask for the "Down/Stay" position.

  Begin the "Down/Stay" exercise with Level 2. Use the same collar and body positions as you did for "Sit/Stay." The only difference will be if the dog gets up from the "Down" position you will need to use your foot on the lead to make the correction.

- Once the dog is holding the "Sit/Stay" and "Down/Stay" positions consistently, you can begin to introduce a variety of distractions to the exercise. See the following chapter for ways to introduce distractions.

- You can gradually increase the distance for both the "Sit/Stay" and the "Down/Stay" with the use of a 30-foot-long line. Replace the 6-foot leash with the long line using the same steps in Level 3. Progress at 2-foot increments. Don't try for too much too soon. Never work on the amount of time you are asking the dog to hold the position while increasing the distance at the same time. Focus on one or the other.

11

OUT IN THE WORLD: HEEL AND WORKING WITH DISTRACTIONS

If your dog is to be a full-fledged member of your family, you will want her to accompany you whenever and wherever possible. Dogs hate to be left behind, and they waste no time letting you know how abandoned they feel if you head out without them. If your dog has learned the basic lessons of communication, you should be proud and happy to take her with you at every opportunity, because her manners will make her good company.

There is yet one more behavior—a graceful way to be out in the world together—that is very useful for the two of you to learn.

THE SEVENTH PRACTICE: HEEL

Heeling is a precise way of walking on a lead without pulling. I use it whenever I'm going to be in a busy area, to keep my dog safe and to keep her from interfering with passersby. Heeling is place-specific; you want your dog's neck and shoulder to be even with your leg at all times. Although it is traditional to have a dog heel on the left (a requirement in obedience competitions), I leave it up to the individual to decide which side will work best.

If for any reason you want your dog always to heel on your right side, you will need to change the training collar, or it will not release. You accomplish this by making sure that the collar is in the shape of the letter Q when you're facing the dog, before you put it on. Before you proceed, test the collar to make sure it releases.

Goal: Your goal for this exercise will be to have your dog walking on a loose lead at your side, with her neck and shoulders even with your leg. This will allow her to move in synchrony with you at all times, quickening her pace when you turn right, and easily dropping back to allow you to go around her when you turn left. She will sit automatically when you stop, unless she has a problem like hip dysplasia or belongs to a breed that cannot sit comfortably. In these cases, the dog can simply stand quietly in place.

A *preliminary exercise—using your body energy to cue your dog:* The way you use your body will be an important factor in the success of this exercise. You need to stand erect, your energy balanced and collected. To experience the difference between being fully conscious and present in your body and being out of touch with your self, practice the Heel with a friend.

- Hold your friend's hand and, assuming the role of leader, walk as if you are lost in another world, aimlessly change your pace from slow to quick, turn unexpectedly, and stop abruptly. Do this for several minutes, and then compare notes. Generally, the person who is being led feels as if she is being hauled around like a sack of grain and cannot anticipate your actions or follow you easily. This experience can give you a sense of what it is like for your dog to heel if you are not using your body to cue her correctly.
- Now align your shoulders over your hips, pull yourself together, stand up straight, and do the same exercise. Imagine that you are sending out a beam of energy from your solar plexus that is lighting the way ahead. As you change your pace or direction, mentally signal your intention to your friend, and moving from your center of gravity, which is just below your navel, turn by rotating your whole body in order to help send a cue. Keep your body relaxed. Stand up straight and keep your shoulders aligned over your hips.
- Envision that you and your partner are moving together like two professional dancers or skaters. In order to achieve this harmony, you have to be aware of the energy of your partner. This is what you will want to achieve with your dog; you are two individual beings, harmoniously joined and moving in a synchronized energy space.
- Compare notes again with your friend. This time, because energy is being exchanged, the whole exercise feels completely different. Carry this same presence of mind into your practice with your dog and you will notice an immediate improvement in her ability to follow you. Your friend will easily be able to anticipate and accommodate your change of pace and direction without any interference.

Practice guidelines: I teach Heel very slowly, in increments of 2 or 3 minutes, moving forward only a short distance at a time. After enough praising, the dog eventually learns that being in that specific place next to you is what earns her your attention. Once she understands this much, I begin to add changes of pace, right and left turns, and full about turns.

After a puppy has learned to walk on a lead without pulling, it is fine to give, at random, a very simple 1 or 2 minute introduction to this exercise. However, do not put too much emphasis on it with very young puppies four months and under. It is more important that puppies be given time simply to absorb and deal with their surroundings.

Practice this exercise in a variety of locations.

Things to check before you begin:

- Be sure the training equipment is on correctly.

- Be sure the leash is adjusted with a loop of slack in it.

- Hold leash with both hands together, palms down.

- Practice the hand signal: with your dog on your left, sweep your left hand straight forward in the space between the dog and you. Give the hand signal simultaneously with the verbal signal just before you begin to move.

- If you are using a food reward, have a few dozen pea-size treats in an easy-access pocket.

"Hand Position for 'Heel'"

Mental and emotional preparation:

- Get yourself quiet and focused by taking a few deep breaths.

- Clarify your intent. Visualize your dog moving with her neck and shoulders even with your leg, walking on a loose leash without pulling, giving you part of her attention at all times. See the two of you coming to a stop, and your dog sitting to wait for you to move forward again. (I strongly suggest that you record this exercise ahead of time and listen to the tape while doing your practice visualization.)

- Increase the power of your intention: experience the happiness that you and your dog will share as your mutual understanding grows.

- Remind yourself that your posture, tone of voice, eye contact, and timing will be the most important elements in the session. If these are fully executed, you will not need to give as many physical corrections.

Open and honor the practice: Energize your symbol.
Technique:
Part One: Moving Straight Ahead and Stopping with "Sit":

- Put the collar high on the dog's neck with the rings underneath the chin and a loop of slack in the leash. Fold the leash and hold it in both hands, palms down.

- If you have a very small puppy or a toy breed, stabilize the leash by holding it in your right hand while cupping your left hand around the length of the lead like a tube, so that the leash can slide up and down with ease.

- Give the corrections with your right hand and use your left hand to keep the leash from interfering with or bumping the dog.

- Have the dog sit beside you. When you are ready to begin, visualize that you have created an energy bubble of space around yourself and another bubble around your dog. Now join the two and put them inside yet another bubble. This will be the energy field within which the two of you will do this exercise.

- Before you move forward, say your dog's name and "Heel" in a cheerful and emphatic tone of voice and give the hand signal at the same time. Then begin moving forward with purpose and confidence, keeping your body erect but relaxed and not rigid. Remember to hold the leash in both hands whenever you are giving corrections. At other times you will be using the hand nearest the dog to give guidance.

- If you see that your dog is beginning to drift from the defined area, correct her while she is in the act, if you failed to anticipate the move. Repeat "Heel" and, using the leash, guide her back to position.

- If your dog starts to drift wide, away from your leg, take a quick step slightly sideways in the opposite direction and give the leash a light pop. This will bring your dog back. Praise her

"Visualizing an Energy Bubble for 'Heel' "

immediately, smile, and use your symbol as soon as your dog is back in position.

- If your dog is lagging behind you, lower your hand slightly, pop the leash straight forward, and quicken your pace a little bit. You need to lower your hands, because pulling upward on the leash tends to hold your dog back, even while you are asking her to move forward. Lowering your hands and popping the leash straight forward opens up a space for your dog to do just that. Praise her as soon as she comes into position again.

- If your dog is pulling ahead, pop the leash quickly downwards and across your right hip, while at the same time making a half-halt with your body. Again, smile, praise, and use your symbol as soon as the dog adjusts her position. Keep the energy flowing.

- Reach down with the hand closest to the dog and pat your leg to give your dog an idea of where you want her to be. Keep visualizing throughout the exercise. I keep up a running chitchat in a warm, steady tone of voice: "Heel! That's it. Good for you. Right there! Great! That's what I'm looking for."

- After ten or twelve steps, slow down. As you begin to come to a halt, shorten the leash with your right hand so your dog cannot move ahead, and have your left hand ready to guide her if her rear end starts to swing out sideways. This way, you both will end up facing forward, with the dog's neck and shoulder area still in position beside your leg.

"Coming into 'Sit' from 'Heel' "

- Just before you stop completely, transfer the shortened leash briefly to your left hand, while your right hand gives the signal for Sit: sweep your right hand very deliberately from your right side, across the front of your body, in front of the dog's face, and up.

- When the dog sits, immediately loosen up on the lead and praise her.

- Once your dog figures out that she should sit every time you stop, you will be able to leave the leash slack and use the hand signal alone. Eventually, you will not need to say "Sit" or use a hand signal. Your dog will automatically sit as a part of the signal to Heel.

- If you have timed your signal correctly, your dog should be sitting as you come to a complete halt. Praise her quietly, use your symbol, and if desired, give her a food reward.

- If you need to reposition the collar in order to better direct your dog, do this each time you stop, while the dog is sitting.

- When you are ready to start up again, say, "Heel," and move briskly forward while visualizing and patting your leg with your left hand to indicate where you want her.

- At random times during the exercise, whenever your dog is responding correctly, be sure to smile, send your symbol, and praise her. Watch your timing so that you are not praising your dog when she is out of position.

Part Two: Turning Right:

- You will execute turns by cuing your dog with your body position and by changing your pace.

- Just before you make a right-hand turn, visualize to your dog that the turn is coming up, and think about what you are going to do and how you will do it.

- Increase your pace before you begin to turn. This will speed your dog up so he can maintain his position more easily through the turn.

- Encourage your dog by patting your left leg as you repeat the verbal cue, make a quarter-turn to the right, and return to a normal pace.

- Once your dog has practiced several right turns and is starting to grasp the idea, begin to alternate between this exercise and all of the other skills you have learned. Use your own body and energy field to help your dog maintain his position beside you:

- If your dog is moving too slowly or hanging back, use more right hand-turns in order to cue the dog to keep up with you. Turn right and persuade the dog to stay with you by giving a quick pop on the leash. Do not pull or swing her around on turns. Put a lot of animated energy into your voice and body language and move briskly.

- The tendency is to walk faster with dogs that forge, and slower with those that lag. You need to do the *opposite* to maintain the desired balance of energy.

- Remember to change your pace and direction frequently to keep her attention. Make it a game and have fun!

- When the lesson is over, let your dog know that she can relax her focus and say, "Free!" with a big smile and an animated tone in your voice.

Part Three: Turning Left:

- Begin by practicing without your dog. Put your left hand at your side where your dog will be, and put your weight on your left foot. Keep your body erect.

- Bring your right knee across your body in a swinging motion, and touch your left hand with your right knee. Repeat several times. By pivoting your body and swinging your knee in front of where your dog will be, you are creating a barricade in front of the dog to prevent further forward motion and causing him to turn to the left to avoid colliding with the barrier. Keep your motion flowing. Do not stop once you have turned. Let momentum carry you and the dog through the turns.

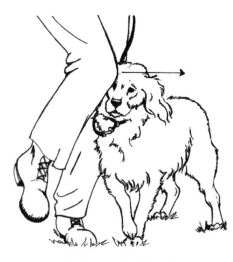

"Making the Left Turn"

- If you have a small dog, you will be using the *side* of your lower leg or foot to create this barrier, which will be at the level of the dog's muzzle. Never use the tip of your toe!

- Now repeat this action with your dog. As you slow down slightly and prepare for the left turn, put your weight on your left leg, and bring your right knee, leg, or foot in front of her face so that she is blocked, creating a barrier in front of her that she must turn left to avoid. Do not shorten up or hold her back with the leash.

- Be sure your dog is in the proper place and moving briskly before you turn, or he might drop behind you and come up on your right side. If your dog has moved out of position and ahead of you, you cannot execute a left turn correctly!

- Complete the turn, following through with your body, and continuing to move forward.

Extra notes:

- Remember that you must cue your dog to slow down in anticipation of the turn left and to speed up in anticipation of the right turn. You will do this by briefly changing your pace *before* you turn. Eventually the dog will change pace automatically all by herself.

- Practice heeling when you take your dog out for a walk. I require the dog's focused attention for only three to five minutes at a time when I teach this exercise. If we are moving straight ahead, I make the exercise interesting and fun by changing my pace, stopping, making turns, weaving back and forth, and reversing direction. When we need a break, I stop, and give my release signal—"Free!" Then I say, "Let's go," and we continue walking in a more relaxed fashion. If I see a car, a bicyclist, or a jogger heading our way, I ask the dog to sit, and then we heel again for a few minutes. When the car or person has passed, I again ask for the Sit. I praise the dog, give the release command, and resume the walk with "Let's go."

Close and honor the practice.

If you are not communicating well during training: If you are not getting the expected results, stop, detach from the situation, and analyze everything. Decide what you need to change, get centered and refocused, and then try again.

SPECIFICS

If your dog continues to forge and pull on leash:

- Are there too many distractions?
- Slow everything down; your dog could be feeling anxious because she does not yet understand what you want.
- Are you under the dog's point of motivation with your corrections?
- Increase the number of left turns that you make into the dog's path, and use your knee or lower leg as described in the exercise. This will slow the dog down and put her back in heel position.

If your dog is lagging and refusing to move forward with you:

- Pop the leash and move briskly forward.
- Be sure to release the pressure on the collar as soon as the dog moves forward.
- Be sure to give lots of praise when your dog moves forward.
- Pat your leg to encourage the dog to keep up with you.
- Hold a food lure in your left hand. Keep that hand slightly ahead of the dog, and keep the dog's neck and shoulder even with your leg.

- Increase the number of turns you make away from the dog's path; pop the leash before you turn to encourage her to keep up with you as you turn.

If your dog is jumping on you:

- Say "Off" in an emphatic, disapproving tone of voice.
- If necessary, give a downward pop on the leash.
- Stop all forward motion until the dog settles down.
- Be sure you do not get caught up in your dog's disrupted energy, but remain calm, centered, and focused on doing the exercise correctly.
- When your dog has settled, start up again as if absolutely nothing has happened.

If your dog is grabbing the leash with her mouth:

- Stop all forward motion.
- Say "Off" or "Leave it" in an emphatic, disapproving voice.
- If the dog persists, repeat the reprimand and give a firm pop on the leash, checking first to make sure that nothing metal is in the dog's mouth.
- Be sure you do not get caught in your dog's disrupted energy; remain calm, centered, and focused on doing the exercise correctly.
- As soon as the dog has released the leash from her mouth, acknowledge her correct response by saying a quiet "Thank you." Then say "Heel" in a cheerful, emphatic voice.
- Begin moving forward with purpose and confidence, as if absolutely nothing has happened. Keep your focus on your goal and not on the things that get in the way of your goal.

If your dog swings out in front to face you when you ask for the Sit:

- Shorten up on the lead so she has to stop beside you.
- Do a half turn to the left as you come to a stop.
- Work the dog close to a wall or a fence to keep her from swinging her rear end out of position.

- Eliminate the hand signal for Sit and just use the verbal cue.
  Use your left hand like a guardrail on the far side of her body to
  keep her sitting straight and close beside you.

Puppies

I rarely do this exercise for more than a few minutes, and never with
puppies under eight weeks old. I have found that using a food lure is
usually the easiest way to help puppies grasp the idea of staying in
one position next to you:

TEACHING HEEL WITH A FOOD LURE

Hold a treat in front of the dog's nose to keep her in position. This will also
teach her how to follow you in turns. (This approach can be hard on your
body if you have a very small dog, because it requires you to bend over for a
prolonged period of time. You can use a clothespin to attach the food lure to
the end of a dowel if bending over is too difficult.)

This method does not use a leash, so it is best to practice indoors. If you
practice outside, put the dog's leash on her and attach it to your belt so that
you have both hands free.

Technique:

- Put one treat in your left hand and several more in your right.

- You will use the hand nearest the dog to lure her ahead by holding the treat in front of her nose, the back of your hand facing
  forward as you move ahead. Keep that hand slightly in front of
  your leg to position the dog with her neck and shoulders even
  with your leg. *Do not hold the treat up high; this will cause the dog
  to jump for it.*

- Remembering to visualize the behavior that you are looking for,
  hold the lure in position, say "Heel," and move forward a few
  steps. As your dog follows, praise her liberally.

- Use your other hand to lure her into a Sit or to help her make a
  right-hand turn. As you come to a stop, move your left hand to
  your stomach, out of the way. Say "Sit" and bring your right
  hand slowly and deliberately across your body, in front of the
  dog's face, and then up over her head. When her nose follows

the lure—which will cause her to sit down—praise her and then give her the treat.

To make a right-hand turn with a lure:

- Move your left hand out of the way to in front of your navel, and bring your right hand, which will also be holding a treat, in front of the dog's nose to bring her a little bit forward. Lead the dog around to the right. When you are facing straight again, switch back to using your left hand to lure her.

- If she is trying to move too fast or too far ahead, put your left hand down in front of her as a barrier to hold her back and slow her pace.

- Once she understands what you are looking for, you can begin to wean her from the food by putting it in a pocket rather than having it in your hand. Begin to move with your hands in a natural position for walking. Use only the hand and verbal signal. From then on, save the food for her fastest and best response. At other times, give her plenty of praise, but no treat.

The Real Test: Working with Distractions

A dog's ability to thoroughly commit to the job that she has been taught to do, can be awe-inspiring. Seeing Eye dogs, police dogs, and dogs that do search-and-rescue work are all wonderful examples of a level of training so complete that the animal can be trusted with a person's life. Although not every dog has the temperament to do such work, a major factor is the amount of time the trainer has spent reinforcing basic training in the face of all kinds of distractions.

In order to ensure that I have taught a dog to the best of my ability, I follow three basic principles:

1. *Teaching:* one thing at a time. This is to create a basic understanding of the connection between a signal and a behavior.

2. *Training:* instilling a consistent response with repetition, corrections, and lots of praise. Most people consider that a dog at this level is trained. However, this is not proven unless the dog has been tested.

3. *Testing:* the use of distractions in order to make sure the dog understands that I expect the same response every time, regardless of what is happening around us.

If you don't achieve that degree of communication with your dog, the things she has learned will be more like tricks than reliable behaviors, and therein lies the danger. Thousands of dogs die every year because their owners overestimate the dog's ability to do what she's told in a wide variety of situations. They believe that if their dog listens to them when they are alone at home, she will respond in other environments as well.

If something unexpected comes up, like a scary noise, an encounter with another dog, a stranger at the door, or someone on Roller Blades passing you as you walk down the street, you want your dog instantly to look to you for guidance. She will learn to do this only if you proof her out over and over in many different situations. Each time the dog chooses any option other than responding to you, you will interrupt her behavior and redirect her to a more acceptable choice.

It is important to emphasize that the dog must, if safety allows, have the freedom to experience the consequences of her choices. A dog absolutely must not be restrained from investigating a distraction, but she must be given a corrective pop on the leash to help her understand that there is a connection between a distraction and a correction. If going near a distraction makes her feel mildly uncomfortable, because it causes a correction, then she will feel less safe and secure than when she avoids it and listens to you. She will believe that she has made the most self-rewarding choice, because you always give her love and approval whereas other encounters in the world produce the opposite effect.

This is another example of the dog functioning at the third level of consciousness. Once she prefers to look to you for guidance, rather than hurtling into an unknown situation, she will be at a level of understanding that ensures her safety.

The following tests use distractions with applications of basic behavior rules. These will show you if there are weak areas in your training. Dogs with excitable temperaments tend to find it more challenging to stay focused on you when something comes along that stimulates their instinctive responses. They need a lot of help learning to think a situation through. If you keep your focus on the dog's point of motivation and try to be proactive, you will be able to create a good support for this learning.

"Come" with Distractions

Goal: Your goal in this exercise is to help your dog learn to come to you in every situation. You will test her by asking her to come when you see that her full attention is on the distraction instead of on you. Choose distractions that will be common to the area where you live, such as other dogs, joggers, baby carriages, kids playing ball in park, wildlife, and other pets.

Practice guidelines: Do this exercise at least once daily for 10 to 15 minutes a session with dogs four months of age and over. For puppies eight to sixteen weeks of age, practice only 5 to 8 minutes.

Practice with different distractions, and in a variety of locations, each with its own combination of sights, sounds, and smells.

Things to check before you begin: Have your dog on a 30-foot line, and choose a place to practice that has a variety of distractions. You may wish to begin in your own backyard—for example, with children playing or with a friend walking another dog around on a leash.

Mental and emotional preparation:

- Get yourself quiet and focused by taking a few deep breaths and relaxing your mind and body. Clarify your intent.

Open and honor the practice: Energize your symbol.
Technique:

- With your dog on the long line and the rest of the line thrown out behind you on the ground, say "Let's go," and begin moving forward.
- For the duration of the exercise, continuously let out and take up the line rather than always holding it at the same length. Dogs are great at judging distance because they are predator animals, and need to gauge how far they are from prey. You don't want to teach her that that the correction will only happen at predictable lengths of the line.
- Keep your long line free of knots. Be careful not to pop the line if it is wrapped around one of your dog's legs; you could do some muscle or tendon damage. It is okay to pop the line if it is only under one leg or under the dog's belly. If you notice that she is hung up in some way, immediately go and free her before continuing the lesson.
- As soon as you see that your dog is completely distracted by something she sees, hears, or smells, instantly say her name in a fairly loud voice to get her attention, and give the cue "Come." Put a strong note of urgency in your voice, as if something terrible is about to happen.
- As "Come" is leaving your lips, pop the line, and visualize the dog leaving the distraction and coming to you.

- The timing of voice and correction is very important because you want to interrupt your dog immediately and not have to give two corrections, which will weaken the message.

- As soon as she responds, pour on the praise while she comes to you, and again after you have her collar safe in your hand.

- If your dog starts toward you and then stops to check out the distraction, give a sharp verbal reprimand, "Leave it!" the instant you see her focus switch.

- Be aware that reeling your dog in like a fish can create resistance. Use the line to interrupt and redirect.

- Say the dog's name and "Come" again in a pleasant tone of voice.

- Repeat the correction as many times as needed, until your dog voluntarily leaves the distraction and comes to you.

- Avoid pulling the dog away from the distraction. That defeats the purpose of the exercise!

- Begin to praise immediately when you see her heading in your direction. Do not wait until she reaches you. Encourage her all the way.

Extra notes: I don't ask a dog to come over and over again without reason. I wait for the moments when she is totally focused on some distraction. An interruption at the right time creates the belief that distractions and corrections go together.

Close and honor the practice.

If you are not communicating well during training: If you are not getting the expected results, become the detached observer, analyze the situation, refocus, and try again.

SPECIFICS

If your dog starts to come and then turns back, give an appropriate verbal reprimand such as "Hey," "Wait," or "Leave it," and then repeat "Come." Give the reprimand in a sharp tone, and make your "Come" lively and inviting. Take up the slack on the line, and repeat your signals with as many corrections as needed.

If your dog simply cannot detach from the distraction, or if you see that your dog cannot hear you because the distraction is so enticing, then concentrate on close work. Restraining her will only serve to intensify her interest. Shorten the line and continue making firm corrections with the dog closer to you, and use the reprimand, "Leave it!" until the dog mentally disengages from the distraction. Then say "Come" once more.

It is typical for people to avoid a particular distraction because it is too hard to get your dog to listen to you. Whenever I encounter this kind of situation, I always say, "Great! This gives me a chance to do some meaningful work in getting the dog to learn to listen to me at all times." I repeat the work with the distraction and repeat the corrections over and over until the dog is able to accomplish the behavior I am looking for. I stay calm and keep visualizing her doing it correctly. As soon as she follows through, I praise her and this ends the session on a positive note. Later in the day, or on the next day, I repeat the distraction work again, to see if the dog remembers what she learned.

WHEN CAN YOUR DOG GO OFF-LEASH?

Before you can reliably trust your dog off-leash, you will need to expose her to a wide variety of distractions over a period of two to five months, depending on the dog's personality, age, and breed. Some dogs never get there. This frequently applies to dogs who, by breeding, are extremely independent or who are hunting breeds with an instinct that absolutely overrides everything else when there is prey around.

I usually tell people that if they are having to make a lot of corrections on the line, common sense says that if the line were not there, the dog would not be either. The line therefore, needs to be there for the dog's safety.

Even though it is obvious that dogs enjoy being able to run at great speeds, investigate things, and have freedom, unfortunately, we are living in a day and an age when many areas are not safe enough to allow the dog to have that experience. If you want to give your dog room to run, find a place that will allow her to do this. If you live in a city, there may be a park with a fenced dog run, where people can allow their dogs to play off-leash. If you are in a rural area, you may be able to find a group of people who would like to join you in establishing a large enclosed field where dogs can have a measure of freedom in a safe place.

Puppies

Go very slowly with very young puppies. This is an exercise for the more mature dog.

I once had a woman named Sarah in my classes who had been allowing her partially trained dog to run off-leash because she was vicariously experiencing a sense of freedom by watching him run and play. Freedom was a very important issue for her in her own life. Unfortunately, when her dog was running one day, he was hit by a car. He was not badly injured, but Sarah quickly saw that she had foolishly risked his life. She signed him up for training classes and determined that he would not run off leash again until she was sure she could control him with verbal cues to keep him safe.

When people give their dogs freedom off the leash before they are mentally responsible to handle it, good training is undermined. For example, when a dog is walked on leash to a meadow and then set free to run, these sessions of "freedom" usually end with coaxing, yelling, and struggles for control if she has not been trained to come every single time her human calls. This is reverse training, because the dog learns that Come costs her the freedom she craves. This is not true freedom. Real freedom will exist for the dog when her immediate and consistent compliance with your signals no longer makes a leash or long line necessary.

The same issue applies when you allow your dog to run loose outside in your yard and then bring her back in when you call, "Come." If you already have a dog who is resistant to coming to you, it is a good idea to break that pattern by calling her to you many times, praising her each time she comes, and then immediately releasing her to play again.

If you are out for a walk in a safe space where the dog can run free, it is also a good idea to reinforce the training by putting the dog on a leash for part of the time and then releasing her again.

I never allow my dogs off leash until I am absolutely certain that they understand and will respond to all of my signals without exceptions. All of my dogs, whether they are puppies or adult rescued dogs, start out on leashes and long lines whenever I take them outside, even in my three-acre fenced yard.

If you cannot count on your dog's response when you need her to come inside when called, secure her on a tie-out, or put her on a long line inside a fenced yard. It is much easier to gather up a dog when there is 30 to 50 feet of long line behind her. However, *never* leave her dragging a long line unsupervised; she could get tangled up and hurt.

If you are having a problem getting your dog to come reliably, do the following training setup, which allows you to work on the problem with her while she is out in the yard.

If your dog is on a long line and will not come: If you have left your dog loose dragging a line, and she won't come when you call, you will have to casually position yourself so that you can get hold of the line. *Do not call her until you have the line in your hands.* Be careful not to give her the impression that you are playing a chase game; simply follow her casually, without making eye contact or showing any interest in her, until you can take hold of the end of the line. Then do not haul on the line, but give a very firm correction as you say, "Inside." Use visualization and positive thinking, and do not forget to praise, even though you may be tempted to get irritated by the way she ignored you. Remember that she is doing the best she can with the amount of training she has had up to that point.

Go back in the house for five minutes or so. Then go out and call your dog. If she comes, give her a treat, shower her with praise and then let her go play again, so that she doesn't associate inside with punishment, because obeying ends her freedom. Do this off and on at random so that she doesn't think that responding to you means that she will always have to go right inside. Let her resume playing. Then repeat the exercise several times.

If your dog is out in the yard and you need her to come in, remember to say "Inside," instead of "Come." If she ignores you, do a training setup: put her on a long line when she is out in the yard. If she does not come to the house when you call "Inside," take hold of the end of the line and give her a correction. Repeat the signal, and give her lots of praise as soon as she complies with your request.

If your dog is on a trolley line and runs away when you call: In this case, set up your training exercise so that she is also attached to a long line that will extend the length of the trolley. When she runs away, pick up the end of the long line, give a correction, and keep correcting, visualizing, and encouraging until she comes to you. Give her lots of praise, and then repeat the exercise off and on at random during the time she is outside.

Verbal signals for house and car: If you need your dog to come in, use "Inside." Use "Get in," and "Outside" for your car. Use these verbal cues every time your dog enters or exits any confined space, so that she comes to know them very well and associates them with each action.

Sit with Distractions

LESSON 1: WITH NOISE AND STRANGE OBJECTS

This exercise requires a helper who will create the distractions while you help your dog maintain her focus and sitting position.

Practice guidelines: Take as long as you need to help your dog understand that she should remain sitting until you release her.

Things to check before you begin:

- Your dog will be wearing training equipment.

- You will need a helper. However, if you are aware that your dog has overly shy or aggressive tendencies, it is better to seek help from a professional than from friends.

- Have a number of distractions already on hand: noisemakers (avoid things that will frighten the dog like cap guns), squeaky toys, whistles, bird calls, pull toys, a stroller, a ball to bounce, a wagon, a whistle, another dog.

- Practice the correction for distractions with a friend, or visualize how it is done; it is the same as the correction for Stay. Have the dog's collar high on the neck, rings under the chin. Holding the leash in one hand, drape it over the other hand, and separate your hands quickly with an up-and-down motion. This will create a wave in the leash, which will tap the dog under the chin.

- Have several treats handy in an easy-access pocket.

Mental and emotional preparation:

- Take a few moments with your helper to get quiet and focused. Clarify your intent.

Open and honor the practice: Energize your symbol.
Technique:

- Put your dog in a Sit, and stand in front of her at a distance of about 3 feet. Your helper will walk around the dog with whatever you can devise that will be distracting, but never anything that is overwhelming or frightening. As your dog learns control, you can gradually increase the level and type of distraction.

- While the distraction is going on, hold your focus on your dog, and keep sending quiet, calm energy. Visualize her holding the Sit position and how happy this makes you. Praise her quietly if she holds.

- Be proactive! The moment that you see her *think* about moving from Sit to investigate the distraction, instantly repeat the cue "Sit" and give the correction (see "Things to Check Before You Begin," above). If necessary, instantly reinforce the correction with "Leave it!" Praise as soon as the dog resumes the Sit position.

Puppies

This is an excellent exercise to do with puppies, who need to learn the proper and polite way to behave when asking for and receiving attention.

- Repeat the exercise until she holds. Reactions to distraction can vary quite a bit. If she breaks, do not let this change your energy. Remain focused and repeat the exercise until you see that your dog can do it correctly. Then praise her lavishly, use your symbol, and give her a food reward. Remember to do a detached analysis if there are problems, and to have a closing ritual of appreciation and thanks.

- When your dog understands this basic exercise, take her outside to practice in an area where there are distractions typical of your local environment.

Extra notes: When you create distractions for your dog, use common sense. A bird dog can be taught to hold still while a gun is fired over her head, but her training never starts out that way. Anything new is always introduced very gradually, so that the dog never loses her trust in her human.

LESSON 2: WITH STRANGERS AND AFFECTIONATE GREETINGS

For this exercise you will need a helper, whose job will be to act the part of a stranger who approaches your dog and gives verbal and physical acknowledgment.

Your goal is to teach your dog to exhibit good manners and remain sitting throughout the distraction.

Practice guidelines: Take as long as you need to help your dog understand that she should remain sitting while she receives attention and recognition from people.

Things to check before you start:

- Your dog will be wearing her training equipment.

- Ask a friend who is not well known to your dog to help you.

- Have several treats handy in an easy-access pocket.

Mental and emotional preparation: Take a few moments with your helper to get quiet and focused. Clarify your intent.

- Remind yourself that your posture, tone of voice, eye contact, and timing will be the most important elements in the session. If these are fully executed, you will need fewer physical corrections.

Open and honor the practice: Energize your symbol.
Technique:

- Put your dog in a Sit, holding the lead so that there is about a foot of slack in it, and stand by her side. Both you and your helper should begin to visualize to the dog what is going to happen and the kind of response you are looking for.

- Beginning from 8 to 10 feet away, your helper should approach the dog calmly, without looking directly at her. If she is especially shy or fearful, your helper should approach her obliquely without making eye contact. This approach will be less threatening to her.

- Be proactive! If you see that your dog is about to react to the approaching person by breaking from position, interrupt the thought with a correction.

- If your dog breaks from position as your helper is approaching, the helper should instantly turn his back on her and walk away a few steps. At the same time, you should give a correction and repeat "Sit." Give the reprimand the instant you see that your dog is about to react. Practice this as many times as you need to, until the person can come right up to the two of you while the dog holds her position.

- The helper should now exchange a few words with you, then calmly look down, smile at your dog, extend the back of his hand for her to sniff, and slowly turn it over to rub under her chin or on the side of her neck. This kind of initial contact from underneath is less threatening than if the hand comes from above, over the top of the dog's head.

- If at any point your dog gets overly excited and begins to get up, jump around, or paw or mouth the helper, give a correction while your helper immediately turns and walks away.

- Repeat the exercise as often as is necessary until your dog holds the Sit while being patted.

- Once she can do this, your helper can also quietly praise her. Have a treat in your hand and give it to your helper to give to your dog.

- By giving the treat to your dog, your helper creates pleasant and positive associations with meeting new people. Your dog learns that inappropriate behavior sends people away, and polite, calm behavior brings praise, attention, and treats.

- Release your dog and close the exercise.

Extra notes: All of these distraction exercises can be done with your dog on a Down/Stay instead of a Sit. Use the following correction with Down/Stay work: Stand in front of your dog while someone creates a distraction. If your dog begins to break out of position, immediately put your foot on the lead, right on top of the buckle of the leash. Now bring your heel down to the ground, keeping the leash in the arch of your foot so it acts like a pulley point, and pull the lead under your foot with one or both hands, so that it creates a pressure on the collar, which will bring the dog back down again.

Be sure to keep your weight on the foot that is on the lead. If you have a large dog and he suddenly jumps up, he could knock you off balance if you are not grounded. Be very careful to keep your foot directly under your dog's chest and close to the dog so that there is only a small amount of leash between your foot and the dog. If there is too much leash, the dog could twist around and wrap the leash around your foot or leg. Do not draw your foot back under you, or you will cause your dog to stand to keep from losing his balance.

Repeat the signal "Down/Stay." Praise your dog as soon as she is back in position. When your dog goes down, all collar pressure stops *immediately*. Praise her and use your symbol!

Once your dog is in the Down position and you have stopped the collar pressure, it is a good idea at this stage of training to keep your foot on the lead. Keep your foot in close to the dog's body so that as long as she remains down, there is no pressure on the col-

"The Foot Correction for 'Down' "

lar, but if she tries to get back up before she is released, she will automatically give herself a correction as she rises.

Remember to release the collar pressure as soon as the dog is down again.

INCREASING TIME AND DISTANCE WITH "WAIT"

Once your dog is reliably stopping all forward motion whenever you use the Wait signal in the house, in the car, and on a leash, you can begin to increase the distance between you.

"Wait" while on a walk: Have your dog on a long line, and amble through your yard or out in an open space. Remembering to visualize, use the verbal and physical Wait signals at random, when your dog is beside you, behind you, ahead of you, and coming toward you.

- If your dog is moving by your side, say "Wait," and pass her. If she does not stop, you should immediately turn, use your force field, and hold your hand up in front of her in the Wait signal. Walk forward into her to crowd her back, if necessary. Praise her as soon as she stops all forward movement. Return to her, praise her, and give her a food reward, if you are using one.

- If your dog is ahead of you, she will not be able to see your hand signal, so be sure that your verbal signal is very strong and emphatic. If she does not respond, give a correction with the line. The correct response is to stop all forward motion and remain in place until given another cue, or to stop all forward movement and return to you.

- If your dog is headed toward you, hold your hand up in the Wait signal and use your energy to hold her back. If necessary, rush toward her to stop forward motion and crowd her back to the designated spot.

- Change the distance at which you hold the line to increase the variables in the exercise. You can practice the Wait and the Come exercises off and on during the same session.

- Alternate between going right to your dog and praising her when she stops, or heading off in another direction with the words, "Let's go." Or tell her "Wait," praise her for her response, and then say, "Come." Or say "Wait," walk right past her, and then say "Let's go," just as you pass.

- Always immediately praise your dog for the Wait and use your symbol. Give food rewards for her best and fastest responses only.

Extra notes:

- As long as she stops all forward motion, your dog can stand, sit, or lie down when she is asked to Wait.
- Remember that you need to allow for a reaction-response time. Think ahead of your dog. If you want her to stop at the edge of the lawn, give the signal before she reaches the edge, so that she has time to hear you, process your signal, slow down, and stop.

It takes months of conscientious effort before you can expect to get reliable responses to all of your cues. While you are engaged in the various practices, remind yourself that there is a big difference between Awareness Training and restraining. When you restrain a dog, you are assuming responsibility for that dog's behavior by exerting physical control. When you communicate clearly with a dog, you allow the animal freedom of choice and the consequences of her own actions. She learns to think for herself and bears the responsibility for controlling her instinctual drives. Because you give her so much positive reinforcement while she learns to interpret your directions, she will have a sense of pride and accomplishment, and above all, she will feel acknowledged and understood.

12

CHALLENGES AND INSPIRATIONS: BEHAVIORAL PROBLEMS AND OTHER LIFE LESSONS

This chapter will help you go even deeper into the experience of what a spiritual connection can be between two beings learning a common language, because this section addresses those instances when you can feel helpless, resistant, lost, and stuck. Many, many times, I have been astounded to discover the amount of untapped strength and awareness available in the universe, as long as I hold fast to the knowledge that there is always a reason for things to happen as they do. This applies equally to difficult behaviors in certain dogs that cannot be explained, and to the pain of dogs who are beyond living in harmony with people, and to dogs who run away or get stolen or lost. In all cases, it has been necessary to let go, to become quiet and calm inside, to observe the situation with detachment and interest, and to create an energy of love and positive expectations while asking for help from my higher self. When I do this, the next step always becomes clear, and I am able to proceed with a peaceful mind and heart. And in so doing, I also discover that I have ascended to a new level of perception and personal power that I had never dreamed was possible.

The first kind of challenge I want to address is so-called problem behavior, a label I have difficulty with because it implies that something is wrong with the dog. Often, any discord that arises between a dog and a human is not the dog's fault, so it is unfair to imply that the dog has done something wrong. It is also true that people often create the fear, stress, and anxiety that contribute to inappropriate behavior in dogs. Dogs are often put on an emotional seesaw by people's moods, unpredictable schedules, inconsistent expectations, tension in family relationships, or relocations. They also endure poor quality diets, and inadequate exercise and mental stimulation.

Many people create a one-sided relationship with their dog, wanting her to be there when they need her for companionship, but expecting her to fade into the background when other matters are more pressing. Dogs can have a hard time keeping up with this on-again, off-again relationship.

Having said this, I want to stress that it is imperative that you not ignore early warning signs of problems. They will not go away if you ignore them. For your dog's sake, do not be tempted to think she'll get over it or outgrow it.

Many behavioral problems arise from physical or metabolic conditions that may not be immediately obvious. A health issue can suddenly manifest itself as a behavioral issue, with the result that the dog receives negative feedback for something over which she has no control. A dog in pain, for example, may snap at people who touch her, and it is tragic if people assume that the dog has suddenly turned aggressive and therefore should be gotten rid of.

It is also important to remember that your dog's instincts are always right beneath the surface of any learned behavior, and many things can trigger an instinctive response. Beyond this, you need to consider your dog's personality, intelligence, and personal preferences. You may have her allegiance, but this does not necessarily mean that she will stop snoozing on the couch when you are away or that she'll avoid taking a luxurious roll in the compost heap whenever you let her out in the yard. There may always be some things about your dog that you wish were different, but you need to accept all of what makes her who she is—both the desirable and the undesirable qualities.

My definition of an unacceptable behavior is any action that is a danger or a legitimate annoyance to the public at large. Beyond this, you are free to establish your own rules with your dog; your standards must be consistently maintained, however, and you must take responsibility for the results. If you do not mind having your dog jump up on you or beg for food at the table, do not reprimand her if she does so when you have company. You do need to be aware, however, that certain things you allow, such as getting up on the furniture, could contribute to behavior problems if your dog is experiencing dominance or aggression issues. Be open to the possibility that some things might need to change, either on your part or on your dog's part.

When people bring their dogs to me for behavioral counseling, I always start with an in-depth analysis of the difficulty. My first recommendation is that the dog have a thorough physical checkup. Many behavioral problems have underlying physical or metabolic problems. These may have been tolerated for a long time, but if they suddenly become acute, the dog will often exhibit dramatic behavioral changes because she is feeling unwell.

If the dog gets a clean bill of health, I lead my clients through some intense detective work. Often the complaint is too general: "She's too hyper," or "She's too aggressive." I need to know exactly which specific behaviors are causing the problem, so I ask many questions about the dog's life, including how many people are in the family and what their ages are. I also try to find out if there is any stress in the household—things like illness, divorce, a new family member, or a change in the daily routine. I also ask what kinds of games are played with the dog and whether she is on any medication. I ask about her diet and whether there are other pets. Details like these may not seem to be related, but they make a whole picture, which can be very instructive. The time of day when a behavior takes place can also be significant. A dog might always behave a certain way in anticipation of an event. If the behavior happens within a certain time period after the dog has eaten, it could be food-related, triggered by an allergy, or caused by too much sugar.

Often, behaviors are linked, and if one is changed, others will be changed also. For example, if your dog goes into a frenzy of barking and running up and down the fence when people or cars go by, stopping the running will usually stop the barking and vice versa.

When I have identified all of the contributing elements, I can usually figure out why the dog seems to think that a particular behavior is rewarding. Remember that the dog may need to release tension, relieve boredom, or get attention. You can find solutions to unwanted behaviors by monitoring your dog throughout a day and pinpointing the what, where, and when of a certain action. Once you know the details, you can begin to formulate possible solutions and try them out.

There are other reasons for sudden behavior changes. It is amazing how quickly some dogs—especially very intelligent ones—can learn something new, even though you may not remember how the lesson was taught. Shaman, one of the dogs living with me, recently provided a good example of this kind of learning. My young apprentice, Beth, was helping to bring the dogs back into the house on a rainy day. If the dogs are very dirty or muddy, I put them in their crates to drip-dry before I let them have the run of the house. The dogs willingly go on their own; all they need is to have the door to their particular crate open.

On this particular day, Shaman, who is a Sheltie–border collie mix and very smart, came right in when asked. However, Beth was being extra helpful, so she patted the top of his crate as he came in the door to the room. This is the signal I use when I want a dog to jump up on top of the grooming table.

Being very bright and thinking that he had received a new direction, Shaman leaped to the top of the crate instead of going inside. Surprised by his response, Beth laughed, gave him a big hug, called him "silly dog," and got him down on the floor again. She asked him again to enter his crate, using the same gesture as before. Shaman again complied by leaping to the top of the crate, got another laugh and a pat—and the new trick became a learned behavior.

I did not know that this had occurred, so when later in the day I asked the dogs to go in their crates, I was surprised to turn around and see Shaman proudly sitting on top of his, instead of inside. It took a little retraining to turn things around again!

The impetus behind this kind of behavior change is fairly obvious if you know your dog well. The harder ones to figure out are those where the link is not as direct. In my story of Jessica in an earlier chapter, I described a time when she was ready to devour a UPS driver, and because I intervened, she turned and started to clamp her teeth into my arm, until she thought better of it. This kind of reaction to frustration is known as stress displacement behavior; it occurs when the perpetrator cannot be dealt with directly.

Sometimes the reaction is not all that dramatic; a nervous, insecure dog might begin yawning or scratching or licking her lips when asked to learn something new. Feeling stressed because she does not understand or feel comfortable with what you are asking her to do, she tries to avoid the whole issue. If you see your dog exhibiting this kind of behavior during a training session, you need to slow down, go back a few steps to a place where your dog feels confident, and send lots of positive reinforcement as you again proceed, in order to help her through that stress period.

A few years ago I worked with a case that was a good example of a destructive displacement behavior. A couple named Molly and Dan came to see me about Gilly, their six-year-old German shepherd, who had never been a problem but who had suddenly taken to trashing their house. They had come home from work one day to find the drapes shredded, wallpaper stripped, window casings and doorjambs chewed into splinters, and the couch half eaten. The same thing was repeated and made worse over the next few days, even though they punished Gilly soundly. They were totally mystified and very upset.

"Has anything different happened?" I asked them. Often there has been a stranger like the meter reader, an oil delivery person, or a garbage collector in the yard, moving around the outside of the house. This kind of stimulus can get a dog so excited that she will run around the house scent-marking—in order to reassure herself by marking her territory—or she will tear something apart as a substitute for the invader.

After playing detective for an hour and a half, we finally discovered that Molly had been given a bird feeder for Christmas and had hung it on the porch. Every day, the target area of destruction was on the side of the house closest to the feeder. Most dogs find visiting birds interesting and not traumatic, but as it turned out, birds were not the issue. It seemed that several cats found the feeder a welcome addition to the neighborhood. They were sitting under it on a daily basis, hungrily eyeing the air traffic overhead.

Meanwhile, a frantic Gilly was trying to take the wall down to get at them. Once the feeder was moved out onto the lawn where the dog couldn't see it, the problem was solved and never reoccurred.

Whether your dog is exhibiting a displacement behavior or some other appropriate behavior, you need to keep things in perspective even while you are figuring out what to do about it. Strewing garbage all over your house is not the same thing as taking a bite out of a visitor. People are often infuriated if their dog creates a problem for them, but they make excuses if the problem is directed at others. The old saying, "Love me, love my dog," exemplifies the intense identification that people can have with their animal companions. For this reason, a behavior like garbage-raiding can be taken as a direct and open affront to you while another person's criticism of your dog's car-chasing can feel like a personal attack on your character. It is very typical for people to seek professional help—or just get rid of the dog—when she is doing something that offends them but to turn a blind eye to problems involving other people or their property until a lawsuit is pending. In all cases, the best and only thing to do is to step out of the picture and figure out why things are not working. Only when you have identified the problem can you apply your learning. You can interrupt the behavior as soon as you see your dog thinking about doing it, or you can do setups to retrain and reinforce the behavior you are looking for, and then shower your dog with love and praise when she gives you the appropriate response.

It will not be helpful for me to give prescriptions for specific behavior problems, because there are so many variables. However I will offer a few general statements about the most common areas of discord.

AGGRESSION

People generally wait too long before seeking professional advice when their dog exhibits aggressive behavior. It is common to hope that it will never happen again, or to make excuses in the belief that the dog "didn't really mean it" or "was justified in doing it." Although the incident itself may seem very innocent, it is important to remember that dogs are always willing to test out a new behavior to see whether it works for them. Therefore, ignoring an incident of aggression *always* teaches a lesson.

Here is a common example: Lucky, a dog in his teenage rebellion period, grows up playing tug-of-war with his humans. One day, he suddenly grabs an off-limits object and runs with it through the house. He growls and shows his teeth when his human tries to take the object from him. This is an appropriate challenge to another dog, and Lucky is testing to see what the reaction will be. If his human releases the object and jumps back in alarm, Lucky says to himself, "Wow, look at that! As soon as I used aggressive body language, that person backed off and I got to keep what I took!" He does not forget the psychological rewards of this incident.

If a dog is allowed to get away with any kind of aggressive response—even if it is only in reaction to something that was not his fault—he will probably repeat that behavior, because he has gotten something meaningful out of it. The longer this pattern is allowed to continue, the harder it will be to break. *Always seek professional advice at the first sign of any aggressive behavior.*

DESTRUCTIVE CHEWING

To minimize destructive chewing, it's better to show your dog what to do than to try to teach him what not to do. In my household of thirty dogs, there is a variety of toys and chew objects. If you have a dog who is doing destructive chewing, you can switch his attention from your expensive possessions to his toys by demonstrating their value to your dog. If you play with your dog and act as if you find his toys of great interest, his interest in them will increase also.

Whenever your dog plays with or chews on his toys, acknowledge the behavior. Smile at him, use your symbol, show him how much that kind of activity pleases you. Never take appropriate behavior for granted! *Dogs only do what works!* If a dog receives more attention when he is doing something he should *not* do, like chewing on the chair leg or taking something he shouldn't have, he may consider it better to have negative attention than no attention at all. Then it becomes obvious which kind of behavior will predominate in your home.

SUBMISSIVE URINATION

In the wild, a dog will indicate to another dog that he does not want to fight by throwing himself on his back in a submissive posture. Usually he will also dribble a little urine. Puppies will also urinate to remind older dogs that they are only puppies and not a threat to their elders.

In most cases, submissive urination is a reflection of the dog's temperament and personality. I once worked with a dog who was so insecure that it took the better part of an hour just to get him to be able to sit upright, and hold the posture while attention was paid to him. As soon as anyone looked at him, he wanted to grovel.

It makes no sense to punish a dog who spontaneously urinates; that will only make her more submissive and escalate the problem. Some dogs urinate only when they are reprimanded; others do it when greeting people or when you pat them. If submissive urination is a constant problem, it is best to avoid doing things that will increase the dog's insecurity or unwittingly encourage the behavior. If a submissive dog begins to lower its hindquarters and get into a urinating posture when I approach—which I do obliquely rather than head-on—I immediately turn my back on her and walk away. If a dog throws herself on her back while I am working with her, I ignore her until she achieves a less submissive posture.

This also holds true when you walk in the door after having been away for a time. It is best to ignore a groveling dog at first and allow her to calm down before you greet her. Then lower your body posture by squatting, and call her to you. This is less dominating than going over to her. Avoid direct eye contact; look beyond the dog, or glance down to your side. Use visualization and project to the dog that you know she is capable of feeling and acting happy and confident. Reach out to scratch her under the chin or on the chest, instead of bringing your hand down from above to the top of her head or back, which is more threatening.

Basic communication skills will help a very submissive dog feel more confident and secure because she will gain a feeling of accomplishment and establish her place in the family. At every opportunity, give this kind of dog lots of praise and picture her feeling proud and happy, surrounded by positive energy.

EXCESSIVE BARKING

There are numerous reasons why dogs become excessive barkers: boredom, stress, and genetic predisposition, for example. Some dogs are inadvertently encouraged to do so. As with all behavioral riddles, you have to look for the trigger that reinforces the activity. Remember, negative attention is better than none.

Most dogs can be trained not to bark excessively if you are willing to invest the time and effort. Working with a dog's mind instead of disciplining her body is still a fairly new concept in our culture, which means that many people are still advised that the only solution is to restrain or cause a painful association with the action. There can also be a tendency to look for a quick fix rather than the underlying cause. All of this means that it is still common to stop excessive barking by muzzling the dog, shocking her with a no-bark collar, or worst of all, cutting her vocal cords, which is incredibly cruel. I especially dislike no-bark muzzles, because they can be a threat to the dog's life if she needs to vomit and cannot open her mouth. I will do everything I can to help my clients avoid putting a no-bark collar on their dog.

Once I have ascertained the reason for the barking, I treat it any number of different ways. Flower essences, homeopathic remedies, herbs, diet changes, massage, and repatterning exercises have proven beneficial in a vast majority of cases. Refer to Chapter 13 and ask a holistic vet for advice on your particular dog.

I also show my clients how to interrupt the barking. Some dogs get so worked up—especially if there is more than one involved—that they have a hard time breaking out of the activity, so you have to be proactive; it is easier to stop a dog before she becomes hysterical. Interruptions for barking can range from a stare to a quick pop on a leash to spray from a squirt bottle, a loud noise, or anything that is *mildly* unpleasant and gets the dog's attention. I remind people always to praise the dog instantly, once the behavior is interrupted. Visualizing and staying calm and centered makes an enormous difference as well, because your dog will be looking to you for cues as to what is expected.

A young woman named Alice once came to me with Max, her Jack Russell terrier. She was afraid that she would be evicted from her apartment because the dog barked so much. He barked the whole time she was at work and kept her awake half the night by sounding the alarm whenever he heard people coming and going in the building.

We began by teaching Max a few basic communication cues as well as the meaning of "Quiet" in connection with nonvocalizing behavior. I instructed Alice to keep a leash attached to him so that she could quickly and effectively interrupt the barking whenever he started up. She also learned to spend a lot of time praising Max every time he refrained from barking at nonthreatening everyday sounds. I put him on flower essences and showed her how to do some massage work on him.

Max slept on Alice's bed, so she could use his leash to correct him immediately if he woke her. Within a few nights they were both getting more sleep. When Alice was at work, we resolved the barking issue by putting Max in a crate. It appeared that he was very insecure and a little on the neurotic side, and he had trouble controlling his need to defend the entire apartment building. As soon as we put him in a kennel crate, where he felt safer and much more secure, the incessant barking during the day stopped, and Alice's neighbors were very grateful.

It takes effort and commitment to change a certain behavior, especially if it has been going on for a long time. The change can take weeks, if the behavior is deeply entrenched. Do training setups, rather than just trying to guess when the behavior might emerge. If you cannot repattern the barking during the week because you are at work, create a situation on the weekend that will trigger the barking so that you can address it. Anticipate, then interrupt, redirect, and praise.

These comments are very basic examples of ways this problem can be approached. If you are unable to change the behavior on your own, I strongly recommend that you consult a qualified behaviorist or trainer.

There is now a new no-bark collar (the ABS) that uses plain water or a citronella scent to interrupt a barking pattern. It is far more humane than shock collars. Obviously, I still prefer and strongly recommend training, over any gimmicky product, but if you have a situation where you must quiet your dog immediately (say a problem with neighbors and the police have become involved) you can safely turn to the ABS as a stop-gap measure.

GREETING VISITORS TOO BOISTEROUSLY

It's a familiar routine: someone comes to your door, and because your dog has super-hearing, he barks and rushes to the entrance before you are aware that anyone is there. "Red Alert! Intruder! Everyone come to the door!" he announces, placing himself in the kingpin position. When you respond to his call, he takes pride in the fact that he has gathered the troops. At this point however, the roles get confused. You open the door and the dog's definition of his next job is to decide whether the person is friend or foe. Because the dog is already at the door, you come up behind him. This makes him think that you are backing him up, and escalates the behavior. You grab his collar and restrain him because you don't want him jumping all over the visitor or escaping out the door, and this makes him more determined, because now he cannot accomplish his goal. The visitor often adds to the chaos by leaning over and acknowledging the dog, so the dog gets two signals at once: "Hello! Nice dog!" from the visitor, and "No! Down! Bad dog!" from you Some dogs become so excited that it takes a long time to calm them down.

If the dog is totally out of control and is dragged off and isolated while visitors are there, he may end up resenting them, because their appearance usurps his position in his family. This can lead to aggression, or it can open a Pandora's box of displacement behaviors. In any case, the dog is in charge, and no one gets a chance to have a conversation or do anything else until he is dealt with.

It is embarrassing and annoying to have to go through this drama every time you have company, so the benefits of changing the behavior are rather obvious. However, perhaps the greatest benefit of having a well-trained dog at the threshold to your home is that it gives you a greater measure of protection. When you open your door, a calm, alert dog sitting at your side can be a great deterrent if you don't want that person in your house. If your visitors are friends, neighbors, or relatives, you will not be embarrassed and have to apologize for your dog's behavior.

All of these reasons underscore the importance of teaching your dog his job description for this occasion. He needs to shift his focus and voluntarily give up his position. If he cannot relinquish the door mentally, it will make no sense to drag him away physically.

The technique for teaching good manners at the door is similar to other behavioral exercises in this book. This is also a very practical application of a number of exercises that you have taught your dog thus far. In this case, you will need to enlist the help of your friends, who will "visit" your house.

Prepare yourself mentally and emotionally ahead of time. Put your dog on a 12- to 15-foot-long line, depending on the size and design of your house. This length is important, because you want to maintain some distance from the dog. You will be giving corrections to teach your dog to relinquish his position at the door, and you should not be standing too near him.

Let your dog drag the line around the house under your supervision. If you have more than one dog, work with one only at a time, and put the others in another part of the house where they cannot interfere with your training exercise.

This exercise will need to be taught in small increments. You will teach the dog to: stop barking and vocalizing when you give him the command "Quiet"; leave the door and come to you after he has signaled the presence of a visitor; accompany you to the door and sit quietly by your side while you open it and invite the person to enter; accompany you and your visitor into the living room, where you will put the dog on a Down/Stay until you see that his excitement level has dissipated; and to greet the visitor politely when you signal that he may do so.

The first part of this exercise can be the most challenging, because his excitement level is usually quite high. It may take many practices and possibly more than a week just to fully teach the first part—to stop barking and come away from the door. Do not worry about the time frame; focus on your goal. Hold firm to your intention, and enlist the help of family members and friends. You can do it; have faith!

Technique:

- Have your helper arrive at a predetermined time and announce her presence either by knocking or by ringing a bell or buzzer. The person should do this only once and then quietly wait for the door to open, no matter how long it takes. Be sure the person does not keep knocking or ringing, because the dog will become even more excited, since this is usually the stimulus that triggers the barking in the first place.

- Allow your dog to go to the door and give a couple of warning barks. Then pick up his line, say "Quiet," and tell him to come. If the dog does not give up his place at the door, correct him by popping the line until he responds to you. It does not matter how many corrections it takes, whether two or five hundred;

continue to interrupt his focus until he shifts his attention and comes to you.

Note: It totally defeats the purpose of the exercise if you use the line to physically pull the dog away from the door. If mentally the dog has not voluntarily given up his kingpin position, you have not changed anything on a behavioral level.

- When your dog comes to you, praise him, use your symbol, and signaling, "Let's go," or "Heel," approach the door with him accompanying you on a loose lead.

- If he becomes excited and pulls, or tries to drag you back to the door, immediately pop the lead, turn him away from the door, and walk several steps. Turn back and approach the door again. As long as the dog is approaching the door calmly beside you on a loose lead, continue moving forward. If at any point the dog becomes excited or pulls again, pop the lead and turn away again. Do this as many times as necessary until your dog figures out that the only way he will ever discover who is at the door is to go there with you without pulling on the leash.

- As soon as the two of you reach the door, tell your dog to Sit and Wait. When he complies, open the door and invite your helper to come in.

- At all times your helper should ignore your dog and look only at you.

- Your dog should remain sitting while you and your visitor engage in a mock conversation. If he jumps up, barks, or does anything other than maintaining his position, continue giving corrections until he does as you ask.

- With your dog still on the lead, accompany your guest into a room where you both can sit down. It is a good idea to change the choice of room from time to time.

- Put your dog on a Down/Stay beside you, making corrections if necessary, and continue conversing with your visitor.

- When you see that the dog's excitement level has dissipated, you can give your release signal. Keep the dog's lead on, but allow him to politely greet the visitor. If he starts jumping, pawing, mouthing, or in any way loses control, immediately pick up the lead, give a correction, and put the dog back on Down/Stay for a while. Release him again and let him try the greeting once more.

- After the dog has been calm around your visitor for a short time, stand up and, keeping the line on the dog, accompany the person to the door to say good-bye.

- Repeat the exercise several times in a row in a concentrated period of time—for example, for an hour—with the same person. She should go out of sight of the house for about five minutes and then return to the door. Keep repeating each part of the practice as often as necessary—with men, women, and children, with people he knows, and with strangers—until your dog understands his job description and gives you a consistent response whenever someone arrives at the door.

Extra notes:

- When you first do this exercise, your dog may become so excited that he will need several corrections. Eventually the constant repetitions with the same person will lower his excitement level, and he will notice that he is receiving praise for calmer behavior.

- If a person arrives unexpectedly at your house, don't throw away a week of training because you are caught off guard. Keep a line on the doorknob, so that you can immediately snap it onto your dog and follow through with your usual routine. If you have the kind of household where people walk in without warning, put a sign on the door: Dog in Training—Knock and Wait. Before you open the door, call out to let your visitor know what you need to do and how to proceed.

- If your dog tends to get overexcited when you return home after being away, ignore him completely at first. Give him time to calm down before you greet him. If you do a lot of effusive greeting when you first walk in, you will reinforce any problems the dog may already have in this area. If you ignore him, he will learn that the sooner he calms down, the sooner he will receive your praise and attention.

I once worked with a couple who had a 90-pound golden retriever named Brandy. He was a wonderfully friendly dog but very exuberant and very large and powerful. His biggest problem was that he could hardly contain his joy when people came to visit, and being a golden, he had a real oral fixation, which manifested in his need to jump up and take the visitor's arm in his mouth. He did not do this in an aggressive way, but he loved to hold on to the person and would stand there, wriggling all over and whining and groaning his greetings at the same time. People who did not know Brandy found this very disconcerting!

No matter how many solutions we came up with to correct the behavior, Brandy would still backslide. I decided that, instead of telling him what *not* to do, we would give him something different to do. A basket containing a number of small gift items was placed on a table by the door. Whenever someone rang or knocked, Brandy would race joyfully to grab that basket off the table and then go to the door, where he would sit proudly holding it in his mouth, still wriggling all over and whining, but happily ready to offer a gift to the visitor. His need to show people how utterly delighted he was to see them was satisfied, and he could not take any part of the visitor in his mouth because his mouth was already full of basket. It was a perfect solution!

OTHER BEHAVIORAL ISSUES
I will discuss jumping-up behavior and house-training in Chapter 15.

THE NEEDS OF HANDICAPPED AND RESCUED DOGS
Rescuing a dog from an abusive situation or from a shelter is a generous and courageous act. People who do this often find that they have taken on a major challenge, however, because a dog who has survived traumatic experiences or a lack of socialization is an emotionally wounded animal who needs extra time, love, and patience while he adjusts to a different reality. If you cannot commit to a long-term investment of your time, with the kind of patience, energy, and effort that is often required to bring about a different behavior pattern from this kind of dog, it may be kinder not to take him on in the first place. It is very hard for a dog, who has already experienced stress and trauma, to be brought into a new situation and then have people give up on him and send him back to the Humane Society or pass him on to yet another new family.

Guidelines for working with a rescued dog:

1. Begin by doing a lot of observation, so that you can learn as much as possible about your new dog's temperament and tolerance. It will often take as long as two weeks for a dog to be comfortable enough in his new environment to show you who he really is.

2. Review "Creating Your Symbol" in Chapter 6 to help you develop a deeper connection on an energy level with the dog.

Use your symbol every time you work with your dog; visualize the new possibilities that you desire for that dog's life.

3. Put the dog on flower essences and homeopathic or herbal remedies that are appropriate to treat any physical or behavioral problems that you observe. Some suggestions to get you started are listed in Chapter 13. Putting a dog on a high-quality diet will help facilitate the necessary changes, but introduce dietary changes gradually to avoid any digestive upsets. These additions will contribute to enhancing the dog's sense of well-being, helping him adjust to his new situation.

4. Begin communication exercises to establish trust and respect.

5. Consider changing the dog's name. Dogs adjust very quickly to this, and a new name can often help him get over past experiences that were negative. For example, I once worked with a dog named Patty, whose humans had not been able to house-train her and who had yelled, "Patty, no! Bad dog!" constantly while they punished her. By the time she came to me, she would cringe whenever I said her name, because she expected a reprimand to follow. I changed her name to Sprite, because I felt that she had a happy, bubbly personality under all of her fearful ways. With lots of love and consistency, she did grow into her name, and she became a wonderful companion.

   If the dog was a stray and doesn't have a name, or if you feel the need to change the dog's name, first sit quietly to see if you get the sense of a name from him. I mentally ask, "Do you have a name?" and listen in my mind for a response. Sometimes I get an answer immediately. If I do not, I ask, "Is there a name that you would like to be called?" If still nothing comes to me, I choose a name with positive qualities that will enhance the dog's temperament and personality.

Although it is tragic that dogs are often abused and neglected, realize that it is not helpful to let the dog's past become a crutch that will prevent him from growing into his full potential. Many times people are reluctant to address behavioral issues because they believe that the dog will be further stressed if he is taken through basic training. If the dog does something unacceptable, like jumping on the furniture, the night that you bring him home, correct him immediately. Don't wait, thinking he needs time to adjust. Your aim will be to create a bond of trust and respect. If you start out with one set of rules and then switch them and begin to reprimand just as he is beginning to bond to you, your inconsistency will give him a good reason not to. The only way to change the past is to start in the present and give the dog the skills that will earn him praise and affection. In this way your dog will revel in the new "now" that you create for him.

Working with a handicapped dog: If your dog is handicapped, you will have a similar challenge when it comes to issues of communication or discipline. When you look at your dog, be sure to see beyond the disability and experience the whole self that is there wanting to be understood, communicated with, and respected.

Behavioral problems may be associated with the dog's disability. Deaf and blind dogs, for example, are often easily startled; therefore you need to approach them with an awareness of their special needs. When I teach people to communicate with handicapped animals, we work out special signals depending on the disability. Deaf dogs, for example, respond well to hand signals, and things like stamping your foot on the floor so that their attention is caught by the vibration, or flashing the outside lights of the house when you want them to come in. It is also a very good idea to put a bell on a deaf dog's collar; since he will not be able to hear you call, this will help you keep track of him if he goes out of sight. A deaf dog should also be kept on a tie-out line or in a fenced yard for his own safety.

Many great gifts that handicapped animals bring with them are their example of living life to the fullest, no matter what the physical hindrance. I once worked with a young woman named Elizabeth who was deaf and very bitter about her condition. When she discovered that Oscar, her cocker spaniel, was also becoming deaf, she considered getting rid of him. She could only identify herself through her disability, and this made her feel unattractive and not worthy of receiving love. By the same token, she felt that she could not love a dog who had the same handicap, because it was a cruel twist of fate and too painful to have her deafness reflected back to her.

Despite the loss of his hearing, however, Oscar maintained his zest for life and was a playful and joyous being. His physical body changed, but his essential nature did not. During our session I pointed out that perhaps he wanted to give Elizabeth the gift of his example. I could tell that she was considering my words, but was not convinced. Since Oscar already understood basic training, it was not going to be difficult to teach him hand signals. I showed Elizabeth how to change the way she worked with him, and as I watched them go out the door, I wondered what Oscar's fate was going to be.

Several months went by, and then one day a car pulled up, and a whole new Elizabeth got out, with Oscar trotting right behind her. Elizabeth was smiling and eager to show me how Oscar had learned to follow her signing. Her whole being now spoke to him through her posture, her eyes, the expression on her face, the movement of her hands, and the visualization of her request. Oscar's eyes never left her face, and he followed her directions eagerly. This was a wonderful achievement, but my greatest pleasure was in seeing that Elizabeth now knew that neither sound nor hand gestures are the most important factors in real communication. She also had come to realize, from Oscar's example, that her hearing impairment did not have to prevent her from having a full and joyful life.

Working with an old dog: It is important to remember that, as dogs age, many begin to lose their sight and hearing. This weakening of faculties can come on so slowly that their other senses compensate quite easily, especially if the dog remains in a familiar environment. You may not be aware of the situation at first, but for the safety of your friend and companion, watch for these changes in order to safeguard him from accidents or injuries.

When your dog gets lost: It is a terrible tragedy if a dog runs away, is lost, or disappears from home through theft or by accident. If this happens in your family, there are a number of things you can do that may help to bring your dog back home again. A very distraught client named Elaine showed up at my house recently to ask for help because her Rottweiler, Cody, had been stolen that day out of the yard in front of her house. Her house was at the end of a dirt road, and neighbors reported seeing a shiny new red pickup truck passing their houses, heading toward hers, and driving by again a short time later. It was hunting season, there were many strangers in the neighborhood, and people around here tend to notice things like this.

As with other cases of lost dogs, I always suggest that people immediately blanket the area with flyers describing the dog and offering a reward for his return. Contact every local radio station, humane society, vet clinic, fish and game warden, and police department. Take every opportunity to tell your friends and anyone you meet your dog is missing.

An important side effect of this event was the effect it had on the other people in the training classes. Realizing how they would feel if they were in Elaine's situation heightened the emotional energy, and a number of people reported that their connection with their dog was strengthened because of the tragedy. Because of this increased awareness, people found themselves able to be more tolerant of the small infractions and annoyances that came up in the practices and to focus instead on all of the benefits and joys that were part of their relationship, with very positive results.

Fortunately, there is a happy end to the story: Cody was left off in front of a local police station only a few days from the time he had been taken. Elaine told us all on the last night of class that the amount of intentional energy that we had created to bring her and her dog back together had been an incredible support to her and, along with all of the heat created in the media, had made her feel that the thief had no choice but to let the dog go.

If despite all of your efforts your dog does not return, be sure to maintain a heart connection and do not give up hope. I have found that, after a while, most people seem to intuitively know whether they will be reunited with their dog or not. The most important thing is to keep your energy flowing, receptive, and available to reestablishing your connection on a physical level, even if that seems improbable.

You may find the following exercise helpful:

A Meditation for a Lost Dog

- Sit quietly, breathe in deeply, and exhale slowly several times. Allow your body to relax, and continue to focus on your breathing.

- Allow an image of your dog to come into your consciousness.

- If a sense of fear and loss comes along with the image, acknowledge that those fears are there, and then release them. Remembering that whatever you send out attracts more of what is happening, you want to work only with positive energy. Your connection with your dog goes beyond the physical, so keep your focus on the higher state of awareness that you share.

- When you are able simply to look at your dog, allow your heart to open and a golden beam of light to go to your dog. See that your dog is also sending golden heart energy back to you.

- Visualize that your dog is safe and well and that someday you will be reunited. See your dog being calm and happy, and connected with your energy, no matter where he is.

- End by stating, either silently or aloud, that you are open to the possibility of reconnecting with your dog. Sit quietly for a moment before opening your eyes. Remind yourself to keep the energy positive as you go about your daily business.

It is important to remember that you can never own another life; though you miss your dog, you cannot lose something that was never yours to own. Because we are connected to one another on an energy level all the time, it may help you to realize that there is a good chance that you will engage with your animal's energy again—perhaps in the form of a different animal in the future.

Finally, even if you do decide that you and your dog may not be reunited, remember that miracles can happen in real life and not just in storybooks.

This was the case with Bruce, a client and friend, who took Annie, his border collie along when he went in early winter to visit a friend several hours away from his home. While they were out cross-country skiing down a country road with the dog off-leash, she ran in front of a car and was hit. Terrified and hurt, she took off through the woods, and although Bruce followed a blood trail in the snow and called and called, it grew dark before he was able find her. It snowed during the night and in the morning, the trail was obliterated. He spent more than a week looking for signs of her without success. At last, he sadly concluded that she had probably died of her injuries. He had to return home, but he begged his friend to call him immediately if there was any sign of her.

Bruce tried to stop thinking about Annie, but he could not bring himself to get another dog. Nearly six months went by, and most of those months were wintry and bitter cold. In late spring he returned to visit his friend again, and they began to talk about the incident. His friend mentioned that a farmer up the road had reported that a feral dog had been hanging around his barn. Bruce's head kept telling him there was no way this dog could be Annie. Still, his heart would not let go of the hope that she had somehow survived the winter on her own.

In the end, he just had to know, and he decided to pay the farmer a visit. When he got to the farm, the farmer—who had a good heart and had been leaving food for the dog in the barn because it was so thin—told Bruce that the dog always showed up at twilight and that he was welcome to sit on a hay bale and watch for it.

His heart pounding, Bruce did as the farmer suggested, and after a half an hour, he saw an animal push its way through a broken board at the back of the barn. Bruce saw it was a dog, but in the dim light, he could not make out any details. As the dog neared the plate of food, Bruce called out in a trembling voice, "Annie?" The dog froze for an instant, one paw raised, ears pricked up, and then spun around, scrambled through the opening, and was gone.

Bruce was shaken by the encounter, even though he could not tell if it was Annie or not. He decided not to go back to his home right away, because he wanted to do whatever he could to help the dog, no matter whose it was. If Annie had ended up in such a situation, he would have wanted someone to help her.

Bruce called and canceled his plans for the week, and began to return to the farm each evening. Each time, the dog came, and each time, it ran as soon as it saw there was someone in the barn.

The week went by, and Bruce could stay no longer. He sadly said goodbye to his friend and decided to stop at the farm one last time on his way home. It was almost dark, and when he stepped into the barn, the dog was already there and was eating from the plate of food. She froze when she saw him, but instead of running, she began inching backwards, torn between her fear and her hunger. Bruce could hardly make out the shape in the dim light, but in that single moment, something about her connected with something deep inside him. He crouched down and held out one hand, even as the dog began backing away into the darker shadows, preparing to flee. Bruce hadn't used her nickname before; maybe the lack of conviction had caused him to be less familiar, but now, full of love and hope, he called out to her: "Little Girl?" The dog froze, head held high, every inch of her body alert and listening. Bruce kept up a stream of their special language, "My Little Girl, Annie girl," he crooned, "Annie pretty girl, little love, Annie girl." He would have gone on, but his words were cut off by the whining, wriggling dog who had thrown herself into his arms.

Annie was emaciated, had numerous sores on her body, and walked with a limp as a result of her accident. These were minor problems; the greatest healing, for her and for Bruce, was already accomplished.

Maintaining a heart connection with your dog, no matter where she is, is more of a support system than you might think. I believe that this is true for all relationships; the energy of love between beings who have made a commitment to one another can sustain them in times of injury and fear, can heal confusion and sorrow, and can create a shining path of light to bring the lost back home.

How was it that Annie happened to show up only a quarter of a mile away from the scene of her accident, more than half a year after its occurrence and during the week that Bruce had returned to the area? The fact that she was so thin indicated that she must have lived all of the time on her own in the wild. It was nothing short of a miracle that she had survived one of the worst winters New England had seen in years, both in depth of snow and in weeks of subzero temperatures. No sign of her had been reported by anyone in the neighborhood prior to that time.

Bruce had never given up hoping that someday he would find Annie again. Annie was confused and afraid; she could not understand what had happened to her. But some part of her was still connected to Bruce and that connection must have given her the willpower and the courage to live as well as the ability to sense his presence. Bruce's heart told him how to do the rest.

"Bruce and Annie"

13

CARING FOR YOUR DOG: NUTRITION AND SUPPORTIVE HOLISTIC HEALING PRACTICES

I am dedicated to encouraging people to take control of their dog's health issues and to educate themselves. I give guidance in holistic healing whenever I do a counseling session, and I help provide access to various remedies as well as to dog food and nutritional supplements. My many years' experience has shown me that the healthiest dogs are those whose human companions have a thorough knowledge of their requirements and who do not leave the responsibility entirely up to the veterinarian.

People who bring their dogs to me for holistic counseling have different responses to doing natural healing work. Some of them come because they see that the chemical medications their dog is on are not working very well and they are seeking another approach. Sometimes when people find out that it's not as simple as giving the dog a pill once a day and that they need to be willing to invest time and energy in bringing healing about by doing things like daily massage or acupressure, they choose not to do so. Other times I encounter someone who knows little about natural or energetic healing practices but who is willing to learn to do anything that will help the dog recover or to help an older pet with chronic arthritis to feel more comfortable. While these people may feel a little unsure of their ability to do touch therapy and massage, or to facilitate healing by sending positive energy to their dog, they find that the more they practice, the easier it gets. This gives them confidence, and their bond with their dog deepens through their daily involvement in the healing process. These people enjoy knowing that they are responsible for making their dog more comfortable. In fact, when they see rapid improvement in their dog, they frequently begin to explore natural healing for themselves.

I also encounter people who are already using natural healing methods for themselves and are seeking the same for their dogs. Because they are familiar with the modalities, they already know that these will play an important role in the healing process for their dog.

It is only logical that learning to direct energy would be followed by a concern that the energy that moves through your dog's physical body be able to move freely and be balanced. This does not happen in an unhealthy body.

This chapter includes an overview of basic issues of health care and nutrition, as well as different holistic healing modalities that you can explore as part of your overall relationship with your dog. Because this is a vast field, I hope to give you an introduction that will inspire you to learn more. After summarizing the various approaches, I will offer suggestions for using these for typical behavioral and physical issues like car sickness and injuries as well as for general conditions like arthritis.

It is important to begin with a discussion of nutrition, because this is of primary importance in giving your dog the right kind of care.

I have been professionally involved with dogs since the 1970s. I have watched dogs over the years becoming weaker with each generation. For a long time I have been feeding my dogs natural foods and teaching my clients the importance of holistic nutrition. Almost half of the dogs I see for holistic health counseling have premature degenerative diseases and a very high incidence of cancer along with an increase in a broad range of illnesses including autoimmune, heart, and liver diseases, epilepsy, allergies, and skin problems.

Bad breeding practices may be one reason why many breeds have decreased longevity. The biggest common contributor to this problem, however, is diet. During counseling sessions, whether behavioral or holistic, one of my first questions is "What is the dog being fed?" My concerns about nutrition are shared by many other animal health professionals. Before all else, holistic practitioners now emphasize that proper nutrition is the foundation of health.

According to W. Jean Dodds, a holistic veterinarian in Santa Monica, California, and an internationally renowned expert on immunological diseases in animals, thyroid dysfunction is becoming increasingly common in dogs, with about 80 percent of the cases caused by an imbalance in the immune system. In an article published in the *Proceedings of the 1997 American Holistic Veterinary Medical Association Annual Conference*, she states that, in addition to genetic predispositions, the three major contributing factors are lack of proper nutrition, overvaccination, and exposure to toxins. Clinical studies have shown that dogs with thyroid disease can suddenly develop behavior problems, including aggression, anxiety, compulsiveness, chewing, lethargy, and seizures.

"Although there has not yet been a comprehensive study done on all breeds in the U.S.," says Dodds, "veterinarians generally concur that mid-size and giant dogs' life spans are decreasing." One study conducted by Dodds on Old English sheepdogs revealed that unspayed females in that breed live three years less than their spayed relatives due to diseases like mammary cancer. Dogs, just like humans, are clearly showing the effects of our unhealthy lifestyle. By contrast, most of my dogs live an average of eighteen to twenty-one years, and they are healthy right up until the end, when they usually succumb to the effects of old age.

Health and behavior begin on a cellular level. Depending on the illness, many unhealthy animals can be helped or have their symptoms eased and their behavior modified through nutritional changes and vitamin support. In my private counseling at Hearthside, I have had dramatic results with many animals—particularly those suffering from serious allergies and problems like arthritis, as well as cats with kidney problems—simply by changing the diet and adding a few vitamin and herbal supplements. I often find that even animals who have been on steroids and antibiotics for years no longer need them.

According to holistic veterinarian Bill Pollak of the Fairfield Animal Hospital in Fairfield, Iowa, "[According to my own research, nearly 75 percent] of common diseases in dogs can be eliminated without medical intervention over a period of one year." Dr. Pollak also says, "Encouraging health through enhanced nutrition is the most efficient means of relieving disease.

Pollak and other veterinarians are finding that high-quality nutritional support enables the animal's immune system to throw off lingering chronic disease, which is not possible when the dog is fed on "marginally adequate grain-based commercial pet foods."

Holistic veterinarians who use nutrition as a front-line defense against chronic illness often find that, when a dog is changed from a poor diet to a healthy one, he has to go through a "healing episode," which is defined by Pollak as a "transient, mild appearance of symptoms mimicking disease without the loss of vitality, mental or physical clarity or strength and with the cessation of symptoms without medical intervention." The symptoms are an indication that the body has summoned enough vitality to expel accumulated toxins through the kidney, colon, lungs, or skin.

Processed food has only been around for the last forty years. During this time, our culture has decided, for the sake of economy and convenience, that dogs should exist on a diet of cooked cereal. Yet the dogs' metabolism has been fueled by raw meat for millennia. You have only to look at any dog's teeth to see his carnivorous heritage and to know what his nutritional requirements need to be. Compared with the amount of time that dogs have been on the earth, forty years is not even one blink of an eye. A shift to a predominantly grain-based diet simply cannot work for the dog.

It's not easy for the average person to find the information he needs to make the right choices about his dog's nutrition. The pet food industry is built on misinformation and hype. The labeled contents on products are difficult to decipher, and there is no real consistency or truth in labeling here in the United States.

In *It's for the Animals!* a comprehensive "cookbook" for animals, as well as an impressively comprehensive resource guide to holistic health, writer Helen L. McKinnon says, "My more thorough investigation of commercial pet food was initiated after reading the shocking article 'Does Your Dog Food Bark? A Study of the Pet Food Fallacy' by Ann Martin, which appeared in the March 1995 issue of *Natural Pet* magazine. I read with horror of diseased cats and dogs euthanized, and the barbiturate found unaltered in the end product—my dogs' food. (One small pet-food plant renders 11 tons a week of euthanized dogs and cats which were sold to [a dog food company]!) The animal proteins used in many commercial foods are diseased meat, road kills, contaminated material from slaughterhouses, fecal matter, and poultry feathers all rendered together. Those decomposing animals, condemned material from the slaughterhouses, were 'denatured': soaked in carbolic acid, fuel oil, kerosene and citronella."

McKinnon also reports:

"The mainstay of dry [dog] foods are vegetable proteins which provide little nutritional value; they are nothing more than sweepings and offal from milling room floors left over after processing. Our own U.S. Government agency that is supposed to regulate animal food by setting the guidelines and definitions, is the AAFCO (Association of American Feed Control Officials). Their "Official Publication" states that there are no restrictions on the type of animals which can be used in meals, digest, etc. (meat meal, meat digest, poultry meal, poultry digest, etc.) Any kind of animal can be used, including cats and dogs. Their list of "Feed Ingredient Definitions" includes:

Spray Dried Animal Blood, Hydrolyzed Hair, Dehydrated Garbage, Unborn Calf Carcasses, Dried Poultry Litter (processed animal waste—feces from commercial poultry and litter present on the production floor, Dried Ruminant Waste, Dried Swine Waste, Undried Processed Animal Waste Products (excreta, with or without litter from poultry, ruminants or any other non-human animal), Urea Formaldehyde."

"Commercial Pet food is allowed to have additives, chemicals, excess sugar, and sodium (salt). Martin calls it "Garbage laced with additives" and suggests an additional label on the pet food package: a skull and crossbones insignia!"

The unpleasant truth is that any foodstuff unfit for human consumption is allowed in pet food. It's no coincidence that major food processing companies also make dog food. This allows them to make a huge profit on by-products that would normally be plowed into the ground. In fact, some of this material is so heavily contaminated with herbicides and pesticides, that it is not allowed to go back into the soil. This is the stuff that makes up your pet food!

Of equal concern is the way some animals become your dog's dinner. Many companies use the 4-D's—dead, diseased, dying, or disabled—domestic livestock as a meat source. Pathogens and toxic substances are passed along in the product after processing. Animals destined for human food consumption cannot be slaughtered until ninety days from the time they received the last injections of antibiotics, steroids, and anti-inflammatories. If, however, the animal dies or the decision is made to euthanize it, it's generally sent away to the nearest meat-rendering plant: a pet food company.

Now that I can see energy fields, I've become even more concerned about this situation. It is frightening to see dogs less than a year old come into my classes with energy fields that are lacking a strong vital life force.

This is only a brief sketch of the nutritional issues. If this is happening to dog food, can you imagine the dangers in your own food supply? More reading on the subject is suggested at the end of this book.

FOODS THAT DOGS NEED

The best food you can give your dog is a home-cooked diet of all natural fresh foods. I have been feeding my dogs this diet for years, because I know how critical it is to their health and well-being. Although home-cooking for dogs is more common in Europe, Americans are now beginning to recognize the benefits.

Here is an example of a recipe published by veterinarian Bill Pollak in his article on nutrition in the 1997 January issue of the quarterly journal published by the American Holistic Veterinary Medical Association:

Basic Canine Three-Part Combo: *Balanced generic recipe for a mid-sized canine. This recipe can be halved for small dogs and doubled for large dogs. Feed once daily. Substitutions of different raw meats, grains, and vegetables should be made to ensure a wide range of nutritive elements are available.*

¼ pound (one-half cup) ground chicken, turkey, or beef (heart or muscle okay); liver not more than once weekly

4–6 slices whole natural bread (break up into small pieces) or [cooked] pasta

1 cup whole milk (raw, non-homogenized, if possible)

2 large eggs (optional: ground-up rinsed and dried egg shells)

¼ cup string beans or other vegetables

1 tablespoon vitamin/mineral powder

1 tablespoon ghee, olive, or vegetable oil

1½ teaspoons bone meal, calcium or rinsed and dried eggshells

200 I.U. vitamin E pill

(Optional) ¼ teaspoon tamari, Braggs liquid aminos or a dash iodized salt

(Optional) 1 clove garlic, crushed or minced

(Optional) ¼ teaspoon ginger, licorice and/or cumin

Combine all ingredients, add water if needed. Serve raw or shape and bake at 325° F. until lightly browned (20–30 minutes).

Using organic foods can be a challenge for people who have limited access to them or are on a strict budget. If you cannot afford to buy organic foods, using vegetables and meats found in your local grocery is still vastly preferable to feeding only dry or canned foods. I spare no expense on my dogs' nutrition, and I know I save in the long run, because they are extremely healthy. Animals with on-going health issues are very time-consuming to care for and have very expensive veterinary bills.

Because I'm feeding an average of thirty dogs on a daily basis, I belong to a local co-op where I can buy organic grains in bulk. I also have a large garden every summer so that we have our own supply of fresh vegetables. In addition, I work with a local slaughterhouse which custom grinds the meat according to my specifications.

I use a very large pot for cooking grains like rice, oatmeal, and millet and I cook enough for several days at a time. I also use a combination of raw leaf and root vegetables as well as fresh and dried herbs. I combine the vegetables in the food processor, grind them fairly fine and then store them in glass jars in the refrigerator. I have found that glass keeps things fresher longer, because it allows the food to be at the same temperature that the refrigerator is set for. Plastic insulates foods from the cold, therefore food doesn't keep as long or stay as fresh.

I prepare all of the different ingredients ahead of time a couple of times a week and then have only to combine them when I'm ready to feed. You can use just one or two kinds of vegetables at a time; however, I usually use a combination of ten to twelve in the mix I make for the dogs.

There are advantages to this: on one particularly busy day, I was tired when it came time for my own dinner and didn't really feel like taking the time to make a salad to go with my meal. The gallon glass jar of ground raw vegetables for the dogs caught my eye, partially because it looked so colorful. I took some out and added some salad dressing. It was delicious—similar to a coleslaw, crunchy and full of flavor. I now regularly partake of this same vegetable mix and have found I can completely change the taste by the dressing that I use or the things I add. I have combined the mixture with cream cheese and spread it on bagels, and I've added it to soups and casseroles. So the discovery of this great fast addition of healthy and flavorful vegetables for the dogs has also benefited me.

My strong connection to Native American spirituality, which teaches awareness and respect for our place in the web of life, inspires me to take a moment to give thanks to the universe and honor the plants and animals whose vital energy is present in the food. My desire is that my dogs' systems are nourished with the energy of my awareness that they are blessed by the contributions of other living beings, who give of themselves to continue the circle of life. I use a thought form to energize the food with positive energy.

Home cooking for dogs needs to be done knowledgeably in order to ensure that the diet is balanced and includes all the necessary vitamins, trace minerals, and so forth. There are several good books to assist you. (See the Appendix.)

Can your dog stay alive on predominantly cereal-based commercially produced dog food? Yes, but there is a difference between being alive and being vitally alive. You are responsible for your dog's well-being. Therefore I cannot impress upon you strongly enough the importance of educating yourself about proper nutrition.

HEALING BUSTER

The following story of a client and her dog who came for holistic counseling illustrates the level of health that can be restored through dietary changes and the proper use of supplements.

Jill's Chow, Buster, had a nice temperament, despite the fact that his breed is generally considered tough, aggressive, and dominant. Jill brought

Buster to me after he had turned from a real sweetheart to a monster who attacked other dogs without provocation. When I met Buster, I knew instinctively that he was not innately aggressive. His muzzle looked strange: all of the hair was gone and it was scabby on the top. Buster's energy field seemed contracted around his body instead of radiating out. This dog just didn't feel good.

Jill said that Buster had been diagnosed as having canine lupus and that the vet had put him on steroids and given him a cortisone cream for the skin problem. It didn't seem to be working, however, and his problem was getting worse. I immediately put him on an herbal detoxification program and a fast to help cleanse the toxins from his system. We then introduced dietary changes and flower essences.

In addition to the holistic program, Jill agreed to bring Buster to the next series of classes in order to reinforce their communication skills and have him be with other dogs in a controlled environment. I put Buster on a Halti to give Jill more control, which helped her stop projecting nervous, fearful energy into the situation. Over the weeks, Buster's face cleared up. As his health returned, he became even more responsive to Jill's requests and returned to his previously good-natured self when he was around other dogs. It has now been over a year and there has been no reoccurrence of the previous symptoms. I felt strongly that Buster's aggression was partly due to not feeling well, but also due to the steroids he was given, which often alter behavior dramatically.

PROPER NUTRITION HELPS PREVENT PARASITES

Since I began feeding predominantly meat and raw foods and stopped using any chemicals on the dogs ten years ago, the dogs in my household have not had fleas. Any poisons that you use to eliminate parasites will also weaken or suppress your dog's immune system. Parasites are attracted to the young, because their immune systems are not fully developed, and to the old, whose immune systems are breaking down. If you have a dog with recurring flea infestations, you really need to pay attention to what those fleas are telling you about your dog's health.

Americans are seriously misled about issues like eliminating parasites. Systemics that are put into or on your dog's body and absorbed into the bloodstream are poisons and challenge your dog's immune system. If a product contains enough poison to kill insects—which is not easy to do—common sense tells me that it cannot be beneficial to the overall health of my dog.

Those products make even less sense when used on dogs who are allergic to fleas. A single flea bite can cause an allergic reaction in some dogs, so if the flea has to bite the dog to be killed by the poison, in doing so it triggers the allergic reaction in the dog that you were trying to prevent in the first place. Also, by impairing your dog's immune system with chemicals and poisons, whether given internally or applied topically, you cause parasites to be even more attracted to the dog.

The dogs I live with are so healthy that parasites are not attracted to them. Also, regular vacuuming and wet-mopping will take care of most flea eggs and larvae in your household. (See the Appendix for books on nontoxic parasite control.)

SELECTING AND WORKING WITH A VETERINARIAN

My personal preference is to work with a holistic vet who uses natural methods to help the body return to its natural state of health, with the emphasis on promoting wellness rather than trying to fight disease. I also work with several local allopathic veterinarians who practice conventional medicine and yet are open-minded enough to see the benefits of both forms of veterinary medicine. I don't believe that it always has to be an either/or choice but one that should integrate the best of both.

Until the physical body wears out from prolonged use, its persistent impulse is to heal and rebalance after any infection, disease, or injury. The goal should be to facilitate this natural healing response by using the simplest, least invasive methods possible and then allowing the body to bring itself back into balance and heal itself.

If you choose a veterinarian who follows these principles, you will have made the best choice for your dog's well-being.

We need to rediscover our power to be healers, and we have to assume more responsibility for creating and maintaining our own health and that of our pets, through wise choices of lifestyle and attitudes. I encourage you to learn about the side effects and long-range ramifications of many traditional chemical medicines. I also encourage you to become informed about the holistic options available for treating the same illnesses. Then you can make your decisions based upon what you feel is right for you and your dog.

VACCINATIONS AND OTHER MEDICATIONS

In 1995 the journal of the American Veterinary Medicine Association printed an article questioning the wisdom of annual vaccinations for pets: "There is little scientific documentation that backs up label claims for annual administration of most vaccines. Although it is possible that some vaccines work best when given annually, others need to be given more often, and many others may last for years. The only vaccine routinely tested for minimum durations of immunity is the rabies vaccine."

Humans don't get annual vaccinations, why should animals? Unfortunately, the reason in many cases seems to be economically driven.

When we vaccinate, we limit the animals' ability to develop their immune systems naturally. I vaccinate puppies and then give a booster at one year of age. Other than rabies, which you have to do by law, mine never get vaccinated again. Most people I know who are on a holistic path, vaccinate their pets one time for distemper and parvo; these three diseases are still deadly to animals. After a year a simple vaccine titer blood test can show whether the immunity persists, and if it does, the animal is not vaccinated again. In addition, some holistic vets are turning to homeopathic nosodes as an alternative preventive measure. If you are interested in this alternative, check with a holistic vet.

Other issues to keep track of include:

- *The rabies vaccine:* According to W. Jean Dodds, D.V.M., the federal government is planning to recommend that all states comply with the three-year time frame, but it is not known how soon this might happen. Because rabies is a fatal disease, even though booster vaccinations may be hard on some dogs, the risk has to be taken to protect the public health.

- *Lyme disease shots:* The original Lyme disease vaccine created adverse reactions in many dogs, including painful swelling in the joints. There are newer vaccines which do not appear to cause bad reactions. It is better to forgo the shot entirely, however, because "Lyme disease in dogs tends to be less clinically significant than in humans," says Dodds, "and can be usually controlled with a course of antibiotics."

- *Heartworm medication:* I have not given this to my dogs in almost fourteen years. I tried it when it first came out; I wasn't on the same path that I am now. When I saw how desperately ill it made some of my dogs, I just stopped doing it. The drug used in heartworm preventative medication is an immunosuppressant and can create problems with the whole immune system. In their natural raw foods diet, my dogs are given a lot of garlic and apple cider vinegar, both of which are great natural insect repellents. I also practice good prevention: I keep their immune systems high, so that they are not attractive to parasites, and I don't put them out during heavy mosquito hours in the warm weather months. If we go out camping, I mix up an insect repellent of essential oils like citronella, rosemary, and lavender and put it in a spray bottle. We test for heartworm every spring, and none of my dogs has ever tested positive.

You will have to decide for yourself about the risks, depending on your location and your dog's level of health. New information is developing rapidly on this subject, so you need to educate yourself and keep abreast of all the current information as it becomes available so you can make knowledgeable decisions. (Check the Appendix for suggested resources.)

EXERCISE AND SOCIAL CONTACT

Because dogs are social creatures by nature, they need contact with people and other dogs on a regular basis. If a dog has come from a puppy mill, it can often have behavioral problems associated with not knowing how to relate to its own kind. If a dog spends an entire day in a crate or tied up outside, the loneliness and boredom can cause problems like destructive chewing, excessive barking, and excitability.

If you live alone, there are a number of ways that you can ensure that your dog has a full and stimulating range of friends to interact with. Maureen, one of my clients, and her beagle, Lolly, are a good case in point. Maureen is single, lives in the suburbs, and works in an office, but when she comes home, her dog gets to join her in her other activities whenever possible. Maureen is always looking for opportunities to create an extended family. She will often drop Lolly off at her sister's house, where there is another dog to play with. Several neighborhood children can be trusted to take Lolly out for walks, and they love to play with her in the fenced-in backyard. Sometimes Maureen and Lolly go to a dog park in the city, where there are always other dogs to share a romp.

Lolly gets plenty of exercise because Maureen is a runner, but too many dogs suffer from a lack of real aerobic activity. They have poor muscle tone, are overweight, and are often caught in a downward spiral of lethargy, depression, and increasing health problems. Small dogs are very often in this category, because their human companions carry them everywhere in their arms or in backpacks.

In fact, a small dog can get a lot of exercise indoors. You can sit in a chair, throw a ball down a hallway for a Yorkshire terrier and give him a pretty good workout. A German shepherd wouldn't even start to pant in this situation, because he could cover that same distance in two strides.

If your dog's exercise is neglected during the week, it doesn't help to take him out and run up a mountain on a weekend. Just like people, dogs need to build up to strenuous physical activity, or they can get sports injuries. They need methodical, consistent conditioning.

If you take your dog jogging, think carefully about your choice of routes. Pounding pavement is hard on a dog's pads and joints, and because he is lower to the ground, he is susceptible to all of the exhaust fumes from passing cars.

THE HOLISTIC APPROACH TO HEALTH

My work with holistic healing is geared toward promoting health, promoting rapid healing after an accident or injury, and slowing down degenerative diseases. Before discussing various holistic health options, I would like to mention that one of the most important things you can do for your dog's physical health and emotional well-being is to take good care of yourself! This is important for a wide variety of reasons: if you are stressed out or if there is tension in your household, it is often absorbed and acted out by the dog. I see many families for holistic counseling where the dog is the "identified patient." Once the counseling session begins, however, and all of the complex and myriad relationships within the family begin to surface, it becomes quite obvious what is causing the dog's behavioral problem. I have needed on occasion to go so far as to recommend counseling for the family, because I knew nothing was going to change for the dog until serious issues within the family were resolved.

Frequently, people do not spend time taking care of themselves, but will spend time taking care of their dog. This is a backwards approach. I encourage you to do those activities that make you feel really good, especially if they include spending time with your dog. Surround yourself with a beautiful, peaceful environment that enhances your feeling of well-being, because this in turn truly benefits your dog.

Taking care of yourself will also help healing flow more easily through you, when you practice using your energy to help yourself and your dog feel better.

When I set about trying to heal an animal who is ill, I use methods that I have tried before and observed to be effective, but each interaction will also require an intuitive response for the individual animal. My sense of the individual animal guides me to what it needs. You will begin to get acquainted with your intuitive gifts as you learn Awareness Training. For any serious health issues about your dog, however, seek professional advice at once, while taking note of your own intuitive feelings. You may not trust your answers in the beginning, but write them down anyway, and check the outcome. You will begin to get a sense for your inner yes or no, and you will become more confident about your decision-making process over time.

To give you a sense of the breadth of options available to you in holistic health care, here, briefly, is an overview of some of my preferred healing modalities. If you choose to try any of them with your animals, begin with those that intuitively feel right or make the most sense to you. Numerous alternative health books for animals are available in bookstores; some of my favorites are listed in the Appendix.

Note: These methods are not to be considered substitutes for informed health care from a professional; these are only additions to the healing process.

USING HERBAL MEDICINES

Both people and animals have used plants as the primary form of medicine since the beginning of time. Humans learned a great deal by observing which plants animals ate in the wild. These days, the bark, leaves, stems, berries, and roots of healing herbs can be collected fresh, grown in your garden, or purchased in a store or by mail. Herbs should not be used indiscriminately, because some of them are very potent and should be used only under the guidance of a professional herbalist.

The following are various forms in which herbal medicines are used:

Teas and infusions: Fresh or dried leaves of the plant are steeped in water, and the tea is given orally or sprinkled on food.

Decoctions: Roots, seeds, berries, or bark are simmered in water for about twenty minutes to several hours.

Capsules: The herb is powdered and put in pill form.

Infused oils: These are active plant ingredients extracted in oil for external use as salves, creams, ointments, and massage oils.

Tinctures: These are herbs preserved in alcohol or glycerine and potentized through any number of methods so that the substance becomes highly concentrated. A tincture is administered by placing a few drops in the animal's cheek pouch or in his food. I prefer using herbs in tincture form for internal treatments, because it can be hard to get a dog to drink the amount of tea needed to have an effect, and dried herbs can be powdered and put in gelatin capsules, but is time consuming to do so. I make most of my own tincture formulas, and vary their proportions and uses from dog to dog. Some of my tinctures are listed here:

- *General body tonic.* I make this from dandelion, burdock, yellow dock, yarrow, and nettle tinctures and give it twice a week to help cleanse the kidney-liver function, and to generally nurture and support the vital organs of the body.
- *Immune herbs.* Goldenseal, echinacea, cats claw and astragulus are all very good for boosting the immune system.
- *Herbs for the nerves.* Wild oats, Saint-John's-wort, and chamomile have excellent calming properties. Agrimony is also

good for relieving tension in dogs, especially when the tension is caused by stress from the people they live with

- *Herbs for wound care.* Plaintain is great for wounds. You can crush the fresh leaves and apply them to the injury. I also keep some in my freezer during the winter when fresh ones aren't available to use for treating wounds or for poultices. Yarrow is another great wound herb. It is particularly beneficial for deep cuts with a lot of bleeding, and also works well for blood blisters and bruises. I have used it as a poultice to help reduce hematomas. Calendula in salve or infused oil form is good for scratches and wounds that are swollen, red, and sensitive to the touch.

- *Pain and discomfort.* Willow and meadowsweet were the original aspirin. They contain salicylic acid

TOPICAL HERBAL TREATMENTS

Compresses and poultices are applied to the skin topically to relieve pain and inflammation and to draw out infections. A compress is a soft pad or cloth that has been saturated with an herbal decoction, infusion, or tincture, which has been diluted with water. Compresses are placed directly on the area to accelerate healing of wounds or muscle injuries. Poultices work like compresses, but the whole herb, rather than a liquid dilution, is applied.

Poultices are made (1) by grinding the dry herb into a powder, mixing it with a little warm water to form a paste, spreading the paste on cheese cloth, folding the cloth over herbs to form a receptacle for the poultice, and then applying it to the wound (I usually don't spread anything directly into a deep, open wound), or (2) by simmering about two ounces of the fresh whole plant in a cup of water, pouring the solution over a cloth or putting it in a gauze bag, placing the cloth or bag on the skin, and covering it with additional cloths or towels to hold the heat in. The poultice can be left on for twenty minutes to twenty-four hours.

My most common remedies for topical herbal treatments are:

- *Flaxseed.* Ground seeds are boiled into a paste and then applied to the affected part. This is very effective for drawing out infections as well as porcupine quills.

- *Plantain, burdock.* Good for rapid healing of wounds.

- *Chickweed.* Draws out heat and infections.

- *Honey.* Although honey is not an herb, I frequently mix herbs with it to form a paste that can be applied to wounds to kill infection and to promote rapid healing of the tissue. I frequently combine it with myrrh, goldenseal, and slippery elm. Honey (preferably unprocessed organic) is also a great remedy for burns.

- *Powdered cayenne pepper.* This is good for stopping bleeding; it is applied directly to the wound. It is also excellent for combatting shock; placing a couple of grains of it under the tongue will stimulate circulation.

HOMEOPATHIC MEDICINES

A homeopathic remedy is made by successively diluting and potentizing an herb, a mineral, or an animal substance until the solution no longer contains any of the physical molecules of the original. The energy properties of the substance are released and activated for healing on an energy level. The premise of homeopathy, developed in 1796 by a German physician named Samuel Hahnemann, is that "like cures like," or "whatever causes the symptoms will create the cure."

Dosages: Because homeopathy is an energetic medicine rather than a physiochemical one, the same dosages can be given to humans and animals alike. Animals usually enjoy taking homeopathic remedies because they taste like milk sugar. You can administer the remedies by pouring 2 to 10 of the granules into a cup or into a folded piece of paper to pour into the mouth so they can dissolve on the tongue and gums. They can also be dissolved in a small amount of spring water or put in a small amount of milk or ice cream. After you have administered the remedies, wait ten to fifteen minutes to see how the dog has responded. In acute conditions you can repeat this dosage every ten to fifteen minutes three or four times. When you see that the dog is responding, do not administer any more.

It takes training and skill to diagnose and treat a chronic illness homeopathically, but there are some basic treatments that you can buy in any holistic health pharmacy which many people find extremely effective for acute illnesses. The most common over-the-counter potencies are 6X or 30 C. Higher potencies are available only through a professional homeopath. Extreme body temperatures can inactivate remedies. Homeopathic remedies last a lifetime so you don't have to worry about an expiration date.

Here are some of my favorites:

- *Thuja*—for alleviating vaccinosis; also for warts and growths.
- *Silica*—for expelling foreign objects from the body. *Note:* Don't use this if an animal has internal surgical staples.

- *Arnica*—for bruising or swelling.
- *Apis*—for bee stings and any other hot, red, and swollen condition.
- *Hypericum*—for nerve-ending damage or trauma, for example, if a dog tears a nail off or injures his tail in a car door.
- *Aconite*—for fear or stress.
- *Phosphorous*—for bleeding when the blood is bright red from superficial vessels.
- *Hamamelis*—for bleeding if the blood is dark red, oozing, and passive.
- *Ipecac*—when the bleeding is profuse, gushing, and bright red.
- *Ledum*—for puncture wounds.

FLOWER ESSENCES

"The healing herbs, by comforting, by soothing, by relieving our cares, our anxieties, bring us nearer to the Divinity within. And it is that increase of the Divinity within which heals us."

—Dr. Edward Bach

Flower essences are extremely gentle nontoxic liquid extractions made from flowers and plants. They are the most esoteric of healing remedies, and the hardest for many people to understand. They were developed in 1930 by Dr. Edward Bach (1886–1936), a homeopathic physician and medical researcher. Since then many people have created their own formulas. One of the best-known in this field is Machaelle Small-Wright of Perelandra Center for Nature Research in Warrenton, Virginia. Another is Molly Sheehan of Green Hope Farms in Meriden, New Hampshire.

Flower essences are based on the principle that there is a relationship between the life-force energy of specific flowers, and the energy of the human mind and soul. Their properties are divined intuitively, and their power is very much related to the attitude of the person who is using them.

Certain healers believe that illness actually begins in the emotional energy force field of the aura, before it reaches the body. By treating the invisible levels of disease with energetic medicines, one can often prevent disease from manifesting on the physical level. Flower essences are electrical solutions that work on vibrational energy patterns to strengthen and bring healing, balance, and harmony to energy systems. They address the root causes of many presenting symptoms and are found to be helpful for physical, emotional, and behavioral problems. Consequently, healing can be very complete.

Although flower essences have proven very useful in treating assorted physical and behavioral problems, they are in no way a substitute for veterinary care, proper training, or behavior counseling. They are most helpful when used as part of a total holistic health care program. I personally have witnessed the many benefits of the remedies with my own and clients' animals.

Why do animals need flower essences? One of the wonderful ways that animals help us is by providing the stability of their love and appreciation in the midst of our harried lifestyles and by absorbing the energy of many stressful situations. Dogs are links to nature and to the expanded web of life with which we lose touch.

Animals act as buffers for the stresses that occur in our lives, and they help us by absorbing our emotional "fallout" into their own systems. They can reflect areas of physical or emotional imbalance that we may need to look at in our own lives.

Surely you have noticed how your pet senses and responds to your needs. I believe that dogs and cats can "see" and "smell" our moods. Think about the way anger is expressed in the human body: anger is one of the few emotions that even humans can see. Animals, however, with their finely tuned and more highly developed senses, are aware of even our most subtle changes and are constantly affected by them.

Animals are subject to all the same environmental stresses and pollutants as we are. In fact, because our pets have accelerated metabolisms and do not live as long as we do, they are monitors for the level of health in our environment. For example, 60 percent of animals that lived in homes where the grounds had been treated with a commercial herbicide developed mammary tumors within one to two years.

Animals have a particularly hard time with stress and a poor environment because they do not have the same options for releasing them. In other words, they can't go to the gym, take a long relaxing bath, or "veg out" with a good book. Without outlets for the negative energy they have absorbed, they often fall into patterns of behavioral problems for their owners or develop a disease. It is a documented fact that our pets are so closely influenced by living with us that they often develop our physical problems and diseases.

I encourage everyone to use flower essences before serious problems develop. All of my animals—dogs, cats, horses, guinea pigs, ferrets, birds, and an assortment of wild creatures who frequent my place—get flower essences daily in their food or water. As a result, I have seen more harmony and less friction among various group members, and they have a robust vitality. Even the very old animals are not plagued by the maladies that affect most animals their age. I have seen animals with physical problems that did not respond to standard veterinary treatment be healed with the aid of flower essences. I depend on my own Animal Emergency Care formula for the occasional accident or injury, and I keep it ready at hand at all times.

Hundreds of different essences have been developed since Bach formulated his original ones, the most famous of which is Rescue Remedy, or Five Flower Formula. I use flower essences from several different sources as well as making my own from flowers I grow in my garden or collect in the wild. I make my own formulas, since I find that animals' energy fields are different from those of humans. I have a formula that I call Daily Care and another called Senior Formula that helps with issues associated with the aging process. I also keep stock formulas on hand for ready use with clients' animals that come for counseling. I use them to address issues like separation anxiety, aggression toward people, and aggression toward other animals. There are also formulas to address and support physical problems such as allergies and arthritis. Bach flower essences are readily available for people who are just beginning to explore their use. Check the Appendix for additional sources.

Dosage and administration: Flower essences can be taken internally or externally. They can be administered in drinking water, placed under the tongue, added to a bucket of water and sponged on, dripped on any injured or painful site, or diluted with water and put in food. They can be put in a spray bottle and misted in the room or cage.

To prepare an essence, add 8 to 10 drops of the concentrate to 2 ounces of spring water. You can also drip 8 to 10 drops of concentrate directly on a dog's nose or on the inside of the ear flap where there is less hair.

There is no wrong way to administer these remedies and it is not necessary to be absolutely precise in counting the drops. There are no side effects or toxicity so they cannot be overdosed. There is also no danger in picking a wrong remedy; the worst that will happen is that it won't work.

Keep the essences away from direct sunlight, computers, and microwaves. Do not touch the dropper against any other surfaces, since it can contaminate the essences. If this does happen, run the dropper under cold water for ten seconds before returning to the bottle. If you only have city water, rinse the dropper thoroughly in spring water, because city water is full of chemicals that can affect the efficacy of flower essences. Flower essences are a vibrational energy medicine; therefore, their potency is increased by shaking them, but shake them in a vertical direction only. (Yes, it does make a difference!)

Dilution bottles can be made from stock bottles. Place 1 or 2 tablespoons of brandy or vinegar in a 1-ounce dropper bottle and fill with spring water. Add 6 to 8 drops of each of the desired remedies in the bottle, being sure to shake each of the remedies from the stock bottle before adding them to the combination.

Veterinarian Stephen Blake suggests the following formula for clearing and balancing the energy in a room. Combine the following flower essences in a spray bottle and mist the room or spray into air ducts: 2 drops of Walnut, 2 drops of Crab Apple, 2 drops of Rescue Remedy or Calming Essence, and 2 drops of Wild Rose to 8 ounces of spring water and 2 ounces of vodka. Make this mixture up fresh weekly.

I use this formula in the training area before and between group classes as well as before and between counseling sessions. I use it throughout my home, especially in my office area.

Here are a few of the different essences used for animals, as described by Adrienne K. Moore, D.V.M., in the 1997 proceedings of the American Holistic Veterinary Medical Association Annual Conference:

- Aspen, for animals fearful of the unknown, unfamiliar circumstances and surroundings.

- Beech, for intolerance of any kind—to grasses, insects, weather, or people—also for picky eaters and animals that constantly complain.

- Chestnut bud, to break bad habits; also to increase memory retention and to assist in training.

- Chicory, for overly possessive animals and to assist in letting go of offspring or of a human companion.

- Crab apple, to cleanse wounds.

- Elm, for those who are overwhelmed by travel.

- Honeysuckle, for separation from loved ones.

- Larch, for cowering animals or those lacking in self-confidence.

- Mimulus, for fearful animals.

- Pine, for the animal that tries to please people, yet is often rejected; also for the animal that assumes guilt any time the human companion is absent.

- Red chestnut, for those who fear approaching storms.

- Rescue Remedy or Calming Essence, a combination of five flower essences that is excellent for any and every situation that is traumatic or stressful.

- Rock Rose, for any kind of terror or panic, for overly fearful animals, and for use after any terrifying event.

- Rock Water, for balancing the heart and mind.
- Vervain, for the intense, hyperactive animal that seems to have inexhaustible energy.
- Walnut, for transition and change.
- Wild oat, for depression or boredom.
- Wild rose, for being confined in a small space and/or for adding a sense of fun to life.
- Willow, for resentment in response to lack of attention.

AROMATHERAPY

Aromatherapy consists of the diffusion of a scent by heating an essential oil or by burning incense. The purpose is to stimulate the sense of smell in order to balance or enhance certain mental and emotional states. Aromatherapy is just beginning to be used with animals; it is an area where I prefer to be cautious, because I believe that the way animals experience and interpret scents can be very different from that of humans.

When I am in a situation where I need extra emotional support, I burn lavender or vetiver to help me maintain a calm, centering energy, because my calmness in turn helps the animal. If an animal has an upper respiratory infection, I use an essential oil like eucalyptus in a vaporizer.

Essential oils are derived from plants through steam distillation or cold pressing. These oils are extremely potent and should never be taken internally without extensive professional knowledge of their proper dosage and use. Be sure to store them well out of reach of pets and children. Do not apply them full strength to the skin. They are always diluted in vegetable oil or water before being used as washes or inhalants or for massage.

LIGHT THERAPY

Full-spectrum lighting is as beneficial for animals as it is for people, especially those of us who spend most of our time indoors. I am a strong advocate of full spectrum lighting for health, because our bodies need all of the vibrations of the color spectrum for complete stimulation and balancing of our systems.

COLOR THERAPY

Color has long been known to influence the emotions. I use color therapy with animals both for physiological and psychological reasons. If a client's dog is very hyperactive, I might suggest that his bed, leash, and blanket be green because this color is very balancing to the system. When I treated the Vermont dogs, I gave them colored-light "baths" every day: blue light to calm nerves and reduce fevers, red for vitalizing energy and overcoming lethargy, and green to soothe and generally balance energy. Although I did not treat the rescued dogs with yellow or yellow-orange light, those colors are known to be effective in stimulating the intestinal and digestive functions.

Sound and Music Therapy

In addition to stimulating the senses of sight and smell, there is much evidence that sound can have very strong healing effects. I have found that my animals are responsive to classical music and some of the New Age music. Mozart, Bach, and Handel are very helpful for calming the emotions and balancing energy. I recommend that music be played during training if you and your dog need extra emotional support.

Healing Meditations

Meditations, visualizations, and sending positive energy are always beneficial when doing any healing work with an animal. I counsel my clients to "see" their animals healed, whole, healthy, and vibrant when they are doing any form of healing work. I had one client ask if this wasn't like denial, since she knew her dog was dying of cancer and she was only trying to extend his life and keep him as comfortable as possible. My response was that I always choose to project the image of health and well-being, and therefore I put the image out into the universe as another possibility. Knowing that thoughts have energy, I also want to attract only positive energy to the animal. Please remember that healing can occur in many ways and on many levels that may not necessarily mean making a recovery in the physical sense.

The following meditation can be used to help any animal in distress, especially in situations where you have done all that you can on a physical level, and "only time will tell":

- Take a moment to be by yourself, sit down, and relax. If you think it will be helpful, burn some incense, take a flower essence that has calming and supportive properties, and put on some quiet music.

- Close your eyes and visualize a healing column of light or a circle. Ask to be connected to your higher self and the higher self of your dog. Ask that the Being that watches over all dogs be present to help. This will be a different imagination for each person. I call this being the Overlighting Deva of all dogs, an entity who assists with the energy process and healing. I see the Overlighting Deva as the guardian angel of dogs.

- Once you can feel that the connections are established and the healing energy is in place, invite your dog to enter the energy circle.

- You may "see" your dog appear in the space you created, or you may get a different reaction. You cannot force healing, you can only offer your energy as a support. I have done this meditation and had the animal refuse to come, saying rather that its intention was to leave its body. If this happens, I continue to hold the energy but ask that it be used to facilitate in the transition process

- If your dog comes into your visualization, hold the image of healing energy light in the circle until it seems that it has received all that it wants or needs at that point in time. Visualize that your dog is vibrant with energy and health.

- You can also add the intent that whatever is ill or injured be made whole and well. If the dog has a broken leg, you can visualize the bones growing back together. If he has a wound, you can imagine all of the steps that will occur to make it whole again. If he has an illness, you can imagine it vaporizing and dissipating like fog lifting off a lake in the morning sun.

- When you feel that the energy has shifted, or that you have done all that you can do, close the meditation by sending love and light to the animal and thanks to your higher self and to whatever other powers you have brought into your vision. Close down the circle and come back into the present.

A CASE STUDY

A friend and breeder of Jack Russell terriers named Nancy called me one day about one of her dogs. Bracken had spent the first part of his life alone, confined on a back porch, which created a lot of behavior problems. Once Nancy acquired him, she worked diligently with him, and a very deep and special bond of love grew between them. He had recently developed a puzzling health problem that caused an ugly green mucus to run from his nose. He was obviously in a lot of pain and would yelp if anyone even passed close to him on that side of his body. He was also losing his sense of balance and would frequently be walking along and then suddenly fall over and cry out. I remembered well the feisty little dog with the "get out of my way 'cause here I come" attitude who had been in several of my training classes. When Nancy brought him to see me, I couldn't believe it was the same dog. His eyes were dull, his whole body was contracted, and if I put my hand within a foot of his head, he would scream and cringe. Nancy reported that he seemed to be in pain all of the time, so he hid out in his crate at home, and if any of the other dogs in the house went near him, he attacked them.

She had taken Bracken to a veterinarian, who thought that the cause was an inoperable tumor. Nancy came to me in the hope that I would have some ideas about how to make Bracken more comfortable while she tried to decide what to do.

Bracken's energy field was congested. It was especially cloudy in the area of the head and neck. As I began to slowly and gently move my hands in his energy field, I could feel a lot of heat and prickling sensations on my palms. From the way it felt, I knew the pain was truly excruciating. Realizing I needed to release the places where the energy was blocked in order to ease some of the pain, I gently worked about a foot from his head, stroking the edges of the field, where I could feel the greatest density. I began sending Reiki energy through my hands, and after ten or fifteen minutes, I was able to get close enough to very lightly touch his head. I closed my eyes and turned to my intuition, asking for guidance. When I got my answer, I was mystified. I looked at Nancy, who was watching me intently. "It's very strange," I said. "I don't think it's a tumor. I keep getting the number six for some reason." I closed my eyes and then opened them again and found myself saying, "I think it's a porcupine quill!" I still didn't get the significance of the number six.

Nancy stared at me, eyes wide, and said, "About six years ago, Bracken tangled with a porcupine. You know Jack Russells; they don't back off if you say stop. And you know Bracken; he tried to kill and eat the thing! It took the vet and me two and a half hours to pull all of the quills out."

I felt even more convinced then. "I think porcupine quills are causing the problem," I said, "and I wouldn't be surprised if there were six of them." When I asked for guidance to see if we could use our energy to dissolve them, the answer was no. Then I asked if they could be removed. This time I got a yes.

I looked at Nancy. "Let's give him some flower essences to calm him down. Then we'll use homeopathic silica to help expel the quills and herbs to help boost his immune system. You'll need flaxseed poultices to help draw the area too. And we'll both have to visualize that these things need to move out."

"How am I going to put a poultice on, when I can't even get near that side of his head?" Nancy wondered.

I worked in Bracken's energy field some more. When I stopped, he was calm and looking at me as if a great cloud had lifted from his brain. I gently touched the side of his head and he blinked but never flinched. I ran my finger along his jaw and there was no reaction at all.

"I think you'll be able to touch him now," I said to Nancy.

She gathered him up carefully, took him home, and began the regimen of herbs, tinctures, and poultices. We both visualized that things were going to start moving. A few days later she called: "You wouldn't believe it, but he's got some things that look like egg yolks showing up on that side of his head. What now?"

"Just keep doing what you have been doing," I said, "Let's keep it moving."

She called again two days later. "Now they've shrunk down," she reported with excitement. "They're like hard peas under his skin." I told her to bring Bracken over, and I did some more energy work on him. At the end of the session, I felt convinced. "It's time to take him to the vet and have the quills taken out," I said.

Nancy raised her eyebrows, but I was insistent, so she made an appointment and told the vet she wanted the growths removed, saying that I believed they were caused by quills. He removed them, put the tissue under the microscope, and then came out and spoke with excitement to Nancy: "Can you imagine?" he said, "Those things looked just like little capsules when I took them off, and when I cut them open, there was a quill in every one! And they looked as if they just went in yesterday; they weren't broken down at all."

Nancy told me he then suggested a regimen of antibiotics and steroids, but she declined, so he'd shrugged and said with a smile, "Well, take him back to April!"

Bracken received more herbal medicine and flower essences from me, but I couldn't get rid of a nagging feeling that we weren't completely done even though he seemed pretty much his old self again.

I was right. About a month later Nancy saw him pawing at his nose. He sneezed a couple of times, and a quill fell out. Nancy called a while later to say that Bracken was having trouble again, so we repeated the process with the same results. This time, when Nancy brought the dog to me for a checkup she was laughing. She said that the vet had asked how I did all of this, and she'd found herself in a quandary. "I can explain to him about the poultices and the homeopathic stuff," she said, "but how do I explain to him about the voodoo stuff?"

I laughed and said, "I wouldn't even try." All of this occurred three years ago. Bracken is still with us and is kept on herbal tinctures and flower essences.

The short moral to this story is that encounters with porcupines are much more serious than most people realize. Quills have barbs on them that cause them to migrate through soft tissue, and they can travel around for years, as they did with Bracken. They have even been found in dogs' hearts. I knew of a family that had a shepherd who had become very aggressive, although he had been a kind dog all his life. They euthanized him, and had an autopsy done, only to find numerous quills in the part of his brain that controls aggression. If your dog ever gets a quill in him, put him on homeopathic silica immediately, because it helps expel foreign objects from the body. If possible, also use poultices with a strong drawing power to help draw them out. Animal Emergency Care Flower Essences and Crab Apple Flower Essence will also help.

OTHER WAYS TO ENHANCE YOUR RELATIONSHIP WITH YOUR DOG

Communicating with your hands: One of the most common ways that people touch dogs is to pat them on the head. Actually, according to the dogs I communicate with, this is not a pleasurable experience for them. If you pat yourself on the head firmly and exuberantly you will see that it is rather annoying and does not feel good at all; it is disruptive to the energy field.

The dog's crown chakra is a major energy center, sensitive and open to the cosmos. When your dog is anxious or stressed, you can soothe him by working in his energy field. Do this by placing your dog on your left and using your left hand to make slow dinner-plate-size counterclockwise circles above his head. Keep yourself relaxed and calm as you do this. Staying relaxed yourself also helps your dog relax. Some dogs never need this, but others benefit from it a great deal, especially if you do it during any kind of stressful situation, such as a trip to the groomer, boarding kennel, or vet. The amount of time you spend doing this will depend on your dog. Watch for signals for when it is enough. Never force any kind of energy work on your dog, but respect what is needed or wanted.

You can choose to learn a specific massage technique with your dog, or you can work out your own, simply through experimenting with a loving touch and being sensitive to what your dog likes.

TTouch: Instead of patting your dog, learn to caress her and give her a good body massage. A wonderful method is TTouch, a kind of body work developed by Linda Tellington-Jones, a renowned horse trainer and animal healer, who studied the Feldenkreis method of awareness through movement. Like Feldenkreis, TTouch is based on the idea that memories and habits are stored in the body as a result of being programmed by our emotional reactions. Through touch and movement of the skin and muscles, these old patterns can be released or prevented.

First, try TTouch on someone else so you can get good feedback. Stand behind your partner and rest the palm of one hand gently on her back, with your hand slightly cupped and the tips of your fingers in contact with her back. This hand will be making the circles. Let your other hand rest lightly on another part of their back to close the energy circuit between your body and hers. Picture the face of a clock; gently press and rotate the skin and muscle, starting at six, making a complete circle, going past six again, and stopping at eight. Move your hand slightly to a new spot and repeat. Experiment with varying the amount of pressure; sometimes you will want to be very light and delicate, using only the tips of your fingers, and other times you will be able to work deeper, in areas that are heavily muscled. As you work, stay relaxed and breathe into your circles. To be sure you are doing it correctly, ask the person for feedback on the difference between when you are doing it correctly and when you are not. Do a few rotations with your fingers without completing the circle and have your partner note the difference in the sensation. It is important to keep your other hand resting with light contact on the person while you are doing the circles with the other. To test this out, continue to do the circles, but from time to time remove your other hand from the person, breaking the contact, and then reestablish it.

Switch places so that you can be the one to experience how it feels.

You can now begin to work on your dog. If you have a small dog, you can hold him on your lap. You can do TTouch all over your dog's body. Touch

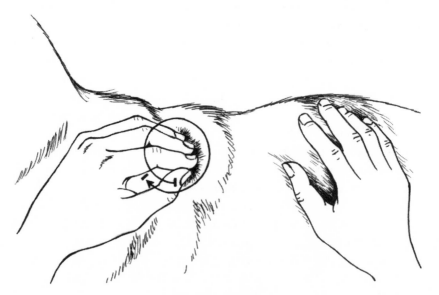

"Hand Circles for T-Touch"

your dog lovingly, and remain open to intuiting what comes back to you in terms of a response. It can be a wonderful way to deepen your relationship.

Whenever you are dealing with a dog who has an aggression problem or a strong aversion to being touched on certain parts of the body, proceed slowly and with caution, or else seek the advice of a professional TTouch practitioner.

If it is a fearful animal, I use TTouch on the dog's hindquarters and tail, where the muscles tend to contract. If it is a dominant dog, I concentrate on the bunched-up muscles of the shoulders and neck. I use TTouch a lot on puppies, to get them used to being handled.

Therapeutic touch: When I described myself working about a foot from Bracken's head, I was using a form of healing called Therapeutic Touch. Developed by an American woman named Dolores Krieger, it is used by nurses in a number of hospitals across America, with premature infants and people who cannot bear physical touch, like burn victims. Therapeutic touch is a magical way to ease pain and promote healing on all levels of the energy field.

The basic techniques of therapeutic touch are as follows: (1) take a couple of deep breaths to relax and get focused; (2) rub your hands together vigorously clockwise for about thirty seconds to create an energy vortex; (3) scan the energy field of the person or dog with your hands to feel for imbalances; (4) ruffle the field with your fingers to break up blocked energy; and (5) smooth the field to promote rebalancing. Also use your hands to send more energy into an area that is depleted, or to pull congested energy out.

Needless to say, this is yet another approach that asks that you let go of limited thinking and stretch out with your feelings. As described earlier, an ability to feel the energy field develops with practice. To experiment with rebalancing your dog's energy, rub your hands vigorously clockwise to create an energy vortex. Then, run your hands gently across the top of her body from nose to tail, staying about three inches above her. Do it several times and see if you can feel sensations of heat, cold, density, any areas that make the palms of your hands feel prickly or sticky, or any other sensations. If the field feels uneven, your dog could be feeling anything from a body ache to a digestive upset. Therapeutic touch allows you to help these kinds of conditions without ever touching the dog at all.

- After you have scanned the dog's entire body and made a mental note of where the various sensations were located, begin to ruffle the field by holding your fingers as if you were going to give the dog a good scratching all down her back. Stay three inches above her body, and do this ruffling action from her head to her tail, making small circles. If you come to an area that makes you feel as if you want to "pick something off" that spot and throw it away, pretend to do so (just don't aim it at another person or animal!). If you find an area that makes you feel as though you want to use your hand to "suction" something out of that area, do so. Trust your intuition.

- When you feel that all of the adjustments have been made, smooth the field by "combing" the same area gently with your fingers, using long, sweeping strokes. Flatten your palms and do it a few more times. Many dogs will stretch out in total bliss or heave deep sighs as you finish. Try it on your children, friends, or on yourself. After you have experienced it a few times, your sensitivity to its effects may increase so that it actually feels as though someone is touching you.

- When you are finished, hold the hands of the person you are working on, or hold the animal's paws in order to ground the energy. Wash your hands in cold water to clear any negative energy that has been released. Silently ask that any negative energy that was removed be transmuted and cleared and replaced with positive energy.

Reiki: Reiki (Ray-key), a worldwide movement that originated in Japan, is taught in workshops all across America and overseas. It is another form of energetic healing. The name literally means "universal life force energy." When you do Reiki, you become a conduit for bringing concentrated and

"Working in the Energy Field with Therapeutic Touch"

amplified healing energy through your body and releasing it through your hands once you place them on specific places on the body of a person or animal. Reiki is similar in concept to the laying on of hands, which is better known in our culture. Although you can learn Reiki positions from a book, you will need to receive the energy attunements from a Reiki master to enable you to channel Reiki energy. You can find listings of Reiki masters in holistic publications, and many places offer free Reiki clinics.

Holistic Health Remedies for Basic Animal Care

FOR BEHAVIORAL ISSUES

- CAR SICKNESS (STRESS)
  - *Flower Essence:*
    - Elm
    - Rock Rose
  - *Homeopathic:*
    - Aconite
  - *Vitamin Supplementation:*
    - B-complex
    - Vitamin C

- COMFORT AFTER ANY EMOTIONAL OR PHYSICAL TRAUMA (I GIVE IT TO MY DOGS AFTER ELECTIVE SURGERY)
  - *Flower Essence:*
    - Star of Bethlehem

- DOGS IN MULTIPET HOUSEHOLDS
  - *Flower essence:* combine
    - Rock Water
    - Vervain
    - Walnut
    - Wild Rose
    - Willow

- FEAR OF LOUD NOISES (E.G., THUNDERSTORMS)
  - *Flower Essence:*
    - Aspen
    - Red Chestnut
    - Rock Rose

- *Herbal:*
  - Chamomile
  - Saint-John's-Wort
  - Stress Formula
- *Homeopathic:*
  - Aconite
  - Naturum Carb or Phosphorus

- HOUSE SOILING PROBLEMS
  - *Flower essence:*
    - Chestnut Bud

- SEPARATION ANXIETY
  - *Flower Essence:*
    - Larch
  - *Herbal:*
    - Saint-John's-Wort
  - *Vitamin Supplementation:*
    - B-complex
    - Vitamin C

- STRESS ANXIETY (E.G., GOING TO THE VET OR GROOMER)
  - *Flower Essence:*
    - Rescue Remedy, Calming Formula, or Animal Emergency Care
    - Elm
    - Rock Rose
  - *Herbal:*
    - Herbal Stress Formula
    - Any of the following single herbs:
      - Flowering Oat Straw
      - Saint-John's-Wort
      - Wood Betony
      - Lavender
      - Lemon Balm
      - Sage
      - Mugwort
  - *Homeopathic:*
    - Aconite

- *Vitamin Supplementation:*
  - B-complex
  - Vitamin C

- STRESS ASSOCIATED WITH BEING CRATED
  - *Flower Essence:*
    - Wild Rose
  - *Homeopathic:*
    - Aconite
  - *Vitamin Supplementation:*
    - B-complex
    - Vitamin C

- STRESS FROM BEING BOARDED OR KENNELED
  - *Color Therapy:*
    - Green (bed, blanket, towel)
  - *Flower Essences:*
    - Honeysuckle
    - Wild Rose
    - Wild Oat
    - Aspen
  - *Homeopathic:*
    - Aconite
  - *Vitamin Supplementation:*
    - B-complex
    - Vitamin C

- SUBMISSIVE URINATING
  - *Flower Essence:*
    - Larch
    - Mimulus
  - *Homeopathic:*
    - Pulsatilla

ACCIDENTS AND EMERGENCIES

- BRUISES AND SPRAINS
  - *Flower Essence:*
    - Star of Bethlehem

- *Herbal:*
  - Plaintain Compress
- *Homeopathic:*
  - Arnica
  - Ruta
- *Other Helpful Treatments:*
  - Chopped Onions (applied to area to control swelling). If the onion begins to smell like vinegar, it's a broken bone. Really!
  - Cold Fresh Tofu (applied directly to the injury is better than ice to draw heat from swelling)
  - RICE: Rest, Ice, Compress, Elevate
  - Turmeric mixed with egg white and applied is as effective as cortisone for acute inflammation (may cause staining).

BURNS

- *Flower Essence:*
  - Star of Bethlehem
  - Rescue Remedy or Calming Formula or Animal Emergency Care
- *Herbal:*
  - Aloe Vera
- *Homeopathic:*
  - Cantharis
- *Other Helpful Treatments:*
  - Honey (applied directly to a burn is an excellent remedy)
  - Vitamin E

- HEAT STROKE
  - *Flower Essence:*
    - Rescue Remedy or Calming Formula or Animal Emergency Care
    - Star of Bethlehem
  - *Herbal:*
    - Chickweed Compresses
  - *Homeopathic*
    - Belladonna

- INJURED EXTREMITIES (E.G., TAIL SHUT IN DOOR)
  - *Flower Essence:*
    - Star of Bethlehem

- Rescue Remedy or Calming Formula or Animal Emergency Care
- *Homeopathic:*
  - Hypericum

- INSECT BITES
  - *Flower Essence:*
    - Agrimony
  - *Homeopathic:*
    - Apis
  - *Other Helpful Treatments: Never squeeze the skin to remove the stinger*
    - Use tweezers to pull it out or the edge of a knife or credit card to lift and scrape it out.
    - Bee stings are acidic; apply paste of bicarbonate of soda and water.
    - Wasp stings are alkaline; use vinegar or lemon juice.

- PORCUPINE QUILLS
  - *Flower Essence:*
    - Star of Bethlehem
    - Rock Rose
    - Rescue Remedy or Calming Formula or Animal Emergency Care
  - *Herbal:*
    - Flaxseed Poultice
  - *Homeopathic:*
    - Silica

- SEIZURES
  - *Flower Essence:*
    - Scleranthus
    - Rescue Remedy or Calming Formula or Animal Emergency Care

- SHOCK
  - *Flower Essence:*
    - Rescue Remedy or Calming Formula or Animal Emergency Care
  - *Herbal:*
    - Cayenne Powder (few grains on tongue)

- TORN NAILS
  - *Flower Essence:*
    - Rescue Remedy or Calming Formula or Animal Emergency Care
  - *Herbal:*
    - Cayenne Powder (applied to injury if bleeding)
  - *Homeopathic:*
    - Hypericum

- WOUNDS, LACERATIONS
  - *Flower Essence:*
    - Rescue Remedy or Calming Formula or Animal Emergency Care
  - *Herbal:*
    - Calendula
    - Cayenne Powder
    - Yarrow
  - *Homeopathic:*
    - Phosphorous, when blood is bright red from superficial vessels
    - Hamamelis, if blood is dark red, oozing, and passive.
    - Ipecac, if bleeding is profuse, gushing, and bright red.
  - *Other Helpful Treatments:*
  - *Minor cuts*
    - *Flower Essence:*
      - Star of Bethlehem
    - *Herbal:*
      - Calendula
      - Yarrow
    - *Other Helpful Treatments:*
      - Clean wound with hydrogen peroxide
      - Plantain or Chickweed or Rosemary Infusion
  - *Puncture wounds*
    - *Flower Essence:*
      - Rescue Remedy or Calming Formula or Animal Emergency Care combined with Impatiens and Crab Apple
    - *Herbal:*
      - Herbal Wash: Of Echinacea or Calendula or Goldenseal or Yarrow or Plantain Tinctures diluted 1 to 5 with water
      - Herbal Immune Tinctures internally:

- Herbal Immune Formula or Echinacea or Astragalus or Goldenseal
- *Homeopathic:*
  - Ledum
- *Other Helpful Treatments:*
  - Clean with hydrogen peroxide
  - Apply slice of onion directly over puncture wound (has strong drawing properties)
  - Garlic (it's high in sulfur and neutralizes toxins from bites)
- *Flower essence combination for any kind of pain:*
  - Star of Bethlehem
  - Beech
  - Impatiens

GENERAL CONDITIONS

- ABSCESSES
  - *Flower Essence:*
    - Crab Apple
  - *Herbal:*
    - Burdock, Yellow Dock and Yarrow (Tinctures mixed together and taken internally)
  - *Homeopathic:*
    - Apis
    - Silica

- ARTHRITIS
  - *Color Therapy:*
    - Green
  - *Flower Essences in combination formula*
    - Agrimony, Beech, Rock Water, Gorse, Impatiens, Oak, Willow
  - *Herbal:*
    - Alfalfa
    - Primrose Oil
  - *Homeopathic:*
    - RusTox
  - *Other Helpful Treatments:*
    - Glucosamine Sulfate
    - Hoka Mix (a nutritional supplement)

- Magnetic
- Massage
- TTouch
- Therapeutic Touch
- CAR SICKNESS (MOTION SICKNESS)
  - *Flower Essence:*
    - Rescue Remedy or Calming Formula or Animal Emergency Care combined with Scleranthus
  - *Herbal:*
    - Ginger

- CONJUNCTIVITIS
  - *Flower Essence:*
    - Crab Apple
  - *Herbal:*
    - Make Compress:
      Add ½ teaspoon powdered goldenseal and ½ teaspoon powdered eyebright to ¼ cup of water
      Cover and simmer 10 minutes.
      Cool to room temperature.
      Soak gauze pads and apply to eyes for 5–10 minutes.
  - *Homeopathic:*
    - Pulsatilla
    - Zincum Metall

- CONSTIPATION
  - *Flower Essence:*
    - Crab Apple (cleansing)
  - *Herbal:*
    - Burdock
    - Flaxseed (ground cooked with small amount of water can be mixed with food)
    - Slippery Elm
    - Yellow Dock (toning action)
  - *Homeopathic:*
    - Sulfur

- HOT SPOTS
  - *Flower Essence:*
    - Agrimony
    - Beech
    - Crab Apple

- *Herbal:*
  - Nettle tincture (taken internally)
  - Powdered Slippery Elm, Goldenseal, and Myrrh (Sprinkle ¼ teaspoon of each on spot after cleaning)
- *Homeopathic:*
  - Sulfur
- *Other Helpful Treatments:*
  - Witch Hazel (applied directly to the area)
  - Regular Tea Bag (moisten and apply directly to the area) tannins contained in tea are drying

- KENNEL COUGH
  - *Flower Essence:*
    - Crab Apple
  - *Herbal:*
    - Mullein
    - Mallow
    - Coltsfoot
  - *Other Helpful Treatments:*
    - 1 tablespoon honey, 1 tablespoon organic apple cider vinegar to a ½ cup water—administer 1–3 tablespoons 2–3 times a day; can be mixed in food

- SPLINTERS, THORNS
  - *Flower Essence:*
    - Crab Apple
    - Impatiens
  - *Herbal:*
    - Flaxseed Poultice
  - *Homeopathic:*
    - Silica

- TONSILLITIS
  - *Flower Essence:*
    - Crab Apple
  - *Herbal:*
    - Herbal Immune Formula
    - Burdock, Yellow Dock and Yarrow (Tinctures mixed together and taken internally)
  - *Other Helpful Treatments:*
    - Garlic
    - Vitamin C

14

GAMES AND GOOD TIMES

It was Rebel's turn in the competition for the title of Companion Dog Excellent of the American Kennel Club obedience trials. Rebel was a top quality Irish setter, and a frequent winner at these shows. In this portion of the competition, I had to throw a white dumbbell over a barrier and then direct Rebel to go and retrieve it for me. He could not see over the barrier, so he had to trust me to know that it was safe for him to leap to the other side. Once over, he had to keep his focus, find and take up the dumbbell, leap back over the barrier, and put the object in my hand.

Rebel was great at this kind of game, and he made a spectacular sight as he flew over the obstacle, his red-gold coat gleaming in the lights, his ears and tail streaming behind him, and his joy in performing shining all over his face. He hit the ground on the other side and stopped short. No dumbbell. It had bounced when I threw it, and landed under a spectator's chair on the sidelines. And the spectator, feeling helpful, had picked it up and now held it on her lap.

Ordinarily, the judge would have stopped us and let us do the sequence over, but she was distracted by something and had somehow missed what had happened. I couldn't do or say anything, or we would risk losing points. Rebel had to figure this one out on his own.

Well, he knew he needed to bring something back, something white, that was sitting on the ground, and he had too much pride to return without completing the task he had been asked to do. He circled a few times before the crowd, then dived under a chair, having found the perfect solution. Seconds later he was flying back over the barrier toward me, a woman's white pocketbook triumphantly clasped in his jaws. The crowd roared with laughter and applauded wildly.

"So that's how you pay your entry fees!" the judge joked. We weren't laughing at Rebel by any means. If anything, Rebel was laughing with us.

Play is soul food for both humans and animals, and dogs have a great sense of humor. In addition, dogs like to have meaningful things to do; it is in their nature to accomplish something on a regular basis, just as it is for humans. In the wild, dogs have the satisfaction of the hunt, as well as all of the games that prepare them for their way of life and solidify their relationships in the pack. Without regular physical, emotional, and mental stimulation, dogs get bored and start to act out. They have self-images. They need to feel proud and confident in their roles in our world.

When I teach a dog a skill or a game, my goal is always to bring out his special talents. If a dog spends a lot of time chasing things, I teach him to retrieve. If he loves to jump, I try him out in agility classes. If he always seems to have something in his mouth, I teach him to carry things for me. I take a natural ability and turn it into an asset for both of us.

While dogs seem to enjoy the attention they receive when they do tricks like shaking hands, playing dead, or sitting up, I find that these behaviors generally are turned into constant solicitations; the dog will pester his human continually by performing in order to get a treat. I think it is more rewarding to find something practical that the two of you can do together.

This is particularly important when you have a dog that is "initiative-smart," as opposed to "trainable-smart." Rebel was an initiative-smart dog: when confronted with a change of plans, he was able to find a solution and still complete his task. By contrast, a trainable-smart dog generally sticks to what he has learned and does not try to take it any further.

When you have a dog that is initiative-smart, it is especially important to keep him happy and motivated to work with you, because if he isn't motivated to do what you ask, he will think of fifty ways to avoid having to do it. Furthermore, you have to be very careful to present new learning correctly, because this kind of dog only needs to be shown how to do something once; whether you presented the task the wrong way or the right way, it becomes a learned behavior.

It is not so much that one type of dog is intelligent and the other is not; the distinction mostly has to do with differences in personality and breeding. Some people like a dog that can learn basic training, but won't try to out-think them beyond the bounds of the established relationship. Others love the challenge of a dog who keeps them thinking and on their toes.

I have both kinds in the pack that lives with me, and they bring different delights and challenges to my life. Amy, my rescued greyhound, was trained to do one thing only—to pursue a lure around and around a racetrack. Yet she has a big heart, and her gentle ways and radiant, peaceful being are a constant balm in my busy household. On the other hand, Tawny the Trickster always keeps me wondering what he'll think of next. Both kinds can learn games very well. Some will go beyond what you teach them and others will give you the same response every time. All dogs love to play, though, and play should be an important part of your relationship.

Before I talk about teaching specific games, I want to say something about two activities that people fall into with their dogs very naturally, sometimes with disastrous results.

The first is tug-of-war, which seems like a very innocent and fun thing to do with your puppy and which dogs do with one another in the pack. It is, in my opinion, one of the worst games that you can play because you are encouraging your dog to use the most aggressive body language he can muster with you. He gives you his most dominant stare, growls, shakes the object, and gives every appearance of being ready to do or die to get final control. People tend to let go first, which makes the dog believe that he has won a dominance contest, and he goes off saying to himself, "Hmm, if I grab, shake, stare at you, and growl, I end up winning."

Invariably, when I counsel people whose dog is biting members of the family, I find that they have been playing tug-of-war with him, without being aware of the lesson they were teaching. This is a particularly dangerous game when children are involved, since dogs do not consider that children have the same ability to set limits that adults do. If things get out of hand and the child is bitten, the dog is often the one who is punished, even to the point of euthanization.

If you have a dog who likes to pull and tug on things, go to a hardware store and buy a fat sisal rope. Tie a big knot in it and hang it from a springy branch. Get your dog interested in the rope and then let him amuse himself. Your dog will spend all day having a great time trying to pull the tree over, and will be very entertaining to watch.

I am sometimes challenged on this issue by people who point out that they never have had a problem with their dog, that he knows the difference between when to play and when not. It is true that there are always exceptions. Nevertheless, I urge my clients to take a clear look at what this kind of game encourages, as well as the possible long-range effects. Is it really a good idea to create a control issue in your relationship?

This concern also applies to heavy roughhousing, which often happens with men and boys and their dogs. A shepherd has a 1,200 pound per inch bite force; it does not make sense to encourage a dog to play rough, particularly because what looks like fun to you can quickly turn into fear or dominance, resulting in aggressive behavior and defensiveness in him. While Dad may be able to hold his own in a physically rough interaction, when the dog transfers the behavior to Mom and young children, the consequences are often dire for all concerned.

Finally, I discourage chase games, including both tag and keep-away. If a dog is used to playing such games with you, he may end up in a dangerous situation and you will be unable to help him because you can't get near him. A case in point: a woman called me early on a Sunday morning, frantic because she could not reach her vet and did not know where else to turn. Her ten-month-old golden retriever had grabbed a packet of double-edged razor blades from the corner of her sewing machine, and had a great time playing keep-away with her all over the house. To her great consternation, the dog chewed up the packet and swallowed all of the blades in his excitement.

I suggested that she immediately take cotton balls, shred them into tiny pieces, soak them in broth or milk, and feed them, bit by bit, to the dog, along with Metamucil. Our best hope was to get the cotton wrapped around the blades before they passed through his system. For several days afterward she monitored the dog's elimination for signs of blood, but fortunately, all of the blades came out in nice little cotton capsules. When the scare was over, I asked her if it was common for her dog to snatch things in the house and run away with them, and she confirmed my suspicions by saying that ever since his earliest puppyhood, her children had played chase and keep-away games with him. It seemed like such innocent fun for kids and a dog, but it could have cost the animal his life.

Examples of better kinds of games that are good for a dog's self-esteem and can ultimately prove helpful to you are retrieving, carrying, and searching games. These can be taught at any time in your training program, once you have established good communication and understanding. When you introduce these skills, follow the principles of Awareness Training as described in previous chapters. Prepare yourself ahead of time physically, mentally, and emotionally. Focus on your timing, give lots of praise, visualize, and use your symbol. Detach and analyze if you are having problems, and always remember to close the practice by honoring and just being with your dog.

TEACHING YOUR DOG TO RETRIEVE

Many dogs love to play this game. If your dog is not interested in fetching balls, you can choose a favorite toy or some other item. Be sure that he really likes whatever you want him to get for you. Remember, all dogs learn something wrong as fast as they learn it right. And this also applies to games.

Technique: To be sure your dog learns to retrieve correctly, put him on a lightweight long line and have several treats in your pocket. Always use a long line; otherwise, you give your dog too many options of what to do with the object. He becomes the one to choose when and how to bring it back, if at all. He may decide to play keep-away, or he may bring it back and decide not to let go of it, which creates a tug-of-war.

- Before you throw the object, have a few treats in your hand, *but do not show them to the dog*. If you do, he may wait for the treat instead of pursuing the object.

- Shake the object you want your dog to retrieve in front of his nose so that his attention is riveted on getting hold of it.

- Throw the object a short distance—not more than 3 or 4 feet. Say "Get it!" with enthusiasm in your voice.

- Allow the line to pass through your hands while your dog goes to the object. As soon as he has it in his mouth, say, "Bring it!" and guide him back to you with the line, using praise and inviting body language.

- If your dog drops the object and won't bring it to you, it is usually because you have started the lesson by throwing the object too far. Work with very short distances until your dog thoroughly understands what the game is all about. You can also try using a different object.

- If he wants to lie down and chew the object, use the line to encourage and insist that he come to you. Do not use corrections; just gently bring him to you. If you keep the distance very short in the beginning, you should have no trouble doing this.

- When the dog is right in front of you with the object in his mouth, hold the treat or the food in front of the dog's nose, and put your other hand under or near his chin, saying, "Give."

- "Give" is an effective signal because the dog learns you mean that he should let go of whatever is in his mouth and place it in your hand. I don't recommend using "Drop it." If the dog drops the object on the ground, it may start a contest as to who gets possession of it again, and your fingers could get inadvertently nipped. I also don't like to keep bending over; I like things to be placed in my hand, so I just hold out the treat, with the other hand under his chin, and the object automatically is delivered into my waiting hand.

- If the dog drops the object instead of placing it in your hand, do not give him a food reward. If you do, he will very likely start dropping the object sooner and farther away from your hand in anticipation of the treat.

- If the dog drops the object on the ground, say, "Get it," again. If the dog follows through, let him have the treat. If he does not pick it back up again, the game is over for that session!

- When the dog has released the object into your hand in order to take the treat, praise him and use your symbol.

- Eventually your dog will figure out that the faster he returns the object to you, the sooner he will get his treat and get to play again.

"Retrieving"

- Once he understands the game very well, you can use treats randomly, and finally not at all, because the enjoyment of the game will be reward enough!

Extra notes: Always quit while your dog is still having a great time and is not physically and mentally exhausted. This is especially important when you play this game in hot and humid weather, or in the water, and also if children are involved, because they may not realize how exhausted the dog is getting. Some dogs will run themselves into the ground chasing after things, and they can get heatstroke or drown. If you stop the game when your dog is still begging to do it one more time, he will always be looking for more fun from you, which will be especially important if you want to teach him to find things.

You may find that there are times when he decides not to give the object right to you when you ask. When this happens to me, I say, "Okay, I guess you didn't want to play that much," and the game is done. I take the dog back in the house, or I go into another room, close the door behind me, and stay there for a short while. I come back out a few minutes later to see if the lesson has sunk in, and if it has, we resume the game. I am always sure to maintain an exchange of respect that says, "If you do for me, I will do for you." And I always give lots of praise and send my symbol when the dog responds to my directions.

Retrieving stationary objects: Begin by securing the dog to something or by having someone hold him on the line. Show him that you have an object by moving it around rapidly in front of him. At first it's helpful if the object is one of his favorite toys or something that he really enjoys playing with. Then go several yards off and drop the object on the ground. Return to the dog and use the request "Get the toy."

Visualize what you are requesting as you release him and allow him to move forward on the line. As soon as he has the object in his mouth, tell him to bring it.

Praise him, say "Give," and take the object from him. Give him the food reward, activate your symbol, and send lots of positive energy.

When the dog goes to the object and picks it up on request, you can begin to utilize a variety of different articles. Be sure to repeat the name of the article that you are using. Eventually you can just use a strong hand signal by extending your arm, pointing to the article, and saying its name. The dog will know which object to bring to you.

"Get it" with specific objects: This exercise becomes especially useful if your dog retrieves specific objects and you teach him their names at the same time. For example, you can say, "Get your ball," or "Get the newspaper," or "Get the pillow." When I am working in the garden and I leave a trowel at the end of the row, all I have to do is to ask Jessie to fetch it for me. She will also bring me brushes and feed buckets when I am taking care of the horses. If I climb into the carriage to go for a drive and find I have forgotten the whip, she will bring it to me so that I don't have to climb down again. When I do a class in agility work for dogs, I put the jumps away, and Jessie collects the plastic cones. She takes tremendous pride in her ability to share in my work.

Playing Frisbee: Dogs love the Frisbee; it makes an excellent retrieving object if you keep two warnings in mind:

1. Always skim the disk low to the ground. Do not be tempted to see how high your dog can jump and twist in midair. For every dog who becomes a Frisbee champion, numerous others suffer serious spine and hip injuries.

2. Use only the cloth Frisbee that is made especially for dogs. This Frisbee is soft and will not lacerate your dog's mouth or bruise his gums when he catches it coming at him at 20 miles an hour.

TEACHING YOUR DOG TO CARRY THINGS

Once your dog has learned to retrieve, you can teach him to carry things for you using the signal "Take it," which means, "I am going to hand something to you, and I want you to take it in your mouth." Follow the cue with "Hold it," which tells the dog that you want him to keep the object until you ask for it. When your dog learns this skill, he can be a real help to you if you need an extra hand. He can even carry a flag in a parade, like Falcon, a dignified Lab-Aussie mix who lives with me, or he can present someone with flowers or a gift. Anything that is in the dog's capacity to carry can be used; this is fun and meaningful work for him, and it earns him lots of attention.

"Jessie carrying a water bucket for me."

Technique: Start the lesson with something easy to carry, like a training dumbbell (found in pet supply catalogs) or a favorite toy.

You can do this exercise outside, with the dog on a leash attached to your belt, or you can work in the house without a leash.

- Hold the object in your hand and move it around the dog, encouraging him to try to pursue and catch it.

- As soon as you see that he is about to take it into his mouth, tell him, "Take it," release your hold on the object, and praise him. Let him hold it in his mouth for a few seconds and continue praising him. Then say, "Give," and when he gives it back, praise him again and give him a treat.

- When your dog begins to get the idea after a number of practices, you can ask him to carry the object over distances. Take it slow and ask the dog to carry for very short distances at first— two steps, then five, and then ten. When your dog can do ten, ask for a little more. If you find that you are asking for too much too soon, scale your expectations back a bit. Remember to build on the small successes first.

- When he's carrying reliably, say, "Hold it. Let's go," and walk one or two steps with your dog, while praising and using your symbol.

- Stop, say, "Give it," and take the object. Praise some more and repeat the exercise.

- Eventually you will be able to simply say, "Take it," and extend your hand with the object. Your dog will automatically open his mouth, receive the object, and hold or carry it for you.

Extra notes: I begin teaching communication signals to dogs from puppy-hood by applying signal or cue words to whatever action is taking place. For example, whenever I give puppies a treat, I say, "Take it." A large part of learning can happen just through these daily interactions and reinforcements.

TEACHING YOUR DOG TO FIND THINGS

Working dogs, especially, love to find things for you, and other breeds often enjoy this activity also. Furthermore, there may be times when you will be very grateful that you have made the effort to teach this skill.

Several years ago I went on a long, arduous climb up a mountain with Jessie and Cider, one of my setters. At the end of a beautiful day, we arrived bone-weary at the base parking lot, only to discover that I had lost the keys to my car on the trail. The prospect of climbing back up and searching the entire trail in the coming darkness was not very appealing, but I had no choice. I took the dogs, and we headed up the mountain. Every now and then, I stopped and reminded them that I needed their help, saying, "Find it." They eagerly put their noses to the ground, but it took nearly an hour of climbing before Cider, to my great relief, found the keys lying in some leaves near a rock. I had rested there and eaten a snack, and I must have pulled something out of my pocket during that time, causing the keys to tumble out with it.

It was another long clamber back down again, but at least we could get in my car at the end, instead of having to hike out for help!

Jessie was the heroine of the hour another time when a client named Marianne put her purse on top of her car at the end of class and, forgetting it, drove off, sending the purse spinning down an embankment and into the underbrush by the road. She did not discover the loss until she stopped for gas. She returned and we searched up and down the driveway, but to no avail. I finally got Jessie, asked Marianne to spend a minute handling a book of hers that we found in her car, and then gave it to Jessie to sniff, saying "Find it!"

Jessie marked the scent, and then began weaving back and forth across the driveway, nose to the ground, but found nothing. When we got to the end of the driveway, Jessie crossed the road and disappeared down over the embankment. I could only see her back moving in the tall weeds and under-brush. Suddenly she stiffened and picked up her pace. I could tell that she had caught the scent, and after a few minutes she came prancing up the bank, carrying the purse carefully in her mouth. Marianne was so impressed that she decided to teach Ringo, her family's mixed-breed, to track also.

Little did Marianne know then that her decision would pay off so well. After you train your dog to find objects, you can also train him to find people, and this is what Marianne did, making a great game of teaching Ringo to track down her three children. The following summer she and her husband took the children, aged six, eight, and nine, camping in a primitive wilderness area. In the early afternoon the three asked if they could explore up a hiking trail that terminated near their tent site. Marianne agreed, but told them to leave Ringo behind, and to only go a little way and then return.

The three set off, and an hour went by, by which time Marianne began to worry. She put Ringo on a long line and told him to go to Billy, her oldest. Ringo happily headed up the trail, and Marianne discovered where the children had gone wrong when she came to a place where the main trail forked with an old logging road. Ringo headed up the logging road, and as time went by, it seemed as though she and the dog covered all of the mountain. From time to time, Marianne would discover her children's tracks in patches of muddy earth, but despite her repeated calls, they did not answer. When she had just about reached the limit of her strength, she discovered that Ringo had led her back to camp again, and there were the three, sitting on a log waiting for her. They had found their way back by themselves. It was not a wasted trip by any means, according to Marianne, for Ringo had followed her children's scent every step of the way, and he received a lot of affection that night for his skill and determination.

The most stirring stories about dogs are those that tell of a rescue. How remarkable that we humans should have the blessing of this kind of dedication and talent in our lives. Whether it is a small thing like some lost car keys or a miracle like the location of a lost child, we should never forget how much is given for so little effort on our part.

You may never need to be rescued like those in my stories; nevertheless, teaching your dog to find things for you is one of the most wonderful ways for you to spend meaningful time together.

Technique: Choose an object made of cloth, leather, or wood, all of which hold scent well, and handle it thoroughly until your scent is on the object and the smell of the object is on your hand.

- Get your dog interested in the scented object by waving it in front of his nose. Make a big deal out of it, so that the dog maintains a focus on the item. You can put him in Stay if he is very used to this behavior, or else you can tie him briefly to something or have someone restrain him on a lead. You want to minimize the restraining aspect of this practice, because your dog will lose his enthusiasm for the game if he is constantly receiving corrections for breaking from position in anticipation of searching for the object.

- Walk a short distance away and, using big gestures to keep the dog's attention, place the object in plain view on the ground.

- Return to your dog and put your slightly cupped hand in front of his nose so that he can smell the object.

- Say, "Find it!" with enthusiasm and make a sweeping gesture with your hand in the direction of the object as you release your dog.

- As soon as your dog has picked the object up, give lots of praise and say, "Bring it," which is the same cue used in retrieving.

- As your dog returns to you, praise him enthusiastically, using your symbol.

- As soon as your dog reaches you, tell him, "Give," and when he releases the object, praise him and give him a treat.

- As soon as your dog learns what the exercise is all about, you can begin extending the distance and, eventually, hiding the object.

TEACHING YOUR DOG TO GO TO A SPECIFIC PERSON

When Marianne sent Ringo up the mountain to look for her children, she used a combination of "Find" and "Go to" training behaviors, which she had taught her dog. With parental supervision, "Go to" can be a great hide-and-seek game for dogs and kids. When you combine it with "Take it," you have another way to include your dog in the work of your household. I sometimes call Jessie, put a note on her collar, and send her out to the barn to look for my assistant, George. Or George may send Jessie to me with instructions to send her back with the hammer. This saves us some footwork, and Jessie has a more interesting day and receives lots of praise and attention.

Technique:

- Restrain your dog by holding on to his collar. You will not need a leash if your dog is performing well with all other signals and if you are practicing in a safe location, but you can use a long line if you are practicing out-of-doors.

- Have the person who will be the target of "Go to" show the dog that she has a treat, then run away from him, stop at a distance, and stand quietly. This person does not call the dog to her.

  Note: It is very important at first to have the target person run away to attract the dog's attention and create a lot of excitement. Later on, she can simply stand quietly at a distance. She should not call the dog or use inviting body language, but simply be visible so that the dog can learn to associate her with her name.

- Say the dog's name, and "Go to George." Release him; both people begin praising while the dog heads to the target person. If the dog hesitates, the target person can say "Come" a few seconds after you have given the "Go to" cue.

- As soon as your dog reaches the person, he gets the treat and more praise.

- Repeat the exercise several times. Use the same person over and over, until the dog makes the association with the name. The target person can go farther and farther away and eventually be out of sight around a corner or find a place to hide.

Extra notes: Do not teach your dog more than one person's name until you are sure he understands the exercise.

WORK AND PLAY WITH MORE THAN ONE DOG

If you have more than one dog in the house, it is important to be aware of each dog's needs in the overall design, because dogs, like humans, can fall into issues of low self-esteem and competition for attention. When you play a game like Retrieve together, be sure that one dog does not consistently get left out by any that are faster and higher-ranking. When you teach your dogs to work with you, give each dog a special job description: one can carry your mail, another can get the newspaper, and another can be the one who always finds things that are lost. If one dog has a special skill, find something else that you can praise and thank him for if he gets too old to do it for you anymore.

I stopped performing with the Sheltie drill team because Tarl and Duke, who were the stars of the show, were getting too old to do things safely, like jump over a lineup of ten other dogs. At first I made the mistake of thinking I could replace them with younger dogs. Whenever I asked another dog to do a job that had formerly belonged to Tarl or Duke, one or the other of the two would break out of the Down/Stay and run in front of the usurper or come up to me, searching my face to try to figure out why I hadn't asked him to do what he had always done so well. It nearly broke my heart to see how bad they felt, as if they were being discarded after years of loyal, unwavering service, so I decided to let them retire in glory, and I disbanded the whole team.

TOYS AND CHEW OBJECTS

A good amount of the dog's natural drive to amuse himself and accomplish something can be satisfied with toys and chew objects. If your dog has a wide assortment of things to play with from puppyhood, there is a good chance that you will not have to deal with the problem of destructive chewing. The more options your dog has to redirect his energy, the less chance that you will have to cope with his expending excess energy at inappropriate times and in undesirable ways.

When you purchase toys and chew objects for your dog, use the same kind of common sense and discretion you would use in buying toys for a child. Not everything on the market is sold with your dog's best interests in mind. Save your your money for well-made objects that will last, rather than buying inexpensive ones that your dog will shred in minutes and that might do him harm.

Balls: A great toy is a hard ball that is too large for a dog to pick up in his mouth. Playing with a ball this size requires that he use his feet and his whole body to try to corral it, and many dogs think this is great fun. It is also an excellent outlet for dogs who love to chase and herd things. A 4-inch-diameter ball works well for the toy breeds, and up to 10 inches is good for big dogs.

Tennis balls are not safe for dogs, especially the ones that are iridescent orange or pink. The chemicals in them are now known to be associated with mouth and throat cancer in many dogs. (In fairness to tennis ball manufacturers, they have never been marketed as a dog toy.) Some dogs can chew a tennis ball up and then swallow the pieces.

Golf balls are also dangerous; large breeds can inhale and choke on them, and if the casing comes off, there are miles of string inside and a small pellet of acid at the core, both of which are hazardous to the digestive system.

A better choice is a ball designed especially for dogs called a Bowser Ball. This toy comes in three different sizes, is nontoxic, will float in water, and will last a long time.

Natural chews—bones, rawhide, and rope: Although I do have some artificial chew toys in my dogs' toy box, my number one preference for a chew toy is a natural one. Ideally it is a smoked beef bone. I get mine from a local slaughterhouse, and when the smoked flavor is gone, I make the bone enticing by stuffing the hollow center with meat or cheese. The bones are easy to clean out with a bottle brush. When I get new ones, I always inspect them to see that they do not have any extra pieces on them that might break off. If I find any, I pry them off before I give the bone to my dogs.

Natural butcher bones are also very popular with dogs. Give only shank or knucklebones, and not the small sliced marrowbones. Always feed these bones raw; if you cook them, they will splinter. If there is a lot of marrow in the bone, I dig some of it out, because a lot at one time can cause diarrhea. If your dog chews on natural bones, his stools may be be white for a few days afterward, because of the bone dust.

Bones are great to give to a dog to occupy him if you are going to be gone for a length of time. It can also be a good idea to reserve the bone only for those times when you are away, because then it becomes a special treat.

I don't like rawhide chews at all. Hundreds of dogs choke on these every year, because rawhide gets as slippery as soap when it is wet, and small pieces easily get caught in the throat. The thin strips that are circular or rectangular are especially dangerous. Knotted rawhide bones can be chewed apart, and then the dog can accidentally swallow the knot. Pigs' ears are also slippery. Rawhide from Third World countries can be heavily saturated with arsenic or formaldehyde toxins. U.S. rawhide is cured with hydrogen peroxide, which is safer, but if the dog gets enough of it in his system, it will cause vomiting, because hydrogen peroxide is an emetic.

Big, solid, pressed rawhide is somewhat safer, but some dogs can still chew and swallow enough quantities as the piece disintegrates to cause blockage in the intestines.

Fresh hoof trimmings are beloved by dogs when the farrier comes to the barn, but dried cow hooves sold in stores break off into sharp pieces and can be like broken glass in your dog's digestive tract. Also, when they get wet from being chewed, they smell as if a whole dairy herd has walked through your home.

Rope chew toys are a lot of fun and wear well. One of my dogs likes to throw a rope toy up in the air and catch it. One time, however, she got it lodged in the back of her mouth, which was very frightening to her. The fibers got caught in her teeth, which was like getting dental floss stuck in yours. Fortunately I was right there and was able to free it quickly. Although this is the only problem I have ever had with a rope chew, I have heard of some dogs shredding them and swallowing the strings. Use your own judgment.

In sum, natural chews can be great; just use good judgment when you purchase them. Furthermore, you don't always have to give your dog a bone; raw carrots and apples can be welcome chews from time to time.

Other toys for fun and mental stimulation: Since I have probably experimented with just about every dog toy on the market, I could spend a long time guiding you through the racks at a pet store. Whenever you introduce a new toy, always spend time watching how your dog will use it before you trust him completely alone with it. General notes include a warning about squeaky toys, which are very entertaining, but if your dog is the kind to tear them apart, monitor him carefully so that he does not swallow the squeaker. Fleece toys are very good to use for retrieving games, and some dogs hang on to them like pacifiers for years. Others rip them to shreds in minutes.

Two final highlights are the Kong and the Buster Cube. The Kong is a hard rubber object that looks like a pile of scoops of ice cream. It has a hole in the middle, where you can put cheese, peanut butter, kibble, or other treats. You can fill it with beef broth in the summer, freeze it, and then give it to your dog outside to lick like a Popsicle. Don't bounce it in the house; it can ricochet unpredictably when it bounces on a hard floor, which makes it a fun and challenging retrieving toy out of doors.

The Buster Cube is a delightful dog toy from Europe. It looks like a solid 8-inch plastic cube with a hole in it. In fact, the inside is designed like the chambered nautilus seashell, with spiraling chambers throughout. You can take a handful of kibble, pour it through the hole and shake the cube to distribute the food; a dial allows you to set the degree of difficulty of release. Any dog that is food-oriented will love to spend hours banging and nosing the cube around, and the more it is abused, the more likely it is that a treat will spill out, which keeps the dog's interest level high. You can put part of your dog's regular food ration in his dish and the rest in the cube, and he can spend the day working for it, which fulfills his instinctual drive. Whenever necessary, you can take the cube apart for cleaning.

Some dogs have trouble figuring out what the Buster Cube is all about at first, so it is a good idea to start with the dial set to minimum difficulty and to use a treat with an enticing smell. This toy is very durable and one of the best creative energy outlets made for dogs.

Whether you are teaching your dog something new, playing a game, or simply sharing your home with him, the principle is always the same: by anticipating problems and redirecting his energy to positive outlets, you will be able to avoid most of the common areas of disharmony that arise between humans and their dogs.

15

THE SPECIAL NEEDS
OF PUPPIES

Few people would disagree that there is something very special about a puppy, whether there is an unusual story in its background or not. When I was a breeder, I loved making sure that any puppies in my care got the right start in life. When I had a bitch with a litter due, I got out my preferred whelping box—actually, it was a large, inflatable child's wading pool—and put it near my bed so that I could keep an eye on her. The circular shape of the pool was a perfect approximation of the nest that the dog makes for herself in the wild. It had three inflatable rings, and because it was soft, and there were indentations between the rings, the chances of a puppy getting caught behind the mother and smothered were minimized—something that can happen too easily with a rectangular wooden or fiberglass whelping box. To further enhance the puppies' safety and comfort, I would also arrange the whelping blankets so that they were saucer-shaped, with a slight depression in the middle, like the nest that a bitch would dig in the wild. Even then, it was important to me to create as natural an environment for the bitch and her puppies as possible.

When the puppies were born, I would check each one over to be sure that it was healthy and thriving, note any markings, and weigh it so that I could monitor its growth. As soon as the puppies were several days old, I would handle them many times over the course of the day, massaging them gently, handling the feet, ears, toes, and tails, and rocking them to help develop their motor coordination. I didn't know anything about Reiki then, but now, if I am caring for a litter, I use it to enhance and balance a puppy's energy and to promote the development of a calm and loving personality.

When the puppies were four weeks old, I put them all together in a pen in the living room, where they received lots of attention from visitors, other dogs, and my cats. They had an area partitioned off where they slept and played, with a door allowing access to a smaller area that had papers on the floor. They instinctively urinated and defecated on the papers from the age of four to five weeks, and, since people passed by constantly, any soiled papers were immediately removed and replaced with clean ones. From the beginning, the puppies were learning to keep their den area clean. This is not the same as paper training which I do not recommend for older puppies. This is simply a way to help very young puppies learn to keep their den clean. The bitch no longer stays with her puppies on a regular basis at this age, so although the pen was just high enough to keep the pups from getting out, she could jump in to check on them and nurse them whenever she wanted to.

When the puppies were six weeks old, I would take the mother and the entire litter along for car rides or out for walks. I wanted them to have the comfort and guidance of adult dogs as much as possible, so sometimes other dogs would go along as well.

When the puppies were about six and a half weeks old, I would begin to take each one off alone with me for short periods of time, so that he would have a chance to develop his own identity and also to minimize the trauma of separation when it was time for it to go to a new home. Puppies that I kept also learned this same lesson, so that they would bond to humans rather than to each other.

I kept my puppies until they were about eight weeks of age, and some until after ten weeks, in order to help them through the fear imprint period. This would depend on the personality of the puppy; since the optimum socialization period is between eight and twelve weeks, it was also important that the puppy have a chance to bond with his new family.

By the time a puppy left my home, it was used to having every inch of its body handled, had been around all kinds of people, including children and an assortment of other animals, was content to sleep and eat alone in its own crate, knew about cats and the rules of older dogs, and understood basic training, especially Come and how to walk on a lead without pulling, so that as much as possible it was functioning confidently and happily as an individual before it left. It also understood the basics of house-training. To lessen the trauma of the first night with a new family, I would rub a cloth all over the puppy's mother and littermates and I would handle it myself, and then send the cloth along for the puppy to sleep with for a week or two. Its kennel crate also went along, as did its collar and leash, health certification, care and feeding instructions, a favorite toy, and a supply of the food he had been on. I always also included free training classes to be sure that the puppy continued to get off to a good start.

People would sometimes call me after they took one of my puppies home, and express concern that the puppy was sick because it did not cry all night like their last dog. I had to reassure them that they had what everyone should have: a well-adjusted, emotionally secure puppy who was ready and eager to become their lifelong companion.

CHOOSING YOUR PUPPY WISELY

I have detailed my puppy-raising methods to help you understand what to look for when you acquire a puppy of your own. Here are some other guidelines.

At the very least, be sure that your puppy has been raised in the breeder's home, with lots of handling and lots of exposure to people and other animals. If a dog is going to be a house dog, he should begin life as one. Educate yourself before you go out looking, and don't be afraid to ask detailed questions about the puppy's background. Visit the place to see if it is clean and whether all of the dogs look healthy. Ask for references from previous clients, take a good, hard look at the temperaments and personalities of the puppy's parents, and trust your inner guidance. If anything at all seems not quite right, walk away.

When people wanted one of my dogs' puppies, I always asked a lot of questions about their lifestyle, habits, prior experience with the breed or with dogs in general, and training experiences. I would try very hard to match the right puppy with the right person or family to ensure compatibility. For example, I wouldn't put an assertive, dominant puppy with an easygoing person who was unlikely to set firm limits.

It is common for breeders to pick out your puppy for you, but you do not have to accept his or her assessment of your needs. Do not go home with a puppy, even if you have reserved it, without spending time with it first to see if there is a soul connection and if it feels like the right one to you.

If you are able to make the choice of a puppy by yourself, be aware of certain emotional traps that may cloud your judgment. Very often people decide either to let the puppy choose them or to rescue the one who seems most to need a home. It is not always advisable to pick the puppy who comes up to you first. This is apt to be one of the more dominant ones in the litter, and it may not fit your personality. Neither is it necessarily a good idea to reach out in sympathy for the shy puppy who hangs back. It is understandable to want to give this kind of dog a good home, but be aware that it could end up being shy about everything in life, or be a potential fear-biter. Personality traits often become stronger with maturity.

Take time to scrutinize the puppies who do not immediately stand out in the pack, those who are more middle-of-the-road. Very often they make the best companions, because they are adaptable.

Even if your intentions are good, it is better not to pick out a puppy for someone else, because that person needs to be the one to make the commitment and to find the soul connection. This also applies to children and puppies: be sure at the very least, that your child has an interest in animals and has spent time with them before. If you have a very young child, resist the idea of using a puppy to teach your child responsibility; it rarely works out, and very young children who aren't capable of caring for themselves can be overwhelmed by a boisterous puppy.

Although I believe in miracles, be aware that puppies from backyard breeding operations and pet shops often come with a wide variety of behavior problems due to the trauma of early separation from the litter, and a lot of repatterning work may be necessary. Depending on the connection and commitment between the dog and the person, these can be opportunities for growth and learning or exercises in frustration and eventual euthanasia for the dog.

If you like the breeder and admire the physical and soul qualities of the mother and father of a litter, you may find a puppy who will turn into a wonderful dog. There is less chance, however, that things will turn out well with a puppy from a pet shop, who is usually a product of an inhumane factory breeding operation called a puppy mill. These operations are similar to other factory farming methods, where breeding animals are confined in small cages and live out their lives doing nothing more than producing offspring. Puppies are removed from their mother when they are very young and confined alone in cages, while she is bred again as soon as possible. The puppy's earliest experience is of feeling lonely and afraid, subjected to the stress of being shipped to a pet shop and isolated in a cage. It misses the education its mother would normally give, as well as the all-important socialization with its own kind.

This deprivation ultimately creates dogs with many behavioral problems. In the past, humane societies used to be the place to find Heinz 57 dogs, but as a result of the activity of puppy mills, kennels, humane societies, and breed-specific rescue organizations today are filled with purebred dogs that have numerous behavioral and congenital disorders.

In addition to the emotional impairment these animals suffer, pet shop puppies are notoriously difficult to house-train. Because they are confined alone in small spaces on display, they become used to urinating and defecating in the same place where they eat and sleep. An inability to house-train is one of the main reasons that dogs are euthanized once they grow out of their small-puppy cuteness. Therefore, an appalling percentage of puppies serve merely for temporary entertainment, like the short-lived bunny rabbits who are bought by the thousands at Easter time.

It is very hard not to want to rescue these puppies from their situation, but as long as people continue to buy them, there will be a market for dogs who, because they are emotionally, psychologically, and genetically impaired, are frequently unable to offer the kind of fulfillment people are looking for in a relationship. The best way to change these inhumane practices is to make them economically and politically unviable.

There are no guarantees that you will end up with the perfect puppy for you, or that it will grow up into the perfect dog. All you can do is to maximize the potential that things will work out. Occasionally a puppy grows into a wonderful dog, despite an incredible amount of stress and trauma in its background. If he has the capacity to do this, that is a strong statement about who he is and what he brings into the world. If you have chosen a dog with problems, because something in your heart told you that the two of you had some growing to do together, then you are starting from the right place together, even if his own beginnings were not ideal.

PREPARING YOUR HOME FOR A PUPPY

Before you bring your puppy home, establish a bathroom area out-of-doors and get a crate for him. If there are a number of family members, discuss the puppy's needs and agree on guidelines for the puppy's care. Put baby gates in the doorways of rooms that the puppy should not enter, attach childproof latches to low cabinets, and block off stairwells and railings that a puppy could slip through and fall. Since the optimum training time is when a puppy is between eight and sixteen weeks, it can be a real setback when a puppy is injured and has to be confined so that it misses out on important experiences that need to take place during an optimal stage of learning.

Puppies learn though observing the activities of those around them and by trial and error. In the wild, they learn skills like hunting by watching and imitating the adult members of the pack. It is very confusing for a puppy to grow up in a human household, because he observes many things that he is not allowed to imitate. He sees people taking out the garbage, but he has to keep his nose out of it. He watches the plugging and unplugging of light cords, but he cannot take them in his mouth, because his sharp puppy teeth could get him electrocuted. Although people can handle houseplants, he cannot, because many plants are toxic to dogs. Even your vitamin pills can be deadly if a puppy swallows them. For all of these reasons, it is important to instruct everyone in the household, as much as possible, to avoid handling things in front of the puppy that may be dangerous to his health and well-being. Clean out the cat litter boxes and fertilize and prune your houseplants when the puppy is napping. Like little children, a puppy explores his whole world with his mouth. Be careful of small toys like Legos, and don't leave anything lying around that the puppy should not play with, including hats, mittens, and shoes.

When Your Puppy Comes Home

Your puppy's training should begin as soon as you bring him home. While you surround him with a feeling of being safe and nurtured, you need to help him learn about himself and where he fits into your household. While you are getting to know your puppy, spend a lot of time observing him, and watch for tendencies like excessive nipping or destructive chewing. At the first sign of any excessively shy or aggressive behavior, get help immediately from a qualified professional.

There are many reasons why I like to teach a puppy, from the very first, to be in a kennel crate. A crate is not a form of punishment, and you should never use it as such. It is the puppy's safe space, his own den within your den. As with children and playpens, the crate allows you to keep the puppy safe while you are busy. A puppy who is used to a crate will feel less stressed when going to the vet or the groomer, where the crate is the most common form of confinement. If you travel with him, he will be happier in his own space, no matter what the form of transportation, and you will be able to relax when you visit friends. When you take him in your car, you can seat-belt the crate in and know that your puppy will have good protection if you get into an accident.

If a puppy learns to spend several hours every day alone in a crate by himself, any separation anxiety will be minimized, because he will learn that he is okay when you are not around. Like most puppies, he will want to keep his space clean, and being crated will help him learn to exert some control over his bladder and bowels while he is being house-trained.

The size of the crate you buy for your puppy will depend on whether you will be using it only during your dog's puppyhood or after he grows up as well. If you get a crate for an adult dog and put a puppy in it, it will be too big and the puppy will be less likely to keep it clean. To solve this problem you can partition off a large crate for a puppy, or you can buy more than one. If the puppy does not like the crate, persevere. It is not a good idea to let him out if he is whining and making a fuss, because he will learn that the more he complains, the sooner he will be let out. Wait until he calms down, and then praise him for being quiet before you take him out again. Visualize to him that he is safe and that this is his special place where he can rest and play.

Feed your puppy in the crate, put him there for naps, and put toys in with him to let him play by himself.

Start with crate-training during the day, not just at night. Put your puppy in the crate for short periods while you are at home as well as when you are away. This will get him into the habit of being alone, and then, if you leave, he will feel less stress. It is hard on puppies if they have constant contact with you, and then none at all for hours. It's best to establish a balance.

HOUSE-TRAINING

The best way to help your puppy learn to control his elimination needs is to give him a consistent routine with clear expectations, just as you would a child. It is unfair to punish him for something that is beyond his control, and it is especially detrimental to do it after the fact.

Whenever possible, I prefer to avoid paper training, because it is like lying to the puppy. He starts out accruing all kinds of recognition and praise when he urinates and defecates in the house, and then, when he gets larger, the rules are switched and he is reprimanded for the same behavior, just at a point when he should be doing some important bonding with you and learning to trust you. It confuses the puppy, and can confuse other young members of the household, too! The most humorous example of this came from a woman named Marcie, who called me, saying she needed some help getting her half-grown puppy, Buffy, house-trained. The puppy would stand in front of Marcie, squat, urinate, and then pop up again and happily wag her tail. Marcie admitted she realized this behavior was her own doing, because that very afternoon, her toddler came over, pulled down his pants, urinated on the floor, and asked if he could have a cookie like Buffy! In order to try to change the situation, Marcie had now started punishing Buffy, which was only making things worse. Fortunately, we were able to solve the problem with vigilance and consistent outdoor time, removing all papers from the floors, timely use of the crate, and by scaling down the level of praise, which was too effusive, and was causing the puppy to urinate in order to please Marcie.

If you have absolutely no way to get your puppy to an outside elimination area during the day, then do not keep the puppy in a crate—it is not humane to keep a puppy crated for more than four hours. Instead, confine him to a small room, mud room, bathroom, or pantry. Masking-tape papers to the floor in the corner farthest from the door to keep them in one spot and so the puppy won't skid them around, chew them up in little pieces, or relocate his bathroom space. This will also keep him from getting his feet dirty and smearing feces on the walls if he jumps up when he hears you coming. Put his toys, a bed, and his water and food dishes in another corner. Use every opportunity when you are home, and especially on weekends, to put him on a leash and take him outside.

It is very important for a puppy to learn to eliminate while on leash. I once had a hysterical call from a woman whose dog was used to having a dog door that led to an outside yard, where he could eliminate whenever he felt the need. Then she took him to the city. He had never eliminated on concrete, while he was on leash, or in a situation where he had to contend with all kinds of people and traffic going by. The dog had not eliminated in the three days and two nights that they had been there, because he was used to being by himself. On my advice, the woman put down a thick layer of newspapers in the bathroom of the apartment where she was staying, and gave the dog suppositories in order to help him release bowels and bladder and avoid a severe case of uremic poisoning.

The desired elements for house-training include putting your puppy regularly in a crate to help him want to control his elimination, keeping him on a schedule, establishing one place out-of-doors where you want him to perform, using a verbal signal to tell him what you expect of him, and monitoring his food and water intake to help avoid accidents.

Every time you take your puppy outside to go to the bathroom, put him on a leash. Say, "Outside," and lead him out to the place you have designated as his bathroom area. You will have to keep this area regularly cleaned of feces, or else your puppy will soon not want to use it. Once you have reached the area, keep the puppy on the leash, and stand there until he goes. Then take him for a walk or play period, and not before. If you walk around beforehand, he will delay eliminating in order to stay outside longer, since he will have learned that as soon as he goes, you will take him back inside.

Use a signal like, "Go potty," "Hurry up," "Get busy," or any phrase that will tell him what you are asking for. Be sure that every member of the family uses the same cue. This will be his signal, so that any time you put him on a leash and go stand with him that area, he knows he will have an opportunity to relieve himself. He will also understand your signal in the future when you stand with him in any other area, whether in the city, while on a car trip, or when visiting friends.

Except for very short-haired dogs, most dogs love to be outside regardless of the weather. Therefore, once he is finished, praise him, and then take him for a short walk, which will reward him for getting his business over with so quickly. If it is cold and the dog is short-haired, his reward will be a nice, warm house as soon as possible! Use your "Inside" signal to tell him when it is time to go in.

When your puppy comes in after having gone to the bathroom, he will usually be good for an hour or two of supervised freedom in a room in the house. Gates across the doors to other rooms are a good idea, so that you do not lose track of him. If the puppy should have an accident on a carpet, put a thick layer of folded paper towels on top of the wet spot and stand on them to force as much urine as possible to soak into the towels. Repeat until there is no more moisture on the towels. Then saturate the area with a solutions of ⅔ cup plain water to ⅓ cup white vinegar. (Test a section of carpet where it will not show beforehand to make sure it will not stain.) Repeat the same process with the paper towels. This combination works best for getting rid of any lingering scent pheromones, which may attract the puppy back to the same spot. If there is a stain, it can often be removed with club soda and the same blotting procedure. Do not rub or you will increase the size of the area. It is also very effective to cut one slice out of a head of *green* cabbage and rub it over the exposed place. Repeat until the stain is gone.

If your puppy has not gone, do not give him unsupervised freedom in the house, or he will very likely have an accident. Instead, put him back in his crate, wait ten or fifteen minutes, and then take him out again. Be sure to praise him well as soon as he performs.

If you catch your puppy in the act of eliminating, stop him by startling him a little. Give your hands a loud clap or stamp your feet and say, "Outside!" Get in the habit of saying "Outside" every time you take your puppy to the door and are about to open it to take him out to go. This will help him make the connection between the word and the place, so that if you interrupt an accident, he will understand that the place is wrong.

Puppies usually eliminate every two hours when they are very young. They need to go soon after they have awakened from a nap, within a few minutes after they have eaten, and after they have been playing hard. Lots of physical activity stimulates the bowel and bladder, requiring more frequent trips outdoors.

Certain factors contribute to house-training difficulties. Monitor his water intake, especially if he seems to need to urinate all of the time. If your puppy is having trouble holding through the night, withhold water after eight or nine o'clock in the evening. If it is summer and very hot, you can give your puppy a couple of ice cubes if he seems thirsty.

If you let your puppy eat whenever he is hungry, it will be impossible to figure out when he needs to go out. Keep him on a predictable schedule, and feed him in his crate, although when he is older, this will not be necessary. Put the food dish in after he is already in, otherwise he may tip it over as he enters the crate. It is also good to do this so that, if you are distracted and don't get to him right away after he is through eating, he will be apt to hold it because he will want to keep his crate clean. It is not advisable to give your puppy water in his crate, or he will turn the crate into a swimming pool.

It is important to keep your puppy free of parasites, because a bellyful of worms and sporadic diarrhea is not conducive to house-training. Nutrition is also important, because poor-quality food can also give your puppy loose bowels and make it difficult to get him on a predictable schedule. Poor-quality food also does not satisfy the puppy's appetite, so he will want to eat more to get nutrients, and much of his dinner will pass undigested through his system. This means that, the more he eats, the more he needs to eliminate, because the food is not being broken down and used to nourish his system.

Puppies are like babies: raising them well is a seven-day-a-week, twenty-four-hour job. House-training has to be regular in order to make progress, which means keeping the daily schedule the same and not sleeping in on weekends!

GETTING THROUGH THE NIGHT

Many people struggle with the problem of young puppies and house-training during the night. I always put the puppy's crate right next to my bed, even if he is not going to end up sleeping in the bedroom. I want the puppy to get into the habit of being in his crate at night, and I want him to be quiet. I also want to avoid the possibility that he will mess in the crate and learn to live with it, which is the exact opposite of what you are trying to encourage him to learn.

Of course, there is no question that your puppy would like to spend his nights cuddled up next to you, but unless you are prepared to share your bed when he reaches adulthood, it is better not to let him do it now, especially, for obvious reasons, while you are still house-training him. Puppies often whine and carry on if isolated in another part of the house and you both will be miserable, so it is a good idea to compromise while he is still growing and let him be near you, but teach him that he has to be quiet.

I keep a leash on top of the crate, and if I hear the puppy fussing in the middle of the night, I immediately get up, snap the leash on, and rush him out the door. If you don't have the puppy on the leash, there is a high probability that he will eliminate before you make it outside.

Since 2:00 A.M. is not the usual time to go for a walk or have a play period with the puppy, I give verbal praise as soon as he eliminates, return to the house, put the puppy immediately back in the crate, and once I'm back in bed with the lights off, I put my hand on top of the crate. I visualize the puppy becoming quiet and going back to sleep, in order to help him calm down.

If the puppy is resistant to settling down, I need to discourage his desire to whine and beg for company. (I will say more about interrupting unacceptable behavior in a bit.) At the first sound the puppy makes, I say nothing, but slam my hand on the top of the crate (fiberglass crates work best), which makes him think that the whole room blew up. If he barks or whines again,

I repeat the action. He soon figures out that every time he opens his mouth, he will cause an explosion, so very quickly, he stops. I then use my symbol and send him my appreciation for being quiet and honoring my need to sleep. Since I am not interacting with him during these times, after one or two nights, he usually settles down and goes right back to sleep as soon as I put him back in the crate. Playing quiet, soothing music may also help both of you get back into a relaxed, sleep-inducing mood.

This approach is much easier on both of you than isolating the puppy in a room where you and your neighbors cannot hear him. If you put the crate several rooms away or downstairs, and your puppy starts barking, you have two choices: you can put a pillow over your head and try to ignore it, or you can get up, turn on some lights, and go and yell at him. Either way, the puppy learns bad habits: if you ignore him, he discovers that he can bark for hours; if you get up, he congratulates himself for turning the lights on and bringing you to see him. Also, it is lonely for him to spend his nights far from you, when he could be nearby, hearing your breathing and knowing that you are near.

Is it cruel to scare the puppy by startling him into silence? It is important to remember that puppies are regularly disciplined by their elders in ways that appear very frightening. A puppy who gets too boisterous around an older dog will quickly see teeth and be bowled over by a ferocious growl. The good thing about this is that he has to learn the lesson only once, and he can immediately put his attention to learning to accept discipline and more positive behavior. In the same way, one or two reprimands from you are not much for him to endure, and they can save you from many torturous nights of lost sleep caused by a crying puppy who can't figure out what your expectations are when the lights go out.

OTHER TRAINING GUIDELINES

If you house-train your puppy and teach him to be quiet at night, you will have overcome two of the biggest obstacles to helping your dog become an agreeable member of your family. In all other cases, you will find that much of your communicating can happen very naturally if you just put a word on a behavior each time you are doing it with the puppy and whenever you see the puppy doing something on his own. When you are ready to feed your puppy, say his name and "Come!" This will create a positive association with that word. I begin doing this kind of patterning with puppies who are only four or five weeks old.

All cues can be taught this way if you are proactive and put the word on the action in the moment just before it is completed. This will enable your formal communication sessions to go much more smoothly, because he will already be used to hearing you use your special voice with the directive tone in it. Praise and acknowledge every single thing that he does that is correct for the rules that you want to teach to him. He will be developing a sense of himself and his ability to connect with you in positive ways.

GOOD WAYS TO AVOID BAD HABITS

It is very easy to get into bad habits with puppies, because they are so adorable. For the sake of the future that you dream of sharing, do not allow yourself or anyone else to tease, roughhouse, or play chasing games with your puppy. Appropriate play should be as described in Chapter 14. Eight weeks is not too early to teach Retrieve, as long as you keep things very simple. Hide-and-seek goes well with teaching Come, because he will get a little anxious when you go out of sight, and will want to find you as fast as possible.

It is best if the puppy does not have the run of the house without supervision, and then he will not have the opportunity to do things that are unsafe or destructive. Get him interested in his chew toys, and resist the temptation to give him one of your worn-out shoes, because he will not be able to discriminate between that object and your brand-new running sneaker. If you are making dinner in the kitchen, give the puppy a bone to chew on while you work, so that he is distracted from wanting to jump up and investigate what you are doing on the counter. Feed him ahead of time, so that he will not pester you while you eat. If you want to sit down and relax in the evening, take him for a walk and then give him a toy to play with first. This will provide him with exercise and stimulation, and he will be more content to spend time by himself, instead of pestering you to see if you will respond.

INTERRUPTING UNDESIRABLE BEHAVIOR

If you catch your puppy engaging in an activity that you want to discourage, use the principles of Awareness Training. Rather than yelling "No!" use constructive directive cues, which tell the puppy what you want him to do. Interrupt the behavior, redirect, and reinforce with praise. Making a loud noise, as in the example of my hand on the crate, is the most common kind of interruption for undesirable behavior when the puppy is off-leash. Other examples include a shake-can noisemaker (an aluminum can filled with pennies, small stones, or beans, with a tape over the hole in the top), smacking a newspaper on a table to create a sudden loud noise, or even stamping your foot or clapping your hands loudly. These are all good ways of getting a puppy's attention. Spanking or striking a puppy is not an acceptable or natural form of discipline—have you ever seen a dog spank another dog? It is meaningless, and although it may relieve your frustration, you can accomplish a lot more with eye contact, body posture, tone of voice, and effective distraction and praise.

It is best not to caress the puppy when he is barking or whining, even if your wish is to calm him. He will interpret your action as approval. Interrupt the activity first, while teaching him the cue for "Quiet." Then you can give him a thankful acknowledgment when he stops. If your puppy cannot contain his energy, create games to redirect him and make sure he gets plenty of exercise, so that he does not need to work off excess energy.

Out of the trash can and off the furniture: A good example of an undesirable behavior that can be avoided if you are proactive is the problem of puppies and trash cans. Ideally, the very first time that he sticks his nose in any kind of waste receptacle, you want him to learn that it is a bad idea. You accomplish this by doing a training setup with an item that you can buy called a Snappy Trap, which looks like a combination mousetrap and fly swatter. You set it open and when it is tripped, the object snaps and pops up in the air, startling the puppy so that he will not want to repeat the experience. There is absolutely no possibility of injury with these; they are used only to interrupt behavior.

To teach your puppy to stay out of any trash can, put your regular garbage can out of the way, and fill a small can with crumpled newspapers and a few meat or cheese wrappers with an enticing smell. (Styrofoam meat trays are not good for dogs to eat, so keep them out of his reach.) Be sure to raise the level of the contents high enough so that the puppy can easily get his head in to explore, which will trigger the traps.

Depending on the diameter of the can, put one or more Snappy Traps on the top of your pile, and spread an opened paper napkin on top of the traps to hide them. The first time the puppy sticks his nose in, the traps will be triggered, there will be an impressive sound, and the paper will fly up in the air. The puppy will back off fast, thinking that there is something in the can that eats puppies for breakfast.

You will need to keep repeating this setup until the puppy understands that it is more self-rewarding to stay away from the can, no matter how enticing a smell is coming from it. When you see that the traps are no longer sprung, you will know that this has happened.

Snappy Traps can also be used to keep puppies from stealing food off of counters or tables, or you can create your own device. For example, instead of a Snappy Trap, you can create a pyramid of aluminum cans on a lightweight board, which spans the top of the can. If they all come crashing down when the puppy noses past them, it will have the same deterring effect.

You can also train your puppy to stay off of furniture by using a smoke alarm as a booby trap. Find the kind that has a protruding test button on the front. Block off all furniture, except for one chair, and place the alarm under the cushion, with a rolled-up hand towel next to it to keep the weight of the cushion from tripping the alarm until the puppy's weight is applied from above.

I want to stress again, that all of these methods are quick, easy, and do not create trauma. Constant anger, yelling, and reprimands are far more injurious to a puppy than a quick lesson, followed by direction to a preferred behavior, and praise. Use common sense when using booby traps, and keep your focus on your long-term goals.

Jumping up: It can be very cute to have a puppy jump up and put his paws on you, as if he is reaching up to you and asking to be nurtured. In fact he is, but many people are not aware of the origins of this behavior. When puppies are little, the bitch nurses them while lying on her side, and there is usually enough room for everyone. When the puppies get bigger, however, space runs out, so she stands, and her puppies jump up and put their paws on her abdomen to nurse, which becomes a self-rewarding behavior. When they are separated from their mother and become part of your life, they will tend to transfer this soliciting behavior to you. This is not much fun if the puppy grows to be a big dog, and it is not a great way to make friends with your company.

The best way to discourage a puppy from learning this habit is to teach him that Sit is the behavior that gets attention. If you see that your puppy is thinking about jumping up on you, be proactive and ask him for a Sit. Then praise him. If he does need a reprimand, say, "Off!" and then ask for the Sit so that you can praise him.

If you have other dogs, it is better not to let your puppy run free with them outside unless you have a fenced yard or are able to supervise them. If you have dogs that are running loose, it is not uncommon for puppies to follow them, not be able to keep up, and then get lost. This also applies to the question of sending your puppy out to play with young children. It is easy for both to wander off from one another, and young children are generally not capable of the kind of supervision that will ensure the puppy's safety.

Mouthing behavior: It is important that you teach your puppy to control the way he uses his mouth around you, especially when you are giving him a treat, and because you may want to use food as a lure in training. When you are holding out a morsel to a puppy, he needs to realize that you do not want him to pinch or grab and that he should not take anything in his mouth without permission.

If a puppy acts like a real piranha when offered a treat, many people jerk the hand back and say, "No!" This kind of response only makes the puppy think he should have moved faster and bitten harder. Rather than risking getting your fingers pinched, it is best to keep the food inside of your closed hand. Allow the puppy to lick and sniff it, but do not let him bite it. If he is getting too pushy, look the puppy right in the eyes, make your voice sound unpleasant, and growl, "Off!" The puppy will think, "Whoa! Big dog! Okay!"

If the puppy puts his nose near your hand, but maintains control over his teeth, praise him and extend the treat on the ends of your fingers saying, "Take it." This will teach him to wait for your signal.

Many puppies will start to mouth your hands if you caress them on the head, neck, and around the mouth. This is disruptive to their energy; also, it is very tempting to snap at things moving and waving about the head. Use gentle, massaging strokes on the body instead. If the puppy persists, stop the attention, which will teach him to stop the behavior.

TEACHING PUPPIES HOW TO GET IN AND OUT OF CARS

It is not unusual for me to be called by people who need help with teaching their grown dogs how to get in and out of cars. When a puppy is little, its humans often either lift him in and out of the car or go through the laborious exercise of placing his front feet on the edge of the seat and then hoisting his rear end in. The puppy learns that this is how cars are entered, and then one day he weighs 80 pounds and his human is going to a chiropractor for back adjustments! As soon as the puppy is big enough, avoid this scenario by using a food lure or a favorite toy to help your puppy learn to scramble in and out on his own—but keep his leash on for safety reasons.

TEACHING PUPPIES ABOUT STAIRS

The same point applies to the use of stairs: use a food lure, and a leash to give guidance and direction. It is easier to teach a puppy to go up, so use the shortest flight of stairs you can find, and put the puppy, facing upward, on the first step down from the top. Have someone stand behind him, in case he stumbles, or do so yourself. Using the lure in front of his nose, lead him up the step, and then give lots of praise. Once he does this well, start him on the second step from the top, and so forth.

Use the same approach when teaching a puppy to go down the stairs: start him on the first step up from the bottom, and use the lure to guide him down. Stay in front of him, ready to catch him if he slips.

PUPPIES AND HOLIDAYS

I often get a lot of calls for help during the holidays because dogs tend to have a hard time with the stress level of the household. This is especially true for the dog's first experience. The schedule is upset, there are more things around that they can't go near, and there is lots of coming and going. If you give your dog presents on a holiday, it can help if he gets a few ahead of time so that he will have something new and interesting to pay attention to.

Adolescent dogs can have a hard time around holidays, and they may create all kinds of ways to try to regain the lost attention. It is important not to let your training slide, because the dog will feel even more insecure.

Be especially vigilant if you have acquired your puppy around a holiday. It is better not to do this if you can avoid it, because all of the chaos at these times makes it difficult to give a puppy the right kind of supervision and care. It is better to wait until the holiday is past to bring the puppy home. Holidays often bring lots of sweets into the home, and chocolate is toxic to dogs. Toys often have small pieces that a puppy can swallow. Christmas trees have light cords that can electrocute if they are chewed, or the puppy can inadvertently get tangled in them and pull the tree over. Tinsel can get twisted in a puppy's intestines and cause death. Batteries are also deadly if they are swallowed. Whenever I had young puppies in my home around Christmastime, I would put Snappy Traps and attach small balloons, blown up as full as they could possibly be, to lower branches of the tree, so that any puppy who decided to chew on a decoration would get a big surprise.

There is a also lot of candy around during Easter and Halloween, as well as other potential dangers like the ingestion of Easter grass and the trauma of groups of costumed children suddenly appearing at the door. Both of these can create stress with ongoing consequences.

LET YOUR PUPPY BE A PUPPY

Almost all problems that people experience with raising a puppy can be avoided if you are vigilant, prepare well ahead of time, and are proactive. Your puppy is a learning dynamo, constantly exploring and looking for activities that will be self-rewarding. If you stay ahead of him, you will eventually have a grown-up dog who has never nipped, chewed the wrong thing, jumped up, had a problem with house-training, or driven you crazy by barking all night.

Even though your puppy needs to start learning the rules of your family as soon as he joins it, don't forget to give him time and space to grow. Technically, the dog's brain is fully developed by the time he is seven weeks of age, but it takes a while for experience and maturity to show him what to do with it. Like children, puppies have a short attention span and are very easily distracted. It takes a while before they can hold their focus.

I would not allow a puppy to get away with inappropriate behavior, but I also do not hold the same expectations for him as I would for a more mature dog. For example, I would never ask a young puppy to hold a Stay for ten minutes, because it would be too hard for him. All of the reprimanding I would have to do to get him to follow through would only turn him into a frustrated and insecure grown-up. Puppies are joyful beings, eager to explore the wonders of their world; I want to encourage that zest and curiosity, because I know it will ultimately give me a more intelligent, responsive, and confident dog. I have seen puppies who have had the wiggle-and-giggle disciplined out of them, and once you take it out, you can't ever put it back. A puppy is only a puppy for a few months, so I concentrate on putting fun and safety first.

CONCLUSION: THE END IS ONLY THE BEGINNING

In mid-July I wanted to go into the upper field to see if any of the yarrow was ready for picking. Life had been crazy, and it was a good time to just slow down on a midsummer afternoon. Jessie and I went alone this time; having such a big family of animals means that I hadn't been spending much time alone with her. The days when we used to team up at shows together are long gone, and now we work hard keeping the Hearthside Animal Center going. It felt good, just the two of us for a change.

It was about four in the afternoon, still pretty hot, even though the sun was now slanting across the dry grass and the trees spread good pools of shade on the edges of the meadow. We took it slow, ambling along, and then reached the end of the field where the woods begin.

I slipped under the electric fence and headed into the cool green light, but Jessie stopped and wouldn't go any farther. I thought maybe she didn't want to go under the fence, so I called her over and told her to do a down so she could crawl under and not get zapped. She came over and did as I asked, but she was hesitant to keep going. I gave her an encouraging rub behind the ears, thinking that this was unlike her. What was going on?

After a little urging, Jessie followed, but instead of bounding ahead as she usually does, she lagged behind. A few minutes later I saw her stumble into the branches of a big fallen tree, and I called her to me, wondering why she wasn't paying attention. We came through the woods and out into the unmowed field on the other side, and still she followed

"Jessie"

behind me, seeming tentative, but not stressed or afraid. Just cautious. I'd never seen her like that.

As we reached a marshy area and a small pond, I headed for the water's edge and began to look for some of the medicinal plants that are July bloomers. After a short search, I checked to see what Jessie was doing, and I saw her standing stock still, her nose in the air, moving her head in a searching way, sniffing for scent. I thought perhaps there was coyote scent in the field, and I called out to her so we could move along. As soon as I said, "Let's go, Jessie," her head snapped around and she came right to me.

I left the pond and went to higher ground, where I found a good patch of Saint-John's-wort, and after filling my basket, I knelt on the ground and began to look for some chickweed. Jessie headed past me about 20 feet away, nose to the ground, and eventually ended up in the middle of a tangle of weeds. When I finally stood up, I saw her in that same strange position, nose in the air, searching.

"Jessie, come," I called, standing still and waiting for her to come bounding to me the way she always does.

She came trotting in my direction. And went right on by, panting a little, a determined look on her face.

It wasn't as though she couldn't see me, the grass was not that high.

"Jessie?" I said, all of a sudden afraid.

She stopped as soon as she heard my voice, turned, and came to me, but the tears were already pouring down my cheeks.

Jessie couldn't see.

I didn't want to believe it. We walked on, and I re-created the same situation, drifting away from her, and then calling her, wanting it to be a fluke. At last I just knelt and threw my arms around her neck and sobbed.

Jessie's whole demeanor changed then, once she realized that I knew. She hung her head and looked deeply embarrassed, as if she had done something wrong. We walked slowly back to the house, taking the road rather than the way we had come so she wouldn't have to negotiate the downfall.

We got through the evening chores, and then I went and sat by the pond with her. I put my arms around her, stroked her thick, soft coat, and tried to find some way to come to terms with the fact that, despite our deep connection, I had been unaware of her condition. I decided she wasn't completely blind, but I doubted that she could see much more than light and shadow. Australian shepherds, as a breed, have several congenital eye problems that sometimes show up in this way. She had compensated for it so well because she knows every inch of the Center by heart. And the other dogs had not given me any indication of a change in her authority.

As Jessie and I sat by the water's edge, the frogs croaking away in the dark, I thought back over the previous months. I remembered how I had used her in my evening classes to demonstrate certain exercises and she had missed my hand signals. I had been excusing this, thinking it was a consequence of her age. She'd had no problem with scent discrimination or the "Find it" and "Go to" exercises; I could send her to George, and George would send her back to me. But unless I said, "That's it, good girl," she was hesitant.

There was now no doubt in my mind that she had deliberately been hiding her condition from me. On the walk, which we had not taken together since the winter, she knew that she would have a hard time in the woods because it was unfamiliar territory to her, and that it would be more obvious to me that she could see almost nothing. She couldn't locate me until I spoke, and I hadn't had a clue until right then that there was anything wrong. Because her other senses were still so good, I had not noticed that her physical capabilities could no longer keep up with the greatness of her spirit.

All of this thinking brought some order back to my world, but I still struggled with a sense of having failed Jessie in some way, because I had not noticed the change. This kept a lump in my throat, and after a while I slipped into that space where she and I can exchange information on the deepest level of all. "Why, Jessie?" I asked. "Why didn't you let me know?"

Jessie sat beside me, regal as ever, her heart radiating compassion, her aura brilliant with light. Her answer was simple, because for her, her job description had always been simple and without question: "I'm your companion and your protector," she said. "I told you this when I came a long time ago and saw that you didn't have a mate to take care of you. I was afraid that if you knew I couldn't see, you would no longer feel safe. It's hard for me now, to know that I cannot do my job as well anymore."

I could not respond, overwhelmed with the thought that Jessie's main concern, as always, was for me. The loss of her sight was far harder for me to accept than it was for her. Obviously she had accepted it a long time ago, and she had adjusted so well that I hadn't even known about it.

I just put my arms around her, and we sat for a long time in silence, leaning into one another.

Jessie is almost thirteen now; I have to face the fact that the physical effects of aging are beginning to show, just as I have had to deal with the blooming and fading of the lives of other great dogs who have given me so much over the years. When I try to come to terms with the impending loss of her physical presence, I can't help getting stuck between philosophy and pure sorrow. I have to remind myself to focus on my conviction that we have shared other earth walks and there is no reason to think it won't be the same in the future. I know that Jessie and I are forever connected on an energy level. I try to follow her example and stay in the moment, grateful for each day she is with me. Jessie will leave her physical body, but I know that I will always be able to connect with her energy in other ways.

Despite all of this, I know I will miss her deeply when she is gone. And I will be helped, as I always am, by all of the other animals, who excel at allowing me to fully express my emotions. Whenever an animal at Hearthside goes back to spirit, the dogs begin a howling salute-and-farewell within a minute or two of the soul departing from the physical form. This happens so often that I know they are connected to what is happening, even though they are not in the immediate area.

Unlike humans, who often try to get over a loss quickly because the grieving process makes them uncomfortable, the dogs gather around me, allowing me the full extent of my emotions. They never try to make me shut down or to tell me to hurry and replace whoever has left. They keep it simple, amplify the experience for me, help me process it, and then together we let it go.

When I look back over my life, I realize that whenever an animal returns to spirit form, it often feels as though it has left so that a new energy or teaching can come in. This lets me know that there is no separation between our worlds, no awkward barrier of different languages, different bodies, and social spheres, or even different dogs; there is only a loving spiritual force that manifests in animal form and consistently flows through my life to inspire and sustain me.

This feeling is borne out when I see how Jessie is grooming Rainbow to take her place. Her knowledge of my needs seems to extend even to this. When I took Rainbow on, I was worried that Jessie would be jealous, because this new dog and I were obviously becoming so close, but they got along beautifully from the very first encounter. Rainbow understood who Jessie was, and immediately accepted her as her teacher, watching her intently, picking up on her leads, and imitating her gestures. Now that Jessie is old and doesn't see as well, Rainbow takes on certain roles for her, always with respect for her teacher's greatness.

Rainbow, rather than Jessie, is the first one now to sound the alert if a stranger comes to the house. Because she is the alpha dog, Jessie has always been at the front of the pack when I open the door, with Rainbow in second place, ready to back her up if needed. Now they stand shoulder to shoulder. Rainbow also joins in with the ear-cleaning ritual now, and if some of the younger dogs get too boisterous in the living room, Rainbow does the disciplining, so Jessie does not have to get up from her place. Every day, Rainbow becomes more mature, nurturing, and secure in her developing leadership role. Last week a younger dog came tearing across the yard when I called and, unable to stop in time, ran into Jessie rather hard. Rainbow flashed around and gave him a firm disciplining. I am witnessing an enduring matriarchy, with one generation passing on responsibility and authority to the next. I need never worry that I will lose the loving and protective web around me; they already have it all worked out.

I feel so humbled when I compare what I have to offer the animals with the gifts they give to me. How can teaching a dog when to sit and lie down on cue equate with having a dog teach me to be more sensitive, present, honest, clear, loving—in short, how to be a better person? Bill Pollak, a holistic veterinarian friend, puts it well: he believes that animals always live with two feet in this world and two feet in the spiritual world. Because they never completely disconnect, they bring so much with them, which is what makes them such marvelous teachers. Our culture attempts to rate animal intelligence lower on the scale than ours, but that is a futile exercise. The language and ways of expression are too different. The issue is not about the amount of intelligence and consciousness in a dog like Jessie; it is about the way the abiding consciousness and presence in the universe shines through Jessie into my life.

When Jessie's moment comes to fly back to spirit, I know that I will be open to still receiving lessons from her, right up to her last breath. This has happened to me several times before. Not too many years ago, Strut, the rescued greyhound described in Chapter 6, had a very clear agenda for his own leave-taking. It was one I have never forgotten.

When I first picked Strut up at the track, I was warned that, beneath his gentlemanly exterior, there was a dangerous madman, who would emerge only when anyone attempted to clip his nails. Then, they told me, I absolutely had to muzzle him or I would be sorry.

I forgot all about the warning, and one day I was trimming everyone's nails and it came to Strut's turn. I picked up his paw very matter-of-factly and, before I could even blink, he bellowed with rage and clamped his jaws down on my wrist. He never broke the skin or hurt me, but he made it quite clear that he could if I wanted to press the issue. We both froze, and then I very, very slowly and quietly put the clippers down. Once they were out of sight, Strut released me. He already had too much respect for me—as well as a truly gentle heart and soul—to do any damage, but if I had persevered, he would no doubt have forgotten his manners.

After a cooling-off period, I put a basket-muzzle on Strut and followed through, because the job had to get done. (This was before I had discovered Awareness Training; I would now put him on flower essences to support him in such situations.) Strut seemed terrified and fought me like a maniac. This was so out of character for him, it boggled my mind. It took two years before he totally trusted that I would not hurt him so that I could finally trim his nails without a restraint and without causing him any stress.

I had an occasion to go back to the track one day to pick up more Greyhounds for placement, and I saw a trainer there whom I had always respected for her humane treatment of the dogs in her charge. I asked her if she remembered Strut, and it was then that I learned the whole story. It seems that he had been such a consistent winner that he was upsetting the odds. Therefore, his nails were sometimes cut all the way down to the pads and then the lesions were cauterized, so that the pain would slow him down. I left the track seething; I find it hard to believe sometimes that humans can be so callous and cruel. Yet when I reached home, Strut was waiting with his gentle ways and complete lack of bitterness, reminding me once again never to stop believing in the power of the heart.

When Strut reached the noble age of fifteen, he began to have trouble rising, and over the next year and a half, it became clear that he was developing spinal myelopathy, a degeneration of the neurological system. Although he had no pain, the muscles were no longer receiving messages from the brain, with the result that he was losing control of his hindquarters. I began massaging him often, and worked his muscles so that they could sustain him as long as possible. Eventually I had to devise a sling so that I could support him when he went outside to relieve himself. Rather than seeming embarrassed by this contraption and my constant tending, Strut retained his decorum and sense of humor. One time he took me for a relentless circling of the yard, as if to say, "In my days of glory, dear April, this was what it was like: around and around and around. . . ."

A day in late winter came when I felt that it would be best to let Strut go. He had been declining for some time, could not support himself at all anymore, was not eating well, and had a digestive disorder. I felt that it would be kinder to put him down than to subject him to the discomfort and embarrassment of not being able to control his bowels. He had always been a dog with great dignity, and he still had his pride, despite his inability to walk by himself.

A friend came over, we dug a grave in a sunny place in the field where the snow had melted, and we carried Strut outside. I hugged and caressed him and then the needle was readied. At that very moment, I felt myself hit by a shock wave, almost as though a horse had kicked me in the head! I rocked back on my heels in wonder, looked at Strut, and saw him looking back at me with an expression of consternation and total disbelief. His message couldn't have been more clear. He was saying, "*What* in the world are you doing? Are you *crazy?*" I had to stop, take him back to the house, and then go back out and fill the hole in, because it was obvious I wasn't going to need it that day. He was so adamant that he was not ready to leave that I had to honor his wishes. Looking at him, I suddenly realized that I had been so involved in wanting to do what I thought was kindest and best for him that I had neglected to ask what he wanted at that point in time.

That night Strut was more like his old self than he had been in months. The diarrhea stopped, he bounced back, and he had less difficulty getting up and walking than he'd had in ages. Two more months went by in this way, until it was spring, and he began, once more, to weaken.

At the beginning of May I was teaching a weekend workshop on Reiki, and I got up early on the second day so that I could meditate before meeting my students. I walked out into the living room and Strut was lying there, so I greeted him saying, "Are you ready to get up and go out, old man?" He just gave me a deep look, and all of a sudden I knew that he wanted to leave. That very day. I thought, "Oh, no, not today," thinking of my students, but he was very eloquent about his need. I felt him say, "Today. I want to go lie in the sun for a while, and then I want to go."

I decided to do the morning portion of the workshop, and then when the spring day was warmest, I would take a longer lunch hour so that I could do as he asked. Two friends who were working with me saw that I was struggling with something, and when they heard, they asked, since they had known and loved Strut for a long time, if they could be with me to also say good-bye and support me. Word spread among the other people in the workshop, and in the end it was obvious that the greatest teaching of the day was going to be done by Strut and not by me. It was one thing to talk about the concept of energy and spirit, which was a crucial part of the training in the workshop; it was another to experience it directly, through the witnessing of a spiritual transition out of the body.

Several people in the class felt fear or confusion about the experience of dying. One woman, who knew and loved Strut from her volunteer work at the Center, was very much afraid of death. She was exploring a spiritual path and insisted that she wanted to be there, but was so terrified that she could not stop shaking and sobbing. There was also a ten-year-old boy visiting whose grandfather had recently died in the hospital. The child had had the event reported to him and had seen that some of his family members were very upset. He was confused and wondered why no one wanted to answer questions like "Where did Grandpa go?" and "Does it hurt to die?" Despite all of the conflicting feelings, everyone wanted to be with Strut in his final moment.

We carried him outside, put him on a big quilt on the ground, and formed a circle around him. Some of us put our hands on him, channeling

Reiki energy into his body to help him ease out of it and spirit-reunite with universal energy.

We stayed present in the moment, all of us searching to contribute our best thoughts and feelings. At the thresholds of life, nothing but the purest expression of your self is needed.

Strut lay on the blanket, absorbing the warm rays of the early spring sunshine, obviously relaxed, happy, and fully enjoying the experience. I remember thinking how peaceful and beautiful he looked as I watched the sunlight glistening on his coat.

We remained that way for some time. Eventually Strut raised his head and turned to look at me. Our eyes met. As I gazed into those large, dark, beautiful, and gentle eyes, so much like those of a deer, I was drawn into the soul behind them, and a wave of love and beauty washed over me. Moments passed, and the look changed and I knew he was ready to leave.

The needle was put into Strut's vein, and he slipped quietly away. No one spoke for several minutes after. Then we breathed again and began to speak in hushed voices, looking to one another for comfort and confirmation of the experience. We were amazed when a number of us recounted that, just as Strut's soul left, it had looked as though a wisp of smoke had risen up from his chest, taken the form of a bird, and disappeared into the sky.

As I looked around the circle of people who had shared this moment with me, I was awed by Strut's timing. He had had a plan that fulfilled who he was, a wise and generous soul to the end. Those who had been so afraid were now looking transported, wide-eyed, and tearful with a mixture of deep relief and wonder.

I was also mystified by the fact that I had not heard the usual howling from the other dogs. I thought about this for several days afterward, and I finally decided it was because Strut was still around; even though his body was no longer of use to him, his spirit had chosen to remain for a while. He used to love having his ears rubbed and would start a funny little humming whenever anyone did this. I used to call it "pushing his humming button." For a long time, when I was working around the Center, I would often sense that he was nearby or pressing against me, or I would think that I heard him. I had only to reach out my hand and say, "Hi, old man, how are you doing?" and I would feel his smooth coat and the press of his bony-backed body at my side. This feeling persisted for several months, and then one day I felt that he had finally moved on to his next piece of work.

Strut did not return again until I found myself spending long hours working on the manuscript of this book. I fell asleep at my table one night and began to dream, or be awake. I could not tell exactly where I was, but images of the whole story of Strut and Eva at the nursing home came, one after another. I had not thought about it in years, and now, every detail was there in living color.

I sat up in my chair, rubbing my eyes, and reached for my pen to get it all down while it was fresh in my mind. As I pondered some of the details, I was suddenly aware that Strut, with a strong, white-haired, piercing-blue-eyed Eva at his side, was standing on the other side of the table.

I rubbed my eyes, I blinked. I blinked again.

Strut stood there. Eva stood there. They were smiling. "Put our story in the book," they said. So I did.

Jessie, Rainbow, Strut, Tarl, Rebel, Tawny, Sequoia, Hawk, Navaho, Princess, Stoff—the list of dogs who have been powerful influences in my life is much, much longer than the few I mention here. There have also been dogs who were just great dogs and who did not seem to need a special relationship with humans. This makes sense to me; I believe that animals, just like people, have evolved to different levels. I've met some dogs who were here on the earth only to fully experience their animal nature. Others, like Jessica, are here for a very specific purpose: to facilitate the development of a new level of awareness between one kingdom and another.

I use the word "facilitate" because it isn't necessarily easy to become more conscious. It is sometimes hard to embrace those experiences that seem to be taking you apart, making you question what you were taught to believe, as opposed to supporting and enhancing your growth. I think that the only way to get through those challenging times is to keep moving and letting go of old and limiting beliefs. The most difficult animals I have worked with have always taught me the most, especially those who pushed all of my buttons and then watched me become frustrated because my present skills wouldn't work with them. They dared me to figure out a different approach. I realize now that those difficult dogs made it possible for me to develop courage, to become fully engaged in each new experience and in the learning process. The more obstacles they created, the greater my commitment grew to understand more.

The process has been like a never-ending spiral; the more I have come to understand, the more I realize I have yet to learn. The desire to keep going deeper is insatiable and is constantly extended by the joy and love that I receive. It is a passion: with each small success, my appetite is whetted to return to my master teachers, who already know the secret of taking delight and being fully present in each moment, no matter how demanding. They help me learn to live in the present, while at the same time detaching from the outcome, not judging, but just fully experiencing.

Out of everything that I have learned, one of the dogs' greatest lessons to me, even more inspiring than their gift of unconditional love, is about forgiveness and trust. I have worked with hundreds of dogs who have been horribly abused and who still have been willing to give me their love. When I look at that heroic offering, that ability to make the leap of faith to become open and vulnerable again, I feel humbled, awed, and know a joy that is hard to put into words. I pray that I will always be worthy to receive such a gift and teaching, and have the courage not only to embrace it but also to offer it to others.

One of the ways that life works is that whenever you think you have figured the important things out, something else can intervene and give you a boost into a whole new way of thinking and being. Several decades ago I had a rewarding life training and showing dogs and horses, and that seemed to be enough. Then I experienced a giant leap in my consciousness which, I see now, was a beautiful symbol of forgiveness and of a new opportunity for growth. Because of that incident, I was put on the path I walk today.

In early spring of 1979 I was giving a benefit performance at the Lebanon Opera House in New Hampshire with my Sheltie drill team. During intermission I was called to the phone. The caller told me that he and his dog had discovered another dog while they were out walking in his field. The strange dog was obviously injured and had staggered off into the woods. The man was calling me because, in those days, I was the local dog control officer.

As soon as we finished the performance, I changed my clothes and went to the place the man had described, but by this time it was pitch dark. I went out searching with a flashlight. The night was cool and full of the fresh smells of spring.

After looking for about half an hour, I found her. I don't know how I found her; it was one of those times when you are drawn to the thing you are looking for. My flashlight revealed the dog silent and unmoving, lying on her side near a tangle of fallen branches on the half-frozen ground.

It was too dark to discover the full extent of her injuries, but I could see that one side of her muzzle and her head were covered with blood. I assumed that she had been hit by a car and had somehow managed to get off the road, into the field, and then into the woods.

As I shined the flashlight on her and began to move closer, the dog tried to rise and then fell back down again. She had lost too much blood to have the strength to run. As my heart filled with concern for her fear and pain, suddenly an old, long-forgotten knowledge woke in me in again. Not since the age of ten, when I had been able to enter into friendship and communication with two squirrels, had I had this sensation. There was a profound shift in my energy and I could not only tell what she was feeling but also sense or feel her actual thoughts.

Out of my heart, I spoke to her, telling her that I did not want to hurt her. I was there to help her.

She must have received my message as clearly as I had hers, because immediately, instead of trying to get away from me, she struggled toward me. She whimpered softly as I held out my hand to let her sniff me and to reassure her that I meant her no harm.

I did not know, in that moment, the horror of how she came to be there. I sat beside her in the dark, placed my hand gently on her back, and suddenly found that the two of us were in a strangely altered consciousness. I was powerfully connected to the world of animals again. It both fascinated and terrified me. Old feelings and sensations flooded back. I felt light-headed and dizzy; I could not connect with my body or my surroundings. I was in another space, another time, another reality.

I began to experience fragments of the dog's story, all mixed in with messages that she was confused and afraid. I struggled to comprehend the images that I was receiving, because she was projecting that she had not meant to do anything bad or make people angry. Even though I didn't know this dog, her energy did not feel like that of a vicious dog who had bitten someone or killed another animal. She felt like the kind of dog who, like so many dogs, was living a half-life without any structure or fulfilled purpose: half her own world, half ours. If she had done anything wrong, it was likely that she had been behaving like a typical dog, digging holes or chewing things up because she had a lot of energy and no other way of entertaining herself.

As my mind continued to be flooded with images, I "saw her" living on a tie-out chain. I saw a shadowy figure of a man come to her, take her off the chain, slip a rope over her head, and lead her out to a secluded location.

Suddenly the images were violently interrupted by what felt like an explosion in my head, followed by several more. Stunned and immobilized, I sat there, trying to process everything that had just happened to me.

When the shock and sensations subsided, I was able to bring my attention back to the dog. I was still under the assumption that she had been hit by a car, and discounted that the person whom I had seen leading her away was involved. I decided that the explosions I had experienced were the dog's impact with a car and the jolts that followed were perhaps from hitting another part of the car or the road.

At that moment it was not part of my reality that someone could ever take his dog out and just shoot her because he didn't want her anymore.

Finding myself able to function again, I realized that I had to get her to a veterinarian, and fast. I took the blanket I had brought along and pulled it around her to try to keep her from going into shock. I was still many years away from knowing about things like holistic remedies for shock.

As I knelt there on the ground and cradled her in my arms, I called out to friends who had joined me in the search, and asked them to bring the backboard—a plywood board with straps and handholds for transporting injured animals—that we had brought with us. I heard them answer, but I could tell by their voices that they were still some distance away, so I simply held the dog and waited and sank once more into thought.

I suddenly just knew: since animals had always given so much to me, I would now dedicate my life to giving back to them.

My friends arrived, and we carefully carried the dog out of the field and drove to the office of a veterinarian friend. He had been at the performance that night and had told me, as I was leaving, to contact him if the dog needed help.

My friend took over, putting the dog on fluids to alleviate shock and to reduce any brain swelling. He doubted that the dog would make it, because she had serious trauma to her head, a skull fracture, a badly fractured jaw, and had lost a lot of blood. He said that he would call the next morning with a report.

It was 2:00 A.M. I left the vet clinic and drove home, exhausted from a day of chores, the performance, and the events around finding the dog. I was still trying to get a perspective on what had happened in the woods in the dark.

As I entered the house, all of the dogs rushed to greet me at the door, welcoming me home with joyful eyes and waving tails and dog kisses. It was then that I finally let go of all of the pent-up emotions of the day, evoked by the pressures of getting the chores done and preparing for the show; the exhilaration of the dogs' performance; the surprise and concern at receiving the phone call; the pain of discovering the injured dog; the flood of feelings as old doors opened again; the sorrow of Tom, the vet, telling me that the dog would probably die anyway.

I sat down on the floor and cried.

The dogs weren't sure how to respond. The more serious ones licked the tears from my face and snuggled against me to comfort me. The more light-hearted ones tried with all of their might to initiate a game by bringing me toys or gently tugging at my hair as if to say, "Don't be sad. Be happy. Be with us!"

I went to bed and spent a restless night, constantly waking with fragmented thoughts about how much I loved and cared for the dogs who resided with me. I thought about their joy at performing; it was as though they knew they were making people both happy and aware of how wonderful dogs are.

And on another level, the dogs seemed to understand far better than I that they were building a bridge between people and animals. I had designed their performances to be educational and to be used at benefit fund-raisers, especially those that promoted animal causes, which helped their own kind.

My thinking shifted to the dog I had found in the woods and how she had come to be there. I had a nagging feeling there was more to the injured dog's story than I knew, but I didn't know what it was. Exhausted, I dozed off and on through the night, and when I woke, I would think of her and instantly be filled with prayers for her life. I now know that when she needed more energy and strength, she sent out an energy SOS to me. I would get flashes of intuition that I immediately and spontaneously responded to with an outpouring of love and compassion. I "sent" that energy to her all night, even though I didn't have a clue about energy or how I was connected to it or that I even had it to send or give. Many years and many lessons from animals would come to pass before I finally "got it," understood it, and allowed myself to embrace it.

I now realize that all through that night, from the moment I met that dog, I was experiencing a profound rebirth of a part of my self. The dog had been abused, and so, in some way, had I, because long ago in childhood, my experiences with the squirrels had been so misunderstood. A part of me had been shut down, and now my powers of intuition were reawakening; I had made an intimate, energetic connection with the dog, and even while we strove together to keep her life energy in her body, her struggles were also my struggles to learn from and forgive my past and grow into a new, expanded way of being.

Morning came, and Tom's call: the dog was alive. The X-ray had revealed four 22.-caliber bullets in her head. Her jaw was broken in several places, and she was missing an eye.

It is hard to explain the feeling that went through me at that point: deep sadness, anger, frustration. There was also a sort of loss of innocence as I came to terms with the horrible cruelty that this dog had endured. I had not encountered that kind of senselessness before. After the news sank in, my commitment deepened: I would do whatever I could do to help that dog find health and a loving home.

Tom explained that the dog would need a tricky and expensive operation to remove the bullets and repair the damage. Although miraculously nothing vital had been hit, the operation might possibly kill her. He wondered who was going to pay for it, and if he should go ahead.

I was plunged into depression. I had no money to spare. I put down the phone, wondering what I was going to do, and then there was a knock on the door.

It was Irina, the secretary and interpreter for the famed Russian writer Aleksandr Solzhenitsyn, who lived in nearby Cavendish, Vermont. She had come over to the United States when Solzhenitsyn defected, bringing along Faulk and Dingo, two large mixed-breed dogs that she had rescued from the streets of Rome.

Solzhenitsyn had two large Saint Bernards who did not get along with Faulk and Dingo, so Irina's dogs boarded with me for the duration of her two-year stay. She had come to visit them, which she did often, because she loved her dogs deeply.

She asked why I seemed so upset. I poured out the whole story to her, and she immediately offered to pay for the surgery, if I thought I could find a home for the dog. I called Tom back right away and gave him the go-ahead. And began praying again. The dog *had* to survive.

She did. I found her name: Second Chance—Chance, for short.

Chance amazed me with her ability to forgive and be loving, cheerful, and trusting despite her traumatic experience. After spending a short recovery time in the clinic, she came to stay with me for a few months and the word was put out that we were looking for a home for her. Her story by now had been reported in the local paper, and I had calls from a number of interested people, but I waited until the perfect family was found. I wanted Chance to be in a home where she would be the only dog, and I wanted to find people who would commit to loving and caring for her for her whole life, so that she would never again have to experience anything other than love and appreciation. She was finally adopted by a couple who had just retired and were home most of the time. They had a large fenced yard and had had dogs all their lives but had recently experienced the death of their canine companion of fifteen years. They needed Chance as much as she needed them. They were also not put off by her missing eye and disfigured face, as were some of the people who had come to see her. Chance lived another seven years. She had a wonderful life.

I think that my experience with Chance was the beginning of knowing in my heart, even if I did not yet know in my head, what my mission in life was to become.

When it became apparent that Second Chance was going to live, I realized that something monumental had taken place, that in different ways we had both been given a second chance. Hers was to live and be with people who truly loved her and whom she could love in return. Mine was the rediscovery of an awareness I had known in childhood, a wondrous connection to the world of animals, and a deepened appreciation for what they give and teach. At the time, I had no idea how things would evolve but somewhere, deep in my heart, I knew that giving other beings a second chance was to take on a very important meaning in my life. I had been given a lesson I would never forget: if you lose the path the first time, you often get a second chance at experiencing love, learning, and even a new life.

My intention for this book has been to share the wisdom I have received from my master teachers. I have put their lessons into words so that you will know what it is possible to learn from your dog. This book is merely a guideline for beginning the adventure. By becoming aware of your power to work with universal energy, and by practicing awareness in each of your interactions, you are allowing yourself to be open and receptive to the unlimited unfolding of your potential.

There is truly no division between where you and I stop and the animals begin. Seek the beauty in life, the wisdom, and the lessons in faith, love, trust, and courage that are brought from the animal kingdom.

There is only the most important teaching of all: in the power of the universal energy of love we are all one.

Blessings—Mitakuye Oyasin

APPENDIX

FOR BROCHURE AND SCHEDULES OF WORKSHOPS AND TRAINING CLASSES
April Frost conducts workshops, retreats, training classes, and lectures. If you would like to be on the mailing list or receive workshop information, please contact:
April Frost
Hearthside Animal Center
RR 2, Box 572
Cornish, NH 03745
Phone: 603-543-3551 Fax: 603-542-3752
email: aprilfrost@cyberportal.net

TO LOCATE A HOLISTIC VETERINARIAN
American Holistic Veterinary Medical Association
2214 Old Emmorton Road
Bel Air, MD 21015
Phone 410-569-0795
email: AHVMA@compuserve.com
    The national source for the latest information on holistic veterinary medicine. A resource center for locating holistic vets in your area. Reviews of presentations at their annual conference are published in a comprehensive journal, which can be purchased for a subscription price of $65.

VIDEO DISCLAIMER
The video: *April Frost, Training That Works for Your Dog* does not cover the same information contained in this book.

SOURCES FOR RECOMMENDED DOG FOOD AND OTHER
NUTRITIONAL SUPPLEMENTS
To obtain a catalog of any of the training equipment, nutritional supplements, natural foods, books, tapes, flower essences or herbal products mentioned in this book, please contact: April Frost
Hearthside Animal Center
RR 2, Box 572
Cornish, NH 03745

RECOMMENDED READING

NUTRITION
Food Pets Die For, by Ann Martin
Give Your Dog a Bone, by Ian Billinghurst
Canine Nutrition, by William C. Cusick
Enzyme Nutrition: The Food Enzyme Concept, by Dr. Edward Howell
Natural Insect Repellents for Pets, People and Plants, by Janette Granger and Connie Moore
Are You Poisoning Your Pets? by Nina Anderson and Howard Peiper

HOLISTIC HEALTH
Dr. Pitcairn's Complete Guide to Natural Health for Dogs and Cats, by Richard H. Pitcairn and Susan Hubble Pitcairn.
It's For the Animals! "Cook" Book *with* the Guided Tour of Natural Care *and* Resource Book by Helen L. McKinnon, A.S.
Vibrational Medicine: New Choices for Healing Ourselves by Richard Gerber, M.D.
Four Paws, Five Directions: A Guide to Chinese Medicine for Cats and Dogs, by Cheryl Schwarz, DVM.
Keep Your Pet Healthy the Natural Way, by Pat Lazurus
Reigning Cats and Dogs, by Pat McKay
The Natural Dog: A Complete Guide for Caring Owners, by Mary L. Brennan with Norma Edkroate
The Holistic Guide for a Healthy Dog, by Wendy Volhard and Kerry Brown
How to Have a Healthier Dog, by Wendell Belfield and Martin Zucker

HERBALISM
Healing Animals with Herbs by John Heinerman
The Complete Herbal Handbook for the Dog and Cat, by Juliette de Bairacli Levy
The Herbal Handbook for Farm and Stable by Juliette de Bairacli Levy

HOMEOPATHY
A Veterinary Materia Medica and Clinical Repertory with a Materia Medica of the Nosodes, by G. Macleod
Homeopathic First Aid for Pets, by Francis Hunter
Dogs: Homeopathic Remedies, by George Macleod
The Treatment of Dogs by Homeopathy, by K. Sheppard
Cats: Homeopathic Remedies, by George Macleod
The Treatment of Cats by Homeopathy, by K. Sheppard

FLOWER ESSENCES
Flower Essences and Vibrational Healing by Gurudas

AROMATHERAPY
Veterinary Aromatherapy by Nelly Grosjean

WORKING WITH CRYSTALS
Working with Crystals by Katrina Raphaell

COLORED LIGHT THERAPY
Crystal Healing: The Therapeutic Application of Crystals and Stones by Katrina Raphaell

BODYWORK AND ENERGY HEALING

The TTellington Touch: A Breakthrough Technique to Train and Care for Your Favorite Animal, by Linda Tellington-Jones with Sybil Taylor

REIKI

Reiki: Energy Medicine by Libby Barnett and Maggie Chambers, with Susan Davidson
Essential Reiki: by Diane Stein

THERAPEUTIC TOUCH

The Healing Touch by Dr. Michael W. Fox
Canine Acupressure: A Treatment Workbook by Nancy A. Zidonis and Marie K. Soderberg

ANIMAL COMMUNICATION

The Little Flowers of Saint Francis, translated by Raphael Brown
Talking with Nature, by Michael J. Roads
Kinship with All Life, by J. Allen Boone
Animal Talk, by Penelope Smith

BEREAVEMENT

The Loss of a Pet, Wallace Sife, new revised edition
Coping with Sorrow on the Loss of your Pet, by Moira K. Anderson
Pet Loss, A Thoughtful Guide for Adults and Children, by Herbert A Nieburg and Arlene Fisher
Pet Loss and Human Bereavement, edited by William J. Kay, Herbert A. Nieburg, Austin K. Kutscher, Ross M. Grey, and Carole D. Fudin

SPIRITUALITY, POSITIVE THINKING

All of Deepak Chopra's books
All of Carolyn Myss's books
Heal Your Body, by Louise L. Hay
You Can Heal Your Life, by Louise L. Hay

ABOUT VACCINATIONS

Who Killed the Darling Buds of May? by Catherine O'Driscoll
Natural Immunity, by Pat McKay
Pet Allergies, Remedies for an Epidemic, by Alfred Plechner and Martin Zucker

One of the best articles I've read so far is by Don Hamilton, DVM, who specializes in Homeopathy. It is reprinted here with his kind permission.

VACCINATIONS IN VETERINARY MEDICINE: DOGS AND CATS

A practice that was started many years ago and that *lacks scientific validity or verification* is annual revaccinations. Almost without exception there is no immunologic requirement for annual revaccinations. Immunity to viruses persists for years or for the life of the animal. Successful vaccination to most bacterial pathogens produces an immunologic memory that remains for years, allowing an animal to develop a protective anamnestic (secondary) response when exposed to virulent organisms. Only the immune response to toxins requires boosters (e.g. tetanus toxin booster, in humans, is recommended once every 7–10 years). And no toxin vaccines are currently used for dogs and cats. Furthermore, revaccination with most viral vaccines fails to stimulate an anamnestic (secondary) response as a result of interference by existing antibody (similar to maternal antibody interference). The practice of annual vaccination in our opinion should be considered of questionable efficacy unless it is used as a mechanism to provide an annual physical examination or is required by law (i.e., certain states require annual revaccination for rabies).[1] (Italics added)

Summary: Yearly "boosters" are unnecessary, provide no benefit if given (will not increase immunity). Thus boosters are either a legal issue (Rabies) or a manipulation issue (inducing clients to come in for examination rather than directly suggesting an examination).

The issue of initial vaccination is less clear than that of boosters. Many clinicians feel that without vaccination they would see outbreaks of disease, particularly canine parvovirus disease. This can be a difficult issue to resolve. A fundamental dilemma is that vaccination in effect leads to weakening of the gene pool, and thus the overall health of a given population. One way this occurs is by allowing individuals to live that would otherwise succumb to disease, such disease being a natural means to "cleanse" and thus strengthen that population. This naturally presents an ethical quandary these days (our understanding of native or aboriginal thinking suggests that letting weak individuals die was implicitly understood to be not only acceptable but proper). Western society values the individual's right to be, therefore we make efforts to save all individuals. Any answer to this question naturally lies with the individuals(s) involved. The second, and more compelling theory of the mechanism of interaction between a vaccine and the body suggests that vaccines "protect" against the acute disease not by preventing the disease but by *changing the form of the disease to a chronic disease*.[2] For example, the panleukopenia virus of cats induces an intense, rapidly progressive malfunction in the digestive tract, leading to vomiting an/or diarrhea. In adult vaccinated animals this transltes into a chronic state of diarrhea and sometimes vomiting. This disease is known as inflammatory bowel disease (IBD), an autoimmune disease of the intestines. IBD has been occurring at near epidemic levels over the past several years; no other reasonable explanation has been proposed for the proliferation of cases of the disease. Vaccinations are known to be a major trigger of other autoimmune processes in susceptible individuals,[3] so it is reasonable to suspect vaccines as a trigger for IBD. Another aspect of panleukopenia virus infection, implied by the name of the virus, is vastly lowered numbers of white blood cells and corresponding immune deficiency. Could the appearance of Feline Leukemia virus disease and later Feline Immunodeficiency virus disease be related to vaccination for panleukopenia during the previous two decades? The logicality of this theory does not allow easy

---

[1] T. R. Phillips, T. R., D.V.M. and Ron Schultz, Ph.D. *Canine and Feline Vaccinations* in *Current Veterinary* Therapy, Volume XI Robert Kirk, D.V.M. and John Bonagura, D.V.M., eds., 1992.

[2] Pitcarin, Richard, D.V.M., Ph.D., A *New Look at the Vaccine Question.* Proceedings of the American Holistic Veterinary Medical Association, 1993.

[3] Dodds, W. Jean, D.V.M., *More Bumps on the Vaccine Road,* Proceedings of the American Holistic Veterinary Medical Association 1995.

dismissal of a relationship, most likely cause and effect. Both of the latter diseases produce low white blood cell counts and immunodeficiency as part of their symptom complexes. Similar connections have been proposed between Canine Distemper virus disease and both kennel cough and Canine Parvovirus diseases as "distemper" includes a pneumonia component as well as severe diarrhea. Chronic coughing is characteristic of kennel cough: parvovirus disease affects the intestines, producing severe diarrhea and vomiting. Additionally, the incidence of inflammatory bowel disease in dogs appears to be on the increase in the past year or two. Vaccination of dogs for Canine Parvovirus has been in effect for fifteen years, contrasted with the much longer history of parvovirus vaccination in cats (Feline Panleukemia virus is a member of the parvovirus family). This portends a frightening future for dogs if the connection is indeed correct. Finally, connections are proposed between vaccination for Rabies and increasing numbers of fearful, aggressive animals. Behavioral problems of the extent seen today are a recent occurrence, being rare only two to three decades ago.[4] Their emergence is coincident with the practice of repeated adult vaccination, suggesting the need to examine that relationship. Aggressive behavior has been observed in dogs for several days following vaccination for rabies, even with non-infectious [killed] vaccines.[5, 6]

As practitioners sharing responsibility for the well being of patients, veterinarians are faced with a challenge when dealing with acute diseases. Vaccinations may prevent these acute diseases, but if the exchange is for a lifetime of chronic disease, is that a viable option? (Viable is from the French *vie,* meaning life, so the question is will the patient live and flourish or simply exist.)

First, remembering that booster vaccines are unnecessary, we can stop all vaccination after one year of age for virtually all diseases. (cf. below; Rabies is required by law so we need to work to change the laws so that they are in accordance with the fact rather than fear.) As repetition naturally increases the likelihood of problems, we can reduce side effects tremendously with no additional risk to the patient, simply by stopping adult boosters. Of course, there will still be some risk involved with even the initial vaccinations, but no risk of contracting the acute disease once the animal is immunized by these first vaccines. See below for duration of immunity to the various diseases for which vaccines are available.

Secondly, all vaccines should be administered as single antigens. (An antigen is something that is capable of eliciting an immune response, in this case a viral or bacterial organism from which a vaccine is produced.) This means not using the polyvalent vaccines which have become so common these days. Natural exposure to diseases is usually one at a time, and the body is probably more successful at responding to only one antigen and producing immunity without adverse effects, rather than responding to a complex of antigens. Therefore, rather than giving a group of antigens together at three to four week intervals, individual components should be given using an alternating schedule with a minimum of repetition. (Cf. below)

Thirdly, only immunize for diseases which meet *all* of the following criteria:

1. The disease is serious, even life threatening.
2. The animal is or will be exposed to the disease.
3. The vaccine for the disease is known to be effective.
4. The vaccine for the disease is considered safe.

Let us take Feline Leukemia virus (FeLV) disease as an example. An indoor only cat will not be exposed as this requires direct, intimate, cat-to-cat contact. Many veterinarians rec-

[4] Young, Arthur, D.V.M., Personal communication.
[5] Blanco, B. Dee, D.V.M., Personal communication.
[6] Hamilton, Don, D.V.M., Personal observation.

ommend immunizing indoor cats against this disease. I feel this is unethical. This disease does not fit criteria number three or four anyway in my experience, so vaccination is unwarrented in most if not all circumstances. Feline Infectious Perritonitis (FIP) virus disease is another disease which fits neither three or four. FIP vaccine has generally been found ineffective and has produced severe side effects. Among the side effects I have observed with both FIP and FeLV is induction of the the clinical disease they were intended to prevent. In dogs, Canine Hepatitis (CH) virus is almost nonexistent (the vaccine virus to prevent CH is Adenovirus-2). Leptospirosis is extremely rare and often not the same serotype used in the vaccine[7] and the bacterin for "lepto" is very prone to side effects. Coronavirus disease was never a serious threat except to dog companions' bank accounts, the same being true for Lyme disease except possibly in very small regions. Kennel cough disease is generally not serious (criteria one), and one study showed immunization to be ineffective or even counterproductive.[8] Immunization should be limited to high risk circumstances, if at all. A similar situation exists with the feline upper respiratory diseases; most are not serious except in very young kittens who contract the disease before vaccines are typically administered. Rabies is another disease for which indoor cats and well-confined dogs have no exposure, so the vaccine is clinically unnecessary although required by law.

Fourth, vaccines should NEVER be given to unhealthy animals. This is a practice that is gaining popularity among veterinarians for some strange reason, and it goes against the recommendations in all vaccine inserts as well as those of virtually all immunologists. This is malpractice in my opinion.

A bolder option is to refuse immunizations entirely, recognizing the inherent risk in administration of even one vaccine into the body, and being willing to accept the risk of not immunizing. While risk does exist if animals are unvaccinated, it can be moderated significantly by feeding better quality foods (home prepared, including fresh, raw meats) and by limiting exposure until the animals are six to eight months of age. An unvaccinated animal will be significantly less likely to suffer from allergies and many health problems. Skin allergic reactions have been associated with vaccine administration,[9] and tremendous numbers of dogs and cats have skin allergies today. Some other diseases for which links to vaccines are known or suspected include epilepsy, thyroid disorders[10] (hyper- and hypothyroidism), chronic hepatitis, renal failure, cystitis or lower urinary tract disease (particularly in cats), autoimmune hemolytic anemia,[11] neurologic diseases such as confusion and inability to be "present," asthma, and so on. In humans sudden infant death syndrome is strongly linked to DPT vaccination,[12] as are attention deficit disease/hyperactivity and autism,[13] among many others including severe brain damage.

Why are vaccines worse than natural exposure? Probably the major factors are the artificial means by which exposure is created with vaccines and the repetition. With few exceptions (primarily rabies and occasionally Feline Leukemia virus or Feline Immunodeficiency

[7] Schultz, Ronald D., Ph.D., American Holistic Veterinary Medical Association Annual Conference, 1995.
[8] Day, Christopher E. I., MRCVS. *Isopathic prevention of Kennel Cough—Is Vaccination Justified?* International Journal of Veterinary Homeopathy, Vol. 2, number 2, 1987.
[9] Scheibner, Viera, Ph.D. *Vaccination: The Medical Assault on the Immune System*, Australian Print Group. Maryborough, Victoria, Australia, 1993, p. 21.
[10] Dodds, 1995.
[11] Ibid.
[12] Scheibner, 1993.
[13] Coulter, Harris, Ph.D. *Vaccination, Social Violence and Criminality*, North Atlantic Books, 1990.

virus), infectious organisms are transmitted via oral and nasal exposure, and this response begins at the oral/nasal level with recognition of a foreign material or organism, followed by initial *non-specific* destruction and elimination of the organism at the local site of exposure as well as within the blood stream whence an organism may not even reach the interior to cause deep illness, but may be successfully repelled at the periphery. In other cases the body would have a lag time of several hours or even days to begin mounting a response before the "invader" reaches interior organs. As a consequence, deeper pathology may be minimized or even averted. This interior organ pathology may be a direct result of the organism, or it may be an indirect result, manifested through antigen-antibody complexes or other immune system components. These components may inadvertently damage body tissues as "innocent bystanders," or may directly attack or invade tissues due to recognition problems (autoimmune diseases). The latter may happen because of similarity between organism structures and host tissues; often this involves the nucleoproteins (DNA or RNA), molecules that are important for controlling activity at a cellular level.

When a vaccine is administered, the organism is injected directly into body tissues, bypassing the local immune responses. When this happens, much of the immune system is rendered useless. The body then must compensate by increasing the activity of the balance of the system, and the defenses begin in a compromised state, with the organism already in the blood stream. Within the blood stream, the primary aspects of the immune system are antibodies, proteins which attach to the organism and assist in its destruction. Although normally only a part of the defenses, these antibodies become heavily responsible in a vaccine (injected) induced invasion, thereby initiating a hyperactive (increased) response. Additionally, the preparation of vaccines often breaks down the integral structure of the virus or bacteria, exposing internal structures such as viral DNA or RNA (depending on the virus) to the immune system, leading to heavy antibody production against these nucleoproteins. Since nucleoproteins are relatively similar in all life forms, the host antibodies may lose the induced hyperactivity of antibody production. The result may be antibody mediated destruction of host tissue, and autoimmune disease. In a natural exposure, antibodies would be directed more at external structures, which are less similar to host tissues thus less likely to induce cross reactions. Incidentally, autoimmune diseases are occurring more frequently than ever; could this be a reason?

Aside from the above considerations, vaccine commonly contain materials other than the organism to which immunity is desired. These materials may be added as preservatives, adjuvants (materials to stimulate immune response, usually added to non-infectious [killed] vaccines), or antibiotics. Preservatives an adjuvants include such toxins and carcinogens as aluminum (alum), mercury (thimersol), and formaldehyde. Also, many foreign proteins are included if the organism was grown on foreign tissue such as chicken or duck embryos. Even more frightening, non-intended organisms are somtimes accidentally incorporated as contaminant "stowaways." In 1995 The Washington Post reported that MMR vaccine produced by Merck & Co. along with some influenza and yellow fever vaccines, contained an enzyme known as reverse transcriptase. This enzyme is associated with retroviruses such as FeLV, FIV, and HIV, and has the capability to alter genetic information, leading to serious diseases such as leukemia and other cancers. These diseases may take years to manifest, so correlation with vaccination may be impossible, masking a potentially causative relationship.

The recommended schedules (age to vaccinate) are from Dr. Schultz, with a few changes as follows: He supports the use of combination vaccines and I strongly do not. He thus recommends in cats to combine Panleukopenia (FPL), Calicivirus (FC), and Rhinotracheitis (FVR) in one schedule; I have recommended to use FVR-FC intranasal vaccine only if needed, and separately from FPL. In dogs he would combine Distemper (CD), Parvo (CPV), and Hepatitis, and possibly Corona and Parainfluenza. I would recommend CD and CPV only, and not combined.

I generally support the use of killed (non-infectious) vaccines, as I feel they have less likelihood for long term damage, but Dr. Schultz presents a strong case for the use of modified live vaccines (MLV) as repetition can be necessary with non-infectious vaccines. With MLV, one dose can have high efficacy. This primarily applies to DC and CPV as non-infectious [killed] Rabies and FP are as effective as MLV. Dr. Schultz's one dose-95% (one dose of vaccine at a given age will successfully immunize 95% of animals) suggestions are as follows.

Canine Distemper (MLV) 10–12 weeks
Canine Parvovirus (MLV) 12–14 weeks
Feline Panleukopenia (non-inf. [killed] OK) 10–12 weeks

Finally, a comment about vaccinations and choice. While the concept of 'owning' an animal is one with which I am uncomfortable, I do recognize that this is how the human-animal relationship is viewed from a legal perspective. Otherwise we certainly can be said to be guardians of our companion animals. Within this framework the choice about vaccination rests with the human who has accepted responsible guardianship. It does not rest with the veterinarian. Another trend of the past few years is coercion of guardians into procedures such as vaccination. This coercion may be blatant, such as refusal to provide services, even emergency care, unless the animal is 'current' on vaccines. Sometimes even critically ill animals are vaccinated upon admission for treatment. More subtle means include induction of fear and/or guilt by asserting (as an authority figure) that companion animals are at risk if not vaccinated yearly, and that failure to comply is evidence of lack of caring. Tactics such as this can create feelings of guilt in the guardian, leading to a fear based decision to vaccinate an animal that is not at risk. This is unethical if not outright malpractice and refusal is an acceptable response. As has been stated above, rabies vaccination is legally compulsive at one to three year intervals, so refusal is a legal risk. Fighting to change these laws, however, is appropriate.

© 1996 Don Hamilton, DVM

Please feel free to copy and disseminate this article, however it must be copied exactly (with no changes) unless written permission is obtained from Dr. Hamilton, author of the forthcoming book *Small Doses for Small Animals: Homeopathy for Dogs and Cats* (North Atlantic Books).

PERFECT HEALTH DIET (PHD)

In alignment with the high standard I have for feeding my dogs, I consider myself very fortunate to have made the acquaintance of Scott Pollack, whose company manufactures Perfect Health Diet (PHD) dog and cat food. I feel totally confident in recommending this food because I know the ingredients are always of the highest quality and because the health of animals is important to Scott. PHD is made by a small company in New York and is shipped by UPS to your door. It is a superior feed, capable of supporting your pet in a very high nutritional range that is far greater than that of products offered by the commercial pet-food industry. The company's responsibility to pets goes beyond claiming that PHD is the optimum diet. Rather, they advocate the implementation of the natural and raw diet with the use of PHD as a supplement. Those who cannot prepare whole foods and who wish to improve their animals' nutritional intake may be assured that PHD is balanced fully nutritious feed, which exceeds all industry standards. PHD is the only commercially manufactured food that I use and recommend to my clients, since I have experienced its far-reaching benefits with the animals in my care. Within a few weeks of starting an animal on PHD, there is usually a noticeable difference in the animal's appearance, vitality level, and behavior.

INDEX

Pack structure, 23, 30, 60, 70–71, 84–85
  and biting, 133
  in feral dogs, 76, 83, 84
  learning in, 315, 332–33
  and play, 297
  rank in, 183
Pain, 95, 143, 285
  and aggression, 241
  herbal treatments for, 272
Parasites, 266–67, 320
Parvo, 268, 349
Patterning, 31, 321
Pheromones, 74
Play, 297–310
  and puppies, 322
  roughhousing, 298
  and toys, 307–310
  tug-of-war, 298
Polarity therapy, 95
Pollack, Bill, 261, 263, 333
Praise, 36, 146, 152, 157
  in corrections, 144, 149
  and directives, 138
  inadequate, 61
  timing in, 151–52, 179
  voice modulation in, 35
Prana, 95
Pressure point, 194, 204
Projection, 1, 32, 94, 98
  of disapproval, 134
  of intent, 104, 185–86
Puppies, 311–27
  adopting, 32, 313–16
  attention span of, 198
  behavior problems of, 32, 314–15, 320–25
  and cars, 325
  developmental stages of, 40–42, 326
  and diet, 320
  house-training of, 317–21
  newborn, 40–41, 311–12
  off-leash training of, 231
  and play, 322
  and separation trauma, 312–14
  and stairs, 325
  and strangers, greeting of, 234
  and submissive urination, 245
  training of, 316, 321–27
    to come, 182
    to heel, 218
    to sit, 193
    to wait, 190
    to walk on lead, 174
  and training collars, 141
  whelping, 311
Puppy mill, 269, 314

Qi Gong, 95

Rabies pole, 69, 71, 74
Rabies vaccine, 267, 268, 349–52

Rehabilitation, of feral dogs, 73–92
Reiki, 73, 82, 83, 95, 281, 286–87
  for puppies, 312
Relationships, dog-human, 3, 11, 53–68, 337
  attitude in, 93–94
  compatibility in, 65–66
  control issues in, 55–60
  and dog behavior, 31–34
  among elderly, 116–19
  and family dynamics, 64–65, 67, 242
  identification in, 244
  and illness, 67–68
  and inconsistency, 60–64, 67
  jealousy in, 64
  quality time in, 66, 114
  roles in, 29–30, 131
  as substitutes, 58
  See also Emotions, dogs' reactions to
Remedies for specific conditions, 287–95
Reprimands. *See* Correction
Rescued dogs, 32, 69–73, 252–53
Respect, 33, 47, 51–52, 56–57, 139, 301
  for animals, 7
  in Awareness Training, 1, 53, 112
  confused with love, 161, 192
  and control in household, 22–23
  establishing mutual, 155–56, 167, 191–92, 253
  and trust, 60
Retrieving, 299–302
  technique for, 300–1
Rewards:
  for desirable behavior, 32, 149–50
  timing of, 151
  for undesirable behavior, 20–21, 42, 153
  See also Food; Praise

Scavenging, 30
Seeing Eye dogs, 26, 227
Self-defense, 30, 43
Senses in dogs, 26–29, 43–44, 79
  body sensitivity, 28, 43–44, 149
  color sensitivity, 27
  development of, 41
  hearing, 27, 43
  motion sensitivity, 27, 177
  night vision, 27
  sight, 26–27, 43
  smell, 26, 27
Separation anxiety:
  and chewing, 32
  and crate training, 316–17
  and emotional dependence, 58
  flower essences for, 276
  in puppies, 312–14
Shedding, 11, 61
Sheehan, Molly, 274
Small-Wright, Machaelle, 274
Snappy Trap, 323
Socialization, 31, 41, 76, 312
  lack of, 162, 252
  and puppy mill dogs, 269, 314

ABOUT THE AUTHORS

April Randall Frost is an animal behaviorist and Reiki master. She has more than thirty-five years' experience working with dogs and horses, and her talent has earned her national recognition both as a trainer and as a handler at the highest levels of competition in the United States and Canada. Her many classes and workshops at her Hearthside Animal Center in Cornish, New Hampshire, are immensely popular. Her training video, *April Frost: Training That Works for Your Dog*, has sold more than 100,000 copies.

Rondi Lightmark is an animal lover and freelance writer who lives in Vermont.